YOUNG, GIFTED AND DIVERSE

Young, Gifted and Diverse

ORIGINS OF THE NEW BLACK ELITE

CAMILLE Z. CHARLES

RORY KRAMER

DOUGLAS S. MASSEY

KIMBERLY C. TORRES

PRINCETON UNIVERSITY PRESS
PRINCETON & OXFORD

Published by Princeton University Press
41 William Street, Princeton, New Jersey 08540
99 Banbury Road, Oxford OX2 6JX

press.princeton.edu

All Rights Reserved
ISBN 9780691237381
ISBN (pbk.) 9780691237459
ISBN (e-book) 9780691237398

British Library Cataloging-in-Publication Data is available

Editorial: Meagan Levinson, Jacqueline Delaney
Jacket/Cover Design: Chris Ferrante
Production: Lauren Reese
Publicity: Kate Hensley, Kathryn Stevens

Cover art: iStock / Maria Voronovich

This book has been composed in Arno Pro

10 9 8 7 6 5 4 3 2 1

CONTENTS

Apart from anything else, I wanted to be able to come here and speak with you on this occasion because you are young, gifted, and black. . . .I, for one, can think of no more dynamic combination that a person might be. . . .though it be a thrilling and marvelous thing to be merely young and gifted in such times, it is doubly so, doubly dynamic—to be young, gifted *and black.*

LORRAINE HANSBERRY, MAY 1964 (1969, 262–263)

THESE WORDS—excerpted from Hansberry's speech honoring the winners of a United Negro College Fund writing contest just months before her death in January, 1965—inspired Nina Simone (with Weldon Irvine) to write the song "Young, Gifted and Black" as a tribute to her friend and to "make black children all over the world feel good about themselves, forever" (King and Watson 2019), because "African American men and women should know the beauty of their blackness" (Garza 2015).

Simone first performed "Young, Gifted and Black" in August 1969 for a crowd of about 50,000 at the Harlem Cultural Festival (the subject of the 2021 documentary, *Summer of Soul*), and recorded it shortly thereafter. The song was a popular hit that was covered by several other artists, including Aretha Franklin's 1972 Grammy-award-winning rendition on her album of the same name. Written and recorded in the midst of the Civil Rights and Black Power Movements, it became an anthem for Black people (Garza 2015; King and Watson 2019).

"You are young, gifted and black"
We must begin to tell our young
There's a world waiting for you
Yours is the quest that's just begun

The song continues to inspire artists: Aretha Franklin's version of the song is sampled or referenced by artists as varied as Big Daddy Kane (1989),

Gang Starr (1992), Heavy D and the Boyz (1992), MC Lyte (1993), Jay-Z (2003), Rah Digga (2004), Lupe Fiasco (2008), and Faith Evans (featuring Missy Elliott, 2014). As part of the song's goal to make all Black children see their great potential, the phrase, "young, gifted and black" understands Blackness as inclusive, expansive, and, importantly, *diverse.*

1

Black Diversity in
Historical Perspective

I don't want to uplift the Black race. I want to uplift people like me.

DARRYL, BLACK MULTIGENERATIONAL NATIVE

If they heard me talk, they would think I wasn't Black enough.

OLIVIA, SECOND-GENERATION NIGERIAN AND
HAITIAN AMERICAN

WHEN WE SPOKE with Darryl and Olivia, they were both attending Ivy League universities. They had proverbially "made it"; their college degrees would solidify their status as part of the American elite and, more specifically, the Black American elite. Yet, each of them laments the complications associated with that status. Their sense of who they are as Black Americans is part and parcel of their lived experiences in families, neighborhoods, and schools and as distinct from one another as can be. The new Black elite is diverse, including multigenerational native Blacks and first- and second-generation immigrants from Africa and the Caribbean, monoracial and mixed-race Blacks, Blacks who are the first in their families to attend college, and those whose parents hold advanced degrees and high-status jobs. They represent the full complement of social-class status and skin tone, and they are disproportionately young women.

Until the early 1990s, social research on racial identity traditionally treated Black Americans as a monolith with little attention paid to intraracial differences (Benjamin 2005). The lingering assumption was that Blacks in America share a common legacy of persecution and subordination linked to African enslavement and Jim Crow segregation. Blackness has long served as a "catchall" category for those who share dark skin and certain phenotypic traits. Psychologists, historians, and sociologists alike sought to understand how Black Americans collectively made sense of their position as a denigrated outgroup at the bottom of the U.S. social hierarchy, unified by generations of oppression. They focused on Blacks' worldviews and ideologies as a reflection of their shared marginalization. For example, Drake and Cayton (1945:390) argued that "'race consciousness' is not the work of 'agitators' or 'subversive influences'—it is forced upon Negroes by the very fact of their separate-subordinate status in American life."

W. E. B. Du Bois (1903) was the first to articulate the duality of the Black experience after Emancipation with his concept of "double consciousness"— the idea that American Blacks are forced to recognize their denigrated social status while simultaneously acknowledging their own worth as human beings. Being a light-skinned man of mixed-racial and immigrant origins himself, Du Bois strove to promote racial uplift within his small, educated cadre of light-skinned, educated young men—which he labeled the Talented Tenth—and to encourage less fortunate Blacks to assimilate into upper-class White Victorian culture in order to elevate their position within the racial stratification system and challenge the color divide.[1]

Black identity in the United States has thus been largely analyzed as a linear construction, based on a simple either-or dichotomy that does not sufficiently capture or explain the multiple facets of what it means to be Black or recognize differences in the Black experience by gender, class, nativity, generation, or experience with segregation. Black achievement and success typically have been thought to require one-way assimilation and acculturation to White norms and values, and Blackness as a racial classification historically has been defined legally and socially by a "one-drop rule" under which any African ancestry limited one's access to rights, resources, and freedom (Davis 2017). Indeed, in the 1896 *Plessy v. Ferguson* decision, the U.S. Supreme Court confirmed that any traceable amount of "Black blood" relegated one to an undifferentiated category of racial subordination.

Given these historical precedents, in the United States, Blackness has been constructed as a "master status" that subjected incumbents to exclusion and exploitation throughout U.S. society (Becker 1963; Hughes 1963). In the words of Supreme Court Chief Justice Roger B. Taney in his 1857 *Dred Scott* decision, Black people are "considered as a subordinate and inferior class of beings who had been subjugated by the dominant race, and, whether emancipated or not, yet remained subject to their authority, and had no rights or privileges but such as those who held the power and the government might choose to grant them." To formalize the precepts of the one-drop rule articulated in the *Dred Scott* and *Plessey* decisions, in 1924 Virginia's legislature passed a "Racial Integrity Act" stating that "the term 'White person' shall apply only to the person who has no trace whatsoever of any blood other than Caucasian" (Washington 2011; Jordan 2014).

In this context, variations in socioeconomic status, skin tone, immigrant origins, and racially mixed ancestry among Blacks became invisible to most White Americans, and in the wake of the Black Power movement of the 1960s, these differences were suppressed for a time within the Black community as well (Hochschild and Weaver 2007). Even though Black activists and scholars have periodically recognized the fact of intraracial diversity, structural racism has consistently limited the academic conversation in ways that explicitly and implicitly linked Blackness with poverty and deficiency and continued to presume a singularity of Black identity and experience (Morning 2011; Go 2018; Williams 2019).

In doing so, scholarship on the Black experience has largely overlooked the Black elite. Social scientists, politicians, and policymakers alike have long defined the parameters of Blackness as a homogeneously disadvantaged experience tied to blocked mobility within a racially stratified system (beginning with slavery) with Blacks unequivocally at the bottom and Whites at the top. This hyperfocus on interracial disparities flattens racial and social-class experiences and "frequently devolves into an either-or debate . . . the dilution of class into a cultural and behavioral category or a static index . . . that fails to capture power relations" (Reed and Chowkwanyun 2012:150). Similarly, a unidimensional focus on interracial disparities treats Blackness as a static identity that is not considered "embedded in multiple social relations" and thus "sidestep[s] careful dissection of how racism . . . [and] race have evolved and transformed" (Reed and Chowkwanyun 2012:151).

The ability to study intraracial diversity within the Black population in the United States, especially in the Black elite, has also been hampered by the absence of reliable statistics on Black nativity, ethnicity, national origin, and other dimensions of Black diversity. Until the 2000 census, most educational and national databases monolithically used "African American" or "Black" in reporting college attendance/graduation rates, neglecting national origin, ethnic identification, and/or intraracial distinctions (Spencer 2011).

Only within the last twenty years or so has the diverse composition and character of the Black population in the United States—and within the Black elite in particular—begun to receive the consideration it deserves as America's racial landscape was transformed by civil rights laws, affirmative action, return migration to the South, and immigration from abroad (Smith and Moore 2000, 2002; Haynie 2002; Rimer and Arenson 2004; Massey et al. 2007; Clerge 2019). In addition, rising Black social mobility and increasing rates of interracial marriage and cohabitation have led to a growing population of multiracial individuals. Today's Black college students come from many different places, with diverse phenotypes and socioeconomic backgrounds.

Although often overlooked, a notable body of qualitative and historical research has focused on the lived experiences of the traditional Black elite, namely the small cadre of multigenerational, native-born Black Americans whose light skin tone, education, relative affluence, and allegiance to "respectability politics" separated them from the rest of Black society (e.g., see Higginbotham 1993; Graham 1999; Moore 1999; Gatewood 2000; Benjamin 2005; Kilson 2014; Thompson and Suarez 2015; Landry 2018). These studies pointed out that the Black elite exists, has long existed, and continues to be an important part of the racial landscape of the United States. However, they tended to follow Du Bois who sought to emphasize Black diversity by focusing on class as the primary differentiator, leaving other dimensions of diversity understudied.

It was Black feminists who introduced the concept of intersectionality, using gender as a lens to argue that focusing on a single axis of inequality is a flawed oversimplification of how systems of racial oppression operate and how people understand their identities in a stratified social structure (see Crenshaw 1989; Collins and Bilge 2016). Yet, we still know relatively little about the origins and the lived experiences of the post–civil rights generation with respect to the other dimensions of diversity that shape access to opportunities and resources and differentially mold the construction of racial identities. Reid (1939) and Bryce-Laporte (1972), for example, argue that Black immigrants historically have been largely invisible in discussions about Black identity. Shaw-Taylor and Tuch (2007) point out that until quite recently, the history of Black immigration has been largely absent from the immigration literature. Clerge (2019) likewise shows how class, migration, and segregation combine to create both global and local understandings of race, color, and status.

Building on that work, here we provide a mixed-methods exploration of diversity within the twenty-first-century Black elite, emphasizing its multidimensionality with respect to racial identity, gender, immigration, skin tone, parentage, social class, and segregation. These are far from the only axes of differentiation, of course. Our data set lacks indicators of sexuality and sexual identity, for example. Nonetheless, in the pages that follow, we hope to contribute to the literature on intraracial diversity by exploring the backgrounds and experiences of a key subset of young Black Americans as they enter adulthood and the nation's professional elite.

Who are the Black elite? What are their demographic and phenotypic characteristics? What do they share in common, and how do they differ? How do their diverse origins and foundational experiences affect their worldviews, including their thoughts on race and responsibility? By exploring these issues both quantitatively and qualitatively, across multiple axes of differentiation simultaneously, we not only reinforce prior findings about the dimensions of difference but also show how the process of entering into the Black elite shapes the way that the next generation of upwardly mobile young Blacks see themselves and their position in the nation's larger system of racial stratification.

The 2008 election of Barack Obama as president of the United States was a watershed moment in U.S. history, not only because he was the first visibly "Black" president but also because of his particular origins. The son of a White American mother and a Black African father who was raised in Hawaii by White grandparents and went on to earn prestigious university degrees, Obama's youthful optimism, Ivy League pedigree, and "nuanced rhetorical style" made him "Barack the New Black" for many Americans (Ford 2009). These qualities enabled him to appeal to a broad "coalition of college-students, hard-core progressives, and political independents" and raise "millions of dollars from small individual donations" (Ford 2009:39).

Obama thus personifies the heterogeneity of the new Black elite, and his presidency came at a critical moment in the evolution of the Black upper class. Four decades after the civil rights movement, many native-born descendants of enslaved people had experienced unprecedented gains in education, enabling them to enter prestigious universities, attain professional occupations, and earn high incomes. At the same time, immigration from Africa, the Caribbean, and Latin America accelerated Black population growth (Waters 1999; Massey et al. 2007; Model 2011; Hamilton 2019) while rising rates of intermarriage created a growing mixed-race population (Rockquemore and Brunsma 2007; Khanna 2011). By the turn of the century, the forces of socioeconomic mobility, immigration, and intermarriage together had generated a very heterogeneous, multihued Black elite (Herring, Keith, and Horton 2004; Charles, Torres, and Brunn 2008; Russell, Wilson, and Hall 2013).

Although the descendants of enslaved Africans, the children of immigrants, and the offspring of intermarried parents have all contributed to the great diversity of the new Black elite, its otherwise heterogeneous members generally share one trait in common: the possession of a college degree, often from a very selective institution. Given that a college education is essential for advancement in today's globalized, knowledge-based economy, the college campus is now the crucible for elite class formation, no less for Blacks than other social groups. Here, we draw on a unique source of data to study the new Black elite in the process of formation at twenty-eight selective institutions of higher education between 1999 and 2003. In doing so, we seek to join others in redirecting scholarly attention away from its myopic preoccupation with the plight of poor Blacks and instead consider internal variation and status differentiation within the Black community, focusing in particular on the new elite emerging on college campuses at the dawn of the twenty-first century.

As we shall see, Black students at selective institutions of higher education are a very diverse lot, far more heterogeneous with respect to socioeconomic status than White students at the same institutions and much more diverse with respect to immigrant and mixed-race origins than the Black population generally (Massey et al. 2003). A light skin tone, a college education, and foreign origins have long been markers of status in the Black community, however. To set the stage for our analysis of Black diversity at selective colleges and universities, we offer a brief history of Black class stratification from the days of slavery up to the civil rights era of the 1960s.

Black Class Stratification Before 1965

Since the days of slavery, light skin tone has given Blacks of racially mixed ancestry an edge over their dark-skinned peers despite the institutionalized construction of race as a master status in American society (Hughes and Hertel 1990; Turner 1995; Hunter 1998; Hill 2000; Herring, Keith, and Horton 2004; Wade, Romano, and Blue 2004; Eberhardt et al. 2006; Hochschild and Weaver 2007). Although "polite" southern Whites typically turned a blind eye to sexual unions between slave owners and enslaved women, they were nonetheless quite common in the antebellum period and produced a cadre of light-skinned offspring who were often granted favored positions on slaveholding estates (Woodward 1981).

Children of interracial unions and their descendants typically provided personal service to the master's family, a relatively privileged status that granted them sustained exposure to elite White culture and society (Gordon-Reed 2008). Given their "acceptable" appearance and the fact that many were the master's own children, these slaves were among the first Black Americans to receive any kind of systematic instruction (Du Bois 1903). They frequently had the opportunity to train as apprentices in various fields under the auspices of their owners, who saw them as "good Negroes" in which investment was worthwhile. At a time when any type of formal education or training was outlawed for the enslaved, "house slaves" thus had a privileged status over that of field slaves (Hill 2000).

Many of them strove to emulate the behavior, speech, and decorum of their masters in order to gain favor, and at times they looked down on their darker counterparts employed elsewhere on the estate who did not enjoy these benefits. Because of their White ancestry, they typically gained their freedom before other enslaved people; their descendants were able to obtain higher paying positions within the White community such as lawyer, doctor, business owner, barber, caterer, and domestic servant (Bullock 1967:1–36). Their visible White ancestry gave them better standing relative to other Blacks, and over the generations, this initial advantage translated into greater access to human and social capital, what Hill (2000) calls "the social origins explanation" for light-skinned privilege.

Free Blacks in the antebellum period were also mostly light-skinned and lived in cities where they also had an elevated status. More than 80 percent of free Blacks in Louisiana were classified as mixed race in 1850, and nationally, a third of free Blacks were classified as "mulatto" in that year's U.S. census, compared with just one out of ten enslaved people (Landry 1987:24). They had relatively close relationships with Whites of similar socioeconomic standing, thus distancing themselves socially from the poor and illiterate Black masses (Moore 1999).

The situation for the small share of Blacks living in the antebellum North was quite different. Above the Mason-Dixon line, the system of slavery was not as entrenched and upwardly mobile Blacks were often able to work and live alongside Whites. At the dawn of the nineteenth century, there were around sixty thousand free Black Americans, most of whom lived in the North, a number that rose to nearly five hundred thousand by 1860 (Pifer 1973:8). During the early nineteenth century, the northern Black elite commonly interacted with similarly stationed Whites, and their children frequently attended integrated schools and played together with White children (Massey and Denton 1993). A fervent abolitionist movement in the North created space for integrationist sentiments, especially in cities such as Boston, New York, and Philadelphia.

During Reconstruction from 1865 to 1876, elite Blacks in the North continued to build status by sending their children to leading public and private
secondary schools where they would receive a first-rate education to prepare
them for the rigors of a predominately White college. A college education was
understood to "both promote the upward mobility of those outside the aristocracy of color and enhance the position of those inside it" (Gatewood
2000:273). Nonetheless, fewer than twenty-five hundred Black Americans ever
graduated from college between 1826 and 1900. Those who did graduate were
held in high esteem and were expected to "represent the race" by taking leadership positions within society. Upper-class Blacks recognized that a high-caliber
education was imperative for sustaining their own high status and ensuring
the future successes of their children.

In the decades immediately following Emancipation, more than 90 percent of
Black Americans remained in the South, where the caste lines of race remained
rigid even during Reconstruction. Members of the southern Black intelligentsia
were forced to send their children to private schools in the North or to one of the
handful of segregated schools that catered specifically to the southern Black elite.
The Avery Normal Institute in Charleston, South Carolina and the Beach Institute in Savannah, Georgia were among the first finishing schools for the children
of prominent southern Blacks who could afford the monthly tuition.

Led by upper-class members of the old free Black population and backed
by the financial support of White philanthropists, the Freedmen's Bureau and
the American Missionary Association provided students with both academic
and industrial training. Black students learned farming, sewing, and home
economics, along with history, government, and philosophy as well as African
American history. Lessons focused on the leadership of prominent Black
Americans who had succeeded in various endeavors despite slavery and segregation and thereby served as models to "uplift the race." Unfortunately, legal
segregation and sharecropping replaced slavery as the principle mechanisms
of racial exploitation in the South after Reconstruction ended in 1877 and the
options for Black students quickly narrowed. In 1875, the Beach Institute, originally founded by the Freedmen's Bureau in 1867, was turned over to the Savannah Board of Education where it became just another underfunded and segregated public school, finally closing its doors in 1919. By the 1880s, the Avery
Institute was the only college preparatory school for Charleston's large Black
population (Drago 1990; Gatewood 2000).

After the demise of Reconstruction, opportunities for elite secondary education moved northward to Washington, DC, where Republican politicians

continued to grant the freedmen and their descendants patronage employment within certain sectors of the federal government. At the center of elite secondary education in the North was the M Street High School in Washington, DC, later renamed Dunbar High School in 1915. Originally chartered in 1870 in the basement of the 15th Street Presbyterian Church by William Syphax, a trustee of the Colored Schools of Washington, DC, the school became the principal training ground for the Washington Black elite during the late nineteenth and early twentieth centuries. Syphax, who was himself a descendant of a "distinguished line" of plantation aristocrats, recognized the importance of a classical education in preparing Black students for the nation's elite colleges and universities (Preston 1935:448).

Most Black faculty members at Dunbar had advanced degrees from Ivy League schools but were unable to obtain faculty positions at White colleges and universities. In 1873, Richard T. Greener, Harvard's first Black American graduate, became the school principal and established a curriculum that trained generations of future Black academics who would eventually teach at Black institutions of higher education (Graham 1999:61; Gatewood 2000:267–272). Other privileged Black parents in the South sent their children to parochial schools that were connected to Black churches in Memphis, Louisville, and Charleston. These schools provided the Black aristocracy with a much better education than that offered by public schools founded by freedmen. The teaching staff at these private Black schools consisted of well-educated Black Americans as well as northern missionary Whites who recognized this "better class of Negroes" as future Black leaders (Du Bois 1903:130).

Despite the surge in school creation and educational advancement during Reconstruction, as Whites consolidated the Jim Crow system of legal segregation in the late nineteenth and early twentieth centuries, opportunities for Black students to receive a college education withered. Prior to the 1960s, never more than 5 percent of adult Black Americans ever held a college degree. Those who did manage to graduate from college became members of a privileged Black intelligentsia, since "access to a college education was clearly the earliest and surest method for earning respect among progressive Whites who were willing to teach Blacks various trades and offer them limited work" (Graham 1999:8).

With access to education at White colleges and universities blocked, most Black Americans before the 1960s attended historically Black institutions such as Fisk University, Howard University, Morehouse College, Spelman College, or the Tuskegee Institute (Du Bois 1903; Lovett 2011). By the end of the nineteenth century, the nation hosted seventy-six Black colleges and universities (the earliest founded in 1837) as well as several Black dental, medical, and law schools. Often founded by northern White religious societies during Reconstruction, these institutions recruited the "best and the brightest" of Black America to produce successive cohorts of Black lawyers, doctors, businessmen, dentists, professors, and teachers who worked in and on behalf of the Black community (Lovett 2011).

Until the civil rights era, Black college graduates were demarcated from other Black Americans not only by their years of schooling but also by their light skin tone, immigrant origins, and multigenerational access to social and human capital (Myrdal 1944; Drake and Cayton 1945; Frazier 1957; Landry 1987, 2018; Hughes and Hertel 1990; Cole and Omari 2003). They comprised a small but formidable group of people who set the stage for political mobilization during the civil rights era (see Landry 1987, 2018; McAdam 1982; Gatewood 2000). Du Bois (1903) famously labeled them the Talented Tenth, describing them as a cadre of "educated mulattoes" and "college-bred Negroes" who could lead the Black race forward to progress (Kilson 2014). Du Bois was himself a member of the northern Black elite. Born into privilege in Massachusetts of White and West Indian ancestry, he was well versed in the culture and mores of upper-class White society. He attended an elite boarding school and earned degrees at both Fisk and Harvard Universities (Lewis 1995).

Du Bois argued that a classic liberal arts education similar to that received by Whites was required to ensure that the "best of this race" would be prepared to spearhead the cause of racial advancement and eventually eradicate White prejudice and segregation. A college education, Du Bois (1903:63) believed, was vital to developing a moral and professional class able to "leaven the lump to inspire the masses" and "raise the Talented Tenth to leadership." A degree from a Black institution such as Howard, Spelman, or Morehouse not only presaged a professional occupation and respectable marriage partner but also carried with it responsibilities for social activism and political leadership. Historical evidence reveals that what Gatewood (2000) labeled an aristocracy of color was part of a dynastic assemblage of affluent mixed-race and immigrant-origin families who experienced a "cross-generational transmission of bourgeois status" as a result of a significant "color-caste dynamic" (Kilson 2014:25–26; see also Du Bois 1903; Kronus 1971).

In other words, prior to the civil rights era, the Black elite developed a "parallel social structure" based on skin color, education, and generations of inherited social status that set them apart from other Black Americans

(Gatewood 2000:4). Until World War I, this small elite group held professional and entrepreneurial occupations and interacted regularly with both a White and Black clientele (Massey and Denton 1993). In this sense, they "straddled the separate Black and White urban worlds . . . until the World War I Era and the beginning of the Great Migration" (Brown 2013:73; see also Myrdal 1944; Drake and Cayton 1945; Frazier 1957).

Although English-speaking Black West Indian immigrants have been a presence in the United States since the 1700s (Johnson 2000; Shaw-Taylor and Tuch 2007), their contribution to elite class formation in Black America has historically been overlooked by scholars and the public alike. According to Bryce-Laporte (1972:31, original emphases), "While black foreigners (and their progenies) have held a disproportionately high number of leadership and successful positions and have exercised significant influence in black life in this country, their cultural impact as *foreigners* has been ignored or has merely been given lip service in the larger spheres of American life. On the national level, they suffer double invisibility, in fact—*as blacks and as black foreigners.*"

Immigration from the West Indies surged during the first decades of the twentieth century, and by 1932, foreign-born Blacks comprised about 4 percent of the Black elite, though only 1 percent of the total Black American population (Reid 1939). Seventy-three percent of all Black immigrants living in the United States were from the West Indies, totaling approximately one hundred and thirty thousand persons (Reid 1939). Black immigration from the Caribbean was highly selective in terms of education, motivation, and aspirations, and most of the new arrivals came from societies in which Blacks were dominant and where race was more of a fluid construct than a caste-like categorization. As a result, the offspring of Black immigrants generally did better educationally and achieved greater upward mobility than native-born Blacks (Reid 1939).

Immigrants coming from British colonies such as Jamaica, Bermuda, and Barbados often earned professional degrees at America's Black colleges and universities, and by 1927, they had established a Caribbean Club at Howard University (Logan 1958). In addition to Du Bois, other well-known Black figures of Caribbean origins include the actor Sidney Poitier, musician Harry Belafonte, Harlem Renaissance writer James Weldon Johnson, congresswoman Shirley Chisolm, Black activist Malcom X, army general and diplomat Colin Powell, Black Power leader Kwame Ture (née Stokely Carmichael), and Nation of Islam leader Louis Farrakhan, just to name a few.

In sum, the descendants of mixed-race enslaved persons, free people of color, and West Indian immigrants dominated the Black aristocracy during the first half of the twentieth century. Their light skin tones, college educations, immigrant origins, and knowledge of White culture set them apart from the mass of Black Americans prior to the civil rights era. Access to education, often through paternalistic relationships with upper-class Whites, along with a shared recognition of the economic and racial barriers faced by all Blacks, was integral to the development of a cohesive Black elite class.

The Great Migration of the twentieth century transformed the Black elite by creating large urban Black communities outside the South that supported a growing middle class of merchants, professionals, and intellectuals (Kennedy 1968; Marks 1989; Lemann 1991; Wilkerson 2010). However, mass in-migration from the rural South hardened the residential color line in cities throughout the North (Lieberson 1980; Massey and Denton 1993). No longer welcome to participate in White society, privileged light-skinned northern Blacks were increasingly relegated to serving the Black community and developing themselves within the confines of the nation's emerging Black urban ghettos. In combination with de jure segregation under Jim Crow in the South, de facto segregation in the North created a rigid racial caste system that limited options for members of the Black elite in White society (Warner 1936; Dollard 1937; Myrdal 1944; Drake and Cayton 1945). It was during this time that the old Black elite lost its privileged status as broker between Whites and the larger Black community (Washington 2011).

Origins of the New Black Elite

Until the middle of the twentieth century, life chances for Black Americans in U.S. society were circumscribed by Jim Crow segregation in the South, de facto segregation in the North, and institutionalized discrimination and exclusion throughout the nation (Massey and Denton 1993; Katznelson 2005; Massey 2007; Rothstein 2017). The situation began to change after World War II, however, with a civil rights movement that began slowly at first but then gathered momentum through the 1950s and 1960s to crest in the 1970s. In 1948, President Harry Truman desegregated the U.S. military, and in 1954, the U.S. Supreme Court eliminated the constitutional foundations for Jim Crow segregation in the South in its *Brown v. Board of Education of Topeka* decision, setting the stage for a civil rights revolution (Williams 1987; Branch 1988, 1998, 2006).

The pace of racial change accelerated during the 1960s, beginning with the passage of the 1964 Civil Rights Act, which outlawed racial discrimination in

labor markets, hotels, motels, restaurants, theaters, and services. The legislation also provided additional resources to promote school desegregation. The
1965 Voting Rights Act prohibited states from restricting the right of African
Americans to vote and authorized federal authorities to enforce Black suffrage
in states characterized by a history of voter suppression. The 1968 Fair Housing
Act banned discrimination in the rental and sale of housing, and beginning in
1969 (Massey and Denton 1993), affirmative action policies were implemented
in an effort to expand Black access to jobs and education through the use of
racially focused targets and recruitment efforts (Skrentny 1996).

During the 1970s, the attention of civil rights leaders turned to discrimination in lending markets. In 1974, the Equal Credit Opportunity Act was passed
to prohibit racial discrimination in mortgage lending and other credit markets,
and it was followed in 1975 by the Home Mortgage Disclosure Act, which
compelled banks to compile data on the race of loan applicants for enforcement purposes. Finally, in 1977, Congress passed the Community Reinvest-
ment Act to end the practice of redlining by which federal housing authorities,
banks, and other lending institutions had color-coded predominantly Black
neighborhoods red to deny residents access to capital and credit, whatever
their race. By the end of the 1970s, racial discrimination had been officially
outlawed in virtually all U.S. markets.

The civil rights legislation passed between 1964 and 1977 greatly expanded
opportunities for aspiring African Americans in education and employment
and led to a surge of growth in the Black middle and upper classes. Figure 1.1
draws on data from the decennial U.S. census and the American Community
Survey to plot the percentage of Black men and women aged twenty-five or
more who held a college degree from 1940 through 2019. As already noted, this
percentage did not exceed 5 percent for either gender until after the civil rights
era. From 1940 to 1970, the percentage of Black Americans holding a college
degree rose very slowly, going from 1.4 percent to 4.2 percent with little difference between Black men and women.

After 1970, however, the percentage of college graduates rose rapidly, dou-
bling to 8.4 percent in 1980, again with little difference by gender. Thereafter,
the increase accelerated further for Black women, with the share holding
at least an associate's degree reaching 19.8 percent in 1990. In contrast, the trend
for Black men did not accelerate and the share of college educated among them
stood only at 11.9 percent in 1990, opening up a large gender gap. Growth in the
share of college-educated Black women flattened during the 1990s, rising to just
20.1 percent in 2000 while the share of college-educated Black men increased

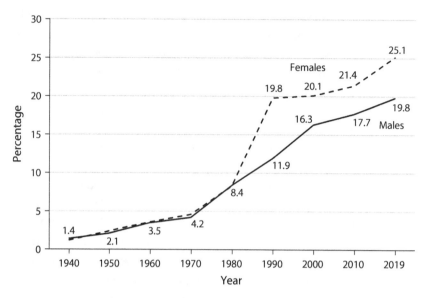

FIGURE 1.1. Percent college educated among Black Americans
Sources: U.S. Census (1850–2010) and American Community Survey (2019)
(Ruggles, Flood, et al. 2021)

and reached 16.3 percent in 2000, thus narrowing the gender gap at the turn of the twenty-first century.

After 2000, however, the increase in the share of college-educated Black men slowed substantially and reached just 19.8 percent in 2019, whereas the upward trajectory resumed for Black women and accelerated after 2010 to propel their share of college graduates to a record high of 25.1 percent in 2019, once again widening the gender gap for college completion. As a class, therefore, the population of college-educated Black Americans has come to be characterized by a very imbalanced sex ratio in which there are 139 college-educated Black women for every 100 college-educated Black men, according to data from the 2019 American Community Survey (Ruggles, Flood, et al. 2021). Among Black college students who were enrolled in U.S. degree-granting institutions in 2019, there were 141 Black women for every 100 Black men (U.S. National Center for Educational Statistics 2020a). The sex ratio is even more skewed at selective institutions. Among Black students attending twenty-eight selective colleges surveyed in 1999 by Massey et al. (2003), there were two hundred Black women for every one hundred Black men on campus.

Although Black incomes continue to lag well behind White incomes, the increasing share of African Americans holding college degrees has led to

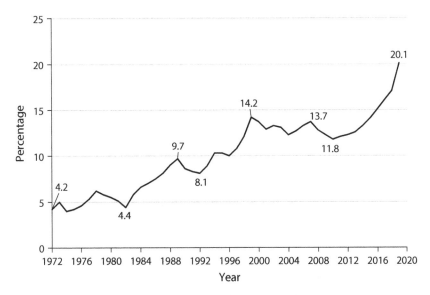

FIGURE 1.2. Percentage of Black households with incomes over $100,000
Source: U.S. Current Population Survey (Flood et al. 2021)

significant increases in household income, as shown in figure 1.2, which draws
on data from the Census Bureau's Current Population Survey to plot the percentage of Black households earning incomes over $100,000 from 1972 to 2019
(U.S. Census Bureau 2020). In 1972, only 4.2 percent of Black households reported earning this much income, and in 1982, the figure was still only
4.4 percent. Thereafter, the share of Black households earning more than
$100,000 rose more rapidly, reaching 9.7 percent in 1989 before turning down-
ward slightly and then recovering after 1992 to reach 14.2 percent in 1999. After
the dot-com bust of 2000, the percentage once again fell but then recovered a
bit to reach 13.7 percent in 2007 when the Great Recession hit. After dropping
back to 11.8 percent in 2010, it then rebounded again to reach an all-time high
of 20.1 percent in 2019.

In sum, from 1972 to 2019, the share of Black households with incomes
above $100,000 rose 4.8 times. Over roughly the same period, the share of
college graduates increased 4.7 times for Black men and 5.5 times for Black
women, thereby greatly expanding the absolute and relative number of affluent, well-educated African Americans. As already noted, however, increases in
income and education were not the only factors reshaping the size and composition of the Black upper class—immigration and intermarriage also played

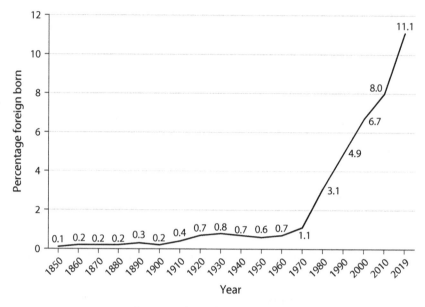

FIGURE 1.3. Percentage foreign born among Black Americans
Sources: U.S. Census (1850–2010) and American Community Survey (2019)
(Ruggles, Flood, et al. 2021)

an important role. Figure 1.3 therefore uses data from the U.S. decennial census
(see Gibson and Lennon 1999 for 1850–1990) and the American Community
Survey to plot the percentage foreign born among Black Americans from 1850
to 2019 (Ruggles, Flood, et al. 2021).

For most of U.S. history, immigrants accounted for a tiny share of all Black
Americans. Prior to 1900, the share never rose above 0.3 percent. Although the
share increased between 1900 and 1930 owing to the arrival of immigrants from
the English-speaking Caribbean, the percentage peaked at just 0.8 percent in
1930, and it was not until 1970 that the share of Black foreigners exceeded
1 percent nationwide, reaching 1.1 percent in that year. Thereafter, the percentage of foreign-born Blacks moved sharply upward, reaching 3.1 percent in 1980,
4.9 percent in 1990, 6.7 percent in 2000, 8.0 percent in 2010, and 11.1 percent in
2019, compared to a value of around 14.6 percent in the U.S. population
overall.

Immigrants invariably are a selected population and not a representative
cross-section of their nations of origin (Hamilton 2019). Non-refugee immigrants tend to be positively selected with respect to observable traits such as
education and health as well as unobservable traits such as motivation,

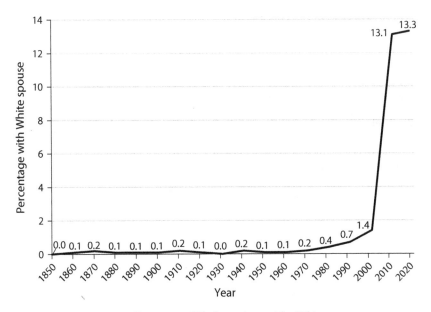

FIGURE 1.4. Percentage of Black marriages with a White spouse
Sources: Gullickson 2006 (1850–2000) and Flood, et al. 2021, U.S. Current Population
Survey (2010 and 2018)

ambition, and willingness to take risks. Given this positive selection, immigrants are generally poised to do better than natives in countries of destination (Hamilton 2019). Although they may begin life in the United States at a lower point in the socioeconomic hierarchy than natives, over time immigrants tend to catch up with and surpass natives on outcomes such as education, occupational status, and earnings (Chiswick 1978), especially if they hail from English-speaking nations (Chiswick and Miller 1998, 2010). Data suggest that this pattern prevails for African and Caribbean immigrants to the United States (Dodoo 1991, 1999; Hamilton 2012, 2013, 2014, 2019), and unsurprisingly, the children of Black immigrants are clearly overrepresented among Blacks attending selective colleges and universities (Massey et al. 2007; Model 2011; Benson 2020).

Although rates of Black-White intermarriage have been quite low historically, in recent years they have risen to generate a growing population of mixed-race individuals who are also overrepresented on the campuses of elite institutions of higher education (Massey et al. 2003). Figure 1.4 draws on data compiled by Gullickson (2006) and the U.S. Current Population Survey (Flood et al. 2021) to show the trend in the Black-White intermarriage rate for

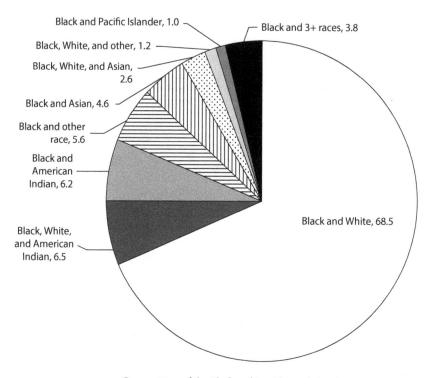

FIGURE 1.5. Composition of the Black multiracial population in 2019
Source: American Community Survey (Ruggles, Flood, et al. 2021)

Black men from 1850 to 2018. From 1850 to 1970, the rate of outmarriage to White women for Black men was exceedingly low, never exceeding 0.2 percent of all marriages. In 1980, however, the rate rose to 0.4 percent and after climbing to 0.7 percent in 1990 and 1.4 percent in 2000 shot upward to 13.1 percent in 2010 and edged up to 13.3 percent in 2018. Among Black Americans, the rate of intermarriage rises with education and is twice as high for Black men compared to Black women; the gender gap widens as education increases steadily as one goes from high school or less to some college to college graduates (Livingston and Brown 2017).

A rise in the rate of interracial marriage inevitably produces growth in the number of persons who report racially mixed origins. According to data from the U.S. decennial census and the 2019 American Community Survey, the number of people reporting mixed racial origins has risen steadily over time, going from 1.7 million persons in 2000 to 3.1 million persons in 2010 and 3.7 million persons in 2015, representing 4.8 percent, 7.4 percent, and 8.4 percent of the total population reporting any Black racial ancestry, respectively (Parker et al. 2015). Figure 1.5 shows the composition of the U.S. Black population reporting two or more races by specific combination of racial origins, as reported on the 2019 American Community Survey (Ruggles, Flood, et al. 2021).

Unsurprisingly given the composition of the U.S. population generally, the most frequently reported origins are Black and White, a combination reported by 68.5 percent of all racially mixed Black individuals in that year. The next largest categories involve American Indian origins, with 6.5 percent reporting Black, White, and American Indian origins and 6.2 percent reporting just Black and American Indian origins. The fourth largest category is Black and "other" race at 5.6 percent, followed by Black and Asian at 4.6 percent, Black, White, and Asian at 2.6 percent, Black, White, and other at 1.2 percent, and Black and Pacific Islander at 1.0 percent. All remaining categories incorporating three or more races together constitute 3.8 percent of the Black multiracial population.

Thus, more than two-thirds of racially mixed Black individuals are the offspring of unions in which one of the partners has married "up" in the American racial hierarchy by choosing a White mate, potentially enabling mixed-race children to tap into the accumulated stock of human, social, and cultural capital from the White side of the family, in addition to whatever stocks of capital may be available on the Black side, thus increasing the diversity and range of resources with which to advance in society. Black-White unions have long been known to be characterized by a "status exchange" in which a partner with a lower racial status but a higher educational status marries someone with a higher racial status but a lower educational status (Merton 1941).

Recent research suggests that this pattern continues for African Americans. Most interracial marriages are homogamous with respect to education, and as just noted, the likelihood of an interracial union increases as education rises. Among those interracially married couples who do report different levels of education, however, husbands and wives from lower racial status groups and higher educational levels generally marry spouses from higher status groups but lower educational levels (Qian 1997; Fu 2001; Torche and Rich 2017). On average, therefore, the offspring of racial intermarriages are likely to have at least one and more likely two parents with a relatively high degree of education.

Studying the New Black Elite

Contemporary research on Black Americans has focused mainly on the plight of the poor and paid little attention to internal variation and status differentiation in the broader Black community (for exceptions, see Gregory 1998; Smith and Moore 2000, 2002; Crutcher 2010; Clerge 2019). Despite a large body of work on racial identity, skin tone stratification, and Black immigration, these literatures are often disconnected from the contemporary study of social class within Black America. It is our goal to unite these literatures through a detailed analysis of data gathered under the auspices of the National Longitudinal Survey of Freshmen (NLSF), a five-wave survey of students who were just beginning their college studies in the fall of 1999 and began receiving their college degrees in the spring of 2003. In doing so, we seek to open a window onto the composition and character of the emerging Black elite of the twenty-first century.

Some thirty-five selective institutions were invited to participate in the survey, which was funded by the Mellon Foundation and the Atlantic Philanthropies (see Massey et al. 2003). Equal-sized cohorts of White, Black, Hispanic, and Asian students were interviewed soon after they arrived on campus and were then reinterviewed over the next four years, during the spring terms of 2000 through 2003. The baseline survey gathered comprehensive data on subjects' social origins, including detailed information about the family, school, and neighborhoods they inhabited at ages six, thirteen, and as seniors in high school, as well as data on their personal perceptions, values, aspirations, and attitudes. The follow-up surveys focused on students' social and academic experiences on campus as they proceeded through college or university, with students who transferred to other academic institutions or dropped out of school being retained as participants in the survey. Having entered college roughly at the age of eighteen, these students today must be around forty years old.

Sampling was stratified by the relative size of the Black student body at each institution. Schools with relatively large Black student populations (1,000+) were assigned a target sample size of 280 respondents (70 individuals from each of the four racial/ethnic groups), those with Black student populations of 500–1,000 got a target size of 200 interviews (50 in each group), those with 100–500 Black students had a target size of 80 respondents (20 in each group), and those with fewer than 100 Black students were assigned a quota of 40 interviews (10 in each group).

In the end, twenty-eight institutions agreed to participate in the study for an institutional response rate of 80 percent. The final sample included sixteen private universities, seven private liberal arts colleges, four public universities, and one historically Black institution (Howard University in Washington, DC). Interviewers approached 4,573 respondents across these campuses and successfully completed 3,924 interviews for an overall response rate of

86 percent. In order to be eligible for inclusion in the sample, a respondent had to be enrolled at the institution in question as a first-time freshman and be a citizen or legal resident of the United States. Here, we focus exclusively on the Black subsample of 1,039 students. To date the NLSF has provided the basis for two books, ten dissertations, and dozens of journal articles. As a result, the survey and its methodology have been well covered in prior publications, especially by Massey et al. (2003: chap. 2 and appendixes) and Charles et al. (2009: appendixes). Additional information is available from the project website at http://nlsf.princeton.edu/.

We originally invited three other historically Black colleges and universities (HBCUs) to participate in the study, hoping to contrast how student social and academic outcomes unfolded over four years in predominantly Black versus majority-White contexts. Unfortunately, Howard was the only institution to accept our invitation, and the small size of its sample (n = 60) is insufficient to sustain separate quantitative analyses comparing social and academic outcomes on predominantly Black and White campuses, and project resources did not permit the extension of qualitative fieldwork to Howard's campus.

Our analyses therefore necessarily focus on the experiences and behaviors of Black students on majority-White campuses. Nonetheless, to represent the experiences of Howard students in our portrayal of the new Black elite, we include them in both our simple descriptive and multivariate analyses. In the latter models, we use a dichotomous measure to indicate the experience of attending an HBCU like Howard and in our interpretations note distinctive departures from the rest of the sample whenever the variable proved statistically significant.

Apart from the relative absence of HBCUs, the twenty-eight institutions in the NLSF well represent the diversity of selective institutions in the United States, which range from rural small liberal arts colleges to urban Ivy League campuses to flagship public universities, which were selected to reflect geographic diversity across the United States. Choosing to attend an HBCU such as Howard is likely related to many of the social and academic outcomes we consider in later chapters. Prior research as well as autobiographical writings generally indicate that being at a place like Howard allows Black students the freedom to explore identities and academics away from the anti-Black racism common to White institutional spaces (e.g., Feagin, Vera, and Imani 1996; Willie 2003; Coates 2015).

In interviews with fifty-five college alumni from Northwestern and Howard Universities from 1967 to 1989, for example, Willie (2003) examined how college experiences had changed for Black students during the twenty years after the civil rights movement. For Northwestern alumni, "experiencing racism was a nearly universal aspect of the college experience . . . although the incidents they describe were not constant and usually not overwhelming, and did not leave most feeling bitter in subsequent years" (Willie 2003:78). Northwestern alumni underscored the importance of getting a first-rate education that gave them increased entrée to the White corporate mainstream. In contrast, Howard alumni stressed the importance of how Howard increased their self-esteem and promoted racial pride. Willie's respondents repeatedly detailed the nurturing, family-like climate at Howard and how faculty and peers valued their intellectual worth; void of racial hostility, the Howard alumni discussed at length how they were able to grow and develop academically and socioemotionally throughout their college tenure.

Willie's (2003) findings represent a common theme in contemporary literature on HBCUs (e.g., Fries-Britt and Turner 2002; Gasman 2008; Kim and Conrad 2006; Palmer, Wood, and Arroyo 2015). Nonetheless, institutional racism still mars the experiences of Howard and other HBCU students. Prestigious predominantly White institutions (PWIs) like Northwestern have large endowments (Northwestern's endowment was over $11 billion in 2020 and the thirteenth largest in the country) thanks to donations from generations of White alumni who have had the opportunity to amass great wealth. Howard, on the other hand, relies largely on government funds to stay afloat, as structural racism has limited its Black alumni base's ability to raise comparable wealth for the institution. Howard's endowment is roughly $700 million and ranks as the 158th largest as of 2020 (National Association of College and University Business Officers 2021). Willie's (2003) interviews revealed that Howard alumni were often left without financial aid or housing because of bureaucratic mix-ups and were forced to sit for hours in the financial aid or housing office to rectify these problems. Black students who opt to attend HBCUs often come from less financially stable backgrounds and are more likely to be first-generation college students. In addition, they possess less academically relevant social and cultural capital than same-race peers who attend selective PWIs (e.g., Palmer and Gasman 2008; Burnett 2020).

In the ensuing chapters, our empirical analyses of the NLSF's quantitative data consist mainly of simple descriptive tables that identify and analyze differences across the dimensions of Black diversity we have identified, exploring variation among students by racial identification, skin tone, nativity, generation, region of origin, gender, social class, and prior experiences of segregation. The analysis begins by describing the dimensions themselves and then in successive chapters we move on to document variation in the traits and characteristics associated with the different dimensions and how they differentiate Black students from one another. In deriving these tables, we first applied the Statistical Analysis System's multiple imputation procedure (*SAS proc mi*) to estimate missing values. Multiple imputation is preferred to listwise deletion of variables with missing data because it allows us to keep a consistent sample size of 1,039 respondents while increasing the validity of estimated values (Allison 2001).

Due to the large number of variables in each chapter, we run a separate set of imputations independently for each chapter. Computing a single set of imputations for all variables was computationally infeasible given the complexity of the imputation algorithm, which rises as the number of missing values increases. Moreover, within each chapter, variables with missing values tend to be theoretically and mathematically related to others also under consideration, providing strong auxiliary variables for the imputation process. For composite scales we constructed from other variables, we first imputed each component variable and then created the scale after imputation. This procedure allows us to include the full sample of Black respondents while avoiding biases that single- or best-subset imputation might otherwise introduce.

Although the analyses presented in each chapter come in the form of descriptive tables, the various dimensions of Black diversity are obviously interrelated and often strongly correlated with one another, leading us to undertake a series of multivariate analyses to tease out which characteristics and outcomes are associated with which dimensions of diversity while holding the influence of all other dimensions constant. Mixed racial origins are strongly associated with a lighter skin tone, for example, while parental education is associated with segregation and nativity and generation are correlated with region of origin; all of these associations are crosscut by gendered differences between Black men and Black women, yielding a plethora of intersections (see Crenshaw 1989; Collins and Bilge 2016).

By shifting to a multivariate framework, we can identify the independent influence of each dimension of Black diversity on outcomes of interest, enabling us to disentangle, for example, the influence of racially mixed parentage from skin tone in predicting racial identity. Multivariate analysis also enables us to consider a broad range of Black intersectionalities, not just by gender but also by racial classification (monoracial or mixed race), nativity and generation, immigrant region of origin, and experience of segregation, thereby revealing the multiplicity of Black collegiate experiences.

The multivariate analyses proceed in sequential fashion following the order of chapters, going from precollege outcomes and experiences and then moving on to consider developments as they unfold on campus, beginning with an analysis of racial identities and attitudes, the parental child-rearing strategies experienced by different students, and their academic preparation for college. In addition to dichotomous indicators of categories of diversity, the multivariate models also include controls for family background factors such as household structure, maternal employment, income, home ownership, and degree of childhood exposure to disorder and violence in neighborhoods and schools. We also include whether a student attends Howard, as the one HBCU in our sample, in our multivariate models and report the significance of those findings in relevant chapter conclusions, as choosing to attend an HBCU is likely to be related to one's upbringing as well as one's experience on campus (Willie 2003). As we move sequentially from chapter to chapter, we add additional controls for other salient variables identified in the prior chapter. At each stage, we perform the same multiple imputation procedure we used in constructing the descriptive tables. All analyses are therefore performed using the unweighted sample of 1,039 Black NLSF respondents. Since the multivariate models are complex and difficult for a general audience to understand, we relegate their specification and presentation to appendix A, and in the text of the book itself, we simply summarize the main results in plain language at the conclusion of each chapter.

In order to provide additional depth and reveal the lived experiences behind the numbers, we also make use of two sources of qualitative data. The first source consists of narratives derived from seventy-eight in-depth interviews with Black undergraduates at two of the participating NLSF institutions. The subjects were full-time students aged eighteen to twenty-two interviewed in two separate waves, with forty-three done on one campus from the fall of 2000 through the spring of 2005 and thirty-five done at the second campus from the fall of 2007 through the spring of 2008. Black students comprised between 5 percent and 6 percent of the undergraduate population at both institutions. To ensure confidentiality, each respondent was given a pseudonym that was attached to all records with no additional identifying information. The last of these interviewees were set to graduate in 2004 from the first institution and in 2011 from the second institution.

Both universities consistently rank among the top institutions of higher education in the annual report published by U.S. News and World Report, with admissions rates of around 26 percent and 11 percent at the time of the baseline survey and SAT averages of 1400 and 1450. Although both are elite private institutions, they are quite different with respect to size, setting, resources, academic climate, and access to Black-oriented activities and extracurricular options. One of the schools is known for its bucolic, small-town setting and its focus on the liberal arts. The other school is touted in college guidebooks as an "urban ivy" and is known for its preprofessional orientation; it is located adjacent to a predominantly Black inner-city neighborhood and sponsors numerous multicultural organizations, including a Black-themed dorm that serves as a hub for Black social and academic life on campus.

In compiling our qualitative data, we made explicit efforts to sample students across class years with different academic interests and a wide range of backgrounds and perspectives. Interviewees, their pseudonyms, and their background characteristics are listed in appendix B. They were located using respondent-driven sampling methods in which initial contacts led to subsequent referrals that were converted into interviews (Glaser and Strauss 1967; Weiss 1994). All interviews were conducted by Kimberly Torres, who spent a great deal of time on the campuses of both institutions attending events and meeting students, not only to conduct interviews but also to discuss ongoing research and elicit feedback from respondents.

Black men were oversampled given that in the institutions surveyed Black women outnumbered Black men by a ratio of two to one (Massey et al. 2003), yielding final interviews completed with forty men and thirty-eight women. All interviews were undertaken using a semistructured guide of open-ended questions (see appendix C). Of those interviewed, 22 percent identified themselves as monoracial Blacks with multiple generations of U.S. residence, 38 percent identified as monoracial Blacks of immigrant origin (born abroad or having at least one foreign-born parent), and 40 percent said they were of racially mixed parentage. Mixed-race interviewees were specifically asked about the race and ethnicity of each parent, and more than half of all mixed-race students also reported immigrant origins.

In designing the interview guide, we used the first-wave NLSF survey instrument as a template, including questions on students' precollege family, neighborhood, and school settings; their academic and social experiences before and during college; the factors that motivated them to attend their respective institutions; the racial and ethnic composition of their peer groups in high school and college; their social and academic adjustment to college; their conceptualization of racial identity; and their perceptions about themselves and others on campus. The guide was divided into sections and designed to gather as much information as possible on each topic. The resulting interviews produced nuanced narrative accounts on each topic and other subjects of interest as they came up, with the interviews often lasting several hours and at times extending over several sessions. Although we did not provide monetary compensation, interviewees were typically offered lunch or dinner as an incentive. The interview response rate was 100 percent, with all respondents contacted agreeing to participate and some even seeking us out to request an interview after hearing about the project from other students.

Without exception, the young adults we spoke to provided rich and detailed accounts of their experiences growing up and living on campus. Their responses were audio-recorded and transcribed in their entirety, and the resulting qualitative data were thematically coded in coordination with the quantitative data to provide continuity between the ethnographic and survey findings. We created a textual database of all interviews and followed open and axial coding techniques devised by the grounded theorists Glaser and Strauss (1967) and Strauss and Corbin (1990). The resulting codes were used to help select narrative quotations that fleshed out and exemplified the quantitative results. A separate numerical data file on the interviewees and their traits was created to enable quantification and comparison with results from respondents to the NLSF survey.

The second source of qualitative data come from eleven focus-group sessions conducted with seventy-five students, including twenty-nine Blacks, twenty-six Whites, and twenty mixed-race persons, all of whom were undergraduate students at the "urban Ivy" university. To guide group-level conversations, the semi-structured interview guide was adapted and tailored to fit the focus-group context and three trained moderators (including Torres) led the group discussions. Six of the focus groups were stratified by race to study in-group conceptions of race and racial identity (with three White groups and three Black groups). The remaining focus groups contained an even mix of Black and White participants in order to examine the extent to which racial context influenced how students from different racial backgrounds discussed race-related topics. Same-race moderators were used for two of the Black focus groups, and Torres moderated all of the White and multiracial groups as well as one of the Black groups.

The focus-group effort was no doubt aided by the fact that Torres had already built rapport with many of the students, as roughly two-thirds of all focus-group members had participated in the interview study. The focus groups included six to ten students each, with sessions lasting one and a half to two hours. Although in-depth interviews are well suited to acquiring detailed information about particular individuals and their experiences, the interviewer mostly determines the content and course of the conversation. In contrast, focus groups allow participants to feed off one another in their responses, thereby taking the conversation in new and different directions that might not have been anticipated by an interviewer, thus enabling an assessment of how group dynamics affect how students respond to questions about race and racial identity.

The overlap between participants in the interviews and focus-group conversations offers a lens for studying how Black, White, and mixed-race students understand race and the diverse ways they actualize their attitudes and beliefs in the company of other students. Although both the interview and the focus-group conversations were loosely guided by semistructured scripts, moderators worked to keep the group interactions as natural as possible by adopting an unrehearsed conversational tone that allowed participants to control the order of the discussion. As a result, the interview and focus groups differ from each other both in how specific questions were framed and in the order in which they were discussed. As with the interviewees, focus-group participants were given pseudonyms prior to the start of each session and conversations were recorded and transcribed in their entirety to enable both open and axial thematic coding.

In the end, our mixed-method approach aids us in providing a more nuanced and intimate portrait of what life was like for Black students on the campuses of selective colleges and universities at the turn of the twenty-first century. Although the data were originally collected to help shed light on the puzzle of minority underachievement, they also offer a detailed snapshot of the new century's Black professional class in the process of formation. At this writing, our interviewees are between twenty-nine and forty years old and presumably have made use of their elite educations to establish themselves as leaders in various endeavors both within and outside the Black community. Our data provide a unique window through which we can observe the diverse origins and varied experiences of the Black American elite as it was coming together in the early twenty-first century, enabling us to move beyond the analytic strictures of race as a master status.

Plan of the Book

Until quite recently, the primary training ground for ambitious young African Americans was on the campuses of HBCUs. In the twenty-first century, however, aspiring Black students have increasingly sought to earn their credentials at elite PWIs—social spaces that prior to the civil rights era were out of reach to most Black students. At present, only around 11 percent of Black college students attend HBCUs compared with 87 percent studying at historically White institutions (McClain and Perry 2017; Reese 2017). In today's knowledge- and information-based economy in which income and wealth are generated through the control, manipulation, and application of data, earning a degree from a selective college or university has become *the* critical step in achieving elite status in the United States for upper-class families, whether Black or White (Reeves 2017).

The extent to which even the rich value an elite education for their children was starkly on display in the college admissions scandal of 2019. Prosecutors around the country discovered that wealthy celebrities, corporate executives, and hedge fund managers were paying under-the-table bribes to ensure the admission of their offspring at top-tier colleges and universities (see Stripling 2019; Taylor 2020). Attending a selective college or university today not only prepares students academically for careers in the nation's upper class, but it also functions as a labeling mechanism that confers elite status and prestige on a rarified few.

Our aim here is to identify the traits and characteristics that differentiate Black students attending selective institutions from one another and to study how their diverse origins influence their social and academic experiences and outcomes before, during, and upon departure from college. In doing so, we seek to understand how intraracial diversity complicates traditional notions of race, class, and social mobility in the new Black professional class.[2] In order to capture the mindsets and experiences of *all* members of the new Black elite, we do not give each element of diversity its own chapter. Instead, we begin in chapter 2 by identifying the key dimensions of diversity, exploring the degree of heterogeneity among Black NLSF respondents with respect to ancestry, racial identification, nativity, generation, skin tone, class status, and gender. We then describe the complex interplay between these dimensions and show how they are associated with differences in parental work histories, family income, and household wealth. This analysis of intragroup heterogeneity sets the stage for a wider exploration of the consequences of diversity for student experiences and outcomes.

Chapter 3 focuses on Black diversity with respect to the level of racial segregation experienced by students during childhood and adolescence. Some NLSF respondents grew up in predominantly minority neighborhoods and attended minority-dominant schools. Others came of age in predominantly

White neighborhoods and White schools, whereas still others grew up in racially mixed residential and educational settings. Roughly 10 percent of our sample lived in predominantly minority neighborhoods but attended predominantly White, often selective, high schools. After documenting how the distribution of Black students across these categories varies by ancestry, identification, nativity, generation, skin tone, and class status, we show how differences in the degree of exposure to neighborhood and school segregation lead to sharp differences in exposure to social disorder and violence during childhood and adolescence.

Chapter 4 moves from the external world experienced by students while growing up to the internal worlds they had constructed for themselves by the time they entered college. We begin by analyzing their views on the relative importance of a Black versus an American identity. We then consider the strength of their common fate identity as African Americans—the degree to which they believe that what happens to them as individuals is linked to the welfare of the Blacks as a group—before turning to their perceptions of social distance or closeness to members of other racial and ethnic groups. After assessing the centrality of different facets of Black identity to Black student respondents, we conclude by examining the degree to which they harbor stereotypes about themselves and other racial/ethnic groups, and whether they think other groups are likely to treat people equally or discriminate on the basis of race.

Chapter 5 considers the diverse pathways by which Black students come to attend selective institutions of higher education. Beginning with their families of origin, we describe how parental child-rearing practices vary across the dimensions of Black diversity as well as the degree to which parents encouraged their intellectual independence and sought to promote their progenies' acquisition of human, social, and cultural capital. After examining what kinds of high schools the students attended and the educational resources those schools provided, we turn to an assessment of students' academic preparation for college as indicated by their high school GPAs and SAT scores. We conclude the chapter by identifying which factors most influenced students' choices about where to apply for college admission and their success in gaining access to a preferred college or university and whether it was a top-ten academic institution.

In chapter 6, we turn to an analysis of students' quotidian lives on campus, examining the day-to-day processes by which race is explored, challenged, reaffirmed, and reimagined through personal interactions on campus with strangers, friends, and romantic partners in different groups. In addition to assessing the frequency of interaction with others through ties of friendship and romance, we assess the range of memberships in different kinds of campus organizations. We also explore the perceived visibility of different groups on campus and assess the intensity and quality of students' interactions with members of other groups. Finally, we assess the perceived degree of racial separation on campus and students' views of the institution's commitment to diversity as an important social and academic goal. In each case, we show how cross-group interactions and perceptions vary across the different subgroups of Black diversity.

Chapter 7 examines some of the downsides of attending elite academic institutions that historically were reserved mostly for Whites. Drawing on survey and interview data, we assess how often Black students were made to feel uncomfortable on campus, heard derogatory racial remarks, and were harassed by different social actors. We also present indicators of the degree to which students felt pressure to reflect well on the race while performing academically and the additional pressure they felt from parental expectations for educational achievement. We then measure the frequency and severity of negative life events that occurred within students' family networks, assess the sense of loss and alienation they might experience in moving from modest circumstances into an elite, privileged environment, the financial debt they may have accumulated over four years of college, and whether they transferred or took time off during their college career. We conclude by adapting a standard index of depression to assess the vulnerability of Black students to mental health issues and how it differs across the various dimensions of Black diversity.

Chapter 8 revisits the racial identities and attitudes respondents expressed at the beginning of college, with an eye toward understanding whether and how the elite college experience changes them. We find that at the end of college—on the eve of ascendance into elite status—the diverse origins of Black students yield far fewer differences in racial identities and attitudes among respondents than were present four years earlier. Their increasingly shared view of race, identity, and structure also gets us—especially via student interviews that criticize outdated models of how to be Black—beyond one-dimensional understandings of Blackness, Black cultural capital, and what constitutes racial authenticity. From the interview data, we learn that the burden of these racial debates about Black legitimacy take a psychic toll on those upwardly mobile young Blacks who come from the most socioeconomically disadvantaged backgrounds and who are less willing to and adept at "fitting in" with the broader campus milieu (Torres and Massey 2012).

Chapter 9 frames the passage of Black students through college to gradua-tion as the end segment of a long educational pipeline stretching back to pre-school and before. The pipeline is leaky, however, and all too many students exit before completing high school much less college, a risk that is higher for Blacks than Whites and much higher for Black men than Black women. The chapter shows that this gendered pattern of leaks continues through college, along with differential exits associated with the other dimensions of Black diversity. Black men are significantly more likely than Black women to transfer institutions and take time off from their studies, thereby delaying their graduation and often preventing it altogether. The same outcomes are more likely for students with less educated parents, those coming from segregated schools and neighbor-hoods, and those of native versus immigrant origin; the differentials are not explained by the plethora of background characteristics we investigated.

Chapter 10 concludes with a systematic review of the differences among Black students across the dimensions of diversity, summarizing how identities, attitudes, upbringing, social experiences, and both the costs and rewards of elite education are unequally distributed by racial identification, nativity, gen-eration, regional origins, skin tone, class background, and prior experiences of segregation. We use that review to push for more research on intraracial diver-sity as well as to hypothesize how exposure to selective institutions pushes Black students toward a shared, cautious optimism about their futures.

Our data show that as they left college in the early years of the twenty-first century, members of the next generation of the Black elite were confident that they had secured a foothold in American society, but we nonetheless caution that their individual success is not evidence of the inevitability of racial pro-gress (Seamster and Ray 2018). Our analyses move beyond a simple descrip-tive portrait to highlight how interactions between identities and contexts generate differences in the experiences of race and racism to create a variety of distinct intersections for students. After sketching out these different expe-riences of race and racism, we consider the future of the Black intellectual elite in light of the structural racial inequalities that unfortunately still persist in the United States.

Our survey respondents and interviewees are now entering middle age, and many are likely managing or own their own businesses, raising children, and choosing their schools while involving themselves in local and national poli-tics and shaping American culture in various ways. Where they are living, how they are raising their families, and what they are accomplishing in their per-sonal and professional lives are likely as diverse as their origins. Vice President

Kamala Harris embodies this diversity, being the Black-identified, light-skinned, biracial daughter of PhD-holding immigrants from India and Jamaica who grew up in a segregated neighborhood and was bused to an affluent White school. This upbringing prepared her to earn college and graduate degrees at two institutions that just happen to be included in the NLSF, enabling her to move on to a career as district attorney, state attorney general, and United States senator from California.

The election of Senator Harris as vice president of the United States puts her in line for the presidency and symbolizes the ascendency of the new Black elite. How Black identity is understood and contested among this twenty-first-century Black elite must keep pace with changing configurations of racial classification, nativity and immigrant origins, skin tone, and gender so as to ensure Black advancement. Knowing where they come from, how they understand themselves individually and vis-à-vis the Black community, and their understanding of their position in American society is crucial to knowing not only the future of the Black elite but the future of American society more generally.

Notes

1. Notably, Du Bois later acknowledged the inadequacy of that vision of racial uplift as overly optimistic both about how White society would respond to the Talented Tenth's education and abilities *and* the Talented Tenth's willingness to sacrifice personal gain for the goal of social justice. As he wrote in a 1948 speech, "In my youth and idealism I did not realize that selfishness is even more natural than sacrifice." Rather than a talented tenth as defined by education, he later emphasized a definition of leadership emphasizing a moral clarity and interracial and international political coalition over his earlier rendition that emphasized educational credentials as the credentialing could too easily become part of a multiracial aristocracy that "regard[s] himself and his whims as necessarily the end and only end of civilization and culture." This later reconsideration and criticism of earlier visions of educated Black leadership, however, is rarely part of the discussion of Du Bois's vision of the Talented Tenth and its place in U.S. society (Du Bois 1948).

2. Throughout the course of this book, we use the terms *Black elite*, *Black professional class*, and *Black upper class* to describe the elevated status of our respondents relative to much of Black America. Whatever their precollege socioeconomic origins, Black students who attend and graduate from a selective college or university not only have brighter socioeconomic prospects, but they are also well credentialed to assume leadership roles both inside and outside the Black community. Our use of the delimiter *Black* nonetheless recognizes how race interacts with class to prevent African Americans from attaining social and economic parity with Whites in the American stratification system due to the legacy of racism in all its economic, political, cultural, and social manifestations (e.g., Landry 1987, 2018; Brown 2013; Thomas 2015).

2

Origins of the New Black Elite

Some days I wake up and I feel African American and then some days I wake up and I feel African.

MALIK, SECOND-GENERATION GHANAIAN AMERICAN

IN OUR QUEST to explore the diversity of the new Black elite, we follow Eric Brown's (2013:10) view that "Black professionals are an important and distinguishable segment of the Black middle class." Until now, little research has considered the unique location of African American professionals within America's racialized class structure. As noted earlier, studies have tended to center on the experiences of economically disadvantaged Black Americans and have paid little attention to other segments of the Black population, which increasingly includes Black immigrants from Africa and the Caribbean, self-identified mixed-race Blacks, as well as Blacks from affluent family backgrounds. The empirical research that does exist is largely qualitative, based on a single site or a sole case study (Gregory 1998; Pattillo 1999; Haynes 2001; Lacy 2007; Brown 2013).

Whatever their familial origins, the Black college students in our sample of selective institutions can be expected to "fulfill all of the criteria of *gradational* definitions of middle class (income, educational attainment, and occupational status)" (Brown 2013:10, emphasis original). Whereas prior research on race has often explicitly and implicitly conceptualized Blackness as a monolithic identity, rising rates of socioeconomic mobility, unprecedented Black immigration from abroad, and increasing rates of interracial marriage have given Black identity a new dynamism. Whereas before the 1960s, the Black elite was small and dominated by an interconnected set of privileged, light-skinned families (Frazier 1957; Graham 1999; Taylor 2017), today's young Black professionals come from many different places, have diverse racial origins and phenotypes, and hail from a variety of socioeconomic backgrounds.

Dimensions of Black Diversity

As noted earlier, given "the homogenizing effect of being Black in America," intraracial differences even today are often "subsumed and overlooked" (Mwangi 2014:1). Immigrant databases and publications on Black immigrants tend not to report place of birth or region of origin, and it was not until 2000 that respondents were able to identify themselves as mixed race on the census (Prewitt 2013). Few statistical databases differentiate Blacks of immigrant origin by generation and instead typically group first- and second-generation immigrants together with multigenerational African Americans for analytic purposes (Waters, Kasinitz, and Asad 2014:371). Hence, we are only slowly beginning to learn about the growing diversity within America's twenty-first-century Black population.

In keeping with these new realities, Black college students in the National Longitudinal Study of Freshmen's (NLSF's) quantitative and qualitative samples exhibit diverse origins, reflecting a wide range of ethnic, racial, class, and immigrant backgrounds. Their varied origins challenge the traditional portrayal of Black people as a monolithic group sharing a singular cultural identity. Being on a college campus, these aspiring Black professionals are well aware of this variation in their social origins. Indeed, in responding to our questions, interviewees often mentioned their multiple racial and ethnic identities as well as their diverse socioeconomic backgrounds. The experiences of our respondents and interviewees illustrate the way that young Black adults on elite campuses today understand the diversity of their own backgrounds and the heterogeneity of their Black peers, and how they draw up this intragroup variation in constructing their identities.

Table 2.1 draws on NLSF survey data to examine the diversity of Black respondents with respect to racial identification, nativity, socioeconomic background, and skin tone. Recall that all NLSF respondents were identified as Black by their college admissions office, presumably because they had checked a box on the application form. Nonetheless, in the initial interview we asked respondents to identify themselves by selecting the racial category that "best describes" their racial and ethnic origins. Possible responses included "mixed" and "other" classifications with spaces provided to write in relevant details. As

TABLE 2.1. Racial identification, immigrant origins, skin tone, gender, and parental education of Black NLSF respondents

Characteristic	Percentage
Racial identification	
Monoracial	84.0
Mixed race	16.0
Race of non-Black parent[a]	
White	63.9
Latino	13.2
Asian	14.5
Other	8.4
Nativity and generation	
Multigenerational native	73.1
Second-generation immigrant	18.4
First-generation immigrant	8.5
Regional/National origin[b]	
Caribbean	51.2
Jamaica	18.6
Haiti	9.3
Trinidad and Tobago	8.2
Guyana	5.4
Other Caribbean countries	9.7
Africa	33.1
Nigeria	17.6
Ghana	6.5
Other African countries	9.0
Other countries/regions	15.8
Skin tone	
Light	24.6
Medium	48.7
Dark	26.7
Gender	
Female	65.1
Male	34.9
Parental education	
No degree	29.5
College degree	30.7
Advanced degree	39.8
Total	1,039

[a] Mixed-origin only; [b] Immigrant-origin only

shown in the top panel of table 2.1, at the time of the baseline survey, the vast majority of Black students considered themselves to be monoracial African Americans, with 84 percent identifying themselves simply as "Black or African American" without qualification; the remaining 16 percent classified themselves as mixed race, a frequency twice that in the total U.S. Black population circa 2000 (Jones and Smith 2001).

In the second panel of table 2.1, we see that among those survey respondents reporting racially mixed origins, 64 percent had a White parent, 13 percent a Latino parent, 15 percent an Asian parent, and 8 percent a parent of some other origin. The third panel reveals that immigrant origins are even more frequent than mixed racial origins, with 18 percent reporting at least one immigrant parent and 9 percent being immigrants themselves. Thus, 27 percent of all Black survey respondents were either in the first- or second-generation of U.S. residence, compared with around 21 percent among all African Americans nationwide at that time (see Bauman and Graf 2003). Among NLSF respondents of immigrant background, a little over half (51 percent) reported origins in the Caribbean, with a third (33 percent) reporting origins in Africa and 16 percent indicating origins in some other world region. Jamaicans constituted the largest national origin group at 19 percent, followed by Nigerians (18 percent), Haitians (9 percent), Trinidadians (8 percent), Ghanaians (7 percent), and Guyanese (5 percent), with 10 percent coming from elsewhere in the Caribbean and 9 percent from somewhere else in Africa.

The foregoing diversity of racial and regional origins yields considerable variety with respect to skin tone, which was assessed by NLSF interviewers using a scale that ranged from 0 (very light) to 10 (very dark) upon completing the baseline survey. Here, we recoded scores from 0 to 3 as "light," those from 4 to 6 as "medium," and those from 7 to 10 as "dark." According to these criteria, nearly half of all respondents (49 percent) had a "medium" skin color and roughly equal proportions fell into the remaining categories, with 25 percent classified as "light" and 27 percent as "dark," with the total exceeding 100 percent because of rounding error. Skin color and phenotype have been found by others to correlate with self-identity and racial self-classification (Korgen 1998; Brown 2001; Rockquemore and Brunsma 2007; Lee and Bean 2010; Khanna 2011; Spencer 2011; Kilson 2014). Racially mixed interviewees who perceived themselves as having a lighter skin tone often opt for a "mixed" rather an exclusively "Black" identity.

Consistent with patterns mentioned in the prior chapter, we see in the next-to-bottom panel that nearly two-thirds of Black NLSF respondents are women.

In addition to ancestry, nativity, skin tone, and gender, the final dimension of Black diversity that we consider in this chapter is socioeconomic status, which we assess here by dividing respondents into three classes based on the level of schooling achieved by the best-educated parent: no college degree, at least one college degree, and at least one advanced degree. As one would expect, Black students with highly educated parents are significantly overrepresented among NLSF respondents. While in the nation as a whole, just 10 percent of adult African Americans held a college degree and another 5 percent held an advanced degree in the year 2000, among the parents of respondents in our sample, the respective figures were 31 percent and 40 percent (Ruggles et al. 2021).

Like Malik's description of his dual self-identity in the opening epigram, interviewees did not necessarily espouse racial identities that were congruent with their actual geographic origins, family backgrounds, or traditional racial categories without qualification. When asked how she self-identified, Olivia opted for both racial and ethnic identities, though when forced to choose, she comes down on the side of race, as indicated by the following exchange:

OLIVIA: I identify myself as Black American but also as Haitian, and also as Nigerian. . . . Those other two more so than Black American.
INTERVIEWER: Okay. So how do you do that? If you were pushed, if someone wants one . . .
OLIVIA: Black.

In her predominately White Long Island suburb and high school, Olivia always felt different from others. She was the only Black student in her Advanced Placement classes and her peer group was exclusively White. When she participated in one of our focus groups, Olivia elected to be in the "Black American" group instead of the "immigrant" one. During the group conversation, however, Olivia identified ethnically as well as racially but in the end considered herself to be more "Black" than anything else.

Darryl, too, preferred to identify himself as "Black" rather than "African American." When asked why, he told us he favored a Black identity over an ethnic one because Black Americans are not viewed through an ethnic lens in the manner of Whites or Asians.

INTERVIEWER: Do you ever use the term *African American*?
DARRYL: No. I might use Afro-American or New African. . . . Well, I've always felt that people who come from any other continent . . . Irish American, Chinese American . . . I feel like African American is sort of

insulting—it's a continent, not a country. . . . I also feel like Americans typically after the second or third generation, you're simply called an American. . . . There's no preface before that, but for Blacks it hasn't been like that. We seem to have this forever-lasting preface . . . so if *I'm Black while an American* [emphasis added]. I understand the ramifications of being Black.

Darryl described his social class as "poor," having grown up in a Bronx housing project with his mother and two younger sisters. At the time of his interview, he was receiving a full scholarship to attend one of the most selective colleges in the country.

Although persons who report racially mixed ancestry, immigrant origins, light skin tone, and high education constitute a relatively small subset of the Black population as a whole, they are substantially overrepresented among students attending selective colleges and universities (Massey et al. 2003, 2007; Charles, Torres, and Brunn 2008). Together, these data highlight the great diversity of young, privileged African Americans coming of age in the early twenty-first century. There is, of course, considerable overlap between segments of the Black population defined on the basis of ancestry, nativity, skin tone, and class, a topic that we explore in more detail in the remainder of this chapter.

Diversity in Racial Identification

Table 2.2 compares the social backgrounds of self-identified monoracial and mixed-race Black respondents. As shown in the top panel, both groups display a similar generational composition, with over 70 percent being multigenerational natives and under 10 percent being first-generation immigrants. Second-generation immigrants, however, are slightly more prevalent among mixed-race persons (24 percent) than among monoracial respondents (17 percent), though the difference is not statistically significant. As one might expect, the greatest difference between the two groups occurred with respect to skin tone (see the second panel). Whereas 16 percent of monoracial respondents were rated as having a light skin tone and 31 percent as having a dark skin tone, the respective percentages among those of mixed race were 72 percent and 5 percent, comprising a highly significant statistical difference between the two distributions. However, there are no meaningful differences in the gender ratio between monoracial and mixed-race respondents. Women far outnumber men in both subgroups.

TABLE 2.2. Social background of Black NLSF respondents by racial identification

Characteristic	Monoracial	Mixed race
Nativity and generation		
Multigenerational native	73.7%	70.5%
Second-generation immigrant	17.4	23.5
First-generation immigrant	8.9	6.0
Skin tone		
Light	15.6%	72.3%***
Medium	53.7	22.3
Dark	30.7	5.4
Gender		
Female	64.6%	67.5%
Male	35.4	32.5
Parental education		
No degree	34.5%	25.3%*
College degree	37.5	36.8
Advanced degree	28.0	37.9
Household structure		
Always both parents in household	50.9%	48.8%
Always single-parent household	18.8	15.7
Ever single-parent household	44.0	46.4
Ever extended-family household	42.3	45.2
Parental work history		
Father always worked full time	86.8%	83.0%
Father ever unemployed	7.0	10.2
Father professional/managerial	47.1	59.0*
Mother always worked full time	62.8	56.9
Mother ever unemployed	19.6	25.9*
Mother professional/managerial	54.9	59.0
Family economic status		
Income less than $50,000	35.8%	36.7%
Income $100,000 or more	24.0	24.3
Parents own home	71.9	73.5
Mean home value	$192,154	$228,311+
Mean annual income	$76,494	$78,198
Total	873	166

+ p < 0.10; * p < 0.05; ** p < 0.01; *** p < 0.001

The fourth panel identifies a significant difference in the distribution of parental education between monoracial and mixed-race Black respondents, though the difference is not as sharp as the contrast we observed for skin tone. Whereas 38 percent of the parents of racially mixed respondents held advanced degrees, the figure was only 28 percent among the parents of monoracial respondents. At the other end of the spectrum, only 25 percent of the parents of racially mixed respondents lacked a college degree compared with 35 percent among the parents of monoracial Blacks. However, we observed no significant differences between monoracial and mixed-race respondents with respect to the household structure they experienced while growing up. Around half came of age in homes where two parents were always present and some 44–46 percent occupied a single-parent household at some point in their first eighteen years, with 42–45 percent at some point experiencing an extended-family household.

We likewise observed few significant employment or economic differences between the two identity groups. On the one hand, the fathers of mixed-race respondents were more likely to work in a professional or managerial occupation (59 percent compared to 47 percent). On the other hand, the mothers of mixed-race respondents were more likely to have been unemployed during the respondent's childhood (26 percent versus 20 percent). There were no real differences, however, between monoracial and mixed-race respondents with respect to income and homeownership, and only a marginal difference in home value.

Thus, beyond the obvious skin color differential between monoracial and mixed-race respondents, the main difference we observe between the two groups is the slightly higher class status of the latter compared to the former (with more college-educated parents and more fathers employed in professional occupations). These educational and occupational differences, however, do not translate into differences in income or wealth (the latter being proxied by the combination of homeownership and home value).

Diversity by Nativity and National Origin

Table 2.3 compares the social origins of first- and second-generation immigrants to those of multigenerational Black natives. The top panel indicates no significant difference between the two groups with respect to racial identification: 16 percent of multigenerational natives reported themselves to be mixed race, compared with figures of 15 percent for first-generation immigrants and 19 percent for those in the second generation. In contrast, we observe significant differences in skin tone when we compare respondents of immigrant versus native origin, with the share being 36 percent dark skinned among those in the first generation and 37 percent among those in the second generation but just 23 percent among multigenerational natives. Likewise, 27 percent of

TABLE 2.3. Social background of Black NLSF respondents by nativity and generation

	Multigenerational native	Second-generation immigrant	First-generation immigrant
Racial identification			
Monoracial	84.5%	80.7%	84.8%
Mixed race	15.5	19.3	15.2
Region of origin			
USA	100.0%	0.0%	0.0%*
Africa	0.0	31.9	35.5
Caribbean	0.0	52.9	47.7
Other	0.0	15.2	17.1
Skin tone			
Light	26.6%	20.4%	17.0%***
Medium	50.4	42.9	46.6
Dark	23.0	36.7	36.4
Gender			
Female	65.5%	64.9%	61.4%
Male	34.5	35.1	38.6
Parental education			
No degree	30.7%	22.2%	34.3%**
College degree	33.0	28.9	23.3
Advanced degree	36.3	49.0	42.4
Household structure			
Always both parents in household	49.1%	56.0%	51.1%
Always single-parent household	19.3	16.8	12.5
Ever single-parent household	45.8	39.8	42.1
Ever extended-family household	38.2	55.5	54.6***
Parental work history			
Father always worked full time	87.6%	84.1%	79.2%
Father ever unemployed	6.8	8.9	10.4
Father professional/managerial	49.3	49.7	48.9
Mother always worked full time	62.8	63.3	49.3+
Mother ever unemployed	20.1	20.9	23.9
Mother professional/managerial	56.4	57.1	48.9
Family economic status			
Income less than $50,000	41.3%	37.2%	54.3%*
Income $100,000 or more	24.4	26.1	16.0
Parents own home	72.6	74.3	64.8
Mean home value	$192,314	$235,210	$160,872+
Mean annual income	$78,732	$77,710	$57,739**
Total	760	191	88

+p < 0.10; * p < 0.05; ** p < 0.01; *** p < 0.001

multigenerational native survey respondents were judged to be light skinned, compared with only 17 percent of first-generation immigrants and 20 percent of second-generation immigrants. However, we found no meaningful gender differences.

Most of the second-generation immigrant Blacks we interviewed also perceived themselves as straddling two worlds: an ethnic world in which they could celebrate their family's culture and traditions and a racial world in which they realized that in society they were indistinguishable from other Black Americans (Waters 1999; Greer 2013; Smith 2014). Yolanda, a dark-skinned freshman was quick to differentiate herself from native-origin Black students because of her known African heritage, insisting that

> I identify myself as African. . . . The traditions, beliefs in which [my parents] live, I was pretty much raised in, with a little twist of some American. . . . Ethnically, I'm African and even deeper than that I'm Sierra Leonian, and even deeper than that, I'm of the Mende and Shabru and Creole tribes.

Yolanda of course recognized that she is initially evaluated by how she looks because her heritage is not immediately known. As she explained, "Everywhere I go, people are seeing my race, but they don't know anything about my ethnicity. . . . I always feel the need to say, like if it comes up, 'Well, my parents are from Africa. I'm African.'"

Malik's parents also instilled in him the cultural traditions and values associated with his Ghanaian heritage; however, he also realized that his dark skin put him on a common footing with multigenerational Black Americans. As he explained:

> Some days, I wake up and I feel African American, and then some days I wake up and I feel African. Because I'm from Ghana—like my parents are both immigrants from Ghana. So some days I'm like, yeah, I'm Ghanaian American. More often, I'm African American, but then some days, I'll be like, oh, I'm African.

Interviewees who self-identified as racially mixed and of immigrant origins expressed the most complex self-identities as they grappled with their ethnic upbringing, foreign origins, and racially ambiguous phenotype. As Charlotte explained:

> I always separate color and ethnicity. . . . Ethnically, I'm more Irish than anything else. And then I'm Indian, Puerto Rican, Black, and a lot of other

things. So that's ethnically what I am. . . . But I guess, racially I'm just brown. I don't know . . . I feel like I never say "I'm Black." I very rarely say I'm mixed. . . . I feel like most people I know that are mixed would just be like, "I'm Black or I'm Black and have a White mom."

Charlotte grew up both in the United States and overseas but attended an international private high school in Atlanta. Her responses correspond to those articulated by other interviewees with racially mixed and immigrant origins, who considered themselves atypical relative to multigenerational native-origin Blacks.

In the fifth panel of the table, we observe significant differences in parental education by nativity. The parents of second-generation immigrants were the best educated, with 49 percent holding an advanced degree and just 22 percent lacking a college degree and 29 percent being college graduates. Thus, a total 78 percent had completed college. At the other end of the spectrum are parents of multigenerational natives: 31 percent of whom had no postsecondary degree and 36 percent of whom had an advanced degree. More members of this group, however, had college-educated parents (33 percent). First-generation immigrants were the most likely to have parents without a college degree (34 percent), but at the same time, 42 percent of first-generation immigrants' parents held advanced degrees, 6 percent more than multigenerational natives' parents.

These educational differences translate into significant economic differences by nativity. First-generation immigrant students came from families with the lowest average income ($57,739), homeownership rate (65 percent), and average home value ($160,872). In contrast, second-generation immigrant students displayed the highest levels of homeownership (74 percent) and home value ($235,210) and the second highest income ($77,710). For their part, multigenerational native students came from families with the highest average income ($78,732) but only the second highest rates of homeownership (73 percent) and mean home value ($192,314).

Given the fact that immigration tends to occur through kinship networks and often reflects strategies of family reunification, it is not surprising that first- and second-generation immigrants were more likely to report living in an extended family at some point during their childhood (around 55 percent) compared with multigenerational natives (just 38 percent). The fathers of first- and second-generation immigrants were also somewhat less likely to have always worked full time, but the differences are not statistically significant.

Differences in maternal employment were marginally significant, with around 63 percent of the mothers of natives and second-generation immigrants reported always to be working full time compared to just 49 percent of mothers of first-generation immigrants.

Table 2.4 moves on to consider differences by national origin, contrasting the social backgrounds exhibited by multigenerational U.S. natives with those reporting immigrant origins in Africa, the Caribbean, and other regions. As shown in the top two panels, racial identification, nativity, and generation differ in obvious ways by region of origin. Respondents from the United States, the Caribbean, and Africa were overwhelmingly monoracial; conversely, nearly half of immigrants from other regions identified as mixed race. By definition, all multigenerational natives were born in the United States to native parents, whereas the other origin groups were either born abroad or born in the United States to immigrant parents. Among respondents of immigrant background, those with origins in Africa and other regions were more likely to be first-generation immigrants compared to respondents of Caribbean origin.

We also observe significant differences in skin tone by regional origin. Among those with an immigrant background, respondents from the Caribbean were most likely to exhibit medium skin complexions (53 percent) compared to both African immigrants and those from other regions (35 percent and 34 percent, respectively). In contrast, African-origin immigrants were most likely to display a dark skin tones (57 percent) and least likely to exhibit a light skin color (9 percent). Those of other regional origins were most likely to exhibit a light skin color (54 percent) and least likely to display a dark skin tone (11 percent). For their part, around half of multigenerational African Americans displayed a medium skin tone with the rest being roughly evenly divided between light-skinned (27 percent) and dark-skinned (23 percent) respondents.

Although African origin respondents may exhibit the darkest skin tones, they also display the highest levels of parental education, with 90 percent of parents holding either a college degree (18 percent) or an advanced degree (71 percent). In contrast, only 67 percent of the parents of respondents of Caribbean origin and 62 percent of respondents of other immigrant origins held college or advanced degrees. Among those of Caribbean origin, 34 percent reported a parent with a college degree and 34 percent reported one with an advanced degree. In contrast, among those of other origins, only 23 percent possessed a college degree, but 38 percent held an advanced degree. At 31 percent, the parents of multigenerational natives displayed the highest frequency lacking a college degree, compared with 33 percent holding a college degree and 36 percent with an

TABLE 2.4. Social background of Black NLSF respondents by region of origin

Characteristic	USA	Caribbean	Africa	Other
Racial identification				
Monoracial	84.6%	84.6%	93.5%	52.3%***
Mixed race	15.4	15.4	6.5	47.7
Nativity and generation				
Multigenerational native	100.0%	0.0%	0.0%	0.0%*
Second-generation immigrant	—	70.6	66.3	65.9
First-generation immigrant	—	29.4	33.7	34.1
Skin tone				
Light	26.6%	15.4%	8.7%	54.5%***
Medium	50.4	53.2	34.8	34.1
Dark	23.0	31.5	56.5	11.4
Gender				
Female	65.5%	66.4%	62.0%	59.1%
Male	34.5	33.6	38.0	40.9
Parental education				
No degree	30.7%	32.2%	10.3%	38.4%***
College degree	33.0	33.9	18.4	23.2
Advanced degree	36.3	33.9	71.4	38.4
Household structure				
Always both parents in household	49.1%	50.4%	63.0%	50.0%+
Always single-parent household	19.3	19.6	10.9	11.4
Ever single-parent household	45.8	47.6	32.6	34.1*
Ever extended-family household	38.2	55.9	55.4	52.3***
Parental work history				
Father always worked full time	87.6%	84.9%	80.7%	80.8%
Father ever unemployed	6.8	8.2	9.7	11.5
Father professional/managerial	49.3	67.0	44.8	44.6**
Mother always worked full time	62.8	63.2	49.4	67.6+
Mother ever unemployed	20.1	18.2	31.5	13.6*
Mother professional/managerial	57.5	54.3	66.1	43.4*
Family economic status				
Income less than $50,000	41.3%	51.4%	31.4%	37.3%*
Income $100,000 or more	24.4	19.1	30.3	19.8
Parents own home	72.8	66.7	70.0	75.0
Mean home value	$192,314	$219,880	$235,210	$193,047
Mean annual income	$78,732	$60,674	$87,642	$72,369**
Total	760	143	92	44

+ p < 0.10; * p < 0.05; ** p < 0.01; *** p < 0.001

advanced degree. These data thus confirm the positive educational selectivity among Black immigrants to the United States (Hamilton 2019).

Laypeople and scholars often consider income and wealth as the best markers of one's social class, and this is true of research on "middle class" Blacks in the United States as well (Lacy 2007; Thompson and Suarez 2015). However, all income and wealth is not equal—intergenerational wealth transfers *combined with* cultural knowledge, especially within the White elite, play a substantial role in differentiating among the highly educated after graduation (Friedman and Laurison 2019). Similarly, income is an inadequate proxy for Black social class—many Black immigrant parents have human, social, and cultural capital through advanced degrees and professional training from their home countries that do not translate into high-income jobs in the United States. As we already know, second-generation immigrant Black students with Anglophone African and Caribbean origins often come from families with high levels of education; the selectivity of immigration from certain countries in Africa, especially, ensures this (e.g., Massey et al. 2007; Capps, McCabe, and Fix 2012; Clerge 2014; Hamilton 2019).

Prior studies show that college-educated immigrant parents are quite knowledgeable and aware of the "culture" and "prestige" of having their children attend competitive postsecondary institutions in the United States and the necessity of attending college in general for guaranteed social mobility (Perna 2000; Griffin et al. 2012). These findings speak to the complexity of social class in the United States as inclusive of the intergenerational transmission of values, attitudes, beliefs, and a worldview that reflect one's family class origins and "habitus," and not necessarily their current socioeconomic condition (Roksa and Potter 2011).

Empirical research on the college-going trajectories of first- and second-generation Black immigrant students and multigenerational native-born students by Bennett and Lutz (2009) confirms a "net [Black] immigrant advantage" regarding enrollment at selective colleges and universities, confirming Black immigrants' somewhat elevated status within the racial hierarchy. Black immigrant students are significantly overrepresented at the most selective institutions relative to their multigenerational, native-born Black American counterparts, despite comprising only about 11 percent of the total Black population in the United States (e.g., Massey et al. 2007; Charles, Torres, and Brunn 2008; Bennett and Lutz 2009; Anderson and Lopez 2018).

Bennett and Lutz (2009:71) contend that the immigrant advantage raises "important stratification questions such as whether college attendance opens doors to the upper echelons of the American occupational structure for some Blacks more than others." Massey et al. (2007) and Charles, Torres, and Brunn

(2008) support these findings, while revealing particular demographic, socio-economic background, and soft skills differences between immigrant and native Blacks that may favor immigrant Blacks' admission to the most elite schools and better credential them for professional careers and higher social status within the new Black elite.

We also observe significant differences across origin groups in the survey data with respect to household structure and parental work history. African-origin respondents were the most likely to grow up in two-parent households, with 63 percent reporting two parents always being present during childhood. In contrast, the figure for all other subgroups hovers around 50 percent. As already noted, the likelihood of living with extended family was much greater among immigrant-origin groups, with frequencies ranging from 52 percent to 56 percent compared with just 38 percent of multigenerational natives, who along with Caribbean-origin respondents were more likely than immigrants from Africa and other regions to have lived in a single-parent household. Although there were no differences in fathers' employment among origin groups, the mothers of African immigrants were least likely to have always worked full time (49 percent compared to values of 63–68 percent among the other groups) and the most likely to have ever been unemployed (32 percent compared to values of 20 percent or lower across the other origins).

Given their high degree of education, it is not surprising to observe the highest average income levels among African-origin parents ($87,642). Although multigenerational native parents exhibited some of the lowest overall levels of education, they paradoxically displayed the second highest average income at roughly $78,732, compared with values of $72,369 for parents of other immigrant origins and $60,674 for parents of Caribbean-origin respondents. The latter also displayed the highest percentage with a family income below $50,000 at 51 percent, compared with values of around 37 percent for other-origin immigrants, 41 percent for multigenerational native parents, and 31 percent for African-origin parents. Thus, the average values reported for first- and second-generation immigrants in table 2.3 often obscure sharp underlying differences by national and regional origin.

Diversity by Skin Tone

Table 2.5 examines differences between subgroups defined on the basis of skin tone. As one would expect, light-skinned respondents were far more likely to report a mixed-race identity than those with medium or dark skin tones.

TABLE 2.5. Social background of Black NLSF respondents by skin tone

Characteristic	Light	Medium	Dark
Racial identification			
Monoracial	53.1%	92.7%	96.7%***
Mixed Race	46.9	7.3	3.3
Nativity and generation			
Multigenerational native	78.9%	75.7%	63.2%
Second-generation immigrant	15.2	16.2	25.3
First-generation immigrant	5.9	8.1	11.6
Region of origin			
USA	78.9%	75.7%	63.2%***
Caribbean	8.6	15.0	16.3
Africa	3.1	6.3	18.8
Other	9.4	3.0	1.8
Gender			
Female	66.0%	68.2%	58.5%*
Male	34.0	31.8	41.5
Parental education			
No degree	28.6%	29.7%	29.8%+
College degree	26.9	33.7	31.3
Advanced degree	44.5	36.6	39.0
Household structure			
Always both parents in household	56.6%	49.2%	47.3%+
Always single-parent household	12.5	20.4	19.9*
Ever single-parent household	38.3	44.9	49.1*
Ever extended-family household	37.5	45.7	42.2+
Parental work history			
Father always worked full time	84.7%	88.3%	83.8%
Father ever unemployed	7.0	8.0	7.4
Father professional/managerial	58.8	49.9	42.3**
Mother always worked full time	54.9	65.5	61.5*
Mother ever unemployed	29.7	19.9	21.8
Mother professional/managerial	60.5	56.7	55.2
Family economic status			
Income less than $50,000	29.8%	43.3%	49.4%***
Income $100,000 or more	31.1	22.6	20.1*
Parents own home	76.6	71.5	69.3
Mean home value	$207,385	$205,365	$174,217
Mean annual income	$89,982	$73,529	$70,468**
Total	256	506	277

+ p < 0.10; * p < 0.05; ** p < 0.01; *** p < 0.001

Whereas 47 percent of all light-skinned survey respondents reported racially mixed origins, the figure was only 7 percent among those with medium skin tones and 3 percent among those with dark skin tones. Consistent with the data in prior tables, dark-skinned respondents were more likely to be of immigrant origin than multigenerational natives. Only 63 percent of dark-skinned respondents reported themselves to be multigenerational natives, whereas the respective figure was 79 percent for light-skinned respondents and 76 percent for those with medium skin tones.

For example, Harrison perceived himself to be of "medium" complexion and physically similar to his Black father but noted that his Black peers on campus often questioned his origins and referred to him as "light skinned." He went on to explain to us that he identifies as "mixed" rather than Black or White: "I consider myself mixed—that is the term I use. My mother's White, my dad's Black and possibly Native American. . . . I'm actually myself just Black and White."

For her part, Megan "checks all that apply" when filling out forms but prefers to answer "I'm Black" when asked about her background because, as she puts it, "the way I look, most people assume that I am." Nonetheless, Megan sometimes identifies as "racially mixed" to reveal her multidimensional heritage, telling us that "I'm very proud of my culture. It's not like I'm waving an Irish flag or I'm going to Africa, but these are things that I like about myself. I mean, it makes me more interested in myself, I guess." Megan was raised in an exclusive suburb of Dallas, Texas with her "Irish American" father and "Black and Native American" mother.

Conversely, Alex defined himself as African American despite his mixed immigrant/native and Black/White origins:

ALEX: I identify myself as African American. I think it's pretty much the truest sense of the word—my mom being [White] American and my dad, Nigerian. I would probably identify more with the African American side because it's what people see.

INTERVIEWER: As a mixed person, how does that influence how you interact with people, because you've got two parents from different backgrounds, right?

ALEX: I don't think it really affects it because people mostly see my skin color and say I'm African American rather than one or the other.

Alex grew up in Cambridge, Massachusetts, in a racially diverse neighborhood and peer group but notes that his skin tone led others to categorize him as African American; other research confirms that among Black immigrants, darker skin tones are associated with adopting a primarily racial self-identity rather than an ethnic one (Vickerman 1999; Waters 1999).

The household structure that survey respondents experienced while growing up also varies systematically by skin tone. As one shifts attention from light to medium to dark skin tones, the percentage always living with both parents falls and the share of ever having lived or always lived in a single-parent household rises. Interestingly, subtle gender differences in skin tone are evident: roughly two-thirds of light-skinned (66 percent) and medium-skinned (68 percent) respondents are women, compared to 59 percent of dark skin-toned respondents, which aligns with research showing that colorism is gendered and that dark skin tones are associated more strongly with school suspensions for Black girls than Black boys, pushing the former off college-bound academic tracks (Hannon, DeFina, and Bruch 2013).

Although skin-color stratification may prevail in the general population, among elite Black students, socioeconomic differences by skin tone are complicated by the high degree of education displayed by African immigrants, who, as we have seen, generally possessed a darker skin tone. Although dark-skinned respondents were more likely than others to come from families earning less than $50,000 per year and displayed the lowest rate of homeownership, they also displayed patterns of parental education that were similar to those of both light- and medium-skinned respondents. Whereas 49 percent of dark-skinned respondents came from families earning under $50,000 per year (compared to respective figures of 30 percent and 43 percent of respondents with light and medium skin tones, respectively) and only 69 percent came from home-owning families (compared to 77 percent and 72 percent of those with light and medium skin tones), 70 percent of those with dark skin tones had college-educated parents (31 percent college degrees and 39 percent advanced degrees), roughly the same as the percentages observed among light- and medium-skinned students. In contrast, we see clear skin-color gradients with respect to household structure, with the share growing up always in a single-parent household being 12.5 percent among students with light skin tones compared with around 20 percent among those with medium and dark skin tones.

Diversity by Socioeconomic Status

Finally, in Table 2.6, we consider differences by socioeconomic status as measured by parental education. Here, we found no significant differences in racial identification, skin tone, or gender between respondents whose parents lacked

TABLE 2.6. Social background of Black NLSF respondents by parental education

Characteristic	No degree	College degree	Advanced degree
Racial identification			
Monoracial	86.5%	83.7%	82.4%
Mixed race	13.5	16.3	17.6
Nativity and generation			
Multigenerational native	76.3%	76.8%	67.8%**
Second-generation immigrant	9.9	6.3	9.2
First-generation immigrant	13.8	16.9	23.0
National origin			
USA	76.3%	76.8%	67.8%***
Africa	3.1	5.2	16.1
Caribbean	15.1	14.9	11.9
Other	5.5	3.1	4.2
Gender			
Female	64.5%	64.8%	65.7%
Male	35.5	35.2	34.3
Skin tone			
Light	22.9%	22.1%	27.9%+
Medium	49.3	52.3	45.5
Dark	27.9	25.6	26.6
Household structure			
Always both parents in household	36.2%	50.7%	61.2%***
Always single-parent household	22.1	22.0	12.5**
Ever single-parent household	56.4	45.1	34.8***
Ever extended-family household	47.9	42.2	39.3+
Parental work history			
Father always worked full time	82.5%	87.7%	86.8%
Father ever unemployed	11.7	6.2	6.5
Father professional/managerial	21.3%	48.4%	73.0%***
Mother always worked full time	61.3	61.6	62.4
Mother ever unemployed	22.6	21.3	24.1
Mother professional/managerial	29.4	56.7	78.5***
Family economic status			
Income less than $50,000	61.9%	49.3%	20.2%***
Income $100,000 or more	6.4	14.7	44.7***
Parents own home	59.8	71.4	82.1***
Mean home value	$135,279	$160,186	$258,793***
Mean annual income	$46,150	$63,591	$110,362***
Total	306	319	414

+ $p < 0.10$; * $p < 0.05$; ** $p < 0.01$; *** $p < 0.001$

a college degree, held a college degree, or held an advanced degree. However, we do observe sharp differences with respect to nativity and generation, national origin, household structure, parental work history, and economic status. The highest status respondents (those whose parents held advanced degrees) were least likely to be multigenerational natives and most likely to be first-generation immigrants compared with middle-status respondents (whose parents hold college degrees) and low-status respondents (whose parents never graduated from college). Whereas more than three-quarters of low- and middle-status respondents were multigenerational natives, the figure was only 68 percent among high-status respondents. Meanwhile, the share of first-generation immigrants rose steadily from 14 percent among low-status respondents to 17 percent among middle-status respondents to 23 percent among high-status respondents.

The monotonic increase in immigrant origins as class rises is complemented by an even sharper increase in African origins with rising parental education. Whereas only 3 percent of lower status respondents were of African origin, the figure rose to 5 percent among respondents of middle status and 16 percent among those of high status. The increase in the prevalence of African origins with rising status was accompanied by a decline in the share of multigenerational natives, which fell from over three-quarters among students whose parents had a college education or less to around two-thirds among those whose parents held an advanced degree; the share of Caribbean students fell from around 15 percent to around 12 percent.

A similar class gradient prevailed with respect to household structure. As parental education increased, the share growing up in two-parent families rose from 36.2 percent to 50.7 percent to 61.2 percent across the three educational categories, while the share always growing up in single-parent families fell from around 22 percent in the first two categories to 12.5 percent in the highest category of parental education. As one would expect, economic status also rose steadily with parental education. The share with fathers and mothers working in professional or managerial occupations steadily rose, for example, with the share of professional-managerial fathers rising from 21 percent to 73 percent moving from low to high status and the share of professional-managerial mothers rising from 29 percent to 79 percent. Likewise, moving from low to high status, the share earning less than $50,000 falls from 62 percent to 20 percent, the share earning $100,000 or more increases from 6 percent to 45 percent, the share of homeowners rose from 60 percent to 82 percent, average income goes from $46,000 to $110,000, and average home value increases from \$135,000 to \$259,000. These data indicate the powerful effect of education in determining objective class status in the United States.

Foundations of the New Black Elite

Social, economic, and demographic trends in the United States since the civil rights era have combined to create a remarkably diverse set of foundations for the new Black elite in twenty-first-century America. As indicated by our survey of young Black adults attending selective colleges and universities in the first years of the new century, the new generation of Black leaders is likely to differ widely with respect to racial identity, nativity, generation, national origin, skin tone, and socioeconomic status. More importantly, this chapter has shown that these dimensions of difference intersect in complex ways to produce more refined and detailed subsets of identity and affiliation within the Black community, likely yielding a plethora of experiences when it comes to race relations on campus.

As we have demonstrated, two categories of racial identity, two genders, three categories of nativity and generation, three categories of skin tone, and three categories of socioeconomic status combine in diverse ways to yield 108 different foundations for identity, perceptions, and behavior ($2 \times 2 \times 3 \times 3 \times 3 = 108$), and these, in turn, can be subdivided for mixed-race persons depending on the race of the non-Black parent and among first- and second-generation immigrants by the national origin of parents. Although this multiplex of diversity holds in Black America generally, it is especially characteristic of those attending elite colleges and universities, persons who will comprise the leadership of the nation's future Black community.

Within the emerging twenty-first-century Black elite, what it means to be Black has moved well beyond an all-encompassing conceptualization of race as a master status in which all persons on the Black side of a color binary share a monolithic racial identity defined in opposition to Whiteness, reinforced by exclusion and buttressed by discrimination. Although exclusion and discrimination clearly still exist, the multiplicity and fluidity of contemporary identities can be expected to condition the experiences of members of the new Black elite and differentiate their trajectories in college and beyond. It is to these varieties of Black experience on college campuses that we turn in later chapters, after first considering the diversity of school and neighborhood compositions experienced while growing up.

3

Experiences of Segregation

I think it's based on how you were raised. I think that's primarily like where you went to school, the kind of people in your neighborhood, what you're used to, you know?

DENISE, BLACK MULTIGENERATIONAL NATIVE

ANDREW'S EARLY YEARS were characterized by racial isolation and poverty. Neither of Andrew's parents went to college, and with both working at low-level service jobs, bouts of homelessness and welfare dependency haunted much of his childhood. Although of mixed Black and White parentage, Andrew identified as Black and explained that his neighborhood and school experiences were also predominantly Black. To help lift the family out of poverty, Andrew's paternal grandmother gave them her home in a predominantly Black and rural area in the Midwest. A football standout, Andrew attended part of middle school and high school there, where he estimated that fewer than fifty of his two hundred high school peers graduated along with him and told us that most of his friends dropped out to work in the local factory or ended up in trouble. When asked about his school experiences, Andrew told us:

> There was one thing about my high school: we didn't have resources. In middle school, I took pre-Algebra [in] seventh and eighth grade and got straight 100s every quarter. They still couldn't do anything with me because we didn't have the resources or anything like that.

Andrew went on to report that a typical classroom had an average of forty-five students and that there were no honors or Advanced Placement (AP) classes available at his school. He was able to attend a prestigious Ivy League university only because of a special college recruitment program that targeted disadvantaged but academically promising minority students. This type of "rags to riches" story—escaping racial isolation and poverty for the Ivy League via a special recruitment program—is culturally popular, and many of our interviewees had similar personal narratives.

In contrast, Carl is the eldest of three sons of a U.S. Army officer. When his father was promoted to colonel, his family moved to an affluent, White enclave outside of Birmingham, Alabama; they were the first Black family in the neighborhood. Carl attended a nearly all-White Christian high school nearby where he and "four or five others" were the only Black students—indeed the only minorities—in the entire student body. He believed his parents sent him there because they thought that "the best [educational] opportunities" were available at private schools. At the time of the interview, his father had just retired, and Carl received no financial aid to attend a very expensive and highly selective university.

Which experience is more common among the new Black elite: Andrew's story of personal uplift from racial segregation and isolation or Carl's experience of early integration into high-status White spaces and schools? Or perhaps something between these two extremes is more common. Here, we show that the new Black elite do not share any particular experience of segregation and we describe how different experiences of childhood segregation reverberate in the social and academic experiences reported by Black students attending elite academic institutions as young adults.

The Rise and Consequences of Segregation

For most of the twentieth century, Black Americans were highly segregated from White Americans, relegated by discrimination to very different residential locations and very different degrees of exposure to neighborhood disadvantage. Prior to the civil rights era, segregation in the South was perpetuated by law and custom following the rigid strictures of the Jim Crow system (Packard 2003). Formally, the legal code in southern states mandated separate facilities for Blacks and Whites in virtually all domains of social and economic life, including education, transportation, employment, accommodation, and all manner of services (Woodward 1957). Informally, social norms and behavioral expectations were institutionalized in private practice to uphold the principle of White supremacy in all interactions between Blacks and Whites, a principle whose violation typically met with swift and often violent retribution (Chafe, Gavins, and Korstad 2001).

Prior to 1900, 90 percent of all Black Americans lived in the South, and levels of Black residential segregation in the North initially were low. Over the course of the twentieth century, however, the great Black migration dramatically increased the size of the urban Black population outside the South and levels of segregation rose precipitously (Lieberson 1980; Wilkerson 2010). Throughout the nation, racial discrimination was progressively institutionalized in the real estate and banking industries to create a de facto system of racial separation characterized by very high levels of residential segregation and neighborhood isolation, yielding a spatial configuration that Massey and Denton (1993) labeled American Apartheid. As of 1980, the degree of segregation was so extreme and so prevalent across multiple geographic dimensions in some metropolitan areas (including Baltimore, Chicago, Cleveland, Detroit, Milwaukee, Philadelphia, Gary, Los Angeles, New York, and Saint Louis) that they coined the term *hypersegregation* to describe it (Massey and Denton 1989).

Legislation enacted during the 1960s and 1970s outlawed racial discrimination in the sale and rental of housing and banned discrimination against Black people and Black neighborhoods in the marketing of home mortgages (Branch 1988, 1998, 2006; Rothstein 2017). In subsequent decades, average levels of Black-White segregation fell, but the reductions were quite uneven (Rugh and Massey 2014). Whereas levels of racial segregation declined in smaller metropolitan areas containing relatively small, affluent Black populations, especially those containing colleges or universities and those housing military bases, they remained stubbornly stuck at very high levels in large metropolitan areas containing large, poor Black populations and characterized by restrictive suburban density zoning regimes and high levels of anti-Black prejudice (Rugh and Massey 2014; Rothwell and Massey 2015).

As of 2010, twenty-one U.S. areas containing one-third of all metropolitan Blacks remained hypersegregated, and half of all urban Blacks lived under conditions of "high" segregation (with a Black-White dissimilarity index above 60; see Massey and Tannen 2015). Blacks also continue to experience limited access to suburbs, and even within suburbs, they display relatively high levels of residential segregation and spatial isolation (Massey and Tannen 2017). Prior to 1990, rising Black socioeconomic status had no effect on the degree of Black-White segregation, and even though levels of Black segregation have now come to decline modestly with rising income, Blacks in the top income quintile are still more segregated than Hispanics in the bottom quintile (Intrator, Tannen, and Massey 2016). Under these circumstances, the social and economic distance between neighborhoods inhabited by affluent Whites and poor Blacks has widened quite markedly over the past forty years (Massey and Tannen 2016; Massey and Rugh 2021).

The ongoing residential segregation of Black Americans is critical to understanding their position in U.S. society because segregation functions very powerfully to undermine Black well-being in four distinct ways (Massey 2018). First, since public schools in the United States are mostly neighborhood based, residential segregation leads directly to school segregation (Reardon and Owens 2014; Massey and Tannen 2016; Reardon 2016); and because public schools are funded by local property taxes, the segregation of Black students within poor, inner-city school districts also concentrates Black students within poorly funded, low-quality schools (Kozol 1991; Fahle et al. 2020; Owens 2020). Continued residential and school segregation thus place African Americans at a distinct disadvantage in today's knowledge-based service economy where earnings vary sharply with education (Tamborini et al. 2015).

Second, segregation interrupts the tight connection between social and spatial mobility that for generations has been a fundamental component of socioeconomic mobility in the United States (Massey and Denton 1985). Societal opportunities and benefits are always distributed unevenly in space so that gaining access to tangible resources such as jobs, housing, and education as well as the intangible advantages of status, prestige, and security inevitably requires residential mobility. By confining Black Americans to a small and disadvantaged subset of neighborhoods, segregation functions to block this avenue of mobility (Massey and Denton 1993; Rothwell and Massey 2015).

Third, segregation undermines the well-being of African Americans by interacting with rising inequalities in the distribution of income and wealth to concentrate disadvantage spatially within Black neighborhoods (Massey 1990; Quillian 2012). Because African Americans have a higher poverty rate than Whites and other groups, their segregation in racially isolated neighborhoods concentrates poverty spatially to create unusually deprived residential environments. As a result, the distributions of neighborhood income experienced by Black and White metropolitan residents hardly overlap, and poor Blacks experience spatial concentrations of poverty that are rarely experienced by the poor of other groups (Peterson and Krivo 2010; Sampson 2012; Sharkey 2013; Massey and Rugh 2021). Even affluent African Americans routinely experience neighborhood conditions that are rarely faced even by the poorest Whites (Massey and Brodmann 2014).

As poverty is concentrated geographically, so are correlates of poverty such as crime, joblessness, delinquency, substance abuse, marital disruption, single parenthood, unwed child bearing, dependency, and public disorder, thus compounding the degree of social disadvantage experienced by African Americans in segregated metropolitan areas (Massey and Denton 1993; Sampson 2012; Sharkey 2013; Desmond 2016). In the end, because of the persistence of Black residential segregation and the concomitant concentration of poverty, neighborhoods have become the nexus for the transmission of Black poverty over the life cycle and across generations (Sharkey 2013; Massey and Brodmann 2014; Sharkey and Galster 2017). Whereas in the 1960s, Duncan (1968) described Black poverty as reflecting the intergenerational inheritance of race, today it is also perpetuated by the inheritance of place, as generation after generation of urban Blacks inhabit segregated neighborhoods characterized by intense racial isolation and high concentrations of poverty (Massey 2013; Sharkey 2013; Cashin 2014; Chetty et al. 2018).

Finally, residential segregation facilitates racial subordination by making discrimination and exploitation easy and efficient. The segregation of African Americans into a contiguous set of racially isolated neighborhoods makes it possible to disinvest in African Americans as a people simply by disinvesting in a place—that is, the discrete urban communities they occupy. For most of the twentieth century, credit and capital were systematically channeled away from Black neighborhoods through practices of redlining that were built into public policy, institutionalized in private practice, and specifically designed to deny African Americans the social and material resources necessary for success in American society (Jackson 1985; Massey and Denton 1993; Ross and Yinger 2002; Katznelson 2005; Rothstein 2017).

Diverse Experiences of Segregation

The Black college students surveyed by the National Longitudinal Survey of Freshmen (NLSF) experienced a diversity of school and neighborhood environments growing up. Some came of age in segregated minority neighborhoods characterized by high levels of concentrated disadvantage; others grew up in White neighborhoods of concentrated privilege; and still others were raised in racially mixed middle- and working-class neighborhoods (Charles et al. 2004, 2009; Massey and Fischer 2006). Given the strong association between residential and school segregation, those respondents who lived in segregated neighborhoods also tended to attend segregated schools (Owens 2020). Nonetheless, as we shall see, parents from segregated neighborhoods at times sent their children to integrated private, parochial, or magnet schools

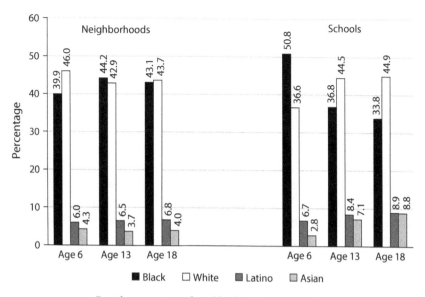

FIGURE 3.1. Racial composition of neighborhoods experienced by Black NLSF
respondents at different ages

as a means of overcoming the link between poor neighborhoods and poorly
performing public schools (Massey et al. 2003).

Figure 3.1 shows the average racial composition of schools and neighborhoods occupied by Black NLSF respondents at ages six, thirteen, and during their senior year of high school (around age eighteen). A neighborhood
was defined for each respondent as the area within a three-block radius
around their home. Although that is an uncommon definition of one's
neighborhood, the NLSF lacked geocoded data for home addresses to link
to a census tract. In a pilot study for the NLSF with such data, students
reported local demographics very similar to census tract data. The correlation coefficient between the census tract Black percentage and that reported
by respondents during their senior year was 0.83, whereas the corresponding correlations for White and Latino percentages were both around 0.79
(Charles, Dinwiddie, and Massey 2004). In addition, although different-
sized proxies for neighborhoods will lead to different reports of local segregation, the patterns of who is segregated from whom does not change
with the size of the neighborhood studied (Lee et al. 2008). In fact, Black
and White respondents living in the same area have very different definitions of their local neighborhood in which Black residents reported a larger

and more inclusive space compared to White residents, regardless of class and tenure (Hwang 2016).

As shown in the bar graphs located on the left side of the figure, the average Black respondent came from a racially mixed neighborhood displaying a rough balance of Black and White residents, with relatively small shares of Hispanics and Asians also present. We see relatively little variation in neighborhood racial composition by age, and during the senior year of high school, on the verge of going off to college, the average Black respondent lived in a neighborhood that was 43.1 percent Black and 43.7 percent White, with Hispanics comprising 6.8 percent and Asians 4.0 percent of all residents, respectively. Note that these figures represent *average* experiences for our respondents, and as we show below, only one-third of the respondents grew up in the sort of mixed neighborhood suggested by these averages. As our sample is of young adults in selective institutions of higher education, they are more likely to live and go to school in more integrated spaces than most Black people in the United States.

In contrast to neighborhoods, the racial composition of schools that respondents attended steadily moved toward integration as they aged. At age six, the average respondent attended a school that was 50.8 percent Black, 36.6 percent White, 6.7 percent Hispanic, and 2.8 percent Asian. By senior year of high school, however, the Black share had dropped to 33.8 percent while the share of Whites had increased to 44.9 percent, and the share of Hispanics and Asians had risen to 8.9 percent and 8.8 percent, respectively. These figures are averages, of course, and they obscure considerable variability in racial composition in by skin tone, nativity, national origin, and socioeconomic status. Table 3.1 explores this underlying diversity by showing the composition of neighborhoods inhabited by members of various Black subgroups during the senior year in high school.

As shown in the top panel, exposure to Black neighbors steadily falls as racial identification shifts from monoracial Black, to mixed race with a non-White parent, to mixed race with a White parent, while exposure to White neighbors correspondingly increases across these same categories. Thus, monoracial Black respondents inhabited neighborhoods that averaged 40.5 percent Black and 42.3 percent White, respectively, whereas mixed-race respondents with a non-White parent inhabited neighborhoods that were 27.4 percent Black and 46.9 percent White; mixed-race students with a White parent inhabited neighborhoods that were 23.9 percent Black and 59.6 percent White. Black respondents were exposed to relatively few Hispanics or Asians

TABLE 3.1. Overall racial composition experienced by various subgroups of Black NLSF respondents during their senior year of high school

Characteristic	Black	White	Hispanic	Asian	N
Racial identification					
Monoracial Black	40.5%***	42.3%***	7.8%***	6.1%***	873
Mixed-race Non-White	27.4	46.9	11.0	9.8	60
Mixed-race White	23.9	59.6	7.1	6.9	106
Skin tone					
Light	29.7%***	52.3%***	7.3%	7.3%	256
Medium	40.2	42.8	7.9	6.3	506
Dark	43.5	39.6	8.2	5.9	277
Nativity and generation					
Multigenerational native	40.9%***	43.5%***	7.0%	5.8%	760
Second-generation immigrant	28.8	49.9	9.6	8.1	191
First-generation immigrant	38.0	38.9	11.2	7.9	88
Region of origin					
USA	40.9%***	43.5%***	7.0%	5.8%	760
Caribbean	37.5	40.7	10.6	7.2	143
Africa	26.6	50.5	9.5	9.5	92
Other	23.6	56.6	10.0	7.7	44
Gender					
Female	39.3%	43.5%	7.8%	6.4%	676
Male	36.7	45.8	7.9%	6.5	363
Parental education					
No degree	49.2%***	33.4%***	9.5%	5.3%	306
College degree	37.4	46.1	7.2	6.4	319
Advanced degree	29.1	53.3	6.8	7.4	414
All Blacks	38.5%	44.3%	7.8%	6.4%	1,039

$^{+}$p < 0.10; * p< 0.05; ** p < 0.01; *** p < 0.001

irrespective of racial identification, though mixed-race students with a non-White parent did display a tendency to live in neighborhoods with slightly more Hispanics and Asians, which is not surprising given that in the NLSF, the non-White parent in question was either Hispanic or Asian.

For example, Jessica, came of age in racially mixed neighborhoods and schools. Growing up in a diverse area outside San Francisco, being racially "mixed" was for Jessica a normative experience. Indeed, she did not identify as Black until college. Her peer group included a number of other mixed-race individuals, and she thought it was commonplace to embrace all aspects of one's background. As she put it:

At home, there's just a lot of other mixed people that I'm close to, who I'm friends with. All of our family friends have mixed kids, so it's just the norm—even just at my high school there were a lot of us. In the Bay Area, there's a lot of mixed people whereas [here], there aren't very many. It's just really not as acceptable as a way to identify and it doesn't have the same kind of meaning, I think, as it does when I'm at home.

The data for neighborhood composition by skin tone are shown in the second panel of the table and are quite consistent with the foregoing pattern in the sense that persons with a light skin tone (many of whom had a White parent) lived in predominantly White neighborhoods (52.3 percent White and 29.7 percent Black with 7.3 percent each for Hispanics and Asians). In contrast, respondents with dark skin tones lived in neighborhoods that were only 39.6 percent White but 43.5 percent Black, with 8.2 percent for Hispanics and 5.9 percent Asians. As one might expect, respondents with a medium skin tone fell in between these two end points, occupying rather diverse neighborhoods that were 42.8 percent White, 40.2 percent Black, 7.9 percent Hispanic, and 6.3 percent Asian.

Ian's experience was even more integrated into Whiteness than Jessica's. Ian is mixed race, but when asked how he self-identified, he told us that he felt "like my experience in the world has made me think I'm White." He explained that he never knew his African American father and did not interact with his paternal kin while growing up. Instead, he lived exclusively with his White mother and socialized with her family members while attending a very "preppy" Massachusetts boarding school where his light skin differentiated him from others in the small population of Black students.

With respect to nativity and generation, we find that second-generation immigrants were most likely to come from predominantly non-Black neighborhoods. The average racial composition for them was 49.9 percent White, 9.6 percent Hispanic, and 8.1 percent Asian. In other words, they inhabited neighborhoods that were more than two-thirds non-Black and just 28.8 percent Black. We observe the largest share of Black neighbors among multigenerational natives, whose typical neighborhood was 40.9 percent Black, 43.5 percent White, 7.0 percent Hispanic, and 5.8 percent Asian. First-generation Black immigrants lived in neighborhoods with relatively equal shares of Blacks and Whites (38 percent versus 38.9 percent, compared with 11.2 percent for Hispanics and 7.9 percent for Asians). On average, respondents from the Caribbean grew up in the most diverse neighborhoods (37.5 percent

Black, 40.7 percent White, 10.6 percent Hispanic, and 7.2 percent Asian). In contrast, those originating in Africa and those in the residual "other" category tended to live in majority-White neighborhoods (50.5 percent and 56.6 percent White, respectively). The respective shares for Blacks were 26.6 percent and 23.6 percent, for Hispanics 9.5 percent and 10.0 percent, and for Asians 9.5 percent and 7.7 percent.

Finally, we observe the clearest differences in the racial composition of neighborhoods by socioeconomic background. As we move from parents without a college education to those with a college degree, to those with an advanced degree, the Black percentage drops from 49.2 percent to 37.4 percent to 29.1 percent, while the White percentage rises from 33.4 percent to 46.1 percent to 53.3 percent. As parental education increases, the share of Hispanics also drops (going from 9.5 percent to 7.2 percent to 6.8 percent) while the share of Asians increases (from 5.3 percent to 6.4 percent to 7.4 percent). Rising socioeconomic status is thus associated with greater contact with more advantaged groups (Whites and Asians) and less contact with disadvantaged groups (Blacks and Hispanics).

In summary, we observe significant differences in exposure to neighbors of different races across the various dimensions of Black diversity. Respondents having a White parent, a light skin tone, a parent with an advanced degree, and a parent from Africa are most likely to live in neighborhoods in which a majority of the residents are White or Asian (see also Alba 2020). In contrast, monoracial, multigenerational Black natives, with dark skin tones, and non-college-educated parents are most likely to live in neighborhoods where Blacks and Hispanics together constitute a majority of neighbors. Falling in between these two extremes are mixed-race respondents with a non-White but non-Black parent, a medium skin tone, college-educated parents and who are immigrants from the Caribbean, who tend to occupy the most racially diverse neighborhoods.

For those from racially diverse neighborhoods, diversity felt like the norm. April grew up in racially mixed circumstances "with African Americans, Latinos, and Whites all on the same block." Her local public high school mirrored the diversity of the neighborhood and contained substantial numbers of both minorities and Whites. When asked to describe the economic circumstances of her neighborhood, April replied, "I don't think it was a doctor kind of neighborhood. . . . I know someone who worked [as a] mechanic. . . . I think there were teachers . . . nothing spectacular." April's parents were married throughout her childhood; when we met her, her father had just retired, and her parents were about to move into a predominately White, middle-class town in southern New Jersey.

Like April—and for most Americans—school segregation mirrors or exaggerates neighborhood segregation (Reardon and Owens 2014; Massey and Tannen 2016; Urban Institute 2018). Nonetheless, some Black NLSF respondents grew up in predominantly minority neighborhoods but attended predominantly White schools. Table 3.2 takes this possibility into account by using both school and neighborhood composition to define four separate categories of experience with segregation during adolescence: respondents who lived in predominantly White neighborhoods and attended predominantly White schools (in which Blacks and Hispanics together comprised less than 30 percent of the population), those who lived in predominantly minority neighborhoods and attended predominantly minority schools (in which Blacks and Hispanics together comprised at least 70 percent of the population), those who lived in and learned in a racially mixed environment (the average populations of the schools and neighborhoods were between 30 percent and 70 percent Black and Hispanic), and finally, those who lived in a segregated-minority neighborhood (at least 70 percent Black and Hispanic) but attended a predominantly White school (no more than 30 percent Black and Hispanic). According to these criteria, 35.4 percent of NLSF respondents grew up in predominantly White schools and neighborhoods, 31.4 percent came of age in racially mixed schools and neighborhoods, and 23.9 percent originated in predominantly minority schools and neighborhoods, with 9.3 percent growing up in minority neighborhoods but attending predominantly White schools.

The first three columns are generally consistent with patterns discerned in earlier tables. Black respondents who are first-generation immigrants, multiracial, with a White college-educated parent, or a light skin tone are likely to have come of age in a predominantly White context, whether these traits are expressed alone or in combination with the others.

In contrast, monoracial, multigenerational-native Blacks, with dark skin tones, and non-college-educated parents are most likely to have grown up in predominantly minority settings, again whether expressed alone or in combination. Finally, our data show that Blacks with a non-White parent, those who are second-generation Americans, and those whose parents hold a college degree tend to live in racially mixed neighborhoods and attend racially mixed schools. Our findings for monoracial and mixed-race Blacks are consistent with other research indicating that mixed-race Blacks with a White parent tend

TABLE 3.2. Overall pattern of segregation experienced by various subgroups of Black NLSF respondents during their senior year of high school

	Pattern of segregation				
	Predominantly White	Racially mixed	Predominantly minority	Minority neighborhood and White school	N
Racial identification					
Monoracial Black	31.7%***	32.1%	25.9%***	10.2%***	873
Mixed-race non-White	45.3	34.3	14.5	5.8	60
Mixed-race White	60.4	23.6	12.3	3.8	106
Skin tone					
Light	48.5%***	28.3%***	15.3%***	7.0%***	256
Medium	32.2	31.3	25.6	11.0	506
Dark	29.4	34.4	28.7	7.6	277
Nativity and generation					
Multigenerational native	30.5%*	34.5%*	25.9%*	9.1%*	760
Second-generation immigrant	29.3	45.0	14.7	11.0	191
First-generation immigrant	35.2	34.1	22.7	8.0	88
Region of origin					
USA	30.5%**	34.5%**	25.9%**	9.1%**	760
Caribbean	32.2	32.2	21.7	14.0	92
Africa	29.4	52.2	13.0	5.4	143
Other	31.8	50.0	11.4	6.8	44
Gender					
Female	31.8%	33.8%	24.7%	9.7%	676
Male	30.6	38.5	22.4	8.5	363
Parental education					
No degree	19.5%***	30.9%***	39.7%***	9.9%***	306
College degree	34.0	33.3	22.2	10.6	319
Advanced degree	48.3	30.3	13.5	7.9	414
All Blacks	35.4%	31.4%	23.9%	9.3%	1,039

$^+$ p < 0.10; * p < 0.05; ** p < 0.01; *** p < 0.001

to live in more diverse residential areas than monoracial Blacks, irrespective of income and education. This research also finds that Black-White multiracials are more likely to reside in predominately white and economically stable areas compared to other Blacks and to experience more interracial contact in their neighborhoods, at school, and over the life course (Holloway et al. 2005; Wright et al. 2013; Davenport 2016).

The next to last column of the table refers to respondents who lived in segregated minority neighborhoods but attended predominantly White schools. Although respondents from all backgrounds are in that category, the most common are monoracial Black respondents, those with a medium skin tone, those whose parents were from the Caribbean, and those whose parents had no more than a college degree.

Segregation and Exposure to Disorder and Violence

Because of racial segregation in housing, Black respondents tend to attend segregated schools which, like segregated neighborhoods, tend to have high concentrations of poverty and to exhibit elevated levels of exposure to disorder and violence (Massey et al. 2013; Massey and Brodmann 2014). Indeed, when levels of exposure to neighborhood crime and violence are compared across groups, the White distribution of neighborhoods hardly overlaps with that of African Americans (Peterson and Krivo 2010). Prior research using data from the NLSF suggests that respondents who reported high levels of exposure to disorder and violence while growing up also experienced more stress in their social networks as college students, given that their kinship and friendship networks extended back into disadvantaged neighborhoods; stress in social networks led, in turn, to poor health outcomes and lower levels of academic achievement (Charles et al. 2004).

The left side of figure 3.2 presents indicators of social disorder that respondents reported witnessing in their neighborhoods at ages six, thirteen, and eighteen. Between 30 percent and 40 percent of respondents recalled seeing homeless people, gang members, drug paraphernalia, and drug dealing within their neighborhoods at ages thirteen and eighteen, up from lower levels at age six. Although marijuana use is now legal in many states, we note that this survey asks about experiences in the late 1980s and the 1990s, when supporting the legalization of any drug was a relatively fringe political opinion. The share of respondents who reported witnessing drug use rose to even greater heights with age, increasing from 15 percent at age six to 32 percent at age thirteen to 55 percent at age eighteen. Witnessing public drunkenness was already quite common at age six, with the share who recalled seeing such behavior being 44 percent and rising to 54 percent at age thirteen before dropping back to 48 percent at age eighteen. Respondents were also asked about graffiti in the neighborhoods they inhabited at age eighteen, and 28 percent recalled seeing it on businesses and 34 percent on homes.

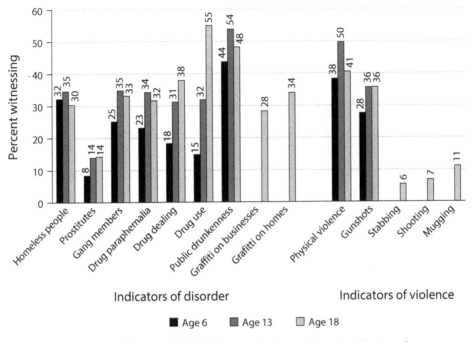

FIGURE 3.2. Percent of Black NLSF respondents ever witnessing indicators of social disorder and violence in their neighborhoods at different ages

The right side of the figure shows the frequency with which indicators of violence were witnessed in respondents' neighborhoods. The share who recalled seeing instances of physical violence rose from 38 percent to 50 percent between ages six and thirteen before falling back to 41 percent at age eighteen; 28 percent recalled hearing gunshots at age six, with the percentage rising to 36 percent at ages thirteen and eighteen. When they were seniors in high school, 6 percent of respondents reported witnessing a stabbing, 7 percent a shooting, and 11 percent a mugging.

Figure 3.3 shows indicators of disorder and violence that respondents reported witnessing in the schools they attended at different ages. In general, the cutting of classes, truancy, alcohol use, and drug use increased with age, as one would expect given adolescent development. The share witnessing students cutting classes rose from 19 percent at age six to 33 percent at age thirteen and 60 percent at age eighteen while the share witnessing students cutting school rose from 21 percent to 27 percent to 49 percent. Alcohol and drug use were reported with much less frequency. The share of respondents witnessing the

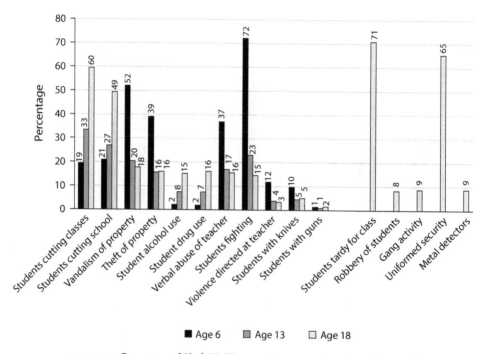

FIGURE 3.3. Percentage of Black NLSF respondents ever witnessing indicators of social disorder and violence within schools they attended

consumption of alcohol in school rose from 2 percent at age six to 8 percent at age thirteen and 15 percent at age eighteen while the share witnessing drug use rose from 2 percent to 7 percent to 16 percent over the same ages.

Other indicators of disorder and violence generally fell with age. The percentage of respondents who recalled witnessing the vandalism of property fell from 52 percent at age six to 20 percent at age thirteen and 18 percent at age eighteen while the share witnessing the theft of property dropped from 39 percent at age six to 16 percent at ages thirteen and eighteen. At age six, some 37 percent recalled witnessing the verbal abuse of a teacher, but this figure dropped to 17 percent and 16 percent at ages thirteen and eighteen, respectively. Likewise, although a large majority (72 percent) of respondents recalled seeing students fighting at age six, the share dropped to 23 percent at age thirteen and 15 percent at age eighteen.

Relatively few respondents recalled witnessing violence directed at a teacher at any age, with the figure being just 12 percent at age six and only 4 percent at age thirteen and 3 percent at age eighteen. The percentage witnessing students carrying knives or guns was also quite low. Some 10 percent witnessed students with knives at age six, compared with only 5 percent at ages thirteen and eighteen, with only 1 percent or 2 percent witnessing students with guns at any age. Finally, 71 percent of respondents remembered students being tardy for class as seniors in high school and 65 percent said their school had uniformed security guards, but only 8 percent witnessed a robbery of a student and 9 percent witnessed any gang activity, while only 9 percent recalled their school containing any metal detectors.

Massey et al. (2003:258–261) developed a series of severity-weighted indexes to capture the degree of exposure to violence and social disorder in schools and neighborhoods. These indexes weighted the frequency with which various transgressions were witnessed by the severity of the transgression using a ratio-level severity scale of crime and delinquency derived by Sellin and Wolfgang (1964) and standardized nationally by Wolfgang et al. (1985). Here, we rely on these scales to analyze the cumulative degree to which Black respondents were exposed to disorder and violence in their neighborhoods and schools over the course of aging from six to thirteen to eighteen.

Figure 3.4 shows indexes for the four categories of residential/school experience defined earlier in table 3.2. On the left side of the figure, average indexes are shown for neighborhood disorder, neighborhood violence, and neighborhood disorder and violence combined. In the middle are average indexes of school disorder, school violence, and school disorder and violence combined. The right side of the figure presents average values for an overall index of exposure to disorder and violence in both schools and neighborhoods. A quick glance at the bar chart reveals that exposure to disorder and violence generally increases as one shifts from White to racially mixed to segregated contexts. The summary index of exposure to neighborhood disorder and violence, for example, stands at 69 among those growing up in predominantly White neighborhoods, 105 among those from mixed neighborhoods, and 154 among those from predominantly minority neighborhoods. For the sake of comparison, going from "rarely" to "sometimes" witnessing drug sales in public is equal to a 20.6-point increase in the disorder scale.

Among respondents from racially mixed or minority neighborhoods who attended a predominantly White school, the index was highest at 164, suggesting that parents are attempting to shelter their offspring from a high degree of neighborhood disorder and violence by sending them to predominantly White schools. Turning to the summary index of school disorder and violence, this strategy appears successful. Whereas the average school disorder-violence

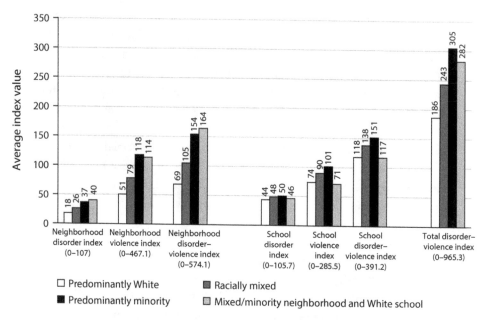

FIGURE 3.4. Indexes of exposure to disorder and violence within schools and neighborhoods by pattern of segregation experienced by Black NLSF respondents during senior year of high school

index rose from 118 for respondents from predominantly White backgrounds to 138 for those from racially mixed backgrounds and 151 for those from predominantly minority settings, it was only 117 among respondents who lived in mixed or minority neighborhoods but attended predominantly White schools.

Likewise, the total disorder-violence index averaged 186 for persons from predominantly White settings and rose to values of 243 and 305 for those coming from mixed and predominantly minority contexts but then fell back to an average of 282 for those from mixed or minority neighborhoods who attended predominantly White schools. By sending their children to predominantly White schools, in other words, parents from mixed and minority neighborhoods not only succeeded in limiting their children's exposure to violence within schools but also were successful in reducing the cumulative total neighborhood and school violence they experienced while growing up.

Interviews confirmed that parents often sent their children to predominantly White schools to protect them from disorder and violence. Rather than coming from backgrounds of affluence, their parents generally had few resources and often went to great lengths to place them into high-quality schools that would protect them from risky neighborhood environments and prepare them for college. John's Bermudan mother decided to send him to a private school from sixth grade onward, hoping to keep him away from the "street life" in the northeastern city where he lived, a strategy he appreciated:

> At a public school, I'm not sure that I would've been able to perform as well academically, just because maybe I would've fallen into a bad crowd or something like that . . . just the way I was headed. Private school probably saved me. . . . It's easy to get caught up in a street life, thug mentality, if that's all you know. You know, my friends, some of them weren't the greatest people. It was like all the White teachers at my [public elementary] school told [my mother], that's where she should send me and pull me out of the school system.

Calvin's Nigerian parents were also worried about him and his older siblings spending time in their poor, segregated New York City neighborhood. His mother held a college degree and his father had earned a two-year degree from a local community college. Like many immigrants, Calvin's father was self-selected for drive, ambition, and grit (Hamilton 2019). He worked very hard and held two jobs—driving a Yellow Cab full time but also preparing people's taxes part time. Calvin explained that "we didn't really associate with, really talk to people around us. Because, you know, it's a lot of drug dealers, a lot of bad influences and my mom was pretty worried."

Calvin said his parents were "strict" about monitoring his whereabouts and did not like him interacting with neighbors outside the confines of their apartment. They also placed a high premium on academic success and helped Calvin get financial aid to attend a prestigious private high school in the Bronx. As Calvin told us, "I suppose . . . it was more just that they were afraid something bad was going to happen all the time." This parenting strategy paid off for Calvin, who earned high marks in high school, completed multiple AP classes, and played three varsity sports, which ultimately earned him admission and a scholarship to a very selective private university.

To gain access to better schooling, parents often sought to move into more integrated neighborhoods or relocate to upscale school districts. Alternatively, they enrolled their children in a public magnet school outside their immediate neighborhood, a strategy that placed significant burdens on many interviewees. For interviewees who lived in racially isolated neighborhoods but attended majority White schools, long commutes to school and back were common. Tiffany, for example, had a two-hour commute each way between her

Bronx neighborhood and the public high school where she was a student in the gifted program, a burden she said she was prepared to bear because "the schools in [my] neighborhood were very, very bad."

Eugene likewise attended a school outside of his majority-Black neighborhood in Alabama. Although he attended a predominantly Black public school in kindergarten and first grade, he told us that

> In second grade, my mother sent me to, for second and third grades she sent me to a predominantly . . . well, it was in the White part of town. So we just can assume it was a predominantly White school. Then in my fourth-grade year, I think the city passed a resolution saying that you basically had to go to your own school . . . in your neighborhood, yeah. And so, fourth and fifth grade I went to a predominantly Black school.

After fifth grade, however, Eugene went on to take and pass a city-wide exam that gained him entry into a competitive magnet middle school from which he was able to enter a selective high school, and "that's how I went back to where I was." Although he described his high school as having some Black students, the majority of the student body was White, and he ultimately graduated with a high GPA and several honors and AP classes under his belt, which propelled him on to college.

Some parents considered this strategy but did not end up following through due to the high costs. For example, LJ was the son of Jamaican immigrants who came to the United States in the 1970s. He lived in the same house for his entire childhood in a poor school district just outside of New York City, where he attended public primary, middle, and high schools. According to him, the few White families in town generally sent their children to private schools, telling us that "there's 3 percent White people living in [name of community]. I think most of the kids of the White families went to private school . . . and they started taking them out, like, in elementary." LJ went on to speculate that "I guess they like, thought they would be—their kids would be safer in private school."

Although LJ's parents also thought about sending him to private school, the high cost of tuition prevented them from doing so. He explained that "my mom thought about sending me to private school . . . 'cause I was, I guess I was acting up in like, eighth grade . . . but it [was] gonna cost too much." Nevertheless, LJ graduated from high school with a cumulative grade point average of 3.8 and was ranked fourteenth in his class of 270; but when he took the proficiency exams for AP credit, he did not earn a passing score on any test.

Differences in Exposure to Disorder and Violence

Table 3.3 concludes our quantitative analysis by examining how exposure to disorder and violence in neighborhoods and schools varies across the various dimensions of Black diversity considered here. For the sake of parsimony, we focus on overall disorder-violence indexes for neighborhoods, schools, and the two combined. The top panel reveals that exposure to neighborhood disorder and violence varies significantly by racial identification, with the average disorder-violence index standing at 111.5 for monoracial Black respondents but only 99.3 for mixed-race respondents having a non-White parent and 94.9 for mixed-race respondents with a White parent. Considering exposure to violence within neighborhoods and within schools and neighborhoods combined, however, we observe no significant differences by racial identification.

The second panel reveals significant differences in exposure to disorder and violence in neighborhoods and in schools, and overall, by skin tone. Whereas the average neighborhood disorder-violence index stood at 97.2 for respondents with a light skin tone, it was 109.6 for those with medium skin tones and 119.4 for those with dark skin tones. Likewise, the total disorder-violence index rose from 228.7 for light-skinned respondents to 239.7 for medium-skinned respondents and 254.4 for dark-skinned respondents.

Although exposure to disorder and violence while growing up clearly varies by racial identification and skin tone, we observe few significant differences by nativity, generation, or region of origin. The only statistically significant finding is that exposure to disorder and violence in schools is greatest for multigenerational natives (with an average index of 134.3) compared to first-generation immigrants (129.5) and second-generation immigrants (124.0). Although we see no significant differences in exposure to neighborhood disorder and violence by nativity or generation, the total disorder-violence index for schools and neighborhoods combined is marginally greater for multigenerational natives compared with first- and second-generation immigrants, owing largely to the significant difference in exposure within schools.

Finally, we observe the sharpest differences in exposure to disorder and violence in schools and neighborhoods by parental education. Whereas respondents whose parents held advanced degrees experienced an average neighborhood disorder-violence index of 86.7, the value rose to 102.3 among those with college-educated parents and 146.2 for those whose parents held no degree. That gap is roughly equal to a one-step increase (e.g., from "rarely" seeing all the forms of violence and disorder" to "sometimes" seeing them) in

TABLE 3.3. Exposure of Black NLSF respondents to disorder and violence in neighborhoods and schools during senior year of high school

	Neighborhood indexes			School indexes			Total disorder-violence index
	Disorder index	Violence index	Neighborhood index	Disorder index	Violence index	School index	
Racial identification							
Monoracial Black	27.8*	83.7	111.5*	46.5	85.3	131.7	243.0
Mixed-race non-White	23.8	75.4	99.3	46.7	86.7	133.5	231.7
Mixed-race White	24.3	73.9	94.9	49.6	83.6	133.3	227.0
Skin tone							
Light	25.4*	73.4	97.2*	47.8	84.8	132.5	228.7*
Medium	27.2	82.2	109.6	45.9	84.3	130.2	239.8
Dark	28.8	90.5	119.4	47.3	87.6	134.9	254.4
Nativity and generation							
Multigenerational native	27.2	83.6	110.4	47.1	87.2***	134.3*	244.5+
Second-generation immigrant	27.0	77.5	104.3	46.7	77.3	124.0	227.9
First-generation immigrant	27.1	80.8	108.5	44.5	84.9	129.5	238.5
Region of origin							
USA	27.2	83.6+	110.4	47.1	87.2**	134.3	244.5
Caribbean	29.4	84.2	113.4	45.4	82.4	127.8	240.6
Africa	24.4	70.4	95.0	47.9	79.1	127.0	222.9
Other	24.8	77.2	102.0	43.9	72.4	116.2	217.9
Gender							
Female	25.0***	72.7***	97.6***	44.7***	81.1***	125.9***	223.5***
Male	31.3	99.7	130.3	50.6	92.7	143.3	273.20
Parental education							
No degree	34.9***	111.5***	146.2***	49.0***	94.3***	143.2***	289.2***
College degree	26.6	75.5	102.3	46.3	85.6	131.9	234.8
Advanced degree	22.0	65.6	86.7	45.5	78.3	123.7	210.1
N							1,039

+ p < 0.10; * p < 0.05; ** p < 0.01; *** p < 0.001

each component of the scale of violence and disorder at the age of eighteen. The respective figures for the average disorder-violence index within schools were 123.7, 131.9, and 143.2, and the total disorder-violence ranged from 210.1 for those whose parents held advanced degrees to 234.8 for those whose parents held only college degrees to 289.2 for those whose parents held no degree.

In sum, while schools were largely similar across social class in terms of disorder and violence, neighborhood segregation and social class differences led to large and meaningful differences in student exposure to violence and disorder which dramatically affect educational outcomes (Sharkey 2018).

Segregation and Culture Shock

Contrasting experiences with integration versus segregation before college are important not only because of the strong association between racial segregation and exposure to violence and disorder but also because of the well-documented phenomenon of "culture shock," which occurs when a student from a segregated background characterized by racial and class isolation encounters the norms, values, and expectations of students and faculty in affluent, predominantly White schools, yielding feelings of racial and class marginality. According to Torres (2009:88), culture shock "is partly a consequence of their encounter with race, but also their encounter with class-based cultural styles that may be foreign to them." Lacking cultural familiarity with elite academia can create serious problems of adjustment that undermine students' well-being and undercut their academic performance (Horvat and Antonio 1999; Kuriloff and Reichert 2003).

In interviews, wealthier students reported comfort in White cultural spaces, in large part because they grew up in White spaces. None of the affluent students we interviewed came from neighborhoods that were predominantly Black *and* affluent; conversely, all of the twenty-seven who came from majority-White neighborhoods and attended majority-White high schools reported that their families owned homes, and most had been homeowners for quite some time. They described their neighborhood backgrounds as upper middle class or affluent and offered tangible examples of their elevated economic standing. Emily, for example, a mixed-race multigenerational native with a White parent, described her parents as medical doctors with incomes "in the top tax bracket." Likewise, James was a light-skinned multigenerational native who described himself as "upper middle class" or "high class" but said that he preferred not to "flaunt" his family's wealth. His father was a prominent businessman with an MBA from Harvard, married to a stay-at-home mother. The family lived in an exclusive Connecticut suburb, and James attended an elite prep school a short distance away. Neither Emily nor James received any financial aid at college. Both were not only comfortable in predominantly White institutions, but wealthy White environments were their norm.

Compared with Black students from racially segregated schools and neighborhoods, those who came of age in White neighborhoods and attended predominantly White, well-resourced public schools, or who came from predominantly minority neighborhoods but attended more advantaged, predominantly White high schools, are at lower risk of experiencing culture shock in college (Charles, Roscigno, and Torres 2007; Carter 2012; Torres and Massey 2012). Jack (2014) refers to students from poor backgrounds who attend advantaged private White middle and high schools as the "privileged poor," in contrast to their "doubly disadvantaged" peers who came to college directly from disadvantaged, racially segregated neighborhoods and schools. Whereas he focuses on students who attended elite private high schools, we broaden the focus to students who lived in predominantly Black or Latinx neighborhoods and attended predominantly White public schools. Typically, those students went to wealthier public institutions (either by traveling to wealthier school districts or as part of magnet programs), and our qualitative data show that these public schools exposed them to the elite White educational institutions, cultures, and peers that Jack emphasized as valuable knowledge for success in elite colleges and universities.

Although exposure to White elites in high school helped students avoid culture shock in college, not being shocked does not mean it is easy to socially integrate. Interviewees who grew up in segregated neighborhoods but went to predominantly White high schools often did so as part of a selective program for high-achieving but economically disadvantaged minorities, such as A Better Chance, Prep for Prep, or City Prep and they experienced culture shock as high school students rather than as college students. Darryl, for example, was one of four children raised by a single mother, who grew up in one of the toughest areas of the Bronx, which he said was plagued by "violence, [a] poor educational system, gangs, drugs" and his childhood was "not easy." Indeed, many of his own family members became entangled in street life.

In the seventh grade, however, Darryl's middle school principal took an interest in him and helped him to gain entry into City Prep, which enabled him to attend an elite boarding school in Pennsylvania. However, it was the first time Darryl had ever interacted with a critical mass of White peers and adults, which was quite a cultural and social adjustment for him. Nonetheless, he recognized the advantage it gave him over other minority students when he arrived at his Ivy League university:

> I think the most significant aid that [name of school] gave me was cultural. . . . It was just being able to socially adjust to the type of institutions

that I intended on applying to for college. You know, just becoming ac-
quainted with the flip-flop-, pop collar-, corduroy-wearing folks. . . .
Understanding the . . . political correctness of these universities and the
superficiality. That's not something they would actively promote, but that
is something that I picked up at [name of school].

Although he valued the cultural capital he acquired at boarding school, Darryl
nonetheless struggled socially and felt that he was "usually misunderstood"
because he was "Black and poor." His closest friends at the school were other
Black young men from lower-class backgrounds.

Denise likewise told us that her experiences at an elite boarding school
prevented her from experiencing culture shock in college. Despite growing up
in a low-income section of the Bronx with a single mother, she feels that "the
kind of life I've had has prepared me for [college]":

I think it's based on how you were raised. I think that's primarily like where
you went to school, the kind of people in your neighborhood, what you're
used to, you know? There are some people here who will talk about how
they went to all-Black schools their whole life and they come to [institu-
tion] and they're kind of like . . . they keep to themselves, they keep to the
Black people. . . . They're not experiencing any other culture, you know?
They see White people, but they're not interacting.

Although Denise was heavily involved in the Black community in college,
most of her close friends did not experience culture shock because they "have
been in similar situations in high school."

Attending an advantaged White high school, however, did not always
provide interviewees with immunity to culture shock. Thomas reported experiencing culture shock at college even though he had attended a selective
private high school near Dallas on a scholarship where his peers were
"mostly White and very wealthy." Nonetheless, he told us that as a college
student he felt

out of place often, especially being a member of an [elite off-campus] club
that only has three Black people. There are "country nights" and "bling-
bling nights" at the club, which make me uncomfortable for different reasons. I have just accepted that I'm going to be one of a few Black people at
these places. The culture shock of being up north, with mainly White
people has been the hardest part of adjusting to college. I don't know if
I will ever fully adjust.

Neither of Thomas's parents went to college, and he recalled being the only Black student in his honors and AP classes. Despite his discomfort on campus, he nonetheless recognized that his high school experiences gave him an advantage over other Black students he met at college:

> Many have a harder time. . . . I think my experience in high school helped me tremendously. Many have never had to deal with the type of people or culture they are thrust into at [institution]. Also, when adding the rigorous course load, it is hard for [them] to become comfortable.

Adam, of mixed racial and immigrant origins, confirmed Thomas's view, telling us quite plainly that he also experienced culture shock when he arrived on his elite campus coming directly from his racially diverse urban neighborhood and school:

> INTERVIEWER: Have you ever experienced culture shock?
> ADAM: Sure. . . . Coming here, in a way, just because it was so different than what I was used to basically. Cultural. Here the dominant culture is White and upper class. I think those two factors permeate everything.

When asked if he was still experiencing culture shock, Adam explained that it had dissipated "because you learn to adapt." During his first semester of college, Adam kept to himself, but over time, he relaxed socially and became friends with non-Black students in his dorm. He eventually joined certain cultural organizations and integrated into campus life, and by the end of his junior year, he had a 3.7 GPA.

Conclusion

In this chapter, we have documented important differences in experiences with integration and segregation among Black students attending selective colleges and universities. Black students who identified themselves as racially mixed with a White parent, had a light skin tone, were second-generation immigrants, and whose parents held advanced degrees were most likely to grow up in a predominantly White neighborhood and attend a predominantly White school. Likewise, interviewees and survey respondents with immigrant origins in Africa were also more likely to come of age in a predominantly White neighborhood and attend White schools, relative to those with origins in the Caribbean. In contrast, their counterparts who self-identified as monoracial, had a dark skin tone, were multigenerational natives, and whose parents never graduated from college were more likely to come of age in a predominantly minority neighborhood and to attend segregated schools.

Finally, those NLSF respondents who were mixed race but with a non-White parent, who had a medium or dark skin tone, were born abroad, and whose parents had graduated from college but did not hold an advanced degree were most likely to have grown up in a racially integrated neighborhood in which neither Whites nor minorities were dominant. A relatively small number of Black students in both the survey and interview samples grew up in racially mixed or segregated minority neighborhoods but attended predominantly White schools.

Because of the effect that racial residential segregation has in concentrating Black poverty spatially, we also showed how different experiences with segregation were associated with different degrees of exposure to social disorder and violence while growing up. In general, such exposure increased as skin tone darkened and was greatest for survey respondents who expressed a monoracial Black identity and least for those who identified as racially mixed with a White parent. Mixed-race students whose other parent was non-White fell in between these end points with moderate levels of exposure to disorder and violence. Exposure to disorder and violence also increased moving from first-generation immigrants to those in the second generation to multigenerational natives. The starkest differences in exposure to disorder and violence, however, were observed with respect to socioeconomic status. Exposure was greatest for respondents whose parents lacked a college degree, lower for those whose parents were college graduates, and lowest for those with parents holding an advanced degree.

These differentials are important because exposure to violence has been shown to have both short-term and long-term effects on human cognition (Sharkey 2018) putting a significant share of Black students at an academic disadvantage (Charles, Dinwiddie, and Massey 2004; Massey and Fischer 2006). Aizer (2007), for example, analyzed a sample of children in Los Angeles neighborhoods and found that exposure to community violence predicted internalizing behavior problems, and likewise Sharkey et al. (2012) found that children were less able to control their impulses and maintain attention during testing in the aftermath of exposure to violence.

Sharkey (2010) also demonstrated that exposure to a homicide within four days of taking a standardized test reduced the performance of Black students in Chicago compared to Black children from the same neighborhoods who were not exposed to homicide, a finding he later replicated in New York City

(Sharkey et al. 2014). Burdick-Will (2013) similarly found that when public school children in Chicago were exposed to higher levels of violence, they performed worse on standardized achievement tests in reading and math. Gershenson and Tekin (2017) found students attending schools within five miles of a shooting in suburban Maryland were significantly less likely to pass their state English and language arts or math assessments. Beland and Kim (2016) found that student performance on English and math assessments declined after exposure to within-school homicides. Lacoe (2016) found that in years when students reported feeling unsafe in school, their performance on standardized achievement tests declined.

In sum, to the extent that segregated neighborhoods display high rates of crime and violence, they can be expected to impair cognition and impede learning while growing up. The collateral consequences of segregation can continue to engulf even those fortunate students who have managed to gain access to an elite college or university. Although these students no longer experience such exposure directly, they nonetheless continue to experience the effects of violent and disordered neighborhoods indirectly owing to the surfeit of stressful life events occurring to people in their social networks.

In addition to the foregoing disadvantages, students coming out of a segregated social world are at greater risk of culture shock (Torres 2009; Jack 2014, 2019) upon arriving on the campus of a selective college or university, leading to experiences of racial and class marginalization that undermine personal well-being and academic performance. In sum, growing up in racially isolated and poor neighborhoods and attending racially segregated schools can be expected to have continuing consequences for aspiring members of the new Black elite, consequences that vary systematically depending on racial identification, skin tone, nativity, generation, and parental socioeconomic status.

4

Identities and Attitudes

I mean, I felt the pressures of an African American kid just 'cause when people see me they don't think I'm African. I mean, it's just that I'm Black. My family tells me I'm American when I'm there; but when I'm here, if they hear that my parents are African, then I'm African. I mean, in the end, Black is, around here, Black is pretty much Black.

ERVIN, SECOND-GENERATION GHANAIAN AMERICAN

IN *The Souls of Black Folk*, W. E. B. Du Bois (1903:3) wrote of a racial "double consciousness" in which African Americans perceived themselves both as Whites saw them (as a stigmatized and denigrated outgroup) but also as they saw themselves (as full human beings worthy of dignity and respect). This duality produced a "sense of always looking at one's self through the eyes of others, of measuring one's soul by the tape of a world that looks on in amused contempt and pity. One ever feels his two-ness." A few years earlier, in *The Philadelphia Negro*, Du Bois (1899:221) also warned against homogenizing Black Americans, noting that "there is always a strong tendency on the part of the community to consider the Negroes as composing one practically homo-geneous mass . . . and yet if the foregoing statistics have emphasized any one fact it is that wide variations in antecedents, wealth, intelligence and general efficiency have already been differentiated within this group."

As Du Bois foresaw, early American social science research indeed adopted a rather monolithic viewpoint on Black identity, focusing on the social, eco-nomic, and psychological experiences of Black Americans *relative* to Whites (Hunter 2015). For example, Robert Park (1923) and his contemporaries (Fer-guson 1938; Horowitz 1939) emphasized the development of Black identity through the common experiences of discrimination and exclusion and came to see Blackness as a "product of assignment" rooted in the historical legacy of slavery and segregation (Eggerling-Boeck 2002:22). In this tradition, Black Americans were viewed as being "identified by skin color and other bodily features . . . [yielding] a self-conscious population that defines itself partly in terms of common descent (Africa as a homeland), a distinctive history (slavery in particular), and a broad sense of cultural symbols (from language to expressive culture) that are held to capture much of the essence of peoplehood" (Cornell and Hartmann 1998:33).

That monolithic conceptualization of Black identity has long hampered research on racial group identities to the exclusion of other salient characteristics such as mixed-race identification, nativity, social class, and segregation, even as there is an equally long history of Black scholars demonstrating the agency of Black individuals and the variation in their worldviews and identities (see, e.g., work by Sellers et al. [2003], within the realm of education and youth; Carter 2005; Warikoo and Carter 2009; Tyson 2011). Mainstream research on Black identity has considered an individual's affinity with only some aspects of group identity, or how people actually see themselves. As prior chapters reveal, however, the generation of Black students at America's top universities come from a wide range of experiences that complicate the assumption of a uniform Black identity. As Cohen (1999) argues in her research on Black politics and the AIDS crisis, the inaccurate assumption of a monolithic Black experience and/or identity has long been used to marginalize specific subpopulations and their needs compared to what are seen as "real" Black issues. Race is a social construction and its expression is always intersectional, depending on the traits and characteristics of the person involved (Collins and Bilge 2016).

Unlike past descriptions of a monolithic Black aristocracy (Gatewood 2000), recent studies suggest that the racial attitudes of young Black Americans in the twenty-first century vary by age, gender, ethnicity, and social class. Differential perceptions of group consciousness and self-concept moderate both in-group and out-group relations (e.g., Benjamin 2005; Khanna and Johnson 2010; Thornton, Taylor, and Chatters 2014; Charles et al. 2015; Jones, Andrews, and Policastro 2015; Davenport 2016). It is the intersection of these different social identities that reveals the complexities of Black identity expression and the nature of Black relationships with Whites as well as Asians and Latinos, not to mention with each other.

In this chapter, we present further evidence to challenge the monolithic conceptualization of Black identity and take note of distinctions as they relate to group stereotypes, perceived social distances, and attitudes on racial inequalities. The quantitative analyses in this chapter draw from wave 1 of the National Longitudinal Survey of Freshmen (NLSF) questionnaire, which was administered very early in the first semester of respondents' freshman year. Survey responses thus reflect their incipient adult identities as formed through childhood and adolescence, including some that we have detailed in earlier chapters; interview responses further clarify the processes through which Black students came to these identities.

In her commentary, Izzy, a second-semester senior, discussed the evolution of her self-identity between high school and college. Of medium complexion with dark, kinky hair, Izzy knew she looked phenotypically Black despite her mixed heritage. Izzy's maternal grandparents emigrated from Poland, and her father was a second-generation Dominican who did not speak Spanish and identified as African American. Izzy said that she grew up with "more Polish traditions than anything else." Both sets of Izzy's grandparents had passed away some time ago; her maternal cousins lived on the other side of the country, and her father's relatives had since migrated to Puerto Rico. Thus, she grew up surrounded by only her nuclear family.

Until college, Izzy had always identified as Black, mainly because she and her brother were the only non-Whites in the local school system and in their suburban Pennsylvania town, and also because she had never known anyone else who was mixed race. In high school, her friends were all White, and she struggled with the fact that their families were better off financially than hers. By the time we met her, though, she explained that she preferred to identify as "mixed" and not "Black" after becoming close with three classmates who are also "Black and White" that she met at preorientation at the start of her freshman year. She told us that she loved being so close to other "mixed friends I could relate to." They all remained best friends through senior year, and Izzy loved going to her African American Studies classes where the majority of the students were Black and Latino. Izzy argued that social class is "a huge factor" in students' experiences at her university because "wealthier Blacks tend to generally hang out with White students" and Izzy described all of her friends "as middle class like me." In chapter 8, we revisit these findings as they relate to survey and interview respondents' identity conceptions after almost four full years of college.

Dualities of Racial Identity

The left-hand side of figure 4.1 summarizes our respondents' answers to a question we posed about "which identity should be most important to African Americans—Black or American?" Only around one-tenth of respondents

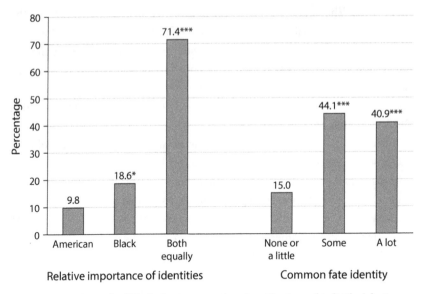

FIGURE 4.1. Strength of Black identity versus American identity and individual destiny versus group fate

(9.8 percent) said that a strictly American identity should be most important, and a little under one-fifth (18.6 percent) said that a Black racial identity should be favored. The remaining 71.4 percent believed that one's racial identity and one's American identity should be considered equally important. Consistent with members of the U.S. Black population, a "hyphenated identity" of Black *and* American appears to be most popular among the young Black adults in our sample generally (Martin 1991; Heilemann 1995; Grant and Orr 1996; Siegelman, Tuch, and Martin 2005; Sears et al. 2008; Cross et al. 2012; Smith 2014).

The wording of this identity item renders it an aspirational question, for it asked about how Black people "should" identify and thus does not reveal how they might actually identify themselves. The right-hand side of figure 4.1 summarizes respondents' answers to a question about the degree to which they see their own fortunes as connected to those of the Black community as whole. Specifically, we asked, "To what extent do you think that what happens to Blacks will affect what happens to you in your life?" This item taps into an important component of Black self-conceptualization known as common fate identity. Rather than simply reflecting an ideal aspiration, it captures core beliefs about Blackness as a racial status and how it determines their own position in society (Blauner 1972; Gurin, Hatchett, and Jackson 1989; Tate 1993; Dawson 1994; Bobo, Charles, and Simmons 2012).

As shown in the figure, 44.1 percent of respondents at the start of college agreed that what happens to Black people as a group affects their own lives "somewhat" and 40.9 percent said it affected them "a lot." Relatively few respondents, just 15 percent, saw little or no connection between the welfare of Black people generally and what happened to them personally. On the cusp of the twenty-first century, therefore, the rising cohort of future Black professionals perceived both the "two-ness" mentioned by Du Bois at the beginning of the twentieth century as well as a powerful sense of connection to the fate of the group as a whole, with at least 85 percent agreeing that their own individual well-being depends at least somewhat on how Black people are treated in the United States generally.

Table 4.1 explores how perceptions about Black versus American identity vary across the different dimensions of Black diversity described in prior chapters. Looking down the right-hand column, we see that irrespective of racial origins, immigrant background, skin tone, gender, socioeconomic status, or experience of segregation, the overwhelming majority of Black NSLF respondents (at least two-thirds) believed that Black and American identities were equally important. Nonetheless, the table reveals subtle but significant differences in the degree of conformity to this balanced acknowledgment of the two identities.

Although both monoracial and mixed-race respondents believed that Black and American identities should be equally important (with 71.0 percent and 74.9 percent choosing this option, respectively), among those respondents who did *not* share this view, mixed respondents tended to favor an American identity (16.2 percent) whereas monoracial respondents favored an unalloyed Black identity (20.2 percent). Consistent with this pattern, identification with both identities dropped as skin color darkened (going from 75.6 percent to 71.5 percent to 68.3 percent as skin tone moved from a light to medium to dark). Over the same progression of categories, the preference for Black identification correspondingly rose (climbing from 11.4 percent to 20.4 percent to 21.1 percent). Compared to men, women expressed both a somewhat stronger commitment to a dual identity than men (73.2 percent compared to 68.7 percent) and a slightly stronger commitment to Black identity (19.5 percent versus 16.4 percent). Only 7.3 percent of women preferred an unhyphenated American identity, compared with 15.0 percent among Black men. Among immigrant-origin respondents, those of African and Caribbean origin were

TABLE 4.1. Relative importance of Black versus American identities among
Black NLSF respondents

Characteristic	Most important identity		
	American	Black	Both Black and American
Racial identification			
Monoracial	8.8%	20.2%	71.0%***
Mixed Race	16.2	8.9	74.9
Nativity and generation			
Multigenerational native	9.5%	17.8%	72.6%***
Second-generation immigrant	9.8	22.2	68.1
First-generation immigrant	14.3	14.9	70.8
Region of origin			
USA	9.5%	17.8%	72.6%***
Caribbean	9.7	23.2	67.1
Africa	11.1	21.6	67.3
Other	16.4	5.2	78.4
Skin tone			
Light	13.0%	11.4%	75.6%***
Medium	8.1	20.4	71.5
Dark	10.6	21.1	68.3
Gender			
Female	7.3%	19.5%	73.2%***
Male	15.0	16.4	68.7
Parental education			
No degree	10.5%	18.0%	71.5%
College degree	11.6	18.0	70.4
Advanced degree	8.3	19.0	72.8
Experience of segregation			
Predominantly White	12.7%	15.7%	71.6%***
Racially mixed	6.1	17.3	76.6
Predominantly minority	11.5	21.8	66.7
Minority neighborhood/White school	8.3	23.8	67.9
N		1,039	

$^{+}$ p < 0.10; * p < 0.05; ** p < 0.01; *** p < 0.001

less likely to see both identities as equally important compared with immigrants from other regions (67 percent versus 78.4 percent).

Finally, respondents who came of age in predominantly White and integrated settings were more likely to see racial and American identities as equal (72 percent and 77 percent, respectively) than Blacks who grew up entirely in segregated circumstances and those who went to predominantly White schools but grew up in minority neighborhoods (about two-thirds in each case). Indeed, those who lived in segregated neighborhoods but attended mainly White schools displayed the *strongest* commitment to a Black identity, with 23.8 percent privileging it above either an exclusively White or dual identity. Among those who grew up entirely in segregated circumstances, the percentage was slightly lower at 21.8 percent (compared with 17 percent among those who grew up in integrated schools and neighborhoods and 16 percent among those who came from predominantly White circumstances). Thus, the racial context that Black respondents experienced while growing up shapes the content of the identities they espouse as young adults.

Table 4.2 turns to an analysis of common fate identity and how it varies across the various dimensions of Black diversity. Although a substantial plurality of both monoracial and mixed-race respondents agreed that what happens to African Americans had "some" influence on their own lives (43.7 percent and 47.0 percent, respectively), once again mixed-race and monoracial respondents who disagreed with this sentiment located themselves at opposite ends of the spectrum. Whereas nearly one-quarter (22.9 percent) of mixed-race respondents perceived little or no common fate identity with Blacks as a group, only 13.5 percent of their monoracial peers did so. Likewise, whereas 30.1 percent of mixed-race respondents reported "a lot" of common fate identity, the figure was 42.8 percent among their monoracial peers. Consistent with this division, although around 43 percent of both medium- and dark-skinned respondents agreed that what happened to African Americans mattered a lot to them as individuals, only 34.8 percent of light-skinned respondents did so.

With respect to immigrant origins, it was respondents in the second generation who reported the greatest common fate identity in their first year of college. Nearly half (49.0 percent) agreed that what happens to African Americans mattered a lot in their own lives, whereas the figure was only 39.5 percent for multigenerational natives and just 34.6 percent among first-generation immigrants. It thus seems that coming to perceive a common fate with native-born Black Americans is part of the assimilation process for Blacks of foreign birth (Waters 1999). As with the question on Black versus American identities, respondents who attended integrated schools but lived in segregated neighborhoods again displayed the strongest Black identity, with just over half (50.5 percent) agreeing that what happens to Blacks generally mattered a lot to them in their own lives.

Experiencing the duality of living in a predominantly Black neighborhood and attending a predominantly White school thus appears to have made

TABLE 4.2. Sense of common fate identity among Black NLSF respondents

Characteristic	What happens to Blacks affects respondent		
	None or a little	Some	A lot
Racial identification			
Monoracial	13.5%	43.7%	42.8%***
Mixed Race	22.9	47.0	30.1
Nativity and generation			
Multigenerational native	15.3%	45.3%	39.5%**
Second-generation immigrant	15.2	35.8	49.0
First-generation immigrant	12.3	53.2	34.6
Region of origin			
USA	15.3%	45.3%	39.5%
Caribbean	12.0	41.5	46.5
Africa	16.1	41.0	42.9
Other	18.2	40.9	40.9
Skin tone			
Light	17.6%	47.7%	34.8%+
Medium	14.7	42.8	42.5
Dark	13.3	43.5	43.3
Gender			
Female	14.5%	43.5%	42.0%
Male	16.0	45.5	38.6
Parental education			
No degree	13.7%	44.6%	41.6%
College degree	17.2	43.7	39.1
Advanced degree	14.2	44.2	41.6
Experience of segregation			
Predominantly White	15.4%	46.0%	38.6%*
Racially mixed	13.7	45.8	40.5
Predominantly minority	18.0	41.2	40.8
Minority neighborhood/White school	10.3	39.2	50.5
N		1,039	

$^+ p < 0.10$; $^* p < 0.05$; $^{**} p < 0.01$; $^{***} p < 0.001$

respondents particularly cognizant of the common fate that binds together all Black people in the United States. In contrast, the figure was only around 41 percent among those who came of age in racially mixed and predominantly minority schools and neighborhoods. As one might expect, those who came of age in a predominantly White milieu expressed the lowest sense of common fate identity, with just 38.6 percent saying that what happens to Black people as a group matters a lot to them as individuals. Nonetheless, only a small minority of Black respondents in any of our categories of segregation

(10.3 percent–18 percent) saw little or no connection between the welfare of the group and their own well-being as individuals.

In sum, responses to our survey questions about American versus Black identity and the existence of a common racial fate confirm the sense of "two-ness" identified by Du Bois, as well as an awareness of the continuing importance of race in determining one's life prospects. At the same time, we nonetheless observe subtle differences in sentiment depending on racial origins, nativity, and the degree of segregation experienced earlier in life, subtleties that were particularly evident in our qualitative interviews. LJ, for example, was quite proud of his Jamaican heritage, but he was also cognizant of the reality that being Jamaican did not render him immune to expressions of racism based solely on phenotype:

> The fact that, like, when you get stopped on the highway, they're not going to say, "Oh, you're Jamaican American, okay?" You're labeled Black, so you, you have to, you know, identify with that. I understand that. . . . If somebody asks me what I am, [I'm] Black . . . but if somebody asks me what, you know, my ethnicity and my race are, I'm Jamaican American.

Likewise, Eugene, who grew up in a Black neighborhood but attended an integrated charter school, explained that however he might see himself, he was nonetheless conscious of the fact that to most White Americans, he was simply "Black":

> People do talk about race; but it's one of those things where the issues that are brought up—like a lot of times the conversations that surround race and racism—the examples that are used and illustrated in those conversations, they're almost always extreme. It's like even if you're African or even if you're West Indian, and you don't come from the same background and don't have the same understanding and concept of American racism, you're still gonna see that issue; or you're still gonna see that event as being racist because it's just so blatantly obvious.

Karen, a multigenerational native, strongly embraced her gender as well as her racial identity and declined to disconnect the two, endorsing the concept of intersectionality by telling us that "I certainly see myself as a Black woman and the two cannot be separated." Yet, as with Eugene and LJ, she felt solidarity and kinship to all Blacks regardless of ethnicity or nativity. As she put it,

> I feel like, especially in America, you're Black regardless of where you're from—if you're fresh off the boat from Ghana or from wherever, you're

Black. . . . I feel like I'm just as connected to Black people. . . . But, yeah, as far as I'm concerned, Black is Black. If you're Black and Hispanic, or you're Black and you're Asian, if you're Black and you're Indian, or you're Black and White, you're still Black as far as I'm concerned.

Karen grew up in two Southern Californian neighborhoods with her mother and four biological brothers, along with her godmother and her four sons. Her father lived some distance away in another part of the state. Both of her child-hood neighborhoods were predominately Black and Latino, but Karen admitted that she did not know any foreign-born or second-generation Blacks until arriving on campus. Her high school reflected the local population of low-income African Americans and Latinos and her peer network was exclusively Black, except for one friend who was biracial, with a White parent.

As we might expect given the survey data, interviewees who were of racially mixed origins perceived emphasizing only part of their parentage as a less attractive option, for the obvious reason that an exclusively Black identity implicitly denied the reality of the other-race parent. As Brad explained,

Yeah. I'm mixed. A lot of times people ask me what I am, and they'll say, "Are you Puerto Rican? Are you Italian?" That's the question that I always get. And I say, "No, I'm mixed. My mom is White and my father's African—and that's that."

As others have documented (see Gibbs 1989; Khanna and Johnson 2010), many Black youth of racially mixed origins perceive adherence to an exclu-sively Black identity to be antithetical to full realization of their own unique identities. When specifically asked about how they identified racially, the ma-jority of mixed-race interviewees did not choose an exclusively Black identity. Instead, they preferred to identify themselves in some intermediate category that indicated mixture and were often quick to point out that they did not want to participate in campus activities that were exclusively geared toward Blacks. They felt that to engage in explicitly Black-oriented activities was too limiting and constituted a disavowal of their more complex heritage. Being Black was only part of who they were, and some, like Blaise, did not have any close Black friends at college. Indeed, he told us he was against participating in any event or organization that was intended primarily for Black students and went on to explain in racial terms his decision to join a predominantly White fraternity:

BLAISE: I never liked that whole . . . like group mentality. . . . Group mentalities are fine, because you know a frat's a group, but I don't like the fact that your, like, number one premise is the fact that you're all Black. . . . Like people try and force you into things 'cause you know, like, that's how . . . society sees you or something.

INTERVIEWER: You don't want to do that?

BLAISE: Yeah, and like that's what's kind of sad about the whole situation 'cause, like, I think our [integrated] frat's good. . . . You know, like I think it's cool . . . if you are like a Black freshman . . . whatever you are (but I'll just say Black for now 'cause we're talking about it), like you feel comfortable. I mean, you see like you know a number of brothers and they're all like, you know they're just cool guys and you don't have to do . . . whatever everyone thinks you should do. I also feel like I'm not, I'm no more Black than I am anything else and you know, I'm just me when it gets down to it.

Although there were a few Black members in his fraternity, Blaise was the only one who identified as mixed race. He believed that the Black-themed dorm on campus—which he felt "encouraged Black separatism" and discouraged racial mixing at campus parties—was to blame for his not having more Black friends.

Growing up in a predominately White enclave of upstate New York with his White mother and older brother, Blaise attended rigorous magnet schools all the way through high school, where he was an academic and athletic stand-out. His high school peer group included three White young men, one young man of mixed Black and White parentage, and one monoracial Black young man. In his youth, Blaise told us that he vacillated between Black and mixed-race identities but ultimately decided to self-identify as both Black and White in high school "when I began to realize the importance of things." Blaise none-theless chose to check the "Black" box when applying to college because he perceived the benefits of doing so in the admission process, revealing to us that

> I've always told people I was mixed, but sometimes, on forms, I would just check Black. . . . I realized I am mixed and I'm denying half of myself every time I fill these [forms] out.

In *The Asian American Achievement Paradox*, Lee and Zhou (2015) also find that Chinese and Vietnamese families and students try to get an edge on the college admissions process, not just through supplemental education (e.g., long hours of tutoring for SAT prep and studying for Advanced Placement [AP] tests) but also through cultural enrichment classes, which often include visits to their "ancestral homelands." They also sign up for "uniquely ethnic" classes in the arts, music, and language to enhance the probability that they will get into the most elite schools (Lee and Zhou 2015:75–77).

Whereas Blaise described a process of self-discovery in high school, Paige's parents always taught both her and her younger brother to embrace their Black and Mexican ethnicities equally. Paige's father was a multigenerational African American and her mother was from northern Mexico. Although neither attended college, her mother did earn a two-year technical certificate. Paige attended a largely White, working-class high school in her Texas hometown. Although it contained a visible Latino minority, she was the only student of color in her honors and AP classes. She described the majority of her classmates as "good ol' boys, like country boys" who generally came from conservative households.

When asked how she identified in terms of race and ethnicity, Paige told us, "Generally, I check two boxes, if they let me. If they don't let me, then I just check 'other.'" Paige told us, however, that she has never checked the "Black" box on any form. In high school, it infuriated her when she had to choose one identity because the computerized form allowed only one selection. She was exasperated that her school classified her only as "Hispanic" and ignored the rest of her ancestry because she felt that "I cannot choose just one." Paige had three close high school friends, one who was White, another who identified as Mexican and White, and a third who was African American. At college, she had some Black men as friends (all athletes) but wasn't very involved in the Black student community. When she spoke to us halfway through her sophomore year, Paige's four closest college girlfriends were White, along with her boyfriend, a football player. Although Paige recognized herself as light skinned, she believed her hair texture "gives away" her racially mixed ancestry.

Blair expressed similar sentiments, and when asked how she self-identified, she stated that she was "mixed with Black and White" origins. As with Paige, both Blair's mother and father always encouraged her to embrace her dual ancestry, and when asked about her race by others, she told us that "I just say, I'm Black and White—but I'd say I wouldn't favor any particular race over the other." On her driver's license, Blair wanted to include both categories, but since that was not an option, she disappointedly chose "other," explaining that

for the driver's license, both of my parents are like—I know my mother feels she's White and so she was, like, "You can't erase me and you can't erase your father either, so you have to put 'other.'" It was interesting because when I asked what they wanted my race to be—Black or White—both my parents at the same time responded, "Other."

Despite also openly acknowledging her African ancestry, Blair did not feel particularly close to her Black college peers. One of her best friends was of Vietnamese and Chinese origin, and she felt especially close to her because she felt this person had also grown up in two different cultures, telling us "she's biracial, too. She goes through the same things. Even though it's not as apparent physically as it might be for me, she's still biracial." What is evident from Blair's comments, as well as those of Blaise's and Paige's, is that all favor a more complex mixed identity over a singular Black one. They believed an exclusively Black identity would not accurately reflect who they felt they were as individuals. Racially mixed interviewees who perceived themselves as having a lighter skin tone often opt for a "mixed" rather than an exclusively "Black" identity.

Our interviews also clarify how respondents' childhoods shaped our finding that second-generation Black immigrants early in college were *least* likely to embrace a dual Black and American identity and were *more* likely to link their fate with that of the race generally. Prior research suggests that immigrant-origin Blacks tend to adopt one of two identity strategies in navigating U.S. society: either adhering to an identity based on national origin (e.g., Jamaican or Haitian) or recognizing themselves as Black and identifying with African Americans, and often these two options are in tension with each other (Waters 1999). When asked how he identified racially and ethnically, as a second-generation immigrant, Malik was conflicted.

Growing up, his parents had instilled in him the cultural traditions and values associated with his Ghanaian heritage, but Malik also realized that his dark skin put him on a common footing with multigenerational African Americans. As noted earlier, he told us, "On some days, I wake up and I feel African American, and then some days I wake up and I feel African." In his affluent neighborhood and predominantly White high school, Malik was one of just a handful of Black students and always felt that his White peers treated him differently because of his dark skin. Nonetheless, at the time of his interview, Malik had few Black friends on campus and socialized mostly with White and Asian students.

Also a second-generation Ghanaian, Ervin grew up with a strong ethnic identity. His parents practiced traditional customs at home, and he initially told us that he identified as "African" because he was "raised in the Ghanaian tradition." Before college, Ervin felt that he stood out in school as the "short Black kid" among his taller multigenerational Black American peers. His suburban southern high school was predominately White with small shares of Asians, Latinos, and Blacks. In Ervin's AP classes, he was the only Black student in living memory, and as a student in both high school and college, he experienced the "pressure of being a Black man" because "inevitably, I'm still a statistic." As he explained,

> I mean, I felt the pressures of an African American kid just 'cause when people see me, they don't think I'm African. I mean, it's just that I'm Black. My family tells me I'm American when I'm there; but when I'm here, if they hear that my parents are African, then I'm African. I mean, in the end, Black is, around here, Black is pretty much Black. People are going to have the same expectations for a Black kid, you know, him being more into sports and music than academics. And so, in that sense, I'm African American.

First-generation immigrants in our qualitative sample expressed less ambivalence about their identity than did those in the second generation. Ashley, for example, was first-generation Jamaican and did not feel she had that much in common with multigenerational African Americans, citing her national origin as being far more salient to her own identity and life experiences. She stated that she had always been surrounded by a critical mass of coethnic friends and had spent most of her life around other West Indians like herself. Ashley preferred the label Caribbean American over any other option, telling us, "For me, it's important . . . 'cause I'm not African American. I'm Jamaican. Like, that's just the way it is. . . . It's just an integral part of my personality." At the time of her interview, Ashley was very active in the Caribbean Student Association on campus and her social circle was composed almost exclusively of other West Indians. From Malik's, Ervin's, and Ashley's comments, it is evident that immigrant-origin interviewees identify themselves racially, ethnically, and nationally in ways that are quite different from multigenerational African Americans.

Suarez-Orozco and Suarez-Orozco (1995) compare how first- and second-generation Latino youth make sense of their minoritized identities as related to academic achievement and their perspectives of success as racialized minorities in the United States. They argue that first-generation Latino youth fare better academically compared to their second-generation peers because a "dual frame of reference" reminds them of the hardships they experienced back home and their idealization of the United States as a place of limitless opportunity. Without this dual frame of reference, Suarez-Orozco and Suarez-Orozco suggest that "acculturated" second-generation Latino youth are more cognizant of racism and ethnic tension from "Anglos" (White students and teachers). They perceive the classroom as "a microscopic version" of broader society "where teachers come from the majority culture and minority students . . . interact in an environment of social inequality" (Suarez-Orozco and Suarez-Orozco 1995:59).

Other explorations of first-generation Black immigrant young adults like Ashley find that they tend to socially distance themselves from Black Americans as a way to preserve their ethnic roots and avoid downward assimilation and the negative effects of White racism as they pursue upward socioeconomic mobility (Waters 1999; Greer 2013; Portes and Rumbaut 2014). New research in the wake of Black Lives Matter finds that corporate organizations preference "visible" Black immigrants with detectable accents over native-born Blacks for higher positions, perceiving the former's "elevated minority status" (Howard and Borgella 2020; Center for Talent Innovation 2021).

As we noted earlier in our analysis of the quantitative data from respondents' first year of college, respondents who lived in segregated communities but attended predominantly White schools exhibited the strongest attachment to an exclusively Black identity and the most intense feelings of a common racial fate. The duality of their adolescent experience evidently exposed them to such divergent social worlds that it underscored the salience of race as a particularly wide gulf in U.S. society. The embodiment of this sentiment was Darryl, a multigenerational native who grew up in a very disadvantaged minority neighborhood in the Bronx but after seventh grade transferred to an elite boarding school in Pennsylvania. Recall that Darryl preferred the label Black over African American and argued that Black people in the United States are not allowed the same options for ethnic identifiers that Whites are. He continued to speak at length about his experiences with racism and discrimination both at school and in his old neighborhood.

Olivia's choice to identify as Black over her immigrant roots at college stemmed from her desire to embrace her racial identity in college after being one of the few people of color at her high school. Although she had originally been assigned to live in a regular dorm, Olivia asked to be put in a Black-themed dorm during her freshman year because she wanted the opportunity to develop a Black peer group. She looked back on high school as a difficult time, telling us that "in general, everyone I was around was White, which was hard. It was a little rough." Olivia especially felt that she missed out on dating in high school because all her friends were White and the few young Black men at her school did not find her attractive because she was not part of their Black peer group. At the same time, her White girlfriends could not empathize with her because they could not conceive of having trouble getting dates, making her the odd person out when it came to romance.

Tia expressed similar sentiments. Although she grew up in a Black, working-class suburb in New Jersey, she was fatigued by being one of just a handful of Black students at her elite prep school:

> When I went to [name of school], I was the only Black person in some of my classes, one of five in my grade, and I just felt like nobody could sympathize with me or even understand me as a Black person.

Despite the fact that the Black community at their respective universities hovered at only around 6 percent of the student body, for Olivia and Tia this share was significantly greater than in their high schools where same-race peers were few and far between. Both women were excited about becoming part of a larger community of other Blacks with whom they could relate and connect. The critical mass of Black students they encountered on campus offered a fresh start where they could meet other high-achieving Blacks from similar class, residential, and educational backgrounds. Their expectation was that skin color would serve as a unifying factor among all Black students (see Torres and Massey 2012).

Black interviewees from segregated neighborhoods and schools arrived on campus with a strong commitment to identifying themselves racially as Black and a strong desire to assert their Blackness in the company of same-race peers. Troy, for example, grew up in a low-income Black and Latino neighborhood in the Bronx and attended a parochial school with a similar racial and ethnic composition. Although his parents were both from Ghana, Troy identified himself as "ethnically African American." He received acceptances from all of his ten top choices but picked his university because he was attracted to the active level of Black student engagement on campus and felt he belonged there.

Troy lived in the Black-themed dorm during his first two years and became very involved in Black student activities on campus. Although he initially felt open to interacting with Whites, he soon concluded that he didn't have much in common with them and instead came to perceive his Black dorm as his "comfort zone":

> Hands down I wanted to make sure I knew the other Black students that were here. Since there weren't a lot, I wanted to know the ones that are here. . . . Everyone likes to come home because home is familiar, home is a place where you know hands down, you know, for the most part you're gonna feel loved, you're gonna feel comfort, and you're home and that's

what made, that's how I felt here. . . . And that's me and that's because of my exposure.

Troy had limited interactions with Whites and Asians on campus, viewing White students in particular as "provincial" and "superficial" because they "don't come out of their comfort zone" to interact with non-Whites. He explained to us what it was like to be Black at his institution:

> What it means to be Black at [name of university] is the understanding that you're going to be a minority number. . . . Because of this, you take pride in your culture, your ethnicity, and celebrate it . . . celebrate being Black and, you know, celebrate [the] label as being Black.

Denise also came from a poor, segregated neighborhood in New York City. Although she had gone to an elite boarding school in another state, she restricted her social interactions to Blacks and Latinos and felt especially distant from Whites:

> Walking down [name of campus walkway], [I see] White people. . . . I find myself looking for people that look like me. . . . To me, [White students] all look the same. White people all look the same to me. I can see the conformity just in their physical being.

Denise identifies as Black and not African American because she believes that her racial identity trumps her Panamanian and southern heritage. She took several African American studies classes in high school and joined clubs and organizations designed for minority students. At college, she considered herself a "spokesman for the Black community" and often talked with her same-race peers about having cultural pride. Denise was vehemently opposed to interracial dating because she thought it prevented "cultural preservation" and thus was a negative influence on the Black community.

In general, for these traditional measures of racial identity, the few divides we see are rooted in family background, be it a connection to a non-American conception of Blackness and identity or via having come from a racially mixed family in which a Black identity meant rejecting or denying the importance of the non-Black parent to one's racial identity. Nonetheless, as these aspiring Black professionals began their collegiate career, it was clear that even though personal background characteristics differentially affected their particular sense of racial identity, they all recognized the importance of racial identity to their futures.

Diversity and Social Distance

Racial attitudes are not only inward looking about one's own identity but also outward looking at with whom one feels close, known in racial attitudes research as social distance. The subject is typically assessed using a question on perceived closeness to people in different groups, defined in the question as "feelings of closeness to similar others in ideas, feelings, and thoughts" (Broman, Neighbors, and Jackson 1988:148). Feeling close to other Blacks is another way of expressing in-group solidarity with same-race peers (Allen, Dawson, and Brown 1989; Demo and Hughes 1990; Parham and Williams 1993; Harris 1995; Thornton, Taylor, and Chatters 2014; Smith and Moore 2000). However, feelings of closeness to in-group members do not necessarily imply perceptions of distance from out-group members, and until recently, not much work examined the extent to which people are actually able to combine feelings of in-group closeness with perceptions of out-group distance (Sellers et al. 1997; Sanchez 2008; Charles et al. 2015).

As with the racial identity measures, we sought to assess respondents' sense of closeness to "one's own and others' group identities" at the beginning of their college careers to gauge how social origins shaped perceptions (Magee and Smith 2013:159). Perceived social closeness or distance measures the desire to interact with members of different groups and reflects the individual's history of prior intergroup contact and interpersonal experiences (Bobo 1988). Social closeness is a by-product of social interactions and is therefore not a static or fixed trait. Social psychologists have long argued that diverse settings can foster beneficial social interactions among dissimilar groups, decrease in-group bias, and erode prejudices and stereotypes about out-groups (Allport 1954; Pettigrew and Tropp 2000).

We therefore asked Black NLSF respondents to indicate on a scale from 0 (very distant) to 10 (very close) the degree of social distance or closeness they perceived between themselves and members of their own group as well as to other racial/ethnic groups (i.e., Whites, Hispanics, and Asians). Unsurprisingly, we found that Black respondents felt closer to other Black Americans, with an average closeness score of 7.3, followed in descending order by Hispanics (5.5), Whites (5.2), and Asians (4.5). Rather than simply asking about broad racial groups in the aggregate, however, we also sought to assess feelings toward specific subgroups of people within each racial category in order to get a sense of the range of feelings about members within each group.

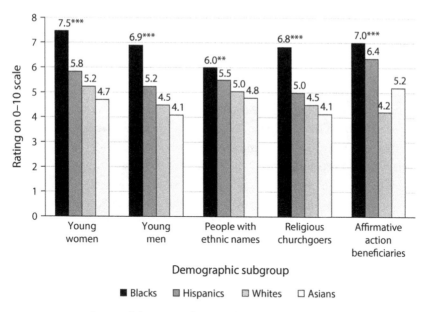

FIGURE 4.2. Perceived closeness to demographic subgroups of the Black, Hispanic, White, and Asian populations

Figure 4.2 thus shows closeness ratings for the groups broken down into various sociodemographic categories defined by factors such as age, gender, ethnicity, and religiosity. With one exception, the closeness ordering of the groups is the same as that just described: Blacks, Hispanics, Whites, and Asians. With respect to young women, for example, with a closeness rating of 7.5 (the highest in the figure) Black respondents felt closest to young Black women, followed by young Hispanic women (5.8), young White women (5.2), and young Asian women (4.7). Although perceived closeness to young men is consistently lower than perceived closeness to young women regardless of race, the ratings follow the same progression as before, moving downward from 6.9 for young Black men, to 5.2 for young Hispanic men, 4.5 for young White men, and 4.1 for young Asian men (the lowest rating in the figure).

When asked how close they felt to people with "ethnic first names," however, Black respondents were more guarded in their evaluations of their own group, rating Blacks with African- or Black-sounding names at just 6.0, compared with closeness ratings of 6.8 to 7.5 for Blacks in the other categories. The progression across groups was nonetheless the same, with closeness ratings for Hispanics coming in at 5.5, Whites at 5.0, and Asians at 4.8. We see the same closeness ordering for religious churchgoing members of each group, with respective ratings of 6.8 for Blacks in this category, 5.0 for Hispanics, 4.5 for Whites, and 4.1 for religious Asians (tied with Asian men for the lowest rating).

The only exception to this progression occurred in the perceived closeness to affirmative action beneficiaries within each group, where feelings toward Black and Hispanic affirmative action beneficiaries followed in the accustomed order, but the ordering of White and Asian beneficiaries was reversed. In this case, the closeness rating went from 7.0 for Black affirmative action beneficiaries to 6.4 for Hispanics in this category but then dropped to a low of 4.2 for Whites before rising back to 5.2 for Asians. Whites, of course, do not normally qualify for racial affirmative action, so it is not entirely clear who Black respondents had in mind when answering the question.

As Massey and Mooney (2007) have noted, however, in U.S. academia there are actually two other sizable affirmative action programs besides those centered on race: legacies (children of alumni who are given favorable treatment in admissions) and athletes (who also receive special attention) (see also Espenshade, Chung, and Walling 2004). Whereas athletes tend to be racially diverse (though less so in selective liberal arts colleges where "White" sports such as lacrosse and squash are common) (see Bowen and Levin 2003), at most schools, legacy students are overwhelmingly White. If legacy students were who Black respondents had in mind when rating closeness to "White affirmative action beneficiaries," then the very low rating assigned to this category of White person would seem to express an estrangement from legacy admissions as a source of White privilege.

Figure 4.3 shifts attention to present closeness ratings for various socioeconomic subgroups in the four racial categories. With respect to class, Black respondents felt closest to middle-class Blacks to whom they gave an average closeness rating of 7.4. Middle-class Hispanics, Whites, and Asians trailed at some distance with respective ratings of 5.9, 5.4, and 5.0. Interestingly, Black respondents gave rich Blacks the same relatively low closeness rating they offered to middle-class Whites (5.4), suggesting some alienation from the wealthier members of their own group. Rich Hispanics received an even lower closeness rating of 4.2, while rich Whites and Asians both received very low ratings of just 3.6. Although they may be on a path of upward socioeconomic mobility by virtue of their admission into selective institutions of higher education, as freshmen Black NLSF respondents, they nevertheless perceived themselves to be quite distant from the wealthy members of any racial group, including their own.

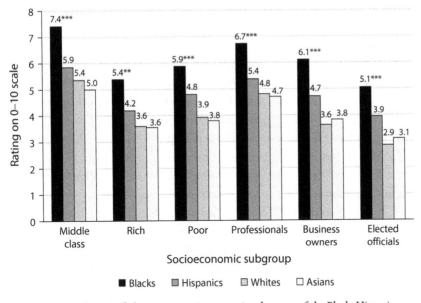

FIGURE 4.3. Perceived closeness to socioeconomic subgroups of the Black, Hispanic, White, and Asian populations

Black NLSF respondents felt only slightly closer to poor Blacks, who received an average rating of 5.9, not nearly as close as they felt to middle-class Blacks (7.4). However, the perceived social distance from the poor of other racial/ethnic groups was even greater, with respective social distance ratings of 4.8, 3.9, and 3.8 for Hispanics, Whites, and Asians. Consistent with their feelings of closeness to middle-class Blacks, respondents also perceived themselves to be relatively close to Black professionals, who received at average closeness rating of 6.7, the second highest value in the figure. As with the class-based ratings, the social distance ratings for professionals of Hispanic, White, and Asian origin were much lower at 5.4, 4.8, and 4.7, respectively. Closeness to Black business owners stood at 6.1, the third highest rating in the figure, and considerably above the respective values of 4.7, 3.6, and 3.8 given to Hispanics, Whites, and Asians who owned businesses.

Black respondents reserved their very lowest closeness ratings for elected officials regardless of race. Even Black elected officials received a middling closeness rating of just 5.1, and the perceived distance from elected officials in other groups was dramatic, especially with respect to Whites. Respondents rated their average closeness to White elected officials at just 2.9, the lowest rating observed for any category displayed in either figure 4.2 or 4.3. However, Asian and Hispanic officials fared little better, with respective ratings of 3.1 and 3.9. Note also that among business owners and elected officials, Asians were seen as socially closer than Whites, who occupied the bottom position in both cases. Early in their freshman year, these young Black adults thus seem to be particularly estranged from White business owners and politicians, two social categories that historically persecuted and subordinated their race.

Despite these few reversals in the ordering of Whites and Asians, within most of the social subcategories, perceived social closeness to Black people went downward from other Blacks through Hispanics and Whites to Asians. Indeed, when we compute average ratings across all the different socioeconomic and demographic categories, we find a mean rating of 7.3 for Blacks, 5.5 for Hispanics, 5.2 for Whites, and 4.5 for Asians. Table 4.3 displays these average ratings of social closeness along dimensions of Black diversity. This operation reveals several notable departures from the standard ordering (highlighted in bold).

For example, mixed-race respondents perceive themselves to be closer to Whites than to Hispanics, reversing the order observed for monoracial Black respondents, who appear to have more in common with members of the nation's other major minority group than with Whites. This is likely because a majority of mixed-race respondents reported having a White parent. In addition, monoracial Black respondents perceive themselves to be significantly closer to other Blacks than their racially mixed peers do (with a closeness rating of 7.5 versus 6.3). At the same time, monoracial Black freshmen also feel significantly more distant from Whites than their mixed-race counterparts (5.0 versus 6.0).

We see a similar pattern in two other cases. Light-skinned Black respondents (many of whom are also of racially mixed origin) likewise see themselves as closer to White people than to Hispanic people, with a closeness rating of 5.6 for the former versus 5.3 for the latter. With a closeness rating of only 6.9, light-skinned respondents also perceive themselves more distant from other Blacks than do their medium- and dark-skinned counterparts (who display respective ratings of 7.5 and 7.4). They also view themselves as closer to White people (with a rating of 5.6) than do those with medium and dark skin tones (4.9 and 5.2, respectively). Finally, although the difference is only marginally significant, light-skinned respondents see themselves as more distant from Hispanic people (5.3) than either medium- (5.5) or dark-skinned (5.6) Blacks do.

The other discrepant ordering occurs with respect to segregation. Respondents who grew up in predominantly White schools and neighborhoods rated

TABLE 4.3. Social closeness to members of different racial/ethnic groups expressed by Black NLSF respondents

Characteristic	Average social closeness rating			
	Blacks	Hispanics	Whites	Asians
Racial identification				
Monoracial	7.5***	5.6***	5.0***	4.5
Mixed race	6.3	**4.9**	**6.0**	4.7
Nativity and generation				
Multigenerational native	7.5***	5.4⁺	5.1	4.4*
Second-generation immigrant	6.9	5.7	5.2	4.8
First-generation immigrant	6.7	5.4	5.2	4.8
Region of origin				
USA	7.5***	5.4⁺	5.1	4.4*
Caribbean	6.8	5.7	5.1	4.6
Africa	7.0	5.7	5.2	4.9
Other	6.7	5.1	5.5	5.2
Skin tone				
Light	6.9**	**5.3⁺**	**5.6***	4.5
Medium	7.5	5.5	4.9	4.5
Dark	7.4	5.6	5.2	4.5
Gender				
Female	7.3	5.5	5.1*	4.4*
Male	7.2	5.4	5.4	4.7
Parental education				
No degree	7.6*	5.5	5.0⁺	4.5
College degree	7.2	5.6	5.1	4.6
Advanced degree	7.2	5.4	5.3	4.5
Experience of segregation				
Predominantly White	6.9***	**5.3***	**5.6****	4.8*
Racially mixed	7.4	5.4	5.0	4.4
Predominantly minority	7.7	5.6	4.6	4.4
Minority neighborhood/White school	7.6	6.1	5.4	4.3
N		1,039		

⁺ p < 0.10; * p < 0.05; ** p < 0.01; *** p < 0.001

themselves to be less close to other Blacks (6.9) than did those who grew up in other circumstances, especially those respondents who grew up in predominantly minority neighborhoods (7.7 for those attending a predominantly minority school and 7.6 for those attending a White school, compared to 7.4 among those whose schools and neighborhoods were racially mixed). Black respondents who came of age in White schools and neighborhoods also saw themselves as closer to White people than Black respondents in other categories of segregation; unlike their peers from mixed or minority neighborhoods (including those who went to White schools), they perceived themselves to be closer to White people than to Hispanic people.

Two other significant relationships prevail in the table (see the panels pertaining to immigrant origins and parental education). First, multigenerational native respondents perceive themselves to be significantly closer to other Black people (7.5) than do either first- (6.7) or second-generation (6.9) immigrants. Second, those whose parents never completed college assigned a higher closeness rating (7.6) to other Black people than those whose parents completed either a college or advanced degree (7.2 in both cases).

Thus, although our survey data suggest that Black students at the beginning of college *generally* perceive social distance to rise moving from Blacks to Hispanics to Whites to Asians, there are several notable exceptions. Mixed-race respondents, those with light skin tones, those of immigrant origin, those who grew up in predominantly White schools and neighborhoods, and those with highly educated parents tended to feel closer to White people and more distant from Black people than their monoracial, dark-skinned, racially-segregated, native-born, lower status counterparts. Our interview data generally buttress these survey findings.

Doug, for example, was a first-generation immigrant who went to a rigorous all-boys boarding school in Ghana. As a freshman, he felt quite comfortable attending an elite U.S. institution of higher education dominated by Whites, telling us that he did not wish to socialize much with native-origin Blacks because he thought they did not make enough of an effort to engage in "cross-cultural exchange":

> Well, from my experience, Black people in America have a very closed community. I don't know if they have a different accent, but it seems like they are all interested in the same kind of music. Like hip-hop, for example, is a unifying factor. Dress and social interests tend to be very similar as well. As a result, they are more of a community. I think for Africans, although we have this shared unity, we don't all speak the same language and we're essentially from different countries.

When asked how he thinks other Blacks on campus perceive him, Doug was not sure because "I actually don't talk a lot to Black students." Indeed, he felt closer to "Ghanaians" or "other Africans" than same-race peers per se; however, Doug's three best friends were nonetheless all White men, though he also did report having three close acquaintances of Ghanaian descent.

Yolanda, a second-generation freshman with parents from Sierra Leone, similarly expressed feeling a certain alienation with respect to multigenerational Black Americans on campus, whom she saw as "cliquish" and "unfriendly" and instead expressed a sense of surprise that White students were so welcoming:

> A lot of the White students here, or at least the one's I've met, have been great. It's like they're nicer than the one's from [name of boarding school]. So, as a matter of fact, I think I've encountered more friendliness from the White people here than from the Black people.

Yolanda told us that she perceived Africans and West Indians to be more "open to hanging out with Whites" because of their more fluid conceptions of race and the "diversity" of Caribbean and African cultures, as opposed to what she saw as the monolith of African American culture in the United States. She went on to describe in some detail the multiplicity of skin tones and ancestries within her own extended family. On campus, Yolanda socialized more with Asians, Whites, and immigrant-origin Blacks rather than with multigenerational African Americans. Blacks of African origin tend to be perceived by many Whites as a "model minority" akin to Asians once their ancestry is known (Ukpokodu 2018).

The large majority of mixed-race interviewees had one Black and one White parent, and in general, they reported feeling close to both heritages and perceived a benefit to having direct knowledge about two different cultures. Maryanna, also a freshman, explained that she liked being mixed because she felt equally part of the Black and White social worlds:

> I think of myself as all the parts that I am. I think of myself as my mom and my dad and my grandparents; but I know that I sort of have that—I don't really know if I identify more as just Black or as like minority.

Maryanna grew up with her White mother in a high-rise building in an affluent area on the Upper East Side of Manhattan. Although not wealthy, she attended well-known magnet schools and the fact that her mother's apartment was rent-controlled enabled them to live a good life without hardship. Maryanna's African American father had an amicable relationship with her mother and visited regularly.

Janice, a mixed-race senior who participated in one of our focus groups, identified as Black and White and felt she didn't fit in with the monoracial Black students because of her predominately White, affluent upbringing. She told us she was glad that she could draw on elements from "both sides" of her family and perceived less stigma associated with being mixed race than with being Black alone:

> I like it because I feel like I can draw from the best of both sides. I really like this about my White culture and I really like this about my Black culture. I like being able to absorb both sides. It's a way to get out of being—it's less of a category than being one race. There's less stereotypes that go with being mixed.

As freshmen, mixed interviewees had an initial sense that being of mixed race was "less threatening" to Whites and recognized that consequently they were able to participate in more integrated peer networks. Neither Maryanna nor Janice believed that they "looked Black," which contributed to their perception of themselves as "different" from other Black Americans.

As we saw in table 4.3, class was also a significant determinant of closeness within and between different groups at the start of college. Compared to Black survey respondents whose parents held college or advanced degrees, those without college-educated parents felt closer to other Black people and less affinity toward White people. Some first-generation college students in fact reported surprise and a certain estrangement from the upper-class Black Americans they encountered on campus. As Greg told us, "I had never been exposed to bourgeoisie Black people—rich Black people, I guess. . . . Because I mean, I knew they existed; I just never met them. You know?"

Julie likewise expressed surprise at the relative affluence of Black students on her campus and saw herself as considerably less advantaged than many of her same-race friends:

> A lot of my friends, like their parents can afford to pay their tuition, you know? They may have a little financial aid, but they don't get as much as, like, I get, you know?

When we checked, 84 percent of our seventy-seven interviewees reported receiving financial aid, though the amounts varied from a few thousand dollars to a full ride (roughly $40,000 at the time). Both Julie and Greg came from working-class families and had grown up in poor, segregated neighborhoods and expressed shock at meeting so many wealthier Black peers when they arrived on campus.

The foregoing discussion indicates that Black identity was far from a monolith for these elite Black students as they embarked on their college careers.

Their varied precollege backgrounds and other intersecting identities link to how they initially articulate and perceive their Blackness—both personally and collectively—just months after separating from their families and high school social worlds. Indeed, we have seen how adherence to a dual Black-and-American identity, recognition of a common racial fate, and social distance evaluations vary systematically depending on the aforementioned dimensions of Black diversity. Now we heed those distinctions here as they relate to group stereotypes and racial attitudes on inequality within this heterogeneous group of young Black adults.

Racial Stereotyping

A variety of negative racial stereotypes have historically been imposed on Black Americans and to a lesser extent on Asians and Hispanics. Stereotypes not only influence how minority group members are perceived by those in mainstream society but also how minority group members see themselves, how they perceive members of other groups, and how they expect members of mainstream society to perceive and act toward them. Moreover, research has shown that one does not have to be a self-defined racist to harbor stereotypical notions and biased inclinations. Stereotypes are deeply embedded within American popular culture and are continuously reinforced in subtle and overt ways in daily life and the mass media, yielding biases that are implicit as well as explicit—lying outside the realm of consciousness as well as being acknowledged and self-consciously expressed (Greenwald and Banaji 1995; Quillian 2006). In a very real way, people growing up in a society rife with racialized memes and images can hardly expect *not* to have stereotypical notions and sentiments etched into social cognition, whether they expressly agree with them or not.

Whenever a negative stereotype about a group exists and is widely understood to exist by members of that group, it has the capacity to influence behavioral outcomes linked to the stereotype in question, yielding a phenomenon known as stereotype threat (Steele 1997). Classic stereotypes about Black Americans are that they are lazy, unintelligent, criminally inclined, and prone to living off welfare (Schuman et al. 1998; Gilens 1999; Bobo et al. 2012). These sorts of stereotypes may be internalized in the form of both explicit and implicit biases, even among Blacks themselves; they can also be externalized in expectations that out-group members will act on these biases and discriminate (Massey and Fischer 2005).

In academia, the internalization and externalization of negative stereotypes about intellectual inferiority have been shown to undermine the academic performance of Blacks and Hispanics, not only in the laboratory (Steele and Aronson 1995; Spencer, Steele, and Quinn 1999; Steele, Spencer, and Aronson 2002) but also in surveys (Owens and Massey 2011). In order to assess the degree to which stereotypes are harbored at the conscious level, we asked Black NLSF respondents at the beginning of college to assess the degree to which various stereotypical traits historically associated with Black Americans applied to their own group as well as to other racial/ethnic groups (i.e., Whites, Hispanics, and Asians).

Specifically, respondents were asked to rate the degree to which members of each group tended to be lazy, unintelligent, welfare dependent, and easily discouraged (to "give up easily" instead of "sticking to it") on a 1 to 7 scale, where 7 indicates that the trait in question applies maximally to members of the target group (e.g., Blacks are very lazy), 1 indicates the opposite (e.g., Blacks are very hardworking), and 4 is a neutral point (in between lazy and hardworking). For each target group, we averaged across each of the four stereotypical traits to create a single index of racial stereotyping toward each group—that is, the extent to which members of that group were seen as lazy, unintelligent, likely to give up easily, and prone to living off welfare (yielding a Cronbach's alpha of 0.787). The resulting indexes are shown by target group on the left-hand side of figure 4.4, which includes a solid horizontal line to indicate the neutral point at which a group is neither seen to exemplify nor contradict the stereotype. Using African Americans as the reference group, asterisks indicate the significance of the difference between the degree of Black self-stereotyping and the extent of Black stereotyping of Hispanics, Whites, and Asians.

As can easily be seen, the stereotype index fell below the line of neutrality for all four racial/ethnic groups, indicating that Black students did not perceive negative stereotypes to apply particularly well to any particular group. To the extent that such stereotypes applied at all, the index of self-stereotyping for Blacks was 3.54, about half a point below the line of neutrality. In general, respondents stereotypically viewed Hispanics more negatively and Whites and Asians more positively. Thus, the Hispanic stereotype score of 3.66 was significantly above that observed for Blacks, suggesting Black respondents perceived Hispanic people to be lazier, less intelligent, more welfare dependent, and more easily discouraged than members of their own group. In contrast, the mean index score of 3.46 for White people was significantly below

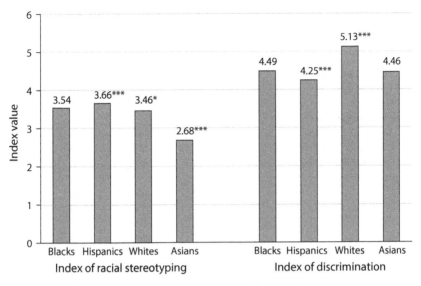

FIGURE 4.4. Measures of racial stereotyping and tendency to discriminate as rated by Black respondents to the NLSF

that recorded for Black people, indicating that respondents saw these stereotypes applying less to White people than to members of their own group. The lowest stereotype score (2.68) was observed for Asians, suggesting that negative attributions about intelligence, motivation, work ethic, and dependency applied least to them. Put another way, Black respondents perceived Asian students to be especially hardworking, intelligent, persistent, and resistant to welfare use, not only relative to members of their own group but to Whites as well, consistent with the "model minority" stereotype (Siy and Cheryan 2013; Wu 2013).

The degree of stereotyping directed at Asian people nonetheless varied along the underlying dimensions of Black diversity. As shown in table 4.4, with a stereotyping index of 2.87 toward Asians, mixed-race respondents were significantly *less likely* to see Asians as particularly hardworking, intelligent, independent, and resilient than their monoracial counterparts, whose stereotyping index toward Asians stood at only 2.65. The negative stereotyping of Asian people was also greater for multigenerational natives (with an index value of 2.72) than for first- and second-generation immigrants (with respective indexes of 2.56 and 2.62). Among first-generation immigrants, those from Africa and the Caribbean generally engaged in less stereotyping (with index values of 2.57 and 2.54) than those from other regions (2.73).

TABLE 4.4. Attribution of stereotypically negative traits to racial/ethnic groups by Black NLSF respondents

Characteristic	Blacks	Hispanics	Whites	Asians
Racial identification				
Monoracial	3.53	3.63	3.44	2.65**
Mixed race	3.57	3.67	3.54	2.87
Nativity and generation				
Multigenerational native	3.53	3.62	3.45+	2.72+
Second-generation immigrant	3.59	3.69	3.33	2.62
First-generation immigrant	3.53	3.69	3.56	2.56
Region of origin				
USA	3.53	3.62	3.45+	2.72*
Caribbean	3.56	3.70	3.51	2.54
Africa	3.56	3.69	3.47	2.57
Other	3.48	3.66	3.49	2.73
Skin tone				
Light	3.52	3.66	3.47	2.74
Medium	3.54	3.63	3.47	2.64
Dark	3.54	3.64	3.43	2.72
Gender				
Female	3.49*	3.59**	3.46	2.64+
Male	3.61	3.74	3.47	2.75
Parental education				
No degree	3.61*	3.71+	3.41	2.63
College degree	3.51	3.63	3.48	2.73
Advanced degree	3.49	3.60	3.48	2.67
Experience of segregation				
Predominantly White	3.51	3.65*	3.56*	2.78
Racially mixed	3.57	3.67	3.41	2.62
Predominantly minority	3.53	3.68	3.42	2.56
Minority neighborhood/White school	3.53	3.58	3.40	2.67
N		1,039		

$+ p < 0.10$; $* p < 0.05$; $** p < 0.01$; $*** p < 0.001$

The table also reveals that the unfavorable stereotyping of Blacks as a group varies with parental education, being least common for those whose parents hold advanced degrees and greatest for those whose parents lack college degrees, with respondents having college-educated parents falling in between. It thus seems that the closer Black respondents are to the typical objects of anti-Black stereotyping (low-status Black Americans), the more they themselves engage in negative anti-Black stereotyping, with the index rising from 3.49 among those whose parents held advanced degrees to 3.51 among those whose

parents graduated from college to 3.61 among those whose parents never graduated from college. The same ordering prevails with respect to the negative
stereotyping of Hispanic people, though the differences are only marginally
statistically significant.

Turning to the influence of prior segregation, we see that Black respondents
who grew up in White, racially mixed, and predominantly minority settings
tend to perceive Hispanic people in more stereotypical terms than those who
grew up in minority neighborhoods but attended White schools (with respective stereotyping indexes of 3.65, 3.67, and 3.68 in the first three instances and
3.58 in the last). In contrast, negative stereotyping of White people was greatest
among respondents who grew up in White schools and neighborhoods (with
an index value of 3.56) compared to those who came from predominantly minority or racially mixed settings (with respective values of 3.41 and 3.42) as
well as relative to those who lived in minority neighborhoods but attended
White schools (with an index value of 3.40). Finally, in terms of gender, Black
men engaged more in the negative stereotyping of Blacks, Hispanics, and
Asians than did Black women, with respective stereotyping indexes of 3.61,
3.74, and 2.75 for men compared with values of 3.49, 3.59, and 2.64 for women.

In addition to asking whether Blacks, Hispanics, Whites, and Asians exhibited stereotypically negative traits, we also asked respondents to use the same
scale to assess whether the members of each group "tend to treat members of
other groups equally, or whether they tend to discriminate against people who
aren't in their group." The resulting average scores are shown on the right-hand
side of figure 4.4. In this comparison, all scores lie above the horizontal line of
neutrality, indicating that Black respondents perceive some tendency for
members of all racial groups to discriminate against out-group members, even
Black Americans, who received a discrimination score of 4.49. Compared to
this benchmark, Hispanics were perceived to be significantly less discriminatory (with an average index value of 4.25), whereas Asians were seen to be
roughly as prone to discrimination as Blacks (index value of 4.46). In this
comparison, it was Whites who stood out with by far the highest average discrimination score of 5.13.

As table 4.5 indicates, however, the perception of White people as discriminatory varied systematically by racial and immigrant origins, skin tone, experience of segregation, and gender. In general, monoracial Black respondents rated
White people as more discriminatory than those of mixed-race origins (5.18
versus 4.83), as did multigenerational natives and first-generation immigrants
compared with second-generation immigrants (5.14 and 5.21 versus 4.79).

TABLE 4.5. Attribution of discriminatory tendencies to racial/ethnic groups by Black NLSF respondents

Characteristic	Blacks	Hispanics	Whites	Asians
Racial identification				
Monoracial	4.48	4.22+	5.18**	4.48
Mixed race	4.58	4.42	4.83	4.40
Nativity and generation				
Multigenerational native	4.47	4.20+	5.14*	4.42
Second-generation immigrant	4.48	4.37	4.79	4.54
First-generation immigrant	4.58	4.38	5.21	4.61
Region of origin				
USA	4.47	4.20*	5.14*	4.42
Caribbean	4.65	4.47	5.14	4.53
Africa	4.43	4.25	5.05	4.59
Other	3.48	3.66	3.49	2.73
Skin tone				
Light	4.48	4.24	4.89*	4.41
Medium	4.47	4.21	5.22	4.42
Dark	4.55	4.30	5.16	4.58
Gender				
Female	4.48	4.24	5.23**	4.51
Male	4.51	4.25	4.94	4.37
Parental education				
No degree	4.44	4.19	5.24	4.41*
College degree	4.51	4.28	5.06	4.34
Advanced degree	4.51	4.27	5.09	4.60
Experience of segregation				
Predominantly White	4.42*	4.21+	5.06+	4.49+
Racially mixed	4.58	4.29	5.18	4.40
Predominantly minority	4.73	4.45	5.35	4.72
Minority neighborhood/White school	4.40	4.17	5.07	4.40
N		1,039		

+ p < 0.10; * p < 0.05; ** p < 0.01; *** p < 0.001

Likewise, medium- and dark-skinned respondents rated White people as more discriminatory than light-skinned students (with values 5.22 and 5.16 versus 4.89 for those with light skin tones). Black women saw Whites as more discriminatory than did Black men (5.23 versus 4.94). Blacks who grew up in mixed or predominantly minority schools and neighborhoods rated Whites as more discriminatory than those who came of age in predominantly White schools and neighborhoods and those who lived in predominantly minority neighborhoods but attended predominantly White schools (with values of

5.18 and 5.35 versus 5.06 and 5.07). Although the perception of White people as discriminatory did not vary by socioeconomic status, the perception of Asian people as discriminators did. Those respondents whose parents held advanced degrees saw Asians as significantly more discriminatory than did those whose parents did not complete college or were college graduates (with an index value of 4.60 compared with respective values of 4.41 and 4.34).

Our findings that mixed-race respondents, those with light skin tones, those who attended predominantly White schools, and those of immigrant origin perceive White people as less discriminatory than their monoracial, dark-skinned, native-origin, segregated counterparts is interesting in light of prior work indicating that the first-listed groups are more vulnerable to stereotype threat. According to Massey and Owens (2014:573), "Students whose 'Blackness' might be less certain—those educated in integrated schools, having a light skin tone or a non-Black parent were more susceptible to the negative influences of stereotype threat . . . than Black students who were monoracial, dark skinned and educated in segregated schools. . . . We also found evidence to suggest that immigrant origins confer a protective effect with respect to the influence of stereotype threat."

For those Blacks with the most sustained exposure to Whiteness and discrimination, the resultant *emotional tax* (Travis, Thorpe-Moscon, and McCluney 2016) can foster context-specific negative prejudices toward Whites. Studies reveal a clear trade-off between the psychic toll of enduring settings where racism is common and the financial benefits of occupational mobility for middle- and upper-class Blacks (e.g., Powers and Ellison 1995; Torres and Charles 2004; Welburn and Pittman 2012; Irizarry 2013; Welburn 2016; Collins 2019). To successfully climb up the hierarchy, Black professionals often must grudgingly wear the "golden handcuffs" to ensure socioeconomic mobility (Collins 2019:93).

Our findings here suggest that the greater vulnerability to stereotype threat of young Black adults who are mixed race, light skinned, of immigrant origin, and raised in integrated settings may stem from the fact that Blacks with these characteristics perceive Whites to be *less* discriminatory and thus feel *more* threatened by stereotyping. Take Agnes, a second-generation immigrant whose parents were from Belize, as an example. Agnes went to a racially diverse public high school in Los Angeles that she described as "30 percent Asian" and "30 percent Black," with smaller numbers of Whites (20 percent) and Latinos (25 percent). She took all honors and AP courses and earned A's with relative ease. Reflecting on her high school performance, Agnes described herself as "lazy . . . but when I gave a little bit of effort, it made me shine, when I really knew I wasn't that spectacular."

During her freshman year of college, Agnes had a White roommate whom she "hung out with all the time." She got to know several of her roommate's friends and they socialized at predominantly White parties and Greek organizations; Agnes pledged a majority-White sorority her freshman year. Academically, though, she struggled some because the difficulty of her schoolwork was much greater than she experienced in high school. Agnes asserted that for her, "racism" was not as big an issue as the "class dimension" on campus:

> You always have to prove that you are not lazy. . . . You are not here because of affirmative action, like you spend your career here defending yourself and defending others . . . especially because it's an area where everyone is supposed to be elite. But it's like you're Black. You got here because of affirmative action. So you have to prove that you are also elite.

Precisely *because* they see Whites as less discriminatory, if they lag in academic performance, they are less likely to blame their shortfall on White prejudice, leading them to place the blame on themselves as individuals and thus confirm a disturbing racial stereotype they actively hope to disprove.

Beliefs about Inequality

Finally, we turn to an assessment of Black NLSF respondents' beliefs about the sources of racial inequality in American society—whether racial disparities stem from differences in individual traits such as skills, abilities, drive, and motivation or differences in external circumstances stemming from prejudice, discrimination, and blocked opportunities. To get at this issue, we presented respondents with five simple statements about the status of African Americans in U.S. society and asked them to rate the extent of their agreement, this time on a 0 to 10 scale: the future looks very promising for educated Blacks; any Black person who is educated and does what is considered "proper" will be accepted and eventually get ahead; when two qualified people, one Black and one White, are considered for the same job, the Black will not get the job no matter how hard he or she tries; many Blacks have only themselves to blame for not doing better in life—if they tried harder, they would do better; and the best way to overcome discrimination is for each individual Black person to be even better trained and more qualified than the most qualified White person.

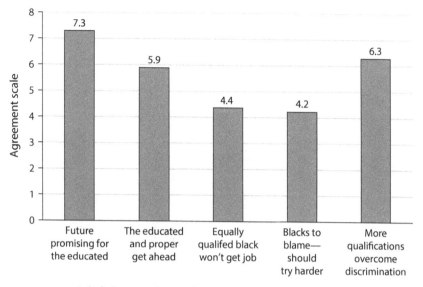

FIGURE 4.5. Beliefs about racial inequality expressed by Black respondents to the NLSF

Figure 4.5 presents ratings for each of these statements. Perhaps unsurprisingly, Black students attending selective colleges and universities thought that the future looked promising for educated African Americans and generally agreed that Blacks who do what is "proper" and "educated" will be accepted and get ahead in life, with respective agreement ratings of 7.3 and 5.9. They expressed considerably less agreement with the view a Black candidate would not be hired when pitted against an equally qualified White person (with a rating of just 4.4), consistent with their faith in the power of education to propel them forward toward a promising future. With a rating of just 4.2, they likewise expressed weak support for the idea that Blacks not doing well in life should blame themselves and just try harder. However, they did rather strongly endorse the idea that the best way to overcome racial discrimination is to gain more training and education than Whites (with an agreement rating of 6.3).

When we examined these ratings along the dimensions of Black diversity, we did not find significant variation in agreement with the statement about the future being promising for educated Blacks, the idea that Blacks who are educated and behaving properly are sure to get ahead, and the notion that a well-qualified Black job applicant will not get the job if there is an equally qualified White candidate. Our attempt to form a scale based on the foregoing items was also unsuccessful. The only significant variation occurred with

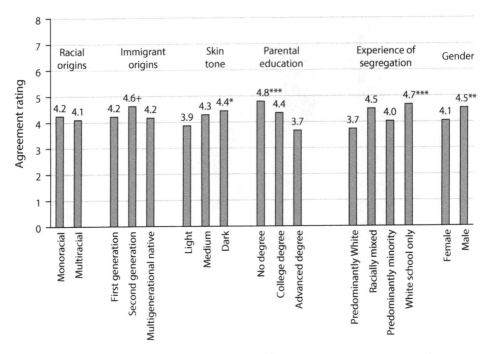

FIGURE 4.6. Extent of agreement by Black NLSF respondents that Blacks are to blame for not doing better and should try harder

respect to the final two statements: the view that Blacks should blame themselves and try harder when not doing well in life and that the best way to overcome discrimination is to get more training and education than Whites.

Figure 4.6 shows variation in ratings of the first of these two items. Although we observe no difference by racial identification, we do detect a marginally significant effect of immigrant origins, with second-generation Black respondents agreeing that the best response to a lack of success is to try harder, with a rating of 4.6 compared with a value of 4.2 for both first-generation immigrants and multigenerational natives. Our finding here is consistent with extant research suggesting that second-generation Black immigrants and their parents are more optimistic in their belief that individual education is the path to success compared either to first-generation immigrants or multigenerational natives (Waters 1999; Portes and Rumbaut 2001; Kasinitz et al. 2009; Model 2011; Waters and Pineau 2016).

Differences were more striking across the other categories of Black diversity. Agreement with the view that Blacks should blame themselves for doing poorly and simply try harder steadily rose as skin color darkened, with the rating being 3.9 for light-skinned respondents, 4.3 for medium-skinned respondents, and 4.4 for dark-skinned respondents. In contrast, agreement dropped with rising parental education, going from 4.8 among those with non-college-educated parents, to 4.4 among those whose parents had finished college, to 3.7 among those parents held advanced degrees.

The view that individual Blacks should blame themselves and try harder for not doing better in life also varied by segregation. Respondents who grew up in predominantly White neighborhoods displayed a low average rating of 3.7, compared to 4.5 among those who grew up in racially mixed schools and 4.0 among those who came of age in minority schools and neighborhoods. The strongest agreement was expressed by those who lived in minority neighborhoods but attended White schools (with an index value of 4.7), echoing our earlier observation that the contrast between a disadvantaged, racially isolated neighborhood setting and a privileged White school experience underscores the size of the racial gap in access to resources, a conclusion also reached by Shedd (2015). In this instance, we find that it prompts them to also advocate greater effort to overcome discrimination. Finally, with respect to gender, it was Black men who agreed that Blacks should blame themselves and try harder whenever they were not doing well (with a rating of 4.5 compared with 4.1 for women).

Figure 4.7 shows how agreement with the idea that Blacks need to be more qualified and better trained to compete effectively with Whites varies across the dimensions of Black diversity. Although all respondents agreed relatively strongly with this sentiment, the level of agreement was significantly greater for monoracial Blacks, whose agreement rating was 6.4 compared with a value of 5.8 for mixed-race respondents. Likewise, the degree of agreement rose as skin color darkened, increasing from 6.0 among those with light skin tones to 6.2 among those with medium skin tones and 6.7 among those with dark skin tones. In general, then, it seems that aspiring Black professionals who lack the racialized advantages of White parentage or a light skin tone are more aware of the continuing power of racism and the barriers to advancement it creates. Hence, they perceive a need for African Americans to compensate by putting out greater effort and acquiring more education, a view that was especially strong among men and those of lower socioeconomic status who attended White schools but lived in minority neighborhoods.

These findings generally accord with prior research suggesting that compared to poor and working-class African Americans, those of upper-middle-class

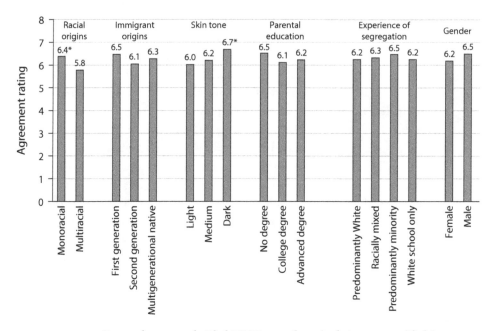

FIGURE 4.7. Extent of agreement by Black NLSF respondents that being more qualified than Whites will overcome discrimination

status tend to articulate a both/and understanding of racial inequality (Benjamin 2005). They attribute racial inequalities to individual characteristics such as a poor work ethic and lack of effort while also recognizing how structural factors act to restrict Black people (Lamont and Fleming 2005; Hunt 2007). This dual consciousness comes to exist as professional Blacks attempt to justify to themselves their elevated socioeconomic position compared to lower class African Americans. Welburn (2016), for example, found that Black interviewees who had struggled and worked hard to make their way up the class ladder favored individualistic explanations for Black success more than those born into the upper middle class.

Consistent with this observation, Tim, a second-generation immigrant freshman from a middle-class family, was quick to share his optimism about the state of the Black community, emphasizing the growing range of opportunities for young Blacks rather than the persistence of racial barriers to be overcome with greater effort:

I think there are less barriers based on race. I think that we definitely have more opportunity. I mean, I think African Americans definitely have more opportunity than they did. Not only under the law, but just as a society, people are more open to Black people being successful.

Although of Kenyan descent, Tim identified as "African American" and grew up in a predominately Black Long Island suburb with his mother. His father passed away at a relatively young age, but both parents had come to the United States for graduate education. With financial aid, Tim was able to attend elite private schools from kindergarten through high school.

Unlike Tim, Karen came from a working-class family and grew up attending segregated schools in minority neighborhoods. When she was asked about the state of the Black community, her response was quite different, admitting that circumstances had improved "to a certain extent" but calling on individual Blacks to continue to push ahead for even greater progress:

> I feel like, you know, Black meant below, inferior, subjugated, and White meant above, superior. And, to a certain extent, it's gotten better. Just being born Black doesn't mean that you're going to have to ride at the back of the bus or drink from the colored water fountain. But it means that you could reach the status of a Condoleezza Rice, or something. . . . I feel like Black people are becoming more aware of that fact as well and of their status in America and, hopefully, their potential power to effect change. Because we do have more power than we give ourselves credit for.

In keeping with this sentiment, Karen was quite active in the Black student community at her university though she did express an openness to engage with non-Blacks on campus. She even revealed that her boyfriend was White and that she enjoyed "hanging out" with some of his friends.

Conclusion

Going away to college marks a crucial time in the transition to adulthood from adolescence for all students attending selective institutions of higher education. As young adults separate from their families and communities, they enter a new stage of personal identity development. Psychologists contend that the residential college experience is a distinct socioemotional stage where individuals explore, develop, and refine certain aspects of their identities to figure out who they really are (Karp, Holmstrom, and Gray 1998; Arnett 2000). Living away from home, many for the first time, late adolescents are free to experiment with different personal and social identities and decide which ones they wish to adopt moving into adulthood. College development theorists argue that intellectual and socioemotional growth of students at four-year institutions is predicated on status individuation and identity exploration (Schwartz, Côté, and Arnett 2005; Syed and Azmitia 2010; Fuligni and Tsai 2012; Arnett 2016).

For aspiring young Black professionals, the predominately White milieu of selective colleges and universities compels them to contemplate their racial identities and self-concepts as members of a distinct racial group. Sustained contact with people of other races forces them to constantly confront issues of race and racial identity as they make their way through campus life. As our findings reveal, Blacks at elite institutions spend a great deal of time and energy contemplating what Blackness means and where they fit into the larger Black community, both on campus and in the world beyond (see Charles et al. 2009; Torres and Massey 2012). Given the diversity of their origins and upbringings, however, the expression of Black identity is not a single, consistent process but one strongly shaped by the social contexts and life experiences students have come before.

Our survey of racial identities and attitudes among elite Black students at the dawn of the twenty-first century generally finds them to be strongly committed to Black culture and identity but with a concomitant desire to achieve success in the American mainstream through education. As they began their collegiate journey, a substantial majority endorsed the equal importance of both Black and American identities, and an even larger share perceived themselves to share a common fate with Blacks as a group. Our respondents generally perceived little social distance from other Black people and, unsurprisingly, felt especially close to young, middle-class, Black professionals, presumably the status group they aspired to join in the near future. At the same time, they were suspicious of those holding influence and power, even when exercised by rich Black people or Black elected officials.

However they felt about their own group, the social distance Black students perceived toward other groups increased moving from Hispanics to Whites to Asians. The primary exception to this ordering concerned White business owners and elected officials, who were seen as more distant even than Asian business owners and elected officials. We also detected a potentially high degree of estrangement from White "legacy" students, whom Black survey and interview respondents appear to perceive benefiting unfairly from a kind of "White affirmative action." Black NLSF respondents nonetheless view the future as very promising for educated Blacks and felt that by gaining an elite education and behaving in "proper" ways, they would ultimately get ahead. Consonant with this view, they were resistant to the idea that Black job candidates would never be accepted over equally qualified Whites, and as a group, they were skeptical of the view that a lack of success could be remedied by accepting blame and simply by trying harder. In sum, they were not unaware of the fact that racial barriers to Black progress still existed, but they felt that the best way to overcome discrimination and exclusion was to be even better trained and more qualified than their White competitors.

Although the foregoing attitudinal profile applies to Black students generally, we nonetheless detected subtle differences between students along the dimensions of Black diversity. Whereas the large majority of respondents preferred to self-identify both as Black and American and also perceived a common fate with other Black Americans, these tendencies were weaker for some students. Specifically, students of mixed race, with light skin tones, who grew up in White or racially mixed settings, and men were all less likely to identify as Black and more likely to label themselves as American. They also perceived themselves to be closer to White people relative to dark-skinned, women from racially segregated backgrounds. The latter were more likely to identify simply as Black and to perceive greater closeness to other Black people and more distance from White people. Second-generation immigrants were also more likely to self-identify as Black, especially those with origins in Africa or the Caribbean.

Interestingly, when all the dimensions of diversity were entered into multivariate models along with controls for family background, differences by skin tone disappear (see appendix tables A4.1–A4.3), suggesting that racial identification, common fate identity, and perceptions of closeness come less from skin tone per se and more from growing up in predominantly White familial, residential, and school settings. Differences by nativity and gender are apparent even after controlling for other dimensions and family background. Compared to women respondents, men are more likely to identify simply as American and to perceive themselves closer to Whites. Likewise, Caribbean respondents, but not those with origins in Africa, were significantly more likely to self-identify as Black.

In addition, multivariate analyses showed that mixed-race students, first-generation immigrants, and men perceived Whites to be less prone to discrimination compared to monoracial native-origin women. Ironically, those who had the most experience with Whites in childhood and adolescence (those who lived in White or mixed neighborhoods and/or attended a White school) saw Whites as more discriminatory, even as they perceived them to be socially closer. Support for the view that Blacks should blame themselves for a lack of success and just try harder was greatest among men and those with darker skin tones, and a dark skin tone also predicted support for the view that Blacks need to be more qualified than Whites to get ahead. Finally, other things being equal, exposure to disorder and violence growing up predicted feeling less closeness to White people and a stronger proclivity to view White people as discriminatory.

Considering its cultural identity as a premier historically Black college and university (HBCU), we expected that students who opted to attend Howard might have markedly different racial identities and attitudes compared to the 90 percent of our respondents who chose to attend a predominantly White institution (PWI). Here and in future chapters, we report results from multivariate models that control for HBCU attendance to test whether students who opt for a selective HBCU report different backgrounds or experiences compared to those who opted for a selective PWI (Willie 2003). The addition of a dummy variable to identify students attending Howard University had little effect on other variables in the multivariate model. Paradoxically, however, Howard students were much more likely than Black students attending predominantly White institutions to self-identify simply as American rather than just Black, even as they perceived a stronger common fate identity, felt more socially distant from White people, and saw White people as discriminatory. In keeping with these views, they also ascribed more strongly to the precept that Black people had to be more qualified than White people to get ahead in American society.

Despite a strong consensus on most issues, the precollege backgrounds and experiences of young, high-achieving Black students clearly affect their worldviews. Those attending selective colleges and universities largely identify with the "double consciousness" originally described by Du Bois (see also Benjamin 2005). However, the sometimes subtle and sometimes large differences across the dimensions of diversity among Black NLSF respondents, suggest that the traditional notion of duality may not go far enough in characterizing the multifaceted nature of Black identity in the twenty-first century. Instead, Blackness today appears to embrace a "set of multiple consciousnesses" and a host of variegated social identities (Rollock et al. 2011:1088).

5

Pathways to Elite Education

There are just things I don't know. I don't know if it's a cultural thing that doesn't have to do with high school. For instance, in class right now, [the professor] is talking about refinancing your house and a mortgage. I have no idea what those things are. I don't know if you learn that in school, but people just bring books up all the time that I've never heard of.

TIFFANY, MULTIGENERATIONAL NATIVE
FROM A POOR BLACK NEIGHBORHOOD

IN RECENT DECADES, critics and advocates of affirmative action—including both scholars and policymakers—have recognized the burgeoning presence of mixed-race, immigrant, and affluent Black students on the campuses of selective colleges and universities and have debated whether "diversity for its own sake" actually redresses racial injustices of the past (Haynie 2002; Massey et al. 2003, 2007; Rimer and Arenson 2004). Some argue, often very forcefully, that these selected subsets of the nation's Black population already have privileged access to human, cultural, social, and financial capital compared with monoracial, native-origin Black people of modest economic circumstances, giving them a clear advantage in gaining admission to selective colleges and universities (Kent 2007; Massey et al. 2007; Charles, Torres, and Brunn 2008; Bennett and Lutz 2009). Onwuachi-Willig (2007:1158), for example, critiques the prevailing system of elite college admissions, arguing that entrance criteria should place less emphasis on "the endpoint of students in their [precollege] academic career" and more emphasis on "the distance between where students started their lives in terms of (dis)advantage, and the point to where they were able to climb in their academic journey."

Recently, a new political movement known as American Descendants of Slavery (ADOS) has emerged among young Black Americans (see Stockman 2019). Its adherents argue that racial affirmative action policies should favor poor people who are descended from enslaved persons present in the United States before emancipation and should not give equivalent weight to the children of recent immigrants from Africa or the Caribbean and other more-privileged subsets of America's Black population (see Stockman 2019). In practice, however, we know little about the varied social and educational pathways that Black students follow as they seek to enter selective colleges and universities. Although we may know something about students' class backgrounds, immigrant origins, and racial ancestry, we do not know how these factors influence the means by which Black families prepare for the college admissions process. We know even less about the strategies and practices Black students and their parents draw on in seeking to gain access to elite institutions of higher education in the United States.

In this chapter, we consider those aspects of child-rearing in three different ways. First, we look at on-the-ground parenting techniques—from questions about whether parents were strict or promoted childhood independence to how well parents knew their child's peers and whether parents engaged in mainstream forms of cultural capital consumption. Second, we consider parents' choice of primary and secondary schools for their children. A key motivator for many White parents is the presumption that White communities have better local schools (Owens 2017, 2018; Bischoff and Owens 2019). As we show in this chapter, many Black parents use their resources or take advantage of nonprofit and scholarship opportunities to gain access to predominantly White schools for their children. We also look at who takes Advanced Placement (AP) courses, perceptions of the difficulty of high school coursework, student grades, and standardized test scores. Third, we consider the final precollege step for the future Black elite: applying to college and what influences respondents' choice of where to attend college, including, as some of our interviews show, the direct influence of parents on that process.

As with most research on Black inequality, empirical works on Black parenting styles have focused mostly on poor, multigenerational African Americans from single-parent households, usually taking White middle-class parents as the reference group (Dickerson 1995; McLoyd et al. 2000; Tamis-LeMonda et al. 2008). This literature labels the child-rearing strategies of less advantaged Black parents as "authoritarian," in contrast to the "authoritative" style common to many middle-class White families (e.g., Baumrind 1972; Berlin, Brady-Smith,

and Brooks-Gunn 2002; Lansford et al. 2004; Murry et al. 2008). Authoritarian parenting is associated with punishment, coercion, and adherence to strict
rules, with retribution to be administered swiftly when rules are broken (Gray
and Steinberg 1999). In contrast, authoritative parenting entails a give-and-
take in which parents set clearly defined rules within a context of affection and
warmth while encouraging age-appropriate autonomy and independence
(Baumrind 1966; Watabe and Hibbard 2014).

Although authoritative parenting styles have been shown to positively
predict children's scholastic performance, motivation, and aspiration (Steinberg et al. 1992; Strage and Brandt 1999; Ingoldby et al. 2003; Turner, Chandler, and Heffer 2009), the circumstances facing many Black families are
quite different than those confronting other American families. Poor Black
parents often must protect their children from the manifold threats of life in
segregated, high-poverty neighborhoods, and *all* Black parents strive to
teach their children how to cope with the racism that still pervades U.S.
society. In doing so, many draw on authoritarian models of obedience intended to counter stereotypes of Black men as angry and violent and Black
women as emotional and disrespectful (McLoyd et al. 2000; Ferguson 2003;
Morris 2007; Froyum 2010).

Research on Black parenting practices suggests that Black parents often
push their sons to suppress expressions of hostility and defiance (Simons et al.
2006) and counsel their daughters to manage their emotions so as "to fit the
expectations of powerful others," stifle "attitudes," and offer "empathy" to
White authority figures (Froyum 2010:45, 50). Black parents tend to keep a
strict watch on their children and seek to limit their movements outside of
home, carefully monitoring their social activities to protect them from risky
social environments (Furstenberg et al. 1999; Lacy 2007; Goldner et al. 2014).
Middle-class Black parents living in the suburbs must also alert their children
to the ever-present risk of being pulled over for "driving while Black" and the
serious, sometimes fatal, consequences that can follow (Tomaskovic-Devey,
Mason, and Zingraff 2004; Sorin 2020; Dow 2019).

Research to date typically posits a dichotomy of two contrasting parenting
strategies: authoritarian and authoritative. Lareau (2003:11–12) famously defines a style of authoritative child-rearing she calls *concerted cultivation* in
which children are taught how to behave in school by speaking clearly, engaging readily in classroom activities, and displaying enthusiasm for learning
while simultaneously communicating respect for authority. Parents are very
involved in their children's lives and seek to engage them in various organized

activities. In contrast, Lareau defines an authoritarian type of child-rearing she calls *natural growth accomplishment*. In this case, parents are less involved in their children's schooling and, outside the classroom, let them engage in unstructured play rather than pushing them into organized activities, allowing them to grow up at their own pace. This strategy, she argues, is common to poor and working-class families who lack the time, experience, information, and resources to teach their children about middle-class norms and expectations, thus putting them at an educational disadvantage.

Lareau (2003) argues that social class and not race primarily determines parenting style. Some critics dispute this claim, asserting instead that Lareau emphasizes White class distinctions that do not accurately reflect how all parenting strategies are racialized, including concerted cultivation (Choo and Ferree 2010; Manning 2019). Studies nonetheless suggest that Black child-rearing practices also vary by socioeconomic status, though findings are somewhat inconsistent (Robinson and Harris 2014). Some studies find that the parenting behaviors of middle- and upper-class Black Americans mirror those of same-status Whites (Bluestone and Tamis-LeMonda 1999; Massey et al. 2003), whereas others suggest that high-status Black parents favor a more relaxed "democratic" style, especially as children enter their teenage years (Smetana 2000; Sampson 2007; Tamis-LeMonda et al. 2008:324).

Factors such as gender, ethnicity, nativity, and skin tone have also been found to affect parenting strategies in Black households, yielding a diverse array of child-rearing practices, sometimes even within the same household (Boyd-Franklin 2003; Wilder and Cain 2011; Smith and Moore 2013). In their longitudinal study of eight hundred Black families, Landor et al. (2013) found a pattern of "gendered colorism" in which dark-skinned boys experienced a more authoritarian and punitive style of child-rearing than light-skinned girls, irrespective of socioeconomic status. Within African and Caribbean cultures, child-rearing tends to be matrifocal and communal, with supervision being shared between mothers and extended kin, many of whom reside in the household. Fathers are often distant figures who provide economic support to children and expect respect and obedience in return (Otterbein 1965; Evans and Davies 1996; Sharpe 1996; Dodoo 1997; Smith and Mosby 2003).

Quantitative studies indicate that mixed-race children are more likely to live in affluent neighborhoods and to attend resource-rich, integrated schools than monoracial children (Doyle and Kao 2007; Charles, Torres, and Brunn 2008; Burke and Kao 2010; Fryer et al. 2012; Wright, Holloway, and Ellis 2013;

Davenport 2016). Harris and Thomas (2002) found that mixed-race young people also tend to have higher GPAs and test scores than their monoracial Black peers, even though their family structures and home environments are more similar to those of Black peers than White peers (Fryer et al. 2012). Ethnographic studies suggest that mixed-race children benefit significantly from a familiarity with "cultural Whiteness" stemming from "access to and an implicit understanding of mainstream cultural capital that permeates all aspects of culture including music, knowledge, language and leisure time activities," thus giving them "a sense of certainty or self-assuredness with cultural authority figures" (Bettez 2002:166). This cultural capital leaves them "well-equipped to use cultural knowledge (sometimes for ulterior motives) to negotiate dominant social situations" (Tutwiler 2016:91–92).

Mixed-race individuals with a White parent also tend to have an economic edge over their monoracial Black peers, owing to generations of material advantage passed down through the White side of the family, giving them greater access to income and inherited wealth as well as a large stock of useful social and cultural capital (Hochschild and Weaver 2007; Norwood and Foreman 2014; Davenport 2016). The racial gap in financial wealth is especially large (Oliver and Shapiro 2006; Conley 2010), making it much more difficult for middle- and upper-class Black families to transfer educational credentials and assets to their children than White families of the same income (Shapiro 2004; Bielby 2012; Shapiro, Meschede, and Osoro 2013; Bowman 2016; Herring and Henderson 2016). The racial wealth gap also limits the size of investment that Black parents can make in their children's educational future and leaves them with less access to information about the college search and application process (Perna 2000; Massey et al. 2003, 2007; Charles, Roscigno, and Torres 2007).

Our goal in this chapter is to analyze the diversity of parenting styles experienced by the aspiring Black students in our quantitative and qualitative data sets and to draw on this information in assessing the diversity of educational experiences and college preparation strategies across different Black subgroups. Since Black men and women are quite likely to experience different child-rearing practices and educational outcomes, we pay particular attention to differences by gender. As noted earlier, Black women outnumber Black men by a factor of two to one among respondents in the National Longitudinal Survey of Freshmen (NLSF), suggesting that pathways into elite institutions of higher education are likely to be highly gendered (Massey et al. 2003; Massey and Probasco 2010).

Diversity in Upbringing

To consider differences in parenting styles, we use indexes originally developed by Massey et al. (2003) to measure three elements of parenting: the extent to which parents cultivate their children's intellectual independence, the strictness with which they dispense discipline, and the degree to which they rely on the use of shame and guilt in child-rearing. We first constructed an index of parental cultivation of intellectual independence using a set of items included on the baseline survey, which asked respondents to rate how often their parents checked their homework and rewarded them for good grades at ages six and thirteen. Other items focused on the senior year of high school (roughly age eighteen) and asked respondents to rate how much their parents believed they should give in during arguments, pushed them to think independently, explained reasons for their decisions, believed that children should not argue with parents, thought adults were always right, and told them they would "understand when they were older." The numerical ratings for each item ranged from 0 to 4 and when added together created a reasonably reliable index (Cronbach's alpha = 0.663) that theoretically ranged from 0 to 64 but in practice varied from 7 to 62. The details of construction are found in appendix B3 of Massey et al. (2003), and average values are shown for different Black subgroups in the first column of table 5.1.

The index of intellectual independence seeks to capture the degree to which respondents are encouraged by parents to think for themselves and stand by and defend their beliefs. Significant differences in parental support for these traits emerge across all but one of the dimensions of Black diversity (gender). On average, the index of parental support for independent thinking was greater for mixed-race than monoracial respondents (40.3 versus 38.3), greater for those with light skin tones (39.3) than those with medium skin tones (38.6) or dark skin tones (37.8), and greater for the parents of multigenerational natives (39.1) than those of first-generation immigrants (36.3) or second-generation immigrants (37.6). Among immigrant respondents, parents from the Caribbean were more supportive of intellectual independence than those from Africa (37.8 versus 36.5); however, multigenerational Black Americans report even more support on average (39.1).

As one might predict, the independence index was also greater for parents holding college and advanced degrees (39.4 and 38.9, respectively) compared with those who lacked a college degree (37.2). In terms of childhood segregation, the parents of respondents who came of age in predominantly White schools and neighborhoods displayed significantly greater support for

TABLE 5.1. Indicators of parental child-rearing strategies experienced by members of different Black subgroups during childhood

	Parental cultivation of intellectual independence index	Strictness of parental discipline index	Parental use of shame and guilt index
Racial identification			
Monoracial	38.3	16.6	9.7
Mixed race	40.3	14.3	9.4
Nativity and generation			
Multigenerational native	39.1**	15.9	9.1***
Second-generation immigrant	37.6	17.4	11.4
First-generation immigrant	36.3	17.0	10.9
Region of origin			
USA	39.1**	15.9+	9.1***
Caribbean	37.8	16.4	11.0
Africa	36.5	17.6	11.9
Other	36.9	18.2	10.9
Skin tone			
Light	39.3*	15.2*	9.8
Medium	38.6	16.2	9.5
Dark	37.8	17.1	9.7
Gender			
Female	38.8	15.0***	9.5
Male	38.0	18.6	10.0
Parental education			
No degree	37.2*	16.4	10.0*
College degree	39.4	16.2	9.0
Advanced degree	38.9	16.0	9.9
Experience of segregation			
Predominantly White	39.8***	15.5*	9.4
Racially mixed	38.1	17.5	9.6
Predominantly minority	37.1	16.0	10.0
Minority neighborhood/ White school	38.9	14.9	9.7
N		1,039	

$^+$ p < 0.10; * p < 0.05; ** p < 0.01; *** p < 0.001

intellectual independence (39.8) than those who grew up in predominantly minority schools and neighborhoods (37.1). Parents of respondents living in racially mixed residential and educational settings fell in between (38.1), as did the parents of those who lived in a predominantly minority neighborhood but attended a White school (38.9).

The next index we consider focuses on the strictness of discipline, also adapted from Massey et al. (2003). It likewise was constructed from items included on the baseline NLSF survey, which asked respondents how often their parents punished them for getting bad grades and for disobeying at ages six, thirteen, and as high school seniors (roughly age eighteen). At ages thirteen and eighteen, respondents were also asked how often their parents limited their time with friends as well as how often their parents forbade them from doing things when they were displeased with them and the extent to which they made their lives miserable for getting poor grades. When combined, the 0 to 4 numerical ratings on each item yielded a scale with a potential range of 0 to 56 that in practice varied from 0 to 46 with a Cronbach's alpha of 0.842 (see appendix table B4 in Massey et al. 2003 for details).

As shown in the second column of table 5.1, the index of disciplinary strictness differed significantly by racial identification, skin tone, experience of segregation, and gender, though not by nativity, generation, or parental education. In general, parental discipline was stricter for monoracial respondents (16.6) than for mixed-race respondents (14.3) and greater for those with dark skin tones (17.1) compared to those with light skin tones (15.2), with medium-skinned students falling in between (16.2). Among foreign-born respondents, differences by region of origin are marginally significant ($p < 0.10$), with parents of African immigrants being slightly stricter (17.6) than those from the Caribbean (16.4).

In terms of prior segregation, parental discipline was stricter in contexts where respondents had less contact with Whites, with index values of 16.0 and 17.5 among respondents coming from minority and mixed settings, respectively, compared with values of 15.5 and 14.9 for those who grew up in a predominantly White context and those who lived in predominantly minority neighborhoods but attended predominantly White schools. This pattern is consistent with research suggesting parental concerns about safety in minority schools and neighborhoods encourage a more authoritarian style of child-rearing intended to keep children close to home and out of danger (Goldner et al. 2014). Studies also indicate that Black parents also tend to be stricter in urban than rural areas, where children are granted more independence (Giles-Sims, Straus, and Sugarman 1995; Bulcroft, Carmody, and Bulcroft 1996; Steele et al. 2005).

Perhaps unsurprisingly, Black men reported stricter parental discipline than Black women (18.6 versus 15.0), the largest absolute difference in the table. Research suggests that Black parents employ strict discipline with boys in an effort to protect them from negative peer influences and the gendered effects of risky neighborhood environments where young Black men are the most frequent victims of crime and violence (Dornbusch et al. 1987; Smetana and Gaines 1999; Thomas and Stevenson 2009; Brewster, Stephenson, and Beard 2013; Dix 2016). Strict discipline also is a protective strategy to try to preempt Black boys getting labeled a "problem student" and to mitigate their disproportionate risk of facing serious disciplinary actions such as suspensions or expulsions. Black girls also appear to be socialized to be more self-reliant and independent than Black boys (Ladner 1971; Staples 1981; McAdoo 1988; Taylor et al. 1990; Hill 2001, 2005).

Although we did not explicitly ask about parenting practices in our qualitative interviews, several students mentioned them in passing. Reports of strict discipline and limit-setting were most common among young Black men hailing from segregated neighborhoods and less affluent, often immigrant backgrounds. Troy, for example, describes his father as a "disciplinarian as far as with [me] growing up." Of Ghanaian ancestry, Troy's parents came to the United States before he and his older brother were born, and the family struggled to make ends meet in a rough section of the Bronx with support from public assistance. Troy's mother had only finished "eighth or ninth grade," though his father had completed "some" college back in Ghana.

Troy's parents worried about his academic success in public schools and thus "sacrificed" themselves to pay for a parochial school in which the other students were similarly racially and economically disadvantaged but in which discipline and order prevailed. Troy recalled that he and his brother "hated" going to Catholic school but never questioned their father's strict preferences on this issue. Mikal likewise described his father as a "tyrant" and, like Troy, he grew up in a troubled minority neighborhood where he attended local schools, which he described as having "metal detectors" and "a lot of fights."

The last column of table 5.1 summarizes results using the index of shame and guilt in child-rearing, again adapted from Massey et al. (2003) and constructed from items on the baseline survey that assessed respondents' agreement with statements about the extent to which parents acted cold when displeased, made them feel guilty for poor grades, did fun things with them, and spent time just talking to them during their senior year of high school. As before, the items were coded 0 to 4 and summed to create an index that theoretically ranged from 0 to 32 and practically from 0 to 31, with a Cronbach's alpha of 0.684 (see table B4 in Massey et al. 2003 for details).

Differences in the use of shame and guilt are large and highly significant with respect to nativity, generation, and region of origin ($p < 0.001$). The use of shame and guilt is greatest among first- and second-generation immigrants (10.9 and 11.4) compared with multigenerational natives (9.1) and was especially pronounced for respondents born in Africa (11.9) and the Caribbean (11.0). In both regions, child-rearing practices tend to be collectivist rather than individualist, with parents and extended kin collaborating to dispense discipline (Evans and Davies 1996; Gyekye 1996; Leo-Rhynie 1996; Dudley-Grant 2001). Shame and guilt are also deployed by parents to encourage respect, obedience, and deference to traditional values. Poor academic performance is seen not simply as an individual failing but as family stigma and a violation of traditional cultural values (Bempechat, Graham, and Jimenez 1999; Mathurin, Gielen, and Lancaster 2006; McAdoo 1997; Brown and Johnson 2008).

Thus, Destiny told us her parents, who were from Belize and never attended college, placed great emphasis on education and stressed how her personal success reflected not only her character but also the values and well-being of her family and culture. As she put it,

> My mother was like, do your work, and do your work, and do your work. . . . I've been learning that immigrant families . . . this is our only chance . . . I just see it in terms of my ethnicity just standing out. I see it in terms of family and how I decide to live my life, what job I decide to go into, and where I decide to live. It was very much contingent on where my family is and how I can be sure that I'm helping us and not bringing us down.

In addition to asking questions about child-rearing practices and disciplinary styles, we also asked a number of questions intended to capture parental efforts to cultivate children's human, cultural, and social capital; once again, we drew on indexes developed by Massey et al. (2003) to assess variation in these efforts across dimensions of Black diversity. Human capital consists of skills and abilities that make people more productive and hence more valuable as economic actors (Schultz 1961, 1981). The classic example of human capital is education (Becker 1964; Blalock 1991), which includes not only formal schooling but also extracurricular activities.

To assess the level of parental involvement in the creation of human capital, the baseline survey asked respondents how often their parents read to them, helped them with their homework, and took them to a library at age six and also whether their parents endeavored to place them in a summer school, a summer educational camp, or a summer enrichment program. They were also asked how often at age thirteen their parents helped them with their homework, took them to a library, participated in a parent-teacher association, and whether their parents placed them in an educational summer camp. Finally, they were asked how often during their senior year of high school their parents checked their homework, helped them with homework, met with teachers, read a daily newspaper, read a Sunday paper, and read a weekly news magazine. Finally, they were also asked about the extent to which each parent pushed them to do their best, helped them with their schoolwork, and encouraged them when they got good grades.

When added together, the numerical ratings for each item produced an index of parental cultivation of human capital with a possible range of 0 to 104 and an actual range of 8 to 70 with a Cronbach's alpha of 0.810 (see appendix B1 in Massey et al. 2003 for details). Results for this index are presented in the first column of table 5.2. Although we see no differences in parental involvement in human capital cultivation by racial identification or skin tone, we do observe significant and often strong differences across the other dimensions of Black diversity. For example, the parents of multigenerational-native and first-generation immigrant Black students were reported to be much more involved in their children's human capital formation than the parents of second-generation immigrants, with respective index values of 46.6 and 46.2 for the former compared and 43.0 for the latter. Parents of African immigrant respondents were especially involved in promoting the education and training of their children, displaying an index value of 47.2.

As one might expect, involvement in human capital formation rises monotonically with parental education, going from an index value of 42.5 for parents with no college degree to 46.7 for parents with a college degree to 48.5 for those with an advanced degree. We also observe stark differences by respondents' experience of segregation during childhood and adolescence. Whereas parents of children from predominantly White schools and neighborhoods displayed a human capital formation index of 47.7, the value was just 43.9 for parents of children from predominantly minority environments. Respondents from racially mixed neighborhoods and schools displayed an index value of 46.2, whereas for those from minority neighborhoods who attended a predominantly White school, the index stood at 46.6. Black parents also appear to have been much more involved in cultivating the human capital of girls than boys, with the index value being 47.2 for women compared with 44.3 for men.

Contemporary research on Black parenting suggests that Black parents, especially Black mothers, socialize their sons categorically differently than

TABLE 5.2. Parental cultivation of human, cultural, and social capital for members of different Black subgroups during childhood

	Index of human capital cultivation	Index of cultural capital cultivation	Index of social capital cultivation
Racial identification			
Monoracial	46.1	9.8***	10.4*
Mixed Race	46.5	11.8	11.2
Nativity and generation			
Multigenerational native	46.6**	10.5***	10.8**
Second-generation immigrant	43.0	10.1	9.9
First-generation immigrant	46.2	7.8	9.8
Region of origin			
USA	46.6*	10.5*	10.8**
Caribbean	44.5	9.1	9.8
Africa	47.2	9.3	9.9
Other	43.5	10.0	10.2
Skin tone			
Light	46.5	11.5***	11.1**
Medium	46.0	9.9	10.6
Dark	46.3	9.4	10.0
Gender			
Female	47.2***	11.0***	10.8*
Male	44.3	8.6	10.2
Parental education			
No degree	42.5***	7.9***	10.4
College degree	46.7	10.1	10.7
Advanced degree	48.5	11.8	10.5
Experience of segregation			
Predominantly White	47.7***	11.3*	10.8*
Racially mixed	46.2	9.7	10.6
Predominantly minority	43.9	8.7	10.2
Minority neighborhood/White school	46.6	10.9	10.3
N		1,039	

$^+ p < 0.10$; $^* p < 0.05$; $^{**} p < 0.01$; $^{***} p < 0.001$

their daughters (Dow 2019). Compared to Black girls, less attention is given to boys' academic and "cognitive" growth. Instead, Black mothers worry more about boys' physical safety and are more wary of potential discrimination by schools and educators. Black mothers also express guilt about boys not having positive masculine role models in the household. They often see athletics as a way out of socioeconomic disadvantage for Black boys and a "masculinity

legitimacy tool" (Faulk, Bennett, and Moore 2017:90), one that offers a posi-
tive "way to circumvent the challenges of behavior with Black male youths,
their performance, and their risk of criminal activity" (Faulk, Bennett, and
Moore 2017:95; see also Mandara, Varner, and Richman 2010; Morris and
Adeyemo 2012; Richardson, Van Brakle, and St. Vil 2014; Voisin et al. 2016;
Williams et al. 2017).

Much of the knowledge required for educational success comes not from
the classroom but from informal interactions and socialization. Parents, of
course, are key actors in identifying and transmitting the knowledge that
people "ought to have." Cultural capital theory contends that wealthy parents
also groom their children to succeed in school by making cultural investments
they expect to help further educational and social success (Lamont and Lareau
1988). Bourdieu (1986:243) asserts that the transmission of cultural capital is
"the best hidden and most socially determinant educational investment."

Knowledge about situationally appropriate dress, manners of speech, and
deportment in high-status settings are forms of cultural capital, and individuals with limited access to elite (White) forms of cultural knowledge tend to be
less well prepared to navigate elite environments. Contemporary research on
cultural capital in the U.S. context has focused on class-based parenting styles
and techniques and how they influence school achievement (Farkas et al. 1990;
DiMaggio and Ostrower 1990; Roscigno and Ainsworth-Darnell 1999; Dumais
2002; Charles, Torres, and Brunn 2008; Cheadle 2008; Condron 2009; Redford,
Johnson, and Honnold 2009; Roksa and Potter 2011; Carolan and Wasserman
2015; Calarco 2018).

For many scholars, cultural capital is considered integral to academic
achievement and "plays an important role in the transmission of socioeconomic advantages across generations" (Kalmijn and Kraaykamp 1996:32).
What constitutes cultural capital is context specific, of course, and since selective colleges and universities are elite institutions, what matters here are *elite*
forms of cultural capital. Crucial to capital's importance is that it is transferable
and can be acquired via other forms of capital (e.g., paying for art lessons or
to attend a concert) and that it is recognizable to the relevant audience. Depending on the audience, any element of societal knowledge may or may not
be useful as cultural capital. The NLSF focused on the audience and setting of
elite colleges, realizing that parents often take action to impart elite cultural
capital to their children to improve their chances of admission and academic
success. It is not that non-elite cultural capital is in any way deficient, just that
it is not particularly useful or valued in the rarefied confines of selective

colleges and universities where traditional markers of "high culture" are dominant. Carter (2003) finds in interviews with Black youth that they recognize both "dominant" capital (that appreciated by elite White institutions) and "nondominant" cultural capital (that common to Black social settings).

One way that parents cultivate "dominant" capital is by taking their children to museums, science centers, plays, and concerts (DiMaggio 1982; Bourdieu 1986; Farkas 1996; Massey et al. 2003). Indeed, Kaufman and Gabler (2004) find that parental museum-going is positively associated with elite college attendance, and Dumais (2002:53) concludes that it "is the parents who hold the key to children's cultural participation by paying for lessons, [and] providing transportation to and from classes." The second column of table 5.2 summarizes intragroup differences with respect to an index of parental cultivation of cultural capital adapted from Massey et al. (2003). At ages six, thirteen, and eighteen, the NLSF baseline survey asked respondents how often parents took them to a museum, plays, concerts, and traveling abroad. At ages six and thirteen, respondents were also asked how often they were taken to a science center and at age six about how often they were brought to a zoo or aquarium. The frequencies were rated on a 0 to 4 scale and when combined yielded an index with both a theoretical and actual range of 0 to 32 and a Cronbach's alpha of 0.890.

According to this index, the parents of mixed-race respondents are much more involved in the cultivation of cultural capital (11.8) than the parents of monoracial respondents (9.8), as are the parents of light-skinned respondents (11.5) relative to the parents of medium- or dark-skinned respondents (9.9 and 9.4, respectively). Likewise, with respective indexes of 10.5 and 10.1, the parents of multigenerational-native and second-generation immigrant Black children are more involved in cultural capital cultivation than the parents of their first-generation-immigrant counterparts (7.8).

As one might expect, parental involvement in the cultivation of children's cultural capital increases steadily with education, with the index rising from 7.9 among parents with no college degree to 10.1 among those with a college degree to 11.8 among those with an advanced degree. Parental involvement is also greater among parents of children who grew up in predominantly White schools and neighborhoods (11.3) or who lived in a minority neighborhood but attended a White school (10.9) compared with parents of those who grew up in minority or mixed settings (8.7 and 9.7, respectively). As with human capital cultivation, Black parenting is gendered with regard to cultural capital formation. Women in our sample report that their parents spent more time introducing them to mainstream cultural capital compared to men, with respective index values of 11.0 and 8.6. Whereas Black girls are more typically socialized to integrate and be independent from an early age, Black boys are more likely to be socialized to stay out of trouble and not confirm negative racial stereotypes about Black violence and criminality than Black girls (Ladner 1971; Staples 1981; McAdoo 1988; Taylor et al. 1990; Hill 2001, 2005).

Social capital refers to productive value that people derive from social ties to others—interpersonal connections and organizational links that facilitate mobility and success within social structures (Granovetter 1973; Bourdieu 1986; Coleman 1988; Stanton-Salazar 1997). According to Portes (1998:6), social capital is "the ability of actors to secure benefits by virtue of membership in social networks or other social structures." Parental involvement in the social lives of children and their interpersonal relationships is central to the cultivation of social capital among young people (Bourdieu 1986; Lareau 2003; Roksa and Potter 2011). To the extent that poor and working-class youth lack ties to college-bound friends or do not have access to well-informed adult mentors and counselors, their educational aspirations and attainments may suffer relative to their middle- and upper-class peers (Neckerman, Carter, and Lee 1999; Carter 2005; Yosso 2005).

Social capital extracted from interpersonal ties may be positive or negative, of course, and research suggests that networks based in settings characterized by concentrated disadvantage are less likely to connect people to opportunities and resources in the wider society and are more susceptible to dangers and risks (see Massey and Denton 1993; Sampson 2012). Recent empirical works reveal that residential segregation is negatively correlated with social capital acquisition. Low-income Black people who remain in poor, concentrated minority neighborhoods often remain "stuck in place" (Sharkey 2013), such that intergenerational poverty continually "shapes inequality through a subtle and pervasive structuring of social relationships" that restricts upward mobility (de Souza Briggs 2002:1; see also Sampson 2012; Ulsaner 2012; Chetty et al. 2014; Wichowsky 2019). A lack of access to social capital from an early age depresses children's cognitive development and later educational achievement (Shaw and McKay 1969; Wilson 1987, 1996; Ellwood 1988; Coleman 1988; Jargowsky and Bane 1990; Edin 1991; Sampson 1992; Ainsworth 2002; Fischer and Kmec 2004; Caughy and O'Campo 2006; Bowen et al. 2008; Johnson 2010; Dufur, Parcel, and Troutman 2013).

In addition, adult role models (teachers, coaches, administrators, and nonparental adult mentors) and close relationships with "pro-academic peers"

also play a vital role "in shaping one's pro-academic identity and future educational aspirations" and thus "facilitate adherence to the educational system's
moral order and ideological foundations," especially within low-income, minority communities (Stanton-Salazar 2011:1082; see also Kaplan 2010; Harper
2008). Qualitative research on the college choices of Black immigrants reveals
that college-going for this group is rooted in parental social and cultural capital, which instills "college expectations" early on (Griffin et al. 2012).

Among Black Caribbean youth, for example, ethnic attachment acts as a
form of social capital to promote achievement and college-going, with coethnic parents and teachers collaborating within networks to place children in
higher quality schools and neighborhoods away from poor minority areas
(Butterfield 2004). Concerns about violence and low educational standards
appear to prompt Black immigrant families to work together, preferentially
seeking out Catholic high schools and top-performing charter and magnet
schools (Butterfield 2004:297–298). Of course, parents cannot completely
control the social lives of their children (see Rich 1998). Nevertheless, parental
oversight of their children's social behavior is a crucial aspect of contemporary
child-rearing strategies.

The third column of table 5.2 presents results for the index of parental cultivation of social capital, again borrowed from Massey et al. (2003) and derived from items of the baseline NLSF survey. We asked respondents how
often their parents talked to their friends at age thirteen and as seniors in high
school and how much they agreed that their mother and father knew their high
school friends. The numerical ratings were added together across items to create an index of social capital cultivation that theoretically ranged from 0 to 18
but in practice ranged from 0 to 16 with Cronbach's alpha of 0.744. Contrary
to what one might expect from Lareau's (2003) work, we observe no differences in social capital cultivation by parental education; although we do observe statistically significant differences on the other dimensions of Black diversity, in absolute terms, they are not very large.

Whereas the parents of mixed-race respondents evinced a social capital
cultivation index of 11.2, for example, the parents of monoracial Black respondents displayed an index of 10.4, significantly different but only slightly lower.
In general, the parents of light-skinned Black respondents, multigenerational
natives, women, and respondents from predominantly White schools and
neighborhoods displayed index values around 11, while the parents of young
men with darker skin tones, immigrant origins, and a more segregated upbringing display indexes around 10.

Overall, the results presented in the preceding two tables reflect the reality that concerted cultivation is a "racialized parenting technique" (Manning 2019:14). That is, the ability and desire of parents to enact that ideal type of parenting reflects not only a class status but also one's racial status. Thus, parents who are more highly educated, as the original theory suggests, are more likely to adhere to a strategy of concerted cultivation, but that is too simplistic a summary. Lighter skin and mixed-race respondents are more likely to experience concerted cultivation prior to entering elite higher education compared with darker skinned monoracial students. Multigenerational natives with parents born and raised in the United States (and thus more exposed to American mores of parenting) are also more likely to follow a concerted cultivation strategy. Finally, survey respondents from both genders experienced qualitatively different parenting strategies, thanks to racialized gender stereotypes that are reinforced in students' high schools and communities (Oeur 2018). Overall, scales built around implicitly White versions of "cultural capital" (like our survey instrument) may miss the cultivation of racialized Black cultural capital and cultural socialization techniques about race and racism and how to succeed in White spaces (e.g., Carter 2003; Lacy 2007; Manning 2019).

Diversity in School Experiences

Virtually all children in the United States attend school well into adolescence, with the large majority graduating from high school around the age of eighteen. According to the U.S. National Center for Educational Statistics (2018), all states and the District of Columbia have compulsory education laws that mandate school attendance at least until the age of sixteen, with eleven states requiring school attendance to age seventeen, and another twenty-five mandating attendance until age eighteen. States generally provide free public education through the twelfth grade, although the quality of schooling varies widely between schools and districts. Given very high levels of school segregation by race and class, educational opportunities are quite limited for poor and working-class children, especially those who are Black or Hispanic (Reardon, Fox, and Townsend 2015; Owens. Reardon, and Jencks 2016). In contrast, White children, particularly (but not exclusively) those from affluent families, are more likely to attend high-performing public schools in well-to-do suburbs or good charter or magnet schools in cities, or very exclusive private academies. In fact, White children from low-income families and children from high-income Black families live in districts with identical economic resources (Brownstein 2016; Owens 2020).

The kind of school a child attends and the quality of education it provides naturally play a critical role in determining the likelihood of entering and graduating from a good college or university and subsequent upward mobility. Not surprisingly, the large majority of Black NLSF respondents attended public schools. At age six, around 69 percent attended a public school whereas 19 percent were enrolled at a private religious school and 12 percent attended a private secular school. At age thirteen, the respective figures were 72 percent public, 17 percent private religious, and 11 percent private secular. By the senior year of high school, 70 percent of Black respondents surveyed were in the public sector, with 15 percent each in private religious and secular academies. Overall, some 53 percent of all Black NLSF respondents spent their entire K–12 education in the public sector, while only 15 percent received their schooling entirely in the private sector.

Table 5.3 shows the distribution of Black NLSF respondents between public, private parochial, and private secular high schools along the different dimensions of Black diversity. These tabulations reveal no significant variation in the kind of school attended by racial identification, skin tone, nativity, generation, or gender. Very significant differences are observed, however, by parental education and childhood experience of segregation. The share of respondents attending public schools falls steadily as parental education rises, dropping from 80.9 percent among respondents whose parents never finished college to 68.3 percent among those whose parents held a college degree, and declining even further to 63.9 percent for those whose parents held an advanced degree. Across the same three levels of parental education, the share of respondents attending religious schools rose from 9.9 percent to 16.7 percent to 17.0 percent, and the share going to secular academies rose from 9.2 percent to 15.0 percent to 18.9 percent.

Turning to childhood segregation, we see that among those who grew up in predominantly White neighborhoods and schools, 61.8 percent went to a public high school, with 18.6 percent going to a private religious school and 19.6 percent attending a private secular school. In contrast, 87.5 percent of respondents who grew up in predominantly minority neighborhoods and schools were in public schools, with just 9.7 percent in religious schools and 2.5 percent in secular academies. The figures for respondents who grew up in racially mixed circumstances were quite similar to those of their counterparts from segregated settings, with 82.2 percent in public schools, 9.6 percent in

TABLE 5.3. Type of high school attended by members of different Black subgroups

	Public	Private religious	Private secular
Racial identification			
Monoracial	69.9%	15.2%	14.8%
Mixed race	72.3	12.7	15.1
Nativity and generation			
Multigenerational native	72.4%	13.4%	14.1%
Second-generation immigrant	62.3	19.4	18.3
First-generation immigrant	69.3	17.1	13.6
Region of origin			
USA	72.4%	13.4%	14.1%
Caribbean	62.9	19.6	17.5
Africa	68.5	15.2	16.3
Other	61.4	22.7	15.9
Skin tone			
Light	68.0%	16.0%	16.0%
Medium	69.0	16.4	14.4
Dark	74.7	19.5	14.4
Gender			
Female	70.3%	14.1%	15.5%
Male	70.2	16.3	13.5
Parental education			
No degree	80.9%	9.9%	9.2%***
College degree	68.3	16.7	15.0
Advanced degree	63.9	17.0	18.9
Experience of segregation			
Predominantly White	61.8%	18.6%	19.6%***
Racially mixed	82.2	9.6	8.3
Predominantly minority	87.5	9.7	2.5
Minority neighborhood/White school	18.1	31.3	50.6
N		1,039	

$^+ p < 0.10$; * $p < 0.05$; ** $p < 0.01$; *** $p < 0.001$

private religious schools, and 8.3 percent in private secular schools. Respondents from minority neighborhoods who attended a predominantly White high school apparently did so by shifting from the public to private sector, with 31.3 percent attending a parochial school and 50.6 percent a secular academy, leaving only 18.1 percent in the public sector (likely some kind of magnet school).

Parental decisions about which schools to send their children are obviously constrained by access to economic resources and information. Public schools are technically free, but there are costs to be paid for access to a high-quality public school in the form of the higher rents, steeper home prices, greater insurance costs, and more burdensome taxes that are required to live in the "right" neighborhood or school district. Apart from the financial barriers that all parents face, Black Americans also face discrimination in real estate and lending markets, yielding additional barriers blocking access to good public schools (Owens, Reardon, and Jencks 2016). Parents in poor neighborhoods who send their children to public charter or magnet schools must contend with higher costs of transportation; unless they receive financial aid, they must also bear significant expenses for tuition and fees to send their children to private schools. Black parents seeking to escape poorly performing public schools thus face a stark trade-off between the cost and quality in education.

Ashley, for example, grew up in a predominately Black and West Indian enclave of Brooklyn where the public schools were not, in her words, "on point" and "students didn't necessarily go to class all the time" but did manage to get in "a lot of fights outside of school." Ashley's mother, however, was a nurse with high educational aspirations for her and her brother, and by strategically picking where to live, she managed to send her children to a majority-White public grade school.

> INTERVIEWER: How did you get to go school in [name of school district]?
> ASHLEY: The address thing worked out. My mom planned this out quite well . . . because she wanted us to go to the best school that we could go to.
> INTERVIEWER: The best school and environment?
> ASHLEY: Ours was the best school in the city, but yes.
> INTERVIEWER: And [name of school] was mostly White?
> ASHLEY: And Jewish.
> INTERVIEWER: Mostly White and Jewish. It is upper class, middle class?
> ASHLEY: I think mid to upper. But on my side, it was, you know, West Indian.

Whereas Ashley's mother managed to secure a spot for her in a high-quality public school by moving just inside of a school catchment line, other interviewees from economically disadvantaged families gained access to costly private schools through special programs or scholarships. Interviewees in this category were typically "discovered" by caring teachers and administrators on the lookout for high achievers in city public schools. As we briefly discussed in the preface, Darryl, a self-described "poor kid from the Bronx," ended up attending a selective boarding school in Pennsylvania:

> It's always a funny story that I share with people. I actually was cutting class one day. I got in trouble. The assistant principal said, "Your grade point average is really high. Why [are] you wasting your time?" and she recommended that I join a program to get away from the Bronx.

Darryl's neighborhood was rife with gangs and poverty. His older sister had dropped out of high school, and his mother worked as a nurse's aide while receiving Section 8 benefits for subsidized housing; he nonetheless managed to escape a failing school system.

In contrast, Emily's parents, a Black American father and a Russian Jewish mother, gained access to high-quality schools by paying the price to move into an affluent, predominantly White community. She identified as Black and was one of a very small number of minority students at her school. As she explained, "There's a small Asian and Hispanic minority contingent, very good schools, very good public schools, a very affluent community." When asked to describe the school system, Emily told us that "it was a really good school system, which counts for a ton. . . . It was a good community to grow up in." Like Emily, most of her peers came from stable, two-parent families with professional jobs and substantial financial resources.

By attending high-quality magnet schools, private academies, or public schools in affluent areas, respondents were able to gain access to educational resources that were largely absent from the public schools that served poor, minority neighborhoods. One important resource is access to AP courses and tests, which have become increasingly salient as a stepping-stone for entry into selective institutions of higher education. A high school transcript that includes AP courses signals to admissions officers a level of academic rigor and college readiness that portends academic success (Judson and Hobson 2015). Unfortunately, racially segregated public schools are less likely to have AP programs due to a lack of funding, lower levels of teacher preparation, and limited student demand (Klopfenstein 2004; Zarate and Pachon 2006; Hallet and Venegas 2011).

Black Americans who attend selective colleges and universities are not representative of Black students generally, of course, and around 83 percent of Black NLSF respondents reported taking at least one AP course in high school, with the average number being 2.5. As shown in the first column of table 5.4,

TABLE 5.4. Indicators of academic preparation for college among members of different Black subgroups

	AP courses	AP tests	Course difficulty	GPA	SAT
Racial identification					
Monoracial	2.5	1.3**	4.4	3.6	1,179**
Mixed race	2.6	1.7	4.5	3.6	1,236
Nativity and generation					
Multigenerational native	2.4	1.3***	4.3*	3.5	1,183$^+$
Second-generation immigrant	2.6	1.3	4.6	3.6	1,217
First-generation immigrant	2.7	1.7	4.7	3.6	1,178
Region of origin					
USA	2.4*	1.3*	4.3*	3.5**	1,183$^+$
Caribbean	2.4	1.5	4.6	3.6	1,189
Africa	2.9	1.7	4.6	3.7	1,170
Other	2.8	1.8	4.9	3.5	1,201
Skin tone					
Light	2.6	1.6**	4.5$^+$	3.6	1,232*
Medium	2.4	1.3	4.3	3.6	1,171
Dark	2.4	1.2	4.5	3.5	1,181
Gender					
Female	2.5	1.4$^+$	4.3*	3.6***	1,190
Male	2.4	1.2	4.6	3.5	1,187
Parental education					
No degree	2.1***	0.9***	4.3$^+$	3.5**	1,145***
College degree	2.5	1.3	4.3	3.6	1,181
Advanced degree	2.8	1.7	4.6	3.6	1,226
Experience of segregation					
Predominantly White	2.8***	1.7***	4.6*	3.6**	1,230**
Racially mixed	2.5	1.3	4.3	3.5	1,175
Predominantly minority	2.2	0.8	4.2	3.6	1,220
Minority neighborhood/ White school	2.2	1.5	4.8	3.4	1,133
N			1,039		

$^+$ p < 0.10; * p < 0.05; ** p < 0.01; *** p < 0.001

however, the number of AP courses taken nonetheless varied significantly by parental education, going from 2.1 among children with parents having no college degree to 2.5 among those with college-educated parents and 2.8 among those whose parents held an advanced degree. Segregation also mattered. Whereas respondents from predominantly White schools and neighborhoods took an average of 2.8 AP courses in high school, the figure was 2.5

for respondents from racially mixed environments and 2.2 for those coming from predominantly minority neighborhoods (whether they attended a White school outside the neighborhood). Although we observe no differences in the average number of AP courses taken by nativity or generation, African-immigrant Black students took more AP courses (2.9) than did respondents with roots in the Caribbean (2.4).

AP credit is not awarded simply by taking courses, however, but by the passing of rigorous AP examinations. In the second column of table 5.4, we see that the number of AP tests passed is less than the number of course taken. The number of AP tests passed rose with parental education, going from 0.9 among those respondents whose parents lacked a college degree to 1.3 among those whose parents had a college degree to 1.7 among those whose parents held an advanced degree. In addition, respondents growing up in predominantly White environments passed 1.7 AP tests while those living in minority neighborhoods but attending predominantly White schools passed 1.5; however, those from predominantly minority settings passed only 0.8 tests on average. Respondents from racially mixed schools and neighborhoods passed an average of 1.3 AP tests.

Although we saw no differences in the number of AP courses *taken* by racial identification, skin tone, nativity, generation, or gender, we do observe significant differences in the number of AP tests *passed*. The number passed was significantly greater for mixed-race than monoracial respondents (1.7 versus 1.3) as well as for respondents with light skin tones (1.6) compared to those with medium or dark tones (1.3 and 1.2, respectively). First-generation immigrants also passed 1.7 tests, compared with just 1.3 for multigenerational natives and second-generation immigrants; the number of AP tests passed was greater for African respondents (1.7) and those of "other" origins (1.8) compared to those from the Caribbean (1.5). Finally, women passed 1.4 AP exams compared to 1.2 exams among men, though the difference was only marginally significant ($p < 0.10$).

These differentials are potentially important since educational research indicates that AP courses and credits foster intellectual growth to put bright young people on track to enter elite postsecondary institutions (Bleske-Rechek, Lubinski, and Benbow 2004). Not only is test success perceived as evidence of academic prowess, but it may also yield college credits or exemptions from equivalent college courses, potentially reducing college expenses and the time to graduation (Mattern, Shaw, and Xiong 2009; Chajewski, Mattern, and Shaw 2011). Given the academic and economic benefits of AP courses and exams, it is troubling that nearly one-fifth of Black NLSF respondents (17.1 percent) took no AP course of any kind during high school.

Nonetheless, the large majority of our qualitative interviewees attended high schools where AP courses were indeed available, and they reported taking a range of courses in the humanities, social sciences, physical sciences, life sciences, computer sciences, and foreign languages. Of course, the number, availability, and quality of the courses varied from school to school and district to district. In total, interviewees mentioned nineteen different AP courses taken at their various schools. The greatest number of AP exams passed by any interviewee was nine.

Although our interviewees all recognized the value of AP courses on their college applications, once they actually matriculated and arrived on campus, that value often seemed to dissipate. Harrison, for example, took seven AP exams and received perfect scores on six at the elite preparatory school he attended. He therefore could have received up to seven course credits upon matriculation, but in the end, he decided against it. Although his advisors told him that "I have the option of doing my degree in three years . . . I didn't want to. It was pretty much like I would have [to have] taken harder classes to fulfill requirements because I had AP credit."

Destiny learned this lesson the hard way. At her urban West Coast high school, she earned a 4.7 weighted GPA and described herself as "always under a book." Although she earned perfect scores on the U.S. history and calculus AP exams, she ultimately regretted cashing in her calculus AP credit since this action ended up forcing her to take a more advanced math course to satisfy her course distribution requirement. As she explained, "It just put me in a higher level of math, which is a bad idea because I don't like math. Bad idea. Waste of time." Although she earned a B+ in the course, she felt the material "was really hard" and "way over my head."

Some interviewees decided against taking AP courses in high school because they did not think they would do well in them or felt they were not really necessary for college applications. Tia, who grew up in a predominately Black New Jersey suburb of Philadelphia with non-college-educated parents, explained that her private day school offered an array of AP courses but that she took only AP biology. Despite getting an A in the class, she opted not to take the exam because "I've never done well in those types of classes . . . yeah, so I figured why waste my money paying for the exam." Denise expressed a similar sentiment, telling us that "when you took the AP course, it was simply to get you to take the AP test. I mean, I wasn't interested in that kind of stuff. . . .

I wasn't really concerned about that. And it was so much of a stress." During her four years at boarding school, Denise did not take any honors or AP courses.

On the baseline survey, respondents were also asked to rate the difficulty of the courses they took in high school on a 0 to 10 scale, where 0 meant not at all difficult and 10 meant extremely difficult. On average, they rated math courses as the most difficult (5.6), followed by courses in science (5.0), foreign languages (4.3), history (4.1), English (4.0), and social studies (3.5), with the average course difficulty being 4.4. The third column of table 5.4 presents average difficulty ratings across dimensions of Black diversity to reveal rather small differences among Black subgroups. On average, men said they took harder courses than women (4.6 versus 4.3); first- and second-generation immigrants took harder courses than multigenerational natives (4.7 and 4.6 versus 4.3), especially when the first-generation immigrants were from regions other than Africa or the Caribbean (4.6). As one might expect, respondents with parents holding an advanced degree took harder courses (4.6) than those with parents who had only a college degree or no degree (4.3).

Among all NLSF respondents, high school GPA has been shown to be the strongest single predictor both of college GPA and the likelihood of graduation (Massey and Probasco 2010). As shown in the fourth column of table 5.4, we observe no significant differences on this indicator of college readiness by racial identification, skin tone, nativity, or generation. GPA is greatest among Africans (3.7), slightly lower for Caribbeans (3.6), and slightly lower still among those from "other" regions (3.5). Although significant effects are also found by parental education, segregation, and gender, the differences are not large. The GPA is slightly higher for respondents with parents holding college or advanced degrees (3.6) than for those whose parents had no degree (3.5), and Black women had a slightly higher GPA (3.6) than Black men (3.5). The widest range is observed across categories of segregation, and paradoxically, it is respondents who came of age *either* in predominantly minority or predominantly White settings that displayed the highest GPAs (3.6). In contrast, those who lived in minority neighborhoods but attended predominantly White schools evinced the lowest GPA (3.4) with respondents from racially mixed schools and neighborhoods falling in between these two bookends (3.5).

The final indicator of preparation for college is the average SAT score, shown in the last column of table 5.4. Here, we observe the same pattern that we observed by level of segregation, with the highest scores among respondents from predominantly White and predominantly minority backgrounds

(1230 and 1220) and the lowest score for respondents attending a White school but living in a minority neighborhood (1133). Once again, those from racially mixed circumstances fell in between (1175). There are no differences in SAT scores by gender or region of origin and only small differences by nativity and generation ($p < 0.10$). In terms of racial identification, SAT scores were higher for mixed-race individuals (1236) and those with light skin tones (1232) compared to monoracial Black individuals (1179) and those with medium or dark skin tones (1171 and 1181, respectively).

Among our in-depth interviewees, Black men who attended majority-White private schools told us that a combination of academic and social challenges prevented them from achieving at the highest academic level. In Kareem's case, he arrived at his exclusive Connecticut boarding school having never interacted with Whites in large numbers. He was surprised to see "only fourteen, fifteen Blacks in the entire school" and the obvious wealth of most in the student body intimidated him. His inner-city Brooklyn middle school had not prepared him well for encounters with these sorts of people, causing him to struggle a lot. As Kareem admitted, "I always struggled in school. . . . like, the more advanced that things are getting, the less easy it is for me to just work harder than everyone else."

In addition to these academic pressures, Kareem also worried about the well-being of his mother and younger brother back home. With no father in the household, he felt he "had a lot of social issues" due to family responsibilities assumed at an early age, such as paying the bills and taking care of his brother. When he first got to his prep school, Kareem revealed that initially he was combative, fighting with peers he thought were against him. As he put it, "When I got to high school, I really had to learn how to talk to people. How do I make friends?" Despite these problems, Kareem worked hard and was "always motivated," graduating from his elite boarding school with an A– average.

Like Kareem, Darryl experienced growing pains during his four years at an exclusive prep school. He was the only Black student in his honors and AP classes and often felt marginalized by his race and class status. In addition, he had a bit of scholarly catching up to do when he arrived at his elite boarding school:

It was just like, most of my days in eighth grade I spent playing either Spades or Uno in the back of the class and playing basketball during lunch period and skipping another period to play basketball. . . . But when I got to [boarding school], it turns out I didn't know anything in any vocabulary, not the first thing about grammar. Yeah, I've never written a five-paragraph essay before. . . . So the only thing I was able to do well in was math because math isn't something you get, or you don't. But I started off with like C, C minuses in English.

Darryl believed his grades did not necessarily reflect his abilities because he had to "deal with a lot of circumstances" that his wealthy White peers did not. In the end, he graduated high school with a 3.1 GPA and chose to attend a very elite university because he wanted to make his family proud as the first one to attend college.

In contrast to Kareem and Darryl, interviewees who attended predominantly minority high schools did not perceive high school to be very difficult despite taking advanced courses and earning high grades. For these interviewees, however, exposure to crime, overcrowding, and social disorder and a lack of scholastic resources put them behind peers at college who graduated from majority-White schools. Respondents who attended White schools uniformly described them as "rigorous" and "challenging" and said their experiences had adequately prepared them for success at college. In contrast, interviewees from segregated schools complained about not gaining the requisite "hard skills" in reading, writing, and math.

In addition to gaining access to hard academic skills, interviewees from majority-White contexts told us they also benefited from the acquisition of "soft skills," such as how to speak in public and how to manage their time, abilities they saw as integral to their success in college. For example, Emily described herself as a "successful student" in her predominantly White high school:

> EMILY: By the end of high school, every teacher knew my name, whether I had them or not. I was on the governing board, so the entire school board for our school district knew me. I was very integrated.
> INTERVIEWER: So did you do a lot of activities?
> EMILY: Yeah. I guess I got involved in the "right ones." . . . So meeting people and I think networking has kind of a manipulative connotation, but . . . I don't think that many kids my age were interested in hanging out with the governing board, but I thought they were pretty cool people.

Emily graduated with a 4.2 weighted GPA from her very competitive high school in a posh, racially homogenous Northern California suburb. Both of her parents were physicians, and Emily described her upbringing as affluent. All of her high school friends matriculated at top colleges and universities. Interviewees at well-resourced public and private high schools such as Emily attended also had the opportunity to engage in an abundance of extracurricular activities—athletics, music lessons, and school clubs—that those who attended less-advantaged schools could not enjoy.

Referring to his scholastic preparation at top-performing public magnet school, Blaise stated that the academic environment there "promote[d] individual thought and creativity. . . . It wasn't like, you know, regurgitating or anything like that for the most part." As a result, when he arrived on the campus of his selective university, he "found it to be an easy transition." He had been in magnet programs since pre-K, had taken a full battery of AP and International Baccalaureate courses during his junior and senior years, and was a talented athlete. He also had excellent role models at home: Blaise's parents both had advanced degrees and worked as educators and administrators in the local public school system.

Interviewees from racially mixed high schools were somewhere in between the extremes represented by Kareem and Darryl, on the one hand, and Emily and Blaise, on the other hand. In retrospect, those who attended racially mixed public schools considered their achievements to be mediocre and felt their work ethic was not equal to that of their peers at college. Although Tiffany did feel that her public, racially mixed high school adequately prepared her for college, she attributed her readiness to the advanced curriculum she selected rather than the school itself, telling us, "I think it's because of the classes I took. Because my AP classes—there was a big drop off between the regular classes and the AP or honors classes. . . . If I hadn't taken the AP and honors classes, I wouldn't have been as prepared because we had excellent teachers. . . . Even my AP English class was basically the same as my writing seminar class now."

Richard described a very different experience. Growing up in a working-class Black suburb in New Jersey with his mother and older sister, he took four AP courses in his junior and senior years but did not pass a single AP exam. In his high school, more than half of his classmates, whom he described as "thuggish," dropped out before graduation. He judged the school to be so bad that "if you could afford to take your kid to another school, you did. . . . The year I graduated, I think our school was ranked fiftieth out of fifty-one schools." He went on to say that "I got the grades and everything. . . . I'd go to school during the day, go home, and just hang out, watch TV, play video games or something, and maybe start my homework that day or right before class. And it would still come out all right . . . it was still good enough."

Although Richard graduated with a 4.0 GPA, repeated bomb threats often canceled or delayed school and high dropout rates and high levels of faculty attrition made learning difficult. In addition, guidance counselors provided little assistance or advice, compelling Richard to navigate the college application process alone. His one saving grace was his mother. Despite not having much education herself, she encouraged him to value education and to achieve scholastically. In his words, "The whole time, my mom was getting on me— how you need to do better, you need to do better in the school. My response was always, 'What's better than an A?' I couldn't actually do better in the school." Given his uncompetitive academic formation, Richard struggled after arriving on campus and had to leave his university for a year because of poor performance. At the time we met him, he had changed his major and was hoping to earn a 2.0 GPA for his junior year.

Andrew reported similar experiences. A football standout, he graduated from a predominately Black high school in the rural Midwest. Although he graduated number one in his class with a 3.8 GPA, Andrew was able to take only one honors class because that was all his school offered. He "didn't even know about AP classes until I came to [name of university]. I heard people—IB and AP—I was like, 'What is that?' They were like, 'What are you talking about? You didn't take AP?'" Like Richard, Andrew found his schoolwork in high school to be easy and he rarely prepared for tests. He learned how to "read and study" at a special summer program for college-bound minority youth, which he credits with helping him earn a 3.0 GPA during his freshman year in college.

For her part, Destiny felt she did quite well at her public, racially mixed high school due to her "work ethic" but felt that she didn't acquire the "cultural knowledge" common to her peers at college. Although she worked very hard to get good grades and her mother checked her homework regularly and encouraged her always to do her best, some things simply could not be learned in the classroom. As Tiffany told us, "There are just things I don't know. I don't know if it's a cultural thing that doesn't have to do with high school. For instance, in class right now, [the professor] is talking about refinancing your house and a mortgage. I have no idea what those things are. I don't know if you learn that in school, but people just bring books up all the time that I've never heard of."

Diversity in College Application Strategies

Regardless of the parenting and schooling they experienced while growing up, all of our survey and interview respondents had set their sights on gaining admission to a selective college or university. For some, gaining admission to an elite institution was a key step in a broader strategy of upward socioeconomic mobility; for others, it was simply following their parents' footsteps into college so they could maintain the affluence and social status they experienced as children. This section explores the college application and admission process and how behaviors differ along the different dimensions of Black diversity.

In the literature on academic counseling, "college fit" refers to a good match not only between a particular institutional curriculum and a student's academic abilities but also between a student's personality and the campus social and cultural environment (Dix 2016). In addition to "fit," students and parents must also consider issues of affordability and access to different sources of financial assistance. Decisions about where to apply and attend depend on a variety of criteria that differ from person to person depending on individual traits and familial circumstances.

The baseline NLSF survey queried respondents about twenty-five different factors that could possibly have influenced their decision making in applying to college. Respondents were asked to rate how important each factor was on a 0 to 10 scale, where 0 is extremely unimportant and 10 is extremely important, and we drew on the resulting ratings to develop six separate measures. An index of the importance of school prestige was computed as an average of ratings given to the importance of a school's academic reputation, admissions standards, course availability, social prestige, and success in placing graduates in jobs, graduate programs, and professional schools. The average rating across the seven items was 6.9 with a Cronbach's alpha of 0.762.

The index of the importance of financial concerns was created by averaging two items that asked respondents how important the cost of college and the availability of financial assistance were in deciding where to apply, yielding an average score of 6.6 and a Cronbach's alpha of 0.701. An index of the importance of racial diversity was likewise derived by averaging two items, one asking about the relative importance of having "enough" Black students present on campus to feel "comfortable" and another asking about the importance of having "enough Black [people]" in the off-campus community. Combining the two measures yielded a mean value of 5.0 and a Cronbach's alpha of 0.762.

An index of the importance of athletics averaged three items asking how important the availability of athletic scholarships, sports opportunities, and the school's athletic reputation were in college decision making, which generated a high Cronbach's alpha of 0.822 but a low mean value of 2.1. The importance of academic support and the importance of social life were measured using single items rather than composite indexes, yielding mean values of 6.6 and 5.7, respectively.

Looking over the foregoing measures, we see that in deciding where to apply to college, the most important factor was institutional prestige, followed by the availability of academic support, cost considerations and access to financial support, social life, racial diversity, and last, athletics. The fact that institutional prestige ranks first is hardly surprising given the multiple advantages associated with obtaining a degree from a prestigious academic institution (Bowen and Bok 1998; Thomas 2000; Massey et al. 2003; Espeland and Sauder 2007). Whatever the origins of our respondents, they shared a common desire either to achieve upward mobility or replicate their parents' elevated class standing, and matriculation at an elite college or university was universally seen as crucial to fulfilling those desires.

Nonetheless, as shown in table 5.5, we observe significant differences in the relative importance of the various factors along the various dimensions of Black diversity. The prestige of the college or university, for example, was more important to monoracial respondents (with importance index of 7.0) than to mixed-race students (6.6). Prestige was also more important to respondents with medium or dark skin tones (with respective indexes of 7.1 and 7.0) compared to those with light skin tones (6.6). It was also more important to women (7.1) than men (6.8). Thus, it would seem that institutional prestige figures more prominently in the decision making of those respondents most subject to the disadvantages of race (being monoracial with a dark skin tone) and gender (women). Although differences by racial identification, gender, and skin tone were statistically significant, however, they were not large and virtually all respondents rated institutional prestige as the most important factor in their decision making, something that also came through in our in-depth interviews. As Thomas put it, "My degree will mean something [after graduation]," while another told us he looked forward to "the reputation, the opportunities afterwards."

The importance of academic support at prospective colleges and universities varied significantly across several dimensions of diversity. Among monoracial Black respondents, the average importance index for academic support

TABLE 5.5. Relative importance of factors influencing choice of college or university by members of different Black subgroups

	School prestige	Academic support	Financial support	Social life	Racial diversity	Athletics
Racial identification						
Monoracial	7.0**	6.7***	6.7	5.7	5.2***	2.1
Mixed race	6.6	5.8	6.3	5.8	3.6	2.2
Nativity and generation						
Multigenerational native	6.9	6.6	6.6	5.7	5.0	2.2*
Second-generation immigrant	7.0	6.6	6.8	5.6	4.7	1.9
First-generation immigrant	7.1	6.5	6.7	5.8	4.9	1.7
Region of origin						
USA	6.9	6.6	6.6**	5.7+	5.0	2.2**
Caribbean	7.1	6.6	7.5	6.1	4.7	1.5
Africa	7.2	6.6	6.1	5.5	5.2	2.0
Other	6.6	6.4	5.6	5.2	4.4	2.2
Skin tone						
Light	6.6*	5.9***	6.4	5.7	4.5**	2.2
Medium	7.1	6.6	6.7	5.7	5.1	2.0
Dark	7.0	7.1	6.7	5.9	5.2	2.2
Gender						
Female	7.1*	6.7*	6.7	5.7	5.2***	1.6***
Male	6.8	6.3	6.4	5.8	4.5	3.1
Parental education						
No degree	6.9	6.9**	7.4***	5.5+	4.8	1.9
College degree	7.0	6.8	6.8	5.7	5.0	2.2
Advanced degree	6.8	6.2	5.9	5.9	5.1	2.1
Experience of segregation						
Predominantly White	6.8	5.9***	5.8***	5.9***	4.6**	2.2
Racially mixed	6.9	6.7	6.8	5.6	5.1	2.1
Predominantly minority	7.0	7.1	7.4	5.3	5.0	2.0
Minority neighborhood/ White school	6.9	6.9	7.4	6.0	5.9	2.0
N			1,039			

+ p < 0.10; * p < 0.05; ** p < 0.01; *** p < 0.001

stood at 6.7 compared to a value of 5.8 for their mixed-race counterparts. The index likewise stood at 7.1 for dark-skinned respondents compared with 6.6 for those with medium tones and 5.9 for those with light skin tones. Likewise, respondents whose parents did not graduate from college rated academic support as more important (6.9) than those with college-educated parents (6.8) and those whose parents held advanced degrees (6.2). With respect to segregation, academic support was most important for respondents from pre-dominantly minority neighborhoods and schools (7.1), followed in descending order by those who grew up in minority neighborhoods but attended White schools (6.9), those who grew up in racially mixed contexts (6.7) and those from predominantly White schools and neighborhoods (5.9). Women also rated academic support as more important (6.7) in thinking about where to apply than men (6.3).

We observe the same differentials with respect to the importance of financial support, though the differences by racial identification, skin tone, and gender are not statistically significant (but are in the expected direction). Financial support loomed very large in the decision making of respondents whose parents lacked a college degree (7.4) relative to those with college-educated parents (6.8) and those whose parents held advanced degrees (5.9). Financial support was also more important for respondents from predominantly minority schools and neighborhoods (7.4) and for those who grew up in minority neighborhoods but attended White schools (also 7.4) compared to those who grew up in predominantly White contexts (5.8) or racially mixed circumstances (6.8). Financial concerns were especially salient among immigrants from the Caribbean (7.5) and native-origin students (6.6), compared with immigrants from Africa (6.1) or other regions (5.6).

Again, it is hardly surprising that academic and financial support are more central to the decision making of those respondents who are most susceptible to the disadvantages associated with race (i.e., dark-skinned, monoracial students from segregated backgrounds), gender (women), and class (first-generation college students), a finding that was also evident in our in-depth interviews. Julie, for instance, came from a family of modest means and told us that "I could apply wherever I wanted, [but] where I went depended on money. . . . Yeah, definitely prestige, but actually going to [name of school], I was gonna have to pay less than going to any other school. . . . It wasn't like I had to weigh prestige against money." Ultimately, it was the university's no-loan policy that readily convinced her "to sign on the dotted line. . . . It was one more push toward [name of school] because they had a no-loan policy, which is just lovely because I can graduate without debt."

Compared with institutional prestige, academic support, and financial support, we see few differences between Black subgroups in the importance of social life. The most significant differences are observed by experience of segregation. Both interviewees and survey respondents from predominantly White backgrounds and those who lived in minority neighborhoods but attended predominantly White schools rated social life as more important (5.9 and 6.0, respectively) than respondents from racially mixed or racially segregated backgrounds (5.6 and 5.3, respectively). Small differences ($p < 0.10$) are observed by region of origin and parental education, with social life being more important for Caribbean immigrants (6.1) and multigenerational natives (5.7) than for immigrants from Africa or other regions (5.5 and 5.2, respectively). Social life was also more important for respondents whose parents had an advanced degree (5.9) than those with parents with just a college degree or no degree (5.7 and 5.5, respectively).

The presence of other Black students on campus and in the community was *much* more important ($p < 0.001$) for monoracial respondents (5.2) than those who identified as mixed race (3.6). A Black presence on campus was likewise more salient for dark-skinned (5.2) and medium-skinned respondents (5.1) than among those with light skin tones (4.5). Campus racial diversity was also more important for women (5.2) than men (4.5), possibly reflecting what multiple Black women interviewees reported: negative experiences with dating in high school because of the relative paucity of Black men in their honors and AP courses. As we explore later in chapter 6, the well-documented dearth of Black men at selective postsecondary institutions still renders dating problematic for Black women (see Massey et al. 2003; Charles et al. 2009; Torres and Massey 2012). With respect to segregation, the presence of a critical mass of Black students was most important to respondents who lived in segregated minority neighborhoods but attended a predominantly White high school (5.9), followed successively by those from racially mixed contexts (5.1), segregated minority contexts (5.0), and predominantly White contexts (4.6).

The fact that racial diversity was most important among survey and interview respondents who came from predominantly Black neighborhoods but attended White schools suggests that they were looking for a way to resolve the contradiction between their prior residential and educational experiences—specifically by choosing a top college that also had a visible Black student population (albeit only around 6 percent of the total student population). Such was the case for Madison, who attended an elite private girl's school in Manhattan but lived in a working-class West Indian neighborhood in Brooklyn. She was explicitly looking forward to interacting with a larger Black student body in college and was delighted to be accepted into an elite institution that fulfilled this criterion. She told us that her trip to campus on visiting day gave her a "gut feeling" that she was making the right choice, and indeed, she went on to say that she "loved" her freshman year and was happy to have made several good same-race friends.

Although students who grew up in predominantly White schools and neighborhoods rated the presence of other Black students as least important relative to other Black subgroups, our interviewee Olivia was an exception, perhaps because unlike most interviewees with this experience, she was neither mixed race nor light skinned. Of Haitian and Nigerian ancestry, she grew up in an affluent White community on Long Island and attended a highly rated public school. She readily identified as "Black" and indeed had a dark skin tone, and although she admitted that institutional prestige was "the biggest factor" in her final selection, she was strongly influenced by the university's Black student population and by its location in a city with a large Black community. She told us she was tired of "being the only Black girl in my classes" and the "only Black girl on my sports team." Like Madison, when she visited the campus, Olivia found the Black students to be very welcoming, and by her senior year, she had held leadership positions in the African, Haitian, and Caribbean clubs, taking full advantage of Black affinity groups relevant to her origins.

More typical of interviewees who grew up in predominantly White circumstances was Blaise, a light-skinned mixed-race interviewee who fully embraced both his White and Black ancestries, asserting that "I'm no more 'Black' than I am anything else." Growing up in an upper-middle-class suburb, he had few Black or other non-White peers. He was recruited by several top football programs and spent his college recruitment visits with athletic team members rather than students at large. Upon matriculating, he pledged a predominantly White fraternity, and his friendship circle mostly included Whites and Asians. Blaise did not regularly socialize with other Black students on campus because he found their communities to be "closed."

Likewise, Bob, a sophomore of Ghanaian ancestry, grew up in London, New Jersey, and rural Michigan. His father worked as an executive for a telecommunications company and his mother was a public school teacher. His family moved to the United States when Bob was in elementary school. Bob applied to his university under its early admission program, attracted by its high academic reputation and focus on undergraduate education. At his prestigious midwestern boarding school, he was active in sports and had a diverse set of friends. Neither racial diversity nor the presence of other Black people on campus factored into his final decision, and he steered away from college activities that were solely Black-oriented, telling us that,

I was involved in Black student groups in high school, but what I found is that it took away from my experience as a whole when I was in high school. Meeting other people and finding if you have points of view that fall outside the group, finding those points of view to be welcomed or marginalized . . . I didn't just come to [name of school] to be with Black students . . . no more than I came . . . to be just with Hispanics or Asians or Jews.

Bob was a member of an elite off-campus club known for its wealthy members and exclusive events. He was one of just a handful of Black members of the club and spent his weekends there socializing with his five closest friends, three of whom were White and two of whom were Black immigrants like he was. Bob said he stayed on the "outskirts" of the Black student community and told us that the "socioeconomic separation" between Black and White students explained the social distance between the two groups on campus.

Darryl could have gone to an Ivy League school with a sizable Black student body in a city with a large Black population, but he instead chose an Ivy League school in a smaller town that had fewer Black residents on and off campus. He explained that being around too many Black peers would put him "in a situation where I know I'm gonna have a lot of fun and neglect school." Given the cultural capital he acquired in boarding school, he thought he could adjust to the university's elite White culture, but during his junior year, Darryl struggled to maintain his GPA in what he saw as an "even more pretentious environment." His core college friends were exclusively Black individuals he described as "Black lower-class people" from "a historically lower-class family or their family just made it."

Tia also left her Black neighborhood to attend a top preparatory school, where she "was the only Black person in some of my classes, one in five in my grade. And I just felt like nobody could sympathize with me, nobody could understand me as a Black person, nobody could understand me as a not poor but lower middle-class person, you know." Like Darryl, she attended college at an elite White institution and formed a peer network that was exclusively Black and was involved in multiple Black-oriented activities, though unlike Darryl, she did not struggle academically.

As already noted, athletics were least important in the minds of Black NLSF respondents in thinking about where to apply for college. Nonetheless, we do observe significant differences by nativity, generation, and regional origin. Multigenerational natives viewed athletics as more important (2.2) than first-generation immigrants (1.7) or those in the second generation (1.9); immigrants from "other" regions rated athletics to be more important (2.2) than those from either Africa (2.0) or the Caribbean (1.5). The starkest difference, however, was between men and women, with an importance index of 3.1 for men compared with a value of only 1.6 for women. In fact, Barry, one of our interviewees placed athletics before all other considerations in deciding where to go, telling us that he chose his school because of "football, prestige, region, and future connections," in that order.

Beyond individual priorities and preferences in selecting a college or university, recruitment efforts by Black admissions personnel and faculty often tipped the scale in students' final decisions, especially for Black students who grew up in segregated circumstances. For example, Eugene, a monoracial, working-class interviewee from a Black community near Birmingham, Alabama, established a close relationship with a Black admissions officer who ultimately inspired him to matriculate.

> INTERVIEWER: And the primary factors that actually convinced you to enroll at [name of school], like if you were gonna list the three most important factors that contribute to your decision to enroll here, what would they be?
> EUGENE: The relationship that I developed with my admissions officer.
> INTERVIEWER: Was this a White admissions officer?
> EUGENE: No, she was Black. It was so interesting that we both were Black.... The admissions, the regional officer for Alabama was Black. We developed a really, really good relationship.... I actually visited, and I actually liked [name of institution]. It seemed like a pretty cool place.... I think if I just came here just off of the top of my head, just to visit here, I don't think I would have come.

Miranda, for her part, was inspired by a teacher at her top-rated public high school to apply to a very elite Ivy League school, despite initial reservations.

> INTERVIEWER: So what were your primary factors in deciding to apply here?
> MIRANDA: Well, actually, like I had a teacher . . . and she lived in [name of place] for twenty-five years and like she taught at [the local] high school and like she loved it and told me [it] would be great for me. And I just remember saying like, "Excuse you, um . . . I'm not going to [name of school]," and I was just like, "They're super pretentious, they're all [] uppity." I was like, "I am not going to an Ivy League

school." . . . I just really did not have the best perception of [name of school]. Um she kept talking to me. . . . I started looking at [name of school] more and I was like, "Fine, you're right," and I applied early. It was so crazy I went from "no, I'm not applying" to applying early.

The baseline survey not only asked respondents about which factors were important in making decisions about where to apply, it also queried about their application strategies and experiences, asking how many applications they filed, how many acceptances they received, and whether they enrolled in their top choice. We then calculated whether that choice is among the ten most selective schools in the NLSF sample. The average Black survey respondent reported submitting 5.7 applications and receiving 4.6 acceptances for an acceptance rate of nearly 88 percent. Some 59 percent were able to enroll in their top choice, with 37 percent entering an Ivy League or other elite private university, 16 percent going to a liberal arts college, and 30 percent entering a flagship state university.

However, as shown in table 5.6, we once again observe significant differences in application behavior and outcomes across the different dimensions of Black diversity. For example, the number of applications submitted differed by nativity and generation, with the average number being greatest among second-generation immigrants (6.8), followed by first-generation immigrants (6.1), and last, by multigenerational natives (5.4).

Due to the larger number of applications they submitted, the same subgroups also received more acceptances, but the rate of acceptance did not differ by nativity or generation; it did, however, vary by region of origin. This time, Caribbean-immigrant Black applicants received more acceptances (5.3) than African and other immigrants (4.9). Black NLSF respondents also exhibit significant differences in college acceptance rates by skin tone, with the rate being 90.5 percent for light-skinned Black respondents compared to 83.9 percent for dark-skinned Black respondents, and 88.2 percent for Black respondents with medium skin tones. These differences, however, were only marginally significant ($p < 0.10$).

The degree to which respondents gained entry to their top choice also varied by skin color. Nearly two-thirds (65.3 percent) of light-skinned respondents were able to enroll in their top choice, compared to 58.1 percent of medium-skinned Black respondents and just over half (53.5 percent) of respondents with dark skin tones. Consistent with this progression, 64 percent of all mixed-race respondents got into their top pick, compared with 58 percent of monoracial Black respondents. Enrollment at a top-choice school also

TABLE 5.6. Indicators of the application strategy and admissions success for members of different Black subgroups

	Number of applications	Number of acceptances	Acceptance rate	First choice	Ten most selective
Racial identification					
Monoracial	5.7	4.7	87.0%	57.6%	32.2%
Mixed race	5.4	4.5	91.0	63.9	34.9
Nativity and generation					
Multigenerational native	5.4**	4.5**	88.2%	59.7%	28.8%***
Second-generation immigrant	6.8	5.5	88.2	57.2	48.2
First-generation immigrant	6.1	4.9	84.7	53.1	31.8
Region of origin					
USA	5.4**	4.5**	88.2%	59.7%**	28.8%***
Caribbean	6.4	5.3	85.0	48.3	44.1
Africa	6.5	4.9	83.4	57.6	50.0
Other	5.8	4.9	93.2	77.1	25.0
Skin tone					
Light	5.4	4.6	90.5%+	65.3%*	34.4%
Medium	5.7	4.7	88.2	58.1	30.8
Dark	5.9	4.6	83.9	53.5	34.3
Gender					
Female	5.8	4.8+	87.0%	56.7%	30.6+
Male	5.4	4.4	88.6	62.3	36.4
Parental education					
No degree	5.8	4.7	87.3%	61.9%	25.4%***
College degree	5.3	4.4	89.0	59.0	28.2
Advanced degree	5.8	4.8	86.8	55.8	41.9
Experience of segregation					
Predominantly White	5.6	4.5	86.3%	57.4%	39.2***
Racially mixed	5.5	4.6	89.5	58.2	28.2
Predominantly minority	5.8	4.6	88.6	58.7	20.6
Minority neighborhood/ White school	6.3	5.1	83.5	59.9	53.9
N			1,039		

+ p < 0.10; * p < 0.05; ** p < 0.01; *** p < 0.001

varied among foreign-born respondents, from a remarkable 77 percent for "other" immigrants, 58 percent for African immigrants, to 48.3 percent for those of Caribbean origin.

Turning to institutional selectivity, we see that the share enrolling in a top-ten school was greater for mixed-race respondents (34.9 percent) than monoracial respondents (32.2 percent). Top-ten matriculation was also higher for second-generation immigrants (48.2 percent) than their first-generation immigrant counterparts (31.8 percent) and multigenerational native Black respondents (28.8 percent). Fully half of African-origin Black immigrants and more than two-fifths of Caribbean immigrants (44.1 percent) attended top-ten NLSF institutions, compared to just 25.0 percent of "other" Black immigrants. As one would expect, access to the ten most selective NLSF institutions rose with parental education. One-quarter of respondents (25.4 percent) with non-college-educated parents attend the ten most-selective NLSF schools, compared to 28.2 percent of Black respondents with college-educated parents and 41.9 percent of respondents whose parents hold an advanced degree.

With respect to respondents' childhood experience of segregation, enrollment in one of the most selective institutions was greatest for Black respondents who grew up in minority neighborhoods but attended White schools (53.9 percent) followed by those who came from predominantly White schools and neighborhoods (39.2 percent) and those from racially mixed backgrounds (28.2 percent); Black respondents from segregated minority neighborhoods and schools were least likely to attend one of the ten most-selective NLSF institutions, at just 21 percent. Although the difference is only modestly significant ($p < 0.10$), Black men appear to have greater access to the most selective institutions than Black women, with 36.4 percent enrolling in a top-ten school compared to 30.6 percent of Black women.

Among our interviewees, those with immigrant parents reported the greatest pressure to enroll at a top-ten institution, especially when the parents were themselves well educated. The physician parents of Albert, a second-generation West Indian who got into several Ivy League schools, actually attempted to block his enrollment at an Ivy institution they considered to be less prestigious, believing that only the most prestigious campus would guarantee him a spot at a top medical school and a superior residency. As he explained to us, "My family strongly wanted me to go to [other more prestigious Ivy League schools], but I had to fight to come to [name of other Ivy League school]. My parents encountered a lot of bias with foreign medical degrees when they came to America and they wanted to put me on the [right track]." In the end, Albert "screamed and shouted and argued with my parents for about three weeks" because he knew [his preferred school] was a better fit for him. He told us that a four-day recruitment visit the university arranged for prospective Black pre-med students sealed the deal in his mind. At the time of the interview, Albert was living in a Black-themed college house, had a cumulative GPA of 3.7, and was in the midst of applying to medical school.

Nia's West Indian parents were also very involved in her college search and wanted her to attend a top school with a strong premed program. Although both her parents were professors at a historically Black college and university (HBCU), they were strongly against Nia attending such a school, with her father actually compiling a list of universities that met his standards:

> My parents kind of, not really, drilled that into my mind, but kind of planted the seed that a name was kind of important. . . . And I felt pressure because I didn't want to disappoint them. Not exactly pressure, but I definitely didn't want to disappoint them.

After Nia got into a good Ivy League school with a strong premed program, her mother lobbied the financial aid office for a better aid package, and after receiving more grant money, Nia's parents told her that she *had* to enroll at that institution.

Madison likewise felt pressure to enter the Ivy League from parents who emphasized the primacy of education and who "pushed" her to succeed. She explained that "my cousin, around my age, he's going to the University of the West Indies, which is very prestigious in the Caribbean. Yeah, there's definitely like, 'Well, you have to continue the line." Kara, a second-generation Nigerian, told us that her father simply *assumed* that she would follow in her older sister's footsteps and attend the same Ivy League school. Kara explained that "my dad's all about bragging. . . . That's why he wants us all to be doctors and stuff like that. . . . 'Hey, I've got two girls at [name of school].'"

Kara's parents both had college degrees from public universities in Texas and had worked hard to move up from "working class" to "lower middle class." A strategic series of residential moves and employment changes brought the family into the Houston suburbs where Kara spent her high school years. Her mother worked as a public school teacher nearby, and her father was a lab technician for a major oil company. Kara ultimately chose an Ivy League school over a top research university in Texas because it gave her the most financial aid, but her parents put more stock in the institution's prestige.

Although first- and second-generation Black children are often pressured to make their parents proud, some native-born parents at times espoused a similar ethos, though it was less likely to be articulated in terms of familial aspirations or cultural pride. Jessica, a self-identified mixed-race woman, grew up in a single-parent, working-class household with her twin brother and

White mother. Although the family struggled to make ends meet, Jessica's mother had graduated from college and was from an affluent background and had very high educational aspirations for her children:

> I mean, my mom definitely pushed us. I mean, it wasn't an overt push—it was kinda like, "Well, if you're not prepared, maybe you should just go to community college. Maybe you should work a year. Think about what you really want to do." And my brother and I were like, "Are you crazy?" But I mean, she definitely wanted us to go. She went to Berkeley, *so she kind of had that knowledge* [emphasis added].

Working-class and lower-middle-class interviewees, especially those from segregated schools and neighborhoods, typically did not have the same access to human, social, and cultural capital as Jessica. Their parents knew little about the college application process, often having never attended college themselves. Darryl's mother, for example, did not participate in the application process at all, and he admits that he felt a bit adrift without familial support. As he told us, "I had no counselors in my family. I had no sort of guidance. I followed my passion the entire time, whether it was choosing my favorite colors for [name of boarding school] or following some sort of namesake for college." Like Darryl, Andrew grew up poor and had limited guidance from either his family or his high school counselors, stating that "I really wanted to make my mom proud, and my dad, especially my dad. . . . Because my dad had already told [my brother and me], 'Don't do what I did—go to college, go to college.'" Andrew was very excited, therefore, to send home his first semester grades from his Ivy League university (all A's and B's) to validate his achievements.

In some instances, non-college-educated, working-class and lower-income parents actively discouraged their children from attending top schools. In addition to a basic lack of knowledge about colleges and college applications, concerns about cost and a desire to have children close to home were reasons interviewees cited for their parents' reluctance to see them move far away. Jeff, a working-class, multigenerational native from Columbus, Ohio, struggled to convince his mother to let him attend an out-of-state institution. At the time of his interview, Jeff's mother was taking classes toward a four-year degree while working full time as a bank clerk, and his dad was a corrections officer who lived apart from the family. Jeff's mother allowed him to apply to only a few local colleges so as to keep the application costs down. She reluctantly agreed to let him apply to one Ivy League institution after a friend told her about the elite cachet of the university in which he ultimately enrolled.

The oldest of nine children, Tiffany grew up with her mother and siblings in the Bronx where her father, a janitor and self-employed electrician, was not a regular presence. Tiffany's dream was to leave her strict religious household to escape having to watch over her younger siblings. She explained,

> It was a very, very strict family. My parents were afraid that I would have outside influences. . . . I mean, my college application process was completely independent of my parents. They had no involvement in it. Like, neither of my parents went to college. Neither of them knew much about the college application process. I'm the oldest . . . so [my mom] actually refused to fill out some of my financial aid forms—actually, all of them. . . . It took other people being really impressed for her to be like, "Wow," and take pride in it.

In the end, Tiffany achieved her dream, receiving a competitive external scholarship for promising students from low-income backgrounds to attend an Ivy League school, which she said was especially helpful in assisting her with the financial aid forms.

Conclusion

This chapter clearly reveals that Black students attending elite postsecondary institutions are not a monolith when it comes to their degree of academic preparation, the strategies they pursue in applying to college, the factors that influence their choice of institutions, and their success in gaining entry into top choices and top schools. Although all the young Black adults in our study share African ancestry and would all be classified as "Black" given America's historical conceptualization of race, we nonetheless observe a significant differentiation of the pathways to college. This differentiation across the dimensions of Black diversity is well captured in the multivariate models presented in appendix A and described in narrative form here (see appendix tables A5.1–A5.5).

With respect to upbringing, we find that Black students who grew up under conditions of class and racial privilege generally experienced a style of child-rearing labeled concerted cultivation, in which parents are intimately involved in supervising their children's education and enrichment (Lareau 2003). However, we also find evidence that such parenting strategies are racialized and that standard measures of concerted cultivation may not accurately reflect the logics and options for Black parenting (e.g., Carter 2003; Choo and Ferree 2010;

Manning 2019). For example, mixed-race students experienced more parental cultivation of cultural capital growing up than their monoracial counterparts. Likewise, the degree of parental involvement in the cultivation of human and cultural capital rose sharply as parental education increased (see appendix tables A5.1–A5.2). In contrast, students who came of age in disordered and violent settings experienced stricter discipline and significantly lower levels of parental involvement in the formation of cultural and social capital. Immigrant origins were similarly associated with less parental encouragement of intellectual independence and less involvement in the cultivation of both human and cultural capital (appendix tables A5.1–A5.2). Black child-rearing patterns are also distinctly gendered, with boys receiving much less parental support for the acquisition of human and cultural capital than girls (Dow 2019).

We also observe differences among Black students with respect to the kinds of high schools they attended and, hence, access to educational resources and the degree of academic preparation for college. We saw in chapter 3 that mixed-race students were far more likely than monoracial Black students to live in White neighborhoods and attend predominantly White schools. Our multivariate models indicate that after taking this fact into account, students of highly educated parents (those holding an advanced degree) are more likely to attend private secular schools as opposed to a public or parochial school (appendix table A5.3). In these more privileged sectors of American secondary education, students earn more AP credits and leave high school with significantly higher SAT scores (appendix table A5.4). Black students of African-immigrant origin earned the highest grades of all, reflecting the great educational selectivity of African immigration to the United States (see Hamilton 2019).

In keeping with the lower levels of parental support they received for the acquisition of human and cultural capital, Black men experienced greater difficulty in their high school coursework than Black women, and they also earned lower grades (appendix table A5.4). Aside from the direct effects of segregation influencing the kind and quality of the school attended, confinement in racially segregated schools and neighborhoods entails greater exposure to social disorder and violence in daily life, which has powerful independent effects. Other things being equal, exposure to greater disorder and violence is negatively associated with the receipt of fewer AP credits, lower GPAs, and worse SAT scores. Compared to other Black students surveyed in the NLSF, those opting to attend Howard University (as we noted in chapter 4, the one HBCU in the sample) were less likely to have gone to a private school, either parochial or secular; in high school, they also received fewer AP credits, earned lower grades, and scored lower on the SAT, despite perceiving coursework to be easier. However, controlling for attendance at this HBCU had little effect on other findings derived from the models (appendix table A5.4).

Given the differentiation of Black educational trajectories by gender, racial identification, nativity, region, class, and segregation, it is not surprising to find significant differences among Black students in their college application strategies (see appendix table A5.5). One way to increase the odds of gaining entry to an elite school is to submit more applications for admission, a strategy assiduously followed by first- and second-generation immigrants both from Africa and the Caribbean, underscoring the centrality of an elite education in the social mobility strategies pursued by immigrant families.

Aside from the number of applications, we found considerable diversity in the institutional attributes that students considered in deciding *where* to apply and attend. As one might predict, campus racial and ethnic diversity was much less important in the decision making of mixed-race than monoracial students, and diversity was less important for men as well. Mixed-race students and men also rated school prestige as less important, along with students whose parents held an advanced degree. In contrast, institutional prestige was more important for immigrant students and those with darker skin tones. The availability of academic support services was less important for men, students with highly educated parents, and those who came of age in White schools and neighborhoods, but more important for darker skinned students. Holding constant family socioeconomic status, financial support was most important for Black students of Caribbean origin, whereas social life was more important for students who grew up in White neighborhoods and schools and those who grew up in minority neighborhoods but attended White schools. Here, we note that students attending Howard University sent out fewer applications than others and weighed prestige, social life, and diversity more heavily in their decision-making compared to other students, and were less concerned with academic support.

In sum, we find diverse pathways to college among aspiring young Black professionals, indicated by significant differences with respect to parental child-rearing practices, degree of academic preparation, strategies for applying to college, and the factors seen as most important for decision-making. Attending college not only marks a psychological transition, but it also involves an important shift in social context. It entails leaving old friends, making new ones, developing romantic interests, and managing academic pressures within an entirely new social setting, and in the next chapter, we examine patterns and processes of social interaction on campus. At the institutions in our sample, Black students not only come into contact with more same-race peers of equal education but also with the diverse kaleidoscope of race and ethnicity that increasingly characterizes U.S. college campuses in the twenty-first century.

6

Campus Social Experiences

You kind of tend to hang out with who you are most comfortable with, and I guess people end up being most comfortable with people who are like them . . . from the same background as they are. . . . All my friends are Caribbean; that's important.

ASHLEY, IMMIGRANT FROM JAMAICA

RECENT SOCIOLOGICAL STUDIES have sought to explain how young Black students seeking to move up in the world learn to navigate elite White settings. Empirical studies done at selective postsecondary institutions indicate that Black students succeed in elite academic environments by developing class-specific repertoires consistent with the "cultures of power" they encounter on campus. At the same time, they simultaneously work to develop and maintain strong connections to the campus Black community (Swidler 1986; Delpit 1988; Neckerman, Carter, and Lee 1999; Moore 2008; Martin 2010; Clerge 2014; Jack 2014, 2019). The intragroup diversity that now characterizes Black students at selective institutions encourages them to experiment with a range of different racial and class outlooks (Greer 2013; Charles et al. 2015). Such experimentation not only serves to socialize students into the Black professional class, but it also serves as their entry point into the larger national elite, which continues to be White dominated.

Socializing while Black

Lacy (2004, 2007) contends that among aspiring Black young people today, attending a selective college or university entails a practice that she calls strategic assimilation in which students cultivate the Black community as a locus for socializing and interpersonal exchange even as they navigate historically White social spaces in search of educational attainment. In this chapter, we ask how much the effort to assimilate strategically stems from intra- versus inter-group experiences and the degree to which precollege origins are associated with differences in the social strategies that Black students deploy on campus. Whereas some Black students may respond to mainstream White college culture by immersing themselves intensively in the campus Black community, others may instead seek to create or maintain racially diverse social networks.

Here, we want to understand the heterogeneous repertoires that high-achieving Black students use to manage life in a social world that in many ways constitutes a dress rehearsal for the professional stage they will enter upon graduation. Specifically, we analyze the diverse social connections to friends, romantic partners, and campus organizations reported by the National Longitudinal Survey of Freshmen (NLSF) respondents and interviewees. Of particular interest are variations in the understanding and enactment of "Blackness" on selective college campuses where race and class intersect to create both opportunities and challenges for aspiring Black students. How students fare in managing social relations during their college years likely foreshadows the degree of their later success in the U.S. stratification system. We also examine whether the racial diversity that Black people encounter at colleges today encourages them to reexamine the nature of their own social ties and organizational affiliations as they prepare to embark on a professional career.

Friendship Networks

Research on the Black collegiate experience often presumes a "generic" racial identity hewn across multiple generations of slavery, segregation, and discrimination, yielding a shared racial consciousness that favors involvement in Black groups and social activities over other types of campus participation (Benjamin 2005; Martin 2010; White-Johnson 2012). The unspoken assumption is that cultural dissonance is a common reality and that the typical response is to withdraw into exclusively Black interpersonal and institutional affiliations for social and psychological support (Solórzano, Ceja, and Yosso 2000; Museus and Quaye 2009; Hurtado et al. 2012; Museus 2014). With few exceptions (Charles et al. 2009; Byrd 2017; Chavous et al. 2018), these studies have largely been qualitative and cross-sectional and have not treated the Black experience on campus as part of a dynamic transition to adulthood that all young people undergo when they arrive on the campus of a selective institution.

TABLE 6.1. Measures of interracial and intraracial association for Black NLSF respondents

Indicator of social association	Mean/Percentage
Race of ten closest college friends	
White	2.4
Black	5.8
Asian	0.8
Latino	0.6
Romantic relationships	
Ever had a steady partner	81.0%
Ever dated outside of own group	66.2
If yes, ever dated a White person	52.4
If yes, frequency of negative reaction (0–3):	
From same-race friends	1.2
From same-race family	0.7
From same-race strangers	1.2
From partner-race strangers	1.3
Negative reaction index (0–12)	4.4
Organizational participation	
In majority-Black organization	58.8
In race-themed organization	20.4
Total	1,039

We begin our analysis by considering the racial/ethnic composition of friendship networks formed by the Black students in our sample. In the spring of their freshman year, respondents were asked to name the race, ethnicity, and gender of their ten closest college friends. Table 6.1 reports the average number of friends named from each racial group (the numbers do not add to ten because some students did not list ten friends). The resulting numbers clearly indicate that Black students favor same-race peers, with an average number of 5.8 close Black friends compared with just 2.4 White friends, 0.8 Asian friends, and 0.6 Latino friends. These findings are generally consistent with those of other studies (Massey et al. 2003, 2007; Fischer 2008; Charles et al. 2009, 2015; Torres and Massey 2012; Arcidiacono et al. 2013).

Qualitative data from our interviews suggest that most Black students arrive at college looking forward to a greater frequency of interaction with educationally similar same-race peers. Although student bodies at most selective institutions remain largely White, the absolute size of the Black student population is often greater than it was in their high schools, especially if they attended a prep school, a magnet school, or took numerous honors and

Advanced Placement (AP) courses. Unlike most high school students, however, college students are all selected on the basis of strong academic interests and abilities, creating a natural foundation for association, especially for elite Black students. In their commentaries, interviewees often shared that college was the first time in which they encountered a critical mass of same-race peers with whom they could affiliate, as well as a variety of Black-affinity clubs and organizations to explore.

Ervin, for example, said he had few Black friends in high school. Most were Asian or White and he found it "really hard to make Black friends." When we met Ervin during the second semester of his freshman year, he reported having ten Black friends, both from his dorm and on-campus organizations, though he did mention three White friends with whom he often socialized. Similarly, Troy, a resident advisor at a Black-themed dorm, told us how excited he had been to arrive on campus after leaving his inner-city Bronx neighborhood where most young people were not college-bound, telling us that "hands down, I wanted to make sure that I knew other Black students. Since there weren't a lot [of educationally motivated students at home], I wanted to know the ones that are here. It's my comfort zone."

Romantic Relationships

Young adults with racially diverse peer networks are generally more open to dating outside their racial or ethnic group than those embedded in homophilous social networks (Fischer 2008; Herman and Campbell 2012). More than fifty years after the legalization of interracial marriage, Black-White unions remain relatively infrequent and are highly gendered (Djama and Kimuna 2014). As of 2010, the frequency of intermarriage was 8.5 percent for Black men and 3.9 percent for Black women (Raley, Sweeney, and Wondra 2015). The gender gap is even wider among college-educated Black Americans; the share intermarried was 30 percent for Black men but just 13 percent for Black women (Livingston and Brown 2017).

Scholars assert that high-status Black Americans have difficulty finding same-race partners because their elevated social-class standing reduces the size of the potential Black dating pool, especially for women (Goldin and Katz 2008; McClendon, Kuo, and Raley 2014). Typically educated at elite schools, Black professionals tend to work in predominantly White organizations, live in integrated neighborhoods, and increasingly are embedded within non-Black social networks, making it difficult to encounter marriageable partners who are "like them" in terms of *both* race and education (Marsh et al. 2007; Cherlin 2009; Banks 2011). Although online dating applications increase the potential size and range of dating pools, selective choices within them systematically reduce the pool of partners considered, yielding a social configuration that is highly segmented by race, gender, class, and sexuality (Currington, Lundquist, and Lin 2021).

Selective college and university campuses offer a unique, closed social setting for aspiring Black students to develop romantic preferences (Charles et al. 2009). Going to college often represents the first time many Black students encounter same-race others who come from different class and residential backgrounds, which is important because as we have seen, romantic relationships are often rooted in peer networks that are quite homophilous with respect to both socioeconomic status and race (Felmlee 2001; Clark-Ibáñez and Felmlee 2004; Levin, Taylor, and Caudle 2007; Edmonds and Killen 2009; Schoepflin 2009; Torres and Massey 2012; Harper and Yeung 2015).

The middle panel of table 6.1 summarizes the dating experiences of Black survey respondents. As can be seen, dating outside the group is quite common, with two-thirds (66.2 percent) reporting at least one interracial date during their freshman year. Among those who dated outside the group, more than half (52.4 percent) said they had gone out with a White person (comprising 34.7 percent of all Black students). For those reporting interracial dates, we also asked how often they had experienced a negative reaction from different categories of people, with the response options ranging from "never" (coded 0) to "sometimes" (1), "often" (2), and "very often" (3). The mean frequency rating for negative reactions from same-race friends and from same-race strangers was 1.2. The same average rating for family members was lower at 0.7 and that for strangers in the partner's group was greater at 1.3.

Altogether, then, the frequency of negative reactions from others ranged somewhere between "never" and "sometimes," suggesting a milieu that was tolerant of interracial dating but with sporadic friction. Adding the separate rating scores across the different categories of social observers (same-race friends, same-race family, own-group strangers, and partner-group strangers) yields a negativity index with a potential range of 0 to 12, with an average score of 4.4 and a Cronbach's alpha of 0.676. In our in-depth conversations, most interviewees told us they were open to interracial dating in theory but that dating outside the group was "not common" in practice, especially when it involved White partners. These reports appear to contradict the survey data, suggesting a gap between perceived norms and actual behaviors. For example,

Jeff, a multigenerational native senior who self-identified as only "marginally Black," explained,

> [Interracial] dating overall, I don't think that happens here [laughs]. Dating, in general, I don't even think that's an issue here. If it does happen, I'm unaware of it. The couples I have seen are very much, from what I can tell, the same race.

Although Jeff described his friends in high school as "diverse," he told us that his collegiate friends were exclusively Black and Latino. Most were people he had lived with since his freshman year, though he did admit to socializing with White students at campus-wide events.

Despite the relative infrequency of negative sanctioning seen in our survey data, interviewees generally felt that interracial dating was not favored within the Black community. Darryl believed that "people who date outside of their race can risk finding themselves ostracized." Although Jeff was a bit more hesitant on this point, he basically agreed with Darryl:

> INTERVIEWER: How do you think interracial dating is perceived by Black students here?
>
> JEFF: I'm not entirely sure. I'd probably say within the community, it would be an insult because you're not "supporting the group" by dating a member of the opposite race.

One person who did date outside the group was Karen; she had a White boyfriend, though he was the only non-Black person in her core social network. Consistent with the concerns intuited by Jeff, she expressed a certain unease about how her romantic choice was perceived by Black peers:

> INTERVIEWER: You said you had a White boyfriend, right?
>
> KAREN: Um-hmm. I don't know if it's an extremely common thing. I can think of a few couples. . . . I feel like I didn't hear a whole lot from Black or White students about it. But that's probably just for the sake of not being inappropriate or rude or whatever the case may be. . . . Or it's something not seriously contemplated or seriously thought about *especially, for me* [emphasis in her voice]. But there was no question of my Blackness because I was clearly, you know, involved in the Black community.

Karen then went on to describe the gender dynamics of dating, sharing a conversation she had with other Black women students:

There's that historical thing about not having enough Black men. . . . So we were going through our senior class and thinking about how many Black men there are. . . . There's like thirty or something, forty—and we were saying how many have dated inside of our senior class. . . . Who the hell are they dating? I don't even know anymore. A few of them are not necessarily dating Black girls. And then, the other ones [who] just aren't dating or have dated Black girls . . . I don't necessarily think we perceive the guys that are dating the White girls or non-Black girls as anything different or negative. But I just think that's me among my friends. That's just our own personal views. I know that it's perceived differently off-campus.

Malik also spoke about the shortage of Black men and its influence on interracial dating options on campus:

There's a very disproportionate number of Black women to Black men. So that's an issue. Like why as a Black male would you choose to date a White woman when there's like four to one, like, Black women to White women, or Black women to Black men?

Although Malik's perception of the skewed sex ratio is a bit of an exaggeration, Black women did outnumber Black men at a ratio of 2:1 at his university at the time of our fieldwork. Malik nonetheless wanted to find a White girlfriend, though his recent advances toward a White woman friend were rebuffed. By way of explanation, he told us that he knew little about the Black social scene because he grew up in an exclusively White setting.

Eugene, for his part, put the onus for not dating on Black women themselves, arguing that their negative stereotypes of Black men made them suspicious of potential romantic partners. It was his opinion that "a lot of Black women feel as though we're not good enough." He also commented on how stereotypes affected the standing of Black men vis-à-vis White men:

I think with White people, particularly White men, it's the whole idea of like the Mandingo as far as you have this Black guy, he's like oversexed, he's coming after your daughter, he's trying to rape your daughter.

For her part, Tia believed that stereotypes of Black women as "exotic" enhanced their attractiveness to White men:

I believe that White males are attracted to [Black] women a lot of times . . . because they want to experiment with . . . whoever they can experiment with before they leave. And a lot of times, Blacks are seen as a sort of exotic . . . female or whatever, and this will be the time to do it . . . because they're not ready to settle down and looking for someone to marry. But that's my opinion!

Tia's social circle was exclusively Black and she was in a long-term relationship with a Black man who did not attend her university. Even though interracial dating clearly happens on campus, our interview data suggest that Black students remain socially uneasy about it.

Extracurricular Activities and Clubs

Elite college campuses customarily host a wide variety of social organizations, sponsored activities, and affinity groups that reflect the diversity of racial, ethnic, gender, cultural, and topical interests in twenty-first-century America. Admissions materials from both universities in the interview sample list several hundred student-run clubs, organizations, and extracurricular activities that cater to a variety of academic, social, and cultural niches. The number of extracurricular opportunities celebrating the cultural, racial, and ethnic diversity of undergraduates at both universities is substantial. Each fall, campus walkways are filled with students manning tables advertising specific organizations and handing out flyers for upcoming events, and representatives are always on hand to explain the mission of their particular group.

At the time of data collection, each of the interview sites listed more than twenty Black-focused organizations. In addition to Black student unions, these included affinity groups for people of Caribbean and African origin, Black fraternities and sororities, gender-specific support groups, Black newspapers, and Black magazines, just to name a few of the many options. Both institutions also sponsored programs for Black professional socialization, including clubs for business-oriented Black students, chapters of the National Society of Black Engineers, special premed tutoring programs, and Africana or African American studies programs, as well as a Black-themed residence hall on one campus housing about two hundred students, mostly but not all Black. Although the other interview setting did not have a Black-affinity dorm, several interviewees referred to informal Black living and social spaces created by Black students for themselves.

During their junior year, we asked survey respondents to list up to two extracurricular organizations to which they belonged and to provide information about the group's purpose and racial composition. Given our focus on intragroup relations, the bottom panel of table 6.1 shows the share of respondents who belonged to an organization in which a majority of members were Black, as well as those that were specifically Black themed or focused. Most respondents (58.8 percent) were involved in at least one majority-Black organization. Given the large number of organizations on most campuses, Black students often belonged to multiple groups and memberships tended to overlap. Many organizations ended up being majority Black not because they were explicitly Black themed, but because they were devoted to interests and causes of interest to Black students, such as community service, gospel a cappella groups, or African and Caribbean cultures. The share of respondents belonging to specifically Black-themed organizations was actually quite low, at around 20 percent.

Dimensions of Black Sociality on Campus

Prior research reveals significant differences in patterns of sociality among Black people depending on their background and upbringing. Friendships, romantic relationships, and patterns of extracurricular affiliation inevitably reflect the complexity of Black identity and the variety of social ecologies that prevail at selective colleges and universities (see Smith and Moore 2002; Massey et al. 2003; Charles et al. 2009, 2015; Torres and Massey 2012). In this section, we undertake a detailed look at how patterns of sociality vary among Black students along the dimensions of racial identification, immigrant origins, skin tone, gender, socioeconomic status, and prior experiences of segregation.

Divergent Friendship Networks

The top panel of table 6.2 shows the number of Black, White, Latino, and Asian friends reported by monoracial and mixed-race survey respondents. Whereas monoracial Black respondents reported an average of 6.2 Black friends and 2.2 White friends in their close friend network, the respective numbers for mixed-race students were 3.9 and 3.8. Students of mixed racial origins were also significantly more likely to report having a Latino or Asian friend. Not only were mixed-race respondents more likely to report having White friends, but the numbers of White and Black friends were much more evenly balanced. In contrast, among monoracial Black respondents, the balance was heavily skewed toward same-race friends; the average number of Black friends

TABLE 6.2. Racial composition of ten closest college friends for Black NLSF respondents by dimensions of diversity

Dimension of diversity	Black	White	Latino/Asian
Racial identification			
Monoracial	6.2***	2.2***	1.3***
Mixed race	3.9	3.8	2.0
Nativity and generation			
Multigenerational native	6.1***	2.2**	1.1***
Second-generation immigrant	5.1	2.6	1.6
First-generation immigrant	4.6	2.8	1.9
Region of origin			
USA	6.1***	2.2***	1.1***
African immigrant	4.9	2.4	2.0
Caribbean immigrant	4.8	2.9	1.6
Other immigrant	4.5	2.8	2.1
Skin tone			
Light	4.8***	3.2***	1.6
Medium	6.2	2.0	1.3
Dark	5.8	2.2	1.5
Gender			
Female	6.1***	2.2***	1.3*
Male	5.3	2.8	1.5
Parental education			
No degree	6.1**	2.0***	1.4
College degree	6.0	2.3	1.3
Advanced degree	5.4	2.8	1.5
Experience of segregation			
Predominantly White	4.9***	3.1***	1.5**
Integrated neighborhood and school	6.2	2.2	1.3
Predominantly Minority	6.6	1.6	1.2
Minority neighborhood/White school	6.5	2.1	1.2

$^+$p < 0.10; * p < 0.05; ** p < 0.01; *** p < 0.001

reported by monoracial respondents had actually increased somewhat since high school (by an average of 0.1, $p < 0.10$). In contrast, no significant change was observed for mixed-race students (here and in the ensuing comparisons, we will not report the statistical tests, just the significance levels).

As shown in the second panel of the table, we also observe significant differences in the composition of close friendship networks by nativity and generational status. The average number of Black friends was greatest for multigenerational natives (6.1) and least for first-generation immigrants (4.6), with second-generation immigrants falling in between (5.1). Conversely, the number of White friends was least among multigenerational natives (2.2) and greatest among first-generation immigrants (2.8), with second-generation immigrants once again falling in between (2.6). Moreover, whereas the average number of White friends reported by multigenerational native Black respondents dropped by a value of 0.4 between high school and college, the decline was less salient among first-generation immigrants (0.2); the number of White friends actually *increased* for second-generation immigrants (by an average of 0.4, $p < 0.01$).

First-generation Black immigrants reported the most Asian and Latino friends, with an average value of 1.9 for their combined total. This finding is, perhaps, unsurprising since both of these groups also include many immigrants. Following close behind were second-generation immigrants with 1.6 Asian and Latino friends; much further behind were multigenerational native Black respondents with 1.1 such friends. Among immigrants, those from Africa on average reported having the largest number of Black friends (4.9) and the fewest White friends (2.4), compared to immigrants from other regions. Moreover, the average number of White friends reported by African immigrants fell by 0.2 persons between high school and college ($p < 0.01$).

Given earlier results showing that mixed-race Black respondents had fewer Black friends and more White friends than monoracial Black students, it is not surprising that light-skinned respondents also reported having fewer Black friends (4.8) than either medium- or dark-skinned respondents (with respective values of 6.2 and 5.8) as skin tone and identifying as mixed race are highly correlated. Furthermore, light-skinned students named more White friends (3.2) relative to their medium- and dark-skinned counterparts (2.0 and 2.2). Although most students with non-Black parents in our sample have a White parent, we cannot parse these respondents out due to small sample sizes. We nonetheless expect that White parentage explains much of the relationship between skin tone and friendship patterns.

At the same time, however, roughly two-thirds of our light-skinned respondents did not report a mixed racial identity, suggesting the potential impact of colorism on Black friendship opportunities. White peers are more likely to seek out and befriend light-skin Black peers who are less "racially salient" (Thornhill 2015) or to hold colorist biases against darker skinned Black peers (Hannon 2015; Maddox and Gray 2002). In addition, the late 1990s and early 2000s saw the rise of the desirability of "racial ambiguity," which may also affect friendship differences by skin tone, given that subjective ratings of physical attractiveness are correlated with large gaps in earnings and other outcomes for Black Americans (Monk, Esposito, and Lee 2021).

With respect to gender, in keeping with prior work showing that the friendship networks of Black women are less diverse than those of Black men, Black women respondents had an average of 6.1 Black friends, 2.2 White friends, and 1.3 Latino or Asian friends, compared with Black men who had an average of 5.3 Black friends, 2.8 White friends, and 1.5 others, a gender differential that was virtually unchanged since high school. Intersectionality helps explain why Black women often have less diverse friendship patterns than Black men. Controlling images of Black masculinity treat Black men as dangerous, powerful, and potentially desirable social connections, whereas controlling images of Black women treat them as quick to anger, desexualized, and intimidating or motherlike, all stereotypes that might make interracial friendships with Black women less desirable to other women. For example, White women's concept of beauty is built largely in contrast to Black women's bodies, which may preclude many opportunities for interracial friendship for Black women on White campuses, where beauty capital is not only about romantic relationships but capital and status more broadly (McMillan Cottom 2019). Combined, skin tone and gender may affect Black women's friendship patterns more than Black men's (Hunter 2002).

We also observe significant differences in the diversity of friendship networks by socioeconomic status. In general, as class status rose, respondents came to have significantly more White and fewer Black friends, with no cross-class differences observed for Latino and Asian friends. Moving from respondents with non-college-educated parents to those with college-educated parents and then on to those with parents holding advanced degrees, the average number of White friends rose from 2.0 to 2.3 to 2.8 and the average number of Black friends fell from 6.1 to 6.0 to 5.4. Despite this significant class differential, the friendship networks of high- and low-status respondents grew more *similar* between high school and college, with the average number of Black friends falling by a value of 0.4 among those with parents who lacked college degrees but rising to reach 0.5 among those whose parents held advanced degrees ($p < 0.001$). At the same time, the average number of White friends increased by a value of 0.1 among those with non-college-educated parents but decreased by a value of 0.4 among those with parents holding advanced degrees ($p < 0.05$).

As with the other dimensions of Black diversity, we also observe significant differences in the composition of friendship networks by the degree of segregation experienced during childhood and adolescence. As one might expect, respondents from predominantly White neighborhoods and schools reported fewer Black friends, more White friends, and more Latino and Asian friends compared to those from more segregated circumstances. Thus, Black survey respondents who came of age in predominantly White schools and neighborhoods reported 4.9 Black friends and 3.1 White friends, while those in the other categories of segregation reported at least 6.2 Black friends and fewer than 2.2 White friends. Between high school and college, the number of Black friends rose by 1.0 and the number of White friends dropped by 1.0 among those from predominantly White schools and neighborhoods. In contrast, the number of Black friends dropped by a value of 1.6 and the number of White friends increased by a 0.9 among those from the most segregated schools and neighborhoods. Thus, overall, the composition of Black friendship networks became more similar to one another between high school and college.

In sum, despite some movement toward equivalence in the composition of social networks between high school and college, we continue to observe systematic differences in friendship diversity among our survey respondents depending on their background characteristics. In general, whiter and more diverse friendship networks prevail for Black respondents who are mixed race, light skinned, with well-educated parents who grew up in more integrated circumstances, especially those who are young men and of immigrant origin. Conversely, friendship networks are less diverse among Black respondents who are monoracial, native born, darker skinned, women, have less-well-educated parents, and who came from racially segregated neighborhoods and schools.

The patterns exhibited for our survey respondents were largely confirmed by our in-depth interview participants, but interviewees also shed light on the subtle interplay between racial identification and sociality on campus to reveal the mediating role played by class and skin color in social interactions. For example, Rachel, who told us she was "half-Jewish and half-Black" and identified as "racially mixed," did not regularly participate in Black-focused activities and reported her ten closest college friends to be a mix of White, Asian, Latino, and West Indian students. She belonged to the most elite White sorority on campus and served as an officer in an affinity group for mixed-race students. Rachel explained that during her freshman year, she was a topic of some conversation among her friends because they "couldn't tell if she was Black." Without consulting her, "they decided I was Hispanic." In discussing her appearance and self-concept she explained,

> I would say probably based on looks and my experience . . . I would be more accepted by the Black group, if it was just [based on] looks. But my

interests are more in common with White people . . . liking *Seinfeld* and different music. . . . I feel like it would be the exact same if I wasn't on campus—like, personality-wise, I'd probably have more in common with White culture.

Other mixed-race students were even more blunt. Both Megan and Emily identified as mixed race and grew up in affluent households, were light skinned, and attended predominately White schools growing up. On campus, they moved in diverse friendship circles that included darker-skinned monoracial Black peers but gravitated toward those Black students who tended to share their socioeconomic background and worldview. As Megan put it, "I'm the Black girl who hangs out with White people." Emily similarly explained that she felt most at ease being with "Black students who feel more comfortable with White people."

Both Megan and Emily suspected that they were not fully accepted by their Black peers and that cultural fluency in White society could be a detriment to establishing relationships with other Black students who did not consider them "Black enough." Indeed, Emily described other Black students as "ethnocentric" and believed they were "resentful" of the fact that light-skinned Black people like her "in the past had been treated better." Although this realization made her feel a bit "uneasy," she nonetheless readily admitted that she, too, had "dealt with White racism and ignorance" just like her monoracial peers.

In contrast, Andrew identified as "African American" despite writing "mixed" on his college forms, largely due to the fact that he grew up under segregated circumstances, telling us that "if someone asks me what race I am, I say that I'm mixed [though] I've always identified with African Americans because that's who I've been around." Andrew graduated from an all-Black high school and knew just two White peers before college. At an admissions event for minority students, he immediately made several Black friends who made him feel comfortable, and on campus, he told us that he "basically stays around Black people exclusively."

INTERVIEWER: Do you feel close to other Black students here?
ANDREW: Most of them—yeah. We talk on a regular basis. . . . Basically, so we're all getting along and stuff like that. . . . You get that connection.
INTERVIEWER: What about mixed students, do you feel close to them?
ANDREW: Not so much. I don't know that many of them. . . . You don't really see them around. There's not that many of us on campus anyway.

INTERVIEWER: Do you think you're more accepted by Black people, mixed people, or White people?

ANDREW: Black people. I'm around them more. I mean, I have those commonalities. I don't know.

For her part, Ashley, a monoracial immigrant from Jamaica, stressed the importance of having friends who shared her ethnicity, culture, and traditions, not just her race:

> You kind of tend to hang out with who you are most comfortable with and I guess people end up being most comfortable with people who are like them . . . from the same background as they are. . . . All my friends are Caribbean—that's important—or [they] have some Caribbean something in them. I don't know if that happened on purpose. Like, my close friends anyway, are all Caribbean.

Caribbean interviewees most typically identified with their immigrant roots and were quite explicit about the importance of having coethnic, immigrant-origin friends. George, of Trinidadian origin, reported that his closest friends in both high school and college were other West Indians and that he was drawn to them because of "their ethnic similarities." However, George also reported having several White friends with whom he regularly socialized at parties and other events. Albert, who traced his origins to Jamaica and Trinidad, told us that his six closest college friends were "all West Indian" but that he also had one close White friend on campus, which was almost the exact configuration of his social network in high school. He attributed the composition of his current friendship network to the overrepresentation of Caribbeans among Black students at his university:

> I find that of the Black people here, a vast good number of them are West Indian. . . . Because [the university] draws from people from New York, Pennsylvania, Jersey, and that is where a lot, 90 percent of all West Indian Black people live in the United States.

Although the statistics Albert referenced are overstatements, Caribbean-origin Black people are, indeed, an important presence in the Northeast and are overrepresented in the region's elite colleges and universities (Rimer and Arenson 2004; Fears 2007; Massey et al. 2007; Bennett and Lutz 2009; Jaret and Reitzes 2009).

Our in-depth interviews reveal that second-generation Black immigrants generally ascribe to what Neckerman, Carter, and Lee (1999) call a *minority culture of mobility*. Raised entirely in the United States in integrated or White settings, they often felt caught between two worlds, one Black and one White. Having well-educated parents, they usually attended private or affluent suburban schools and were accustomed to interacting and achieving in places where people who looked like them were few and far between. They valued and actively celebrated their national and ethnic origins—indeed, their parents instilled it in them—and they were well aware of their distinctiveness relative to multigenerational native Black students. For them, college provided an opportunity to expand their same-race social connections and interact with others, sharing their culture rather than dealing with the challenges of being just one of a few Black students in their community.

At the same time, however, they felt the burden of performing a Black American identity that was unfamiliar to them because they do not share the same legacy of oppression, exclusion, and discrimination. Greg, a second-generation Ghanaian, thought that the unidimensional concept of Blackness as working class and multigenerational American was "manufactured" and fed into a clash about what constitutes "authentic" Blackness in today's world. To him, phenotype was only a small piece of what it meant to be Black:

> If you don't watch the same shows as us, you don't listen to the same music as us. You didn't listen to the same music as us when we were kids. But then if you were watching *Fat Albert*, show's like . . . show's kinda like *Martin*, but . . . sort of like . . . predominately Black shows. . . . So then you'll learn from people you meet. . . . Or, *you'll just fake it. But you have to condition yourself because . . . you can't be Black with all White friends and constantly feel alienated. You have to, I guess, sacrifice or just pacify [yourself] to assimilate* [emphasis added].

For students like Greg, attending to the script of "acting Black" required a lot of effort and time. Malik, also of Ghanaian origin, struggled to make Black friends because he had a "very Anglo speech pattern" and did not know how to speak "Black English" (i.e., Black English Vernacular; see Baugh 1983). He also felt he lacked an "urban African American" cultural repertoire and explained that many of his same-race peers felt that Black people who did not embrace or embody these linguistic and cultural styles were "selling out in a way" or "negating their Blackness."

Multigenerational native interviewees were most likely to report having exclusively Black friendship networks and tended to place a high priority on living and socializing with other Black peers. Most multigenerational native interviewees were from working-class backgrounds and often met their Black college friends at summer programs designed to ease new students' social and academic acclimation to college. April, for example, lived in the Black-focused dorm when she participated in a program for incoming Black students. She enjoyed living there and felt most comfortable socializing with other Black students.

> INTERVIEWER: Are [your friends] mostly from your same racial group?
> APRIL: Um-hmm . . .
> INTERVIEWER: Close friends at [name of university]?
> APRIL: I mean, *all of them are Black* [emphasis added].
> INTERVIEWER: All of them? How about your acquaintances?
> APRIL: They're pretty much all Black, too.

April credits her close friendships with other Black students for "helping me get through [college] alive."

Eugene, also a multigenerational native, explained that he did not care to associate regularly with non-Black peers, telling us, "I mean, if you're *not* Black, I don't pay attention to you. I mean, for me basically I see a bunch of Black people. That's because I purposely zone in on Black people." Like April, he attended the summer program for incoming Black freshman at his university as well as receiving a generous financial aid package. His entire friendship network was Black and he pledged a Black fraternity.

Multigenerational native students also frequently discussed how they stayed in close contact with Black friends from home. Sean, a freshman when we met him, told us that he was struggling to "fit in." Both his closest friends from home had enrolled in historically Black institutions, while he had chosen to leave the West Coast specifically for the experience of an elite Northeastern university. Nonetheless, Sean often talked with his hometown friends and they hung out together regularly over breaks to share their experiences and had plans to live together over the summer in the same segregated neighborhood where they had grown up. As Sean explained,

> I mean like when we first got to college, it was like, man, I wish we were together, 'cause like they're my boys. I met [name] in kindergarten and my friend [name] in fourth grade and it's like our parents are close. . . . We played basketball together from middle school up to about tenth grade. . . . We spent a whole lot of time together, you know? It's like those relationships are like tight-knit relationships. . . . My boys are like my boys.

When we checked in on Sean in his sophomore year, he was living in his institution's Black-themed dorm and was pledging a Black fraternity. Despite having made several Black friends on campus, he still felt closest to his friends from home.

By contrast, Bruce, a light-skinned mixed-race sophomore of Black, Asian, and Italian descent, reported having a very racially diverse peer group that was nonetheless considerably "Blacker" than was his high school social circle. At college, Bruce was surprised by how "easy it was just to approach another Black student," and when we met him, he was the vice president of the mixed-race student organization and reported a relatively balanced mix of White, Black, and mixed-race friends. He was excited about his involvement with the mixed-race student community on campus because, as he put it, "being mixed, I always felt like that was important. I'm proud of being mixed, so yeah, I put that out there." Bruce took pride in the diversity of his peer group and directly linked his self-identity to that diversity:

> Some [Black] people are just predisposed to have more Black friends. They come here and they're like, "Oh, you're Black." I've always been one of those people who is, like, "just because you're Black doesn't mean I'll necessarily be friends with you," you know? I won't immediately take them in just because they're Black.

Bruce belonged to an elite, predominantly White fraternity, but he also participated in several Black-oriented clubs.

Most mixed-race interviewees counted other mixed-race peers among their closest college friends. Candace, a senior, met her closest girlfriends at the start of her freshman year. Candace came from a working-class suburb of Philadelphia, and she and her brother were the only non-White kids in their town. Before college, she identified as Black because she didn't know anyone else with dark skin. After she met her two best college friends, who were also of mixed Black and White origins, she began to self-identify as "mixed."

INTERVIEWER: And how do you racially and ethnically identify?
CANDACE: Since coming to college, I've identified as mixed.
INTERVIEWER: What made you change, or what made you identify that way, as opposed to something else?
CANDACE: Um, because before that, I'd never met any other people who were mixed. So, yeah, I grew up in, my brother and I were the only people who were not White in my town, so . . . Our school is really small, and we were the only non-White people at the school.

INTERVIEWER: So you just considered yourself what?
CANDACE: Black.

After meeting her first mixed-race friend during a preorientation community service trip, she and her new friend ended up meeting their other two future best friends, who were also mixed, a few days later. They soon realized they actually all lived in the same dorm and remained close four years later. As she explained,

> We just started talking and we all just sat and talked for three hours. We all said this. . . . Is this what other people normally feel when they meet someone new? There was so much you didn't have to explain. Yeah, it was an amazing feeling.

At the end of college, Candace had five close friends including three mixed-race and two monoracial Black women.

As in the survey data, the qualitative interviews indicate that prior experience with segregation markedly affected the composition of interviewees' friendship networks on campus. Interviewees who grew up in White neighborhoods and attended White schools reported a clear motivation to make Black friends in college. For example, Olivia lived in an affluent, suburban neighborhood on Long Island, but most of the Black students at her school lived in the poorer "Black part of town." Even though her high school was about 20 percent Black and Latino, her honors courses included no same-race peers: "Everyone I was around was White, which was hard . . . a little rough." Olivia was determined not to repeat this experience in college and was adamant about not being the only Black person in her friendship circle:

> I made a very conscious choice. I did not want to be the only Black girl among White people anymore. And more importantly, I didn't want to feel isolated or ostracized from the Black community. I had done it for so long.

Despite her West Indian and African origins, Olivia identified as "Black" and deliberately sought to create an all-Black friendship network and chose to participate exclusively in Black organizations in college.

Trying to fit in with other Black students was not always enough to succeed. Albert, for example, explained how he had been criticized by some of his same-race peers for not "acting Black" because both his parents were doctors and he did not receive any financial aid.

INTERVIEWER: So where does it come in, is it if you are "not Black enough" does it mean you are not poor enough?

ALBERT: In some people's minds, yeah.

INTERVIEWER: Would someone say that you "are not Black enough"?

ALBERT: Yeah. I mean people tell me that all the time: "Oh, you are bourgie, you live on Long Island," da, da, da. It is something I have contemplated for a while and I just don't really know where it comes from. I tend to ignore it. . . . Among students, there is a very, very large group within the upper-class or middle-class backgrounds, and to me it signals if there were certain groups of students who gravitated away from the more affluent students because they were more affluent. You know you are not Black enough because you have a little more than I do.

INTERVIEWER: So can you break it down in your viewpoint of what it means to be "Black enough" or "not Black enough"?

ALBERT: Well, I don't ascribe to that way of thinking. I think that your being Black is a function of birth and that is it.

Nia came from a solidly upper-middle-class background, grew up with highly educated parents in a predominately White neighborhood, and attended an elite day school. Originally excited to meet other Black students at college, Nia was dismayed that she did not actually like her Black roommate freshman year and that there were "so many different types of Black people" who did not share her worldview. She told us that her White friends from home were "so much more similar to me in the sense that we tend to like the same things, like, we tend to agree on the same ideas." Nevertheless, she was later unnerved by how her White peers were treating her and, as a sophomore, left her predominantly White singing group, where she felt marginalized as the only person of color. By then, her peer network had become exclusively Black and she had joined a Black sorority despite the class distance she felt from many Black students.

In contrast, interviewees from segregated minority schools and neighborhoods often wanted to construct more diverse friendship networks. For example, Tiffany's closest friends at her segregated high school—three Black and three Latino—reflected the school's demographics, not necessarily her preferences. College was her first opportunity to socialize with members of other groups, and as a freshman, she befriended her Puerto Rican and White roommates. And although she was heavily involved in Black organizations and cultural activities on campus, she was also very open to meeting non-Black students.

> TIFFANY: I knew that [name of university] was majority White and I knew it was going to be completely different from my high school, so why would I come and try to make it into my high school? So I totally knew that I would be meeting other people.
>
> INTERVIEWER: And you wanted that?
>
> TIFFANY: Yeah, and I thought that the rest of the world was like that. Actually—this is very naive—but I didn't know that African Americans were called minorities because they're a minority population in the U.S. My friend was, like, "There's 70 percent White people in the U.S., in this country. I was, like, what? This is not where I live, you know? So I was like, "You know what? I'm definitely living in a very limited world right now.

At the end of her senior year, Tiffany's friendship network included four Black, two Puerto Rican, one White, and one mixed Black and Asian friends.

Interviewees from lower socioeconomic status families and segregated neighborhoods but predominately White (usually private) high schools gravitated toward the relatively few Black and Latino students who shared their backgrounds. Darryl, for example, reported having four close friends at his boarding school: two African Americans and two Latinos. Darryl felt close to a "selective group" of ten to fifteen same-race peers at his university because they related to his preferred attire of "Timberlands, Rocawear jeans, and a do-rag." Darryl revealed that he struggled to interact with people who were different from him racially and socioeconomically:

> As close as I can try to get with people outside my condition, not even just Black but Black upper-class people, there seems to be just a misunderstanding. So I don't know. All the people I'm close with are either lower class with a historically lower-class family or their family just made it, so they have a lot of lower-class people in their circle.

But Darryl was confident that due to his boarding school experience, "when I enter any sort of Black professional circles, I'm usually pretty well accepted. I know how to act."

In both our qualitative and quantitative data, therefore, we observe strong and consistent associations between dimensions of Black diversity (racial identification, skin tone, social class, and segregation) and the racial composition of respondents' friendship networks on campus. At the same time, however, differences between monoracial and mixed-race, darker- and lighter-skinned Black respondents obscure significant movement toward more similar college friendship networks compared to their precollege experiences. Those from "Blacker" backgrounds tended to acquire more White friends and those from "Whiter" backgrounds tended to gain additional Black friends.

Divergent Dating Patterns

Table 6.3 continues our analysis of Black social life with a deeper consideration of dating patterns. As already noted, dating tends to be a fraught activity for Black students at selective institutions due to both the complexities of race and the very imbalanced sex ratio among Black students on most college campuses (Massey et al. 2003; Robertson, Mitra, and Van Delinder 2005). Beyond demography, the historical devaluation of Black women as potential partners (hooks 1981; Spickard 1989; Twine 1996; Ferber 1998; Collins 2000; Yancey and Lewis 2009) and the hypersexualization of Black people regardless of gender (Currington, Lundquist, and Lin 2021) renders interracial dating a daunting prospect. It is thus hardly surprising that Charles and colleagues (2009) found that Black students were far less likely than Asians or Latinos to date outside their group, and when they did, it was usually not with White or Asian partners but with Latinos, the group next closest to them in America's current racial hierarchy.

Given the realities of campus demography and the legacy of gendered racism, it is unsurprising that studies reveal Black women to be the least sought-after romantic partners in general (Currington, Lundquist, and Lin 2021) and at selective colleges and universities in particular (Massey et al. 2003). Indeed, on campus, they are the least likely of all race/gender combinations to date interracially. The latter distinction persists even after controlling for the diversity of friendship networks and earlier interracial dating experiences (Keels and Harris 2014). Moreover, across all levels of education, Black men are more open to interracial dating than Black women; college-educated Black men are also more willing to date (and marry) interracial partners of lower socioeconomic status (Raley, Sweeney, and Wondra 2015).

As can be seen in the fifth panel of table 6.3, the gendered asymmetries of the campus dating scene are readily apparent among Black NLSF respondents. Black women were much less likely than Black men to say they had dated interracially (59.4 percent versus 78.9 percent) and were even less likely to date a

TABLE 6.3. Romantic relationships reported by Black NLSF respondents by dimensions of Black diversity

Dimension of diversity	Romantic outcome			
	Had a steady partner	Dated interracially	Dated a White person	Negative response index
Racial identification				
Monoracial	80.6%	61.9%	47.5%***	2.33*
Mixed race	82.9	88.7***	78.4	1.77
Nativity and generation				
Multigenerational native	82.4	63.4*	50.3	2.15
Second-generation immigrant	77.4	76.2	57.4	2.56
First-generation immigrant	76.6	68.5	60.6	2.28
Region of origin				
USA	82.4+	63.4**	50.3*	2.15
African immigrant	68.4	72.2	57.4	2.48
Caribbean immigrant	82.5	71.5	55.4	2.31
Other immigrant	78.2	84.6	70.5	2.31
Skin tone				
Light	84.7*	75.1**	66.0***	1.91*
Medium	82.8	63.5	47.1	2.28
Dark	74.2	62.9	49.7	2.43
Gender				
Female	79.1	59.4***	45.7***	2.18
Male	82.0	78.9	65.1	2.27
Parental education				
No college	81.9	57.9**	43.4**	2.43*
College degree	78.9	67.7	51.2	2.18
Advanced degree	81.9	71.2	60.2	2.10
Experience of segregation				
Predominantly White	80.2	76.3***	66.8***	2.00*
Integrated neighborhood & school	81.7	65.5	49.2	2.36
Predominantly minority	81.0	52.3	35.2	2.43
Minority neighborhood/ White school	81.3	63.5	51.0	2.27

+ p < 0.10; * p < 0.05; ** p < 0.01; *** p < 0.001

White partner when doing so (45.7 percent versus 65.1 percent). There are, however, no gender differences in either the likelihood of encountering a negative reaction for interracial dating or of having a steady romantic partner.

A perusal of the first column in table 6.3 reveals few differences in the likelihood of having a steady partner on any dimension of diversity. The sole exception is skin tone, where the percentage reporting a steady partner was 84.7 percent among light-skinned Black respondents, compared to 82.8 percent and 74.2 percent of those with medium and darker skin tones, respectively. We observe sharper differences with respect to other dating outcomes. Looking at the likelihood of dating interracially and the relative probability of dating a White person, for example, we encounter significant differences along the dimensions of racial identification and immigrant origins. Mixed-race respondents are significantly more likely than monoracial respondents to report dating interracially (88.7 percent versus 61.9 percent), and having chosen to do so, they are also more likely to have dated a White person (78.4 percent versus 47.5 percent). Mixed-race Black respondents were also less likely to experience a negative reaction for interracial dating. Their average negativity score was 1.77 compared with a value of 2.33 for monoracial Black respondents. In neither case, however, was the frequency of negative reactions very high on the 0–12 scale, indicating at best a subtle difference on the continuum from never to sometimes.

The second panel of table 6.3 considers differences by nativity and generation. Here, we see that second-generation immigrants were most likely to date interracially, with 76.2 percent saying they had dated outside the group. Among multigenerational natives, the figure was only 63.4 percent, and first-generation immigrants fall in between these two end points at 68.5 percent. Among immigrants, those from Africa and the Caribbean were less likely to date interracially than those born in other regions, with percentages of 72.2 percent for Africans and 71.5 percent for Caribbean students, compared to 84.6 percent among Black people from other world regions. We observe a similar pattern in the likelihood of dating a White person (57.4 percent and 55.4 percent versus 70.5 percent, respectively). However, we encounter no significant differences by nativity or national origin in the likelihood of experiencing a negative reaction for interracial dating.

Differences in interracial dating by skin tone largely parallel those observed for racial identification. Compared to medium- and dark-skinned respondents, those with light skin tones are more likely to date non-Black partners (75.1 percent versus 63.5 percent and 62.9 percent, respectively). Moreover, among those who do date outside the group, light-skinned Black respondents are much more likely to date a White person (66.0 percent versus 47.1 percent for those with medium skin tones and 49.7 percent for those with dark skin tones). Light-skinned Black respondents are also significantly less likely to report a negative reaction from others, with an average negativity rating of 1.91 compared with mean negativity scores of 2.28 and 2.43 for medium- and dark-skinned respondents, respectively.

We also find significant social class differences in dating behavior. The share who reported dating a non-Black person increased steadily with parental education, rising from 57.9 percent among those with non-college-educated parents, to 67.7 percent among those whose parents completed college, and to 71.2 percent among those whose parents held an advanced degree. The same pattern emerges regarding the share of students who had White partners, which rose from 43.4 percent to 51.2 percent to 60.2 percent across the three educational categories. Respondents with more educated parents were also less likely to report a negative reaction from others for dating outside their race, with an average negativity score of 2.10 for those whose parents held advanced degrees, compared to a mean of 2.18 for those holding college degrees, and 2.43 for those with non-college-educated parents.

In his interview, Eugene said that interracial dating is the "ultimate taboo" because "it breaks the status quo . . . that unwritten rule of just being cordial to each other, of coexisting." Of lower middle-class origins, Eugene grew up in a largely Black suburb in Alabama; neither of his parents had a college degree, and Eugene's college social circle was entirely Black. He even revealed that he regularly made fun of a friend "to his face" for dating an Asian woman. Tia saw a class divide affecting how Black students perceive interracial dating, explaining that "upper-class, wealthy [Black women], come from wealthy families or whatever, and that's basically the only way they'll date White males on this campus. You know what I mean?" Tia believes that because wealthy Black women do not have as many same-race friends and do not regularly participate in Black-oriented activities, they are spared much of the hostility that can accompany interracial dating.

We observe the sharpest differences in dating behavior across the categories of segregation experienced while growing up. Those who came of age in predominantly White schools and neighborhoods displayed the highest likelihood of interracial dating (76.3 percent) and the highest likelihood of dating White partners (66.8 percent). The lowest likelihoods of both interracial dating and dating White partners were observed among those who grew up in segregated schools and neighborhoods (with respective percentages of 52.3 percent and 35.2 percent). In between were respondents who came from racially mixed schools and neighborhoods (with respective percentages of 65.5 percent dating outside the group and 49.2 percent dating White partners). The frequency of experiencing a negative reaction for dating a non-Black partner rose steadily as prior experience of segregation increased. Among those from predominantly White backgrounds, the negativity score was 2.00, compared with values of 2.27 among those who lived in segregated neighborhoods but attended predominantly White schools, 2.36 among those who grew up in racially mixed schools and neighborhoods, and 2.43 for those coming of age in segregated schools and neighborhoods.

In general, then, when it comes to dating, we observe rather sharp differences in the likelihood of interracial dating and in the likelihood of dating White people along all the dimensions of Black diversity, with particularly salient divergences by racial identification, skin tone, gender, socioeconomic status, and prior experience of segregation. Differences by nativity status and national origin are more muted but still evident. In the emerging twenty-first-century Black elite, mixed-race individuals, men, higher status persons, and those from predominantly White schools and neighborhoods are most likely to date outside the group and more specifically to date White people. Students with these same background characteristics are also the least likely to experience a negative reaction for looking outside the group for romance.

Mixed-race interviewees tended to embrace the complexities of their origins and say that their lighter skin tones and "ambiguous" features influenced their choice of partners. For example, Jacob explained that his liberal racial attitudes came from his upbringing as well as his physical appearance. Growing up with his second-generation Cape Verdean mother and Irish American father, Jacob had been taught to take pride in his mixed origins and not choose one over the other.

> INTERVIEWER: How about biracial or mixed students, how is it for them to date other races? Do they do it more?
> JACOB: I think it's probably easier for them.
> INTERVIEWER: Yeah? How so?
> JACOB: Because you don't look as much like one race and I feel, like, you are mixed. At least for me, I don't think of race as something I can't be without, you know? The example is set for me by my folks.

Mixed-origin interviewees were also more likely than their monoracial peers to know and interact with interracial couples, and as already shown, their peer groups included more mixed-race friends. Paige's boyfriend was White and she was close to several other Black students on campus who were involved in interracial relationships.

> INTERVIEWER: What about interracial dating? Does that happen here?
> PAIGE: Well, I think it happens a lot here. I was telling someone, and she was like, "I think you're just seeing it." . . . I know a number of

couples. . . . Like, guys on the football team. [Name] is Black, his girlfriend is from Hungary. Then this other guy [name], who is half-Japanese, half-White, and his girlfriend is half-Irish, half-Black. . . . And then there's a girl from Trinidad that has an Asian boyfriend. . . . Maybe it's just 'cause I see it. I'm one to maybe look for that because of my background and then I'm in an interracial relationship. . . . It's not a big deal.

Of Black and Mexican heritage, Paige has always identified as racially mixed, and because of her light skin and ambiguous features, she often felt socially distant from monoracial Black peers. Consequently, she saw it as "more acceptable" for her to date non-Black men than it was for other, darker-skinned Black women:

I think it's more acceptable to be in an interracial relationship if you're [mixed]. Yeah, like, okay, what are the odds that I'm going to find a Mexican and Black guy—seriously? [laughs]. . . . It seems like . . . it could be more accepted, just because you know you are a product of something that's not [the norm].

Paige's White boyfriend was a football player and her social group included several of his White friends.

Compared to multigenerational natives, immigrant-origin interviewees were also more likely to date interracially, especially with a White partner. Immigrant-origin Black interviewees were inclined to see interracial dating as an "individual choice" but recognized that tolerance for interracial dating "varies among the population." Bob, a Ghanaian immigrant born in London, said that "I think it all depends on background and if you have an idea of Blackness. Like, what fits into that."

Although our mixed-race respondents reflected on light-skin privilege, colorism is also driven by anti–dark skin attitudes or experiences. Malik had especially dark skin, for example, and he often pondered whether it was "because I'm Black" that he couldn't find a woman to date or "hook up with" on campus. During one conversation, he vented his frustrations with the dating scene:

There's been times where, like I'll go out with my friend who's [mixed]. He's African American, like he's darker skinned. . . . I guess when he and I are out together, like we feel . . . we feel differently when we're out. Like, for instance, we went to this sorority party downtown, and when we came back, we were both like really mad because we felt . . . the girls there weren't being like true to us as like attractive men in their interactions with us. You know, I think what our impressions were that there's still like a stigma around like interacting with or dating or, you know, appearing to date or hook up with an African American . . . you know, which kind of enraged the both of us.

Like Malik, other dark-skinned interviewees we spoke to (e.g., Tia, Eugene, Karen, and Denise) also felt romantically "stigmatized" and resented the interracial dating habits of their lighter-skinned peers. Tia complained that "[dark-skinned students] will get dogged pretty much. They'll talk about you to no end. . . . It's hostile, it's a very hostile situation, I know in the Black community." Denise similarly called interracial dating between Black and White partners a "huge conflict" for her because of the negative historical legacy of such relationships and her commitment to racial solidarity and racial uplift.

As noted previously, Black women have historically been stereotyped as hypersexual, fetishized as exotic, acceptable for casual dating or a sexual "hookup" but not for serious, long-term relationships. Sandra, a former member of the swim team who often attended social events and parties with other athletes, told us how she felt when several White football players actively pursued her and her Black women friends explicitly because of their race, and more for sex than any serious romantic attachment:

SANDRA: [Me] and my friends were going to this football house to hang out and like all the guys in the house were really curious about Black women, like dating Black women.
INTERVIEWER: These were White guys?
SANDRA: Yes, White guys—all of them White guys. And also my friend [name]. He's a White guy and I went out to lunch with him like maybe a week or two ago and he was like, "I'm so upset. I never had the opportunity to date a Black woman here." And he was like, "I just want to date—like there's something very exotic about a Black woman right now." I think that, like, whole side of it is just like exoticized. . . . That's the only way I can really explain it.

Destiny shared similar experiences from her freshman year:

I had a really good half-Ecuadorian, half-White friend that I really liked, and I think a lot of the reason that he didn't like me back was I was Black. It was the same reason—oh, you're cool, but Black girl, what? Like, what are we going to talk about? And I felt either ignored, and . . . the only kind of attention was like, "Do you want to come to my room at three o'clock in the morning?" And I was like, "What? I've never been on a date. Like, I've never been kissed before." I was like, "I want to have a nice boyfriend." These White boys were like, "Boyfriend? You can come over, if you want, but what is a girlfriend? What the hell is that?"

Ellen completely agreed with Destiny's viewpoint, telling us, "I plan on dating. I'm not a hookup kind of girl!" And Kareem also noted the persistence of stereotypes about Black women's sexuality on campus and in society more broadly:

Every time you look in a magazine, it's rare that a Black female is portrayed as beautiful. It's usually more like exotic and sexy and borderline pornographic, unless they're really light-skinned and then they'll do the exact opposite and then they'll make them as alike as possible to like, Beyoncé, Ciara.

Kareem admitted very forthrightly that the dating culture on campus "sucks for Black women" because White men only want to "hook up" with Black women and do not consider them as potential life partners. When it comes to committed relationships, monoracial interviewees like Greg, a Ghanaian man born in London, emphasized the importance of racial homophily in long-term relationships:

You can have relationships with someone who you can relate to on a lot of different things, you see eye-to-eye with them, you feel comfortable with them—and that's a Black woman, usually. But if it's just sex, it can be any type of woman.

Among both men and women interviewees, there was a consensus that Black men dated outside the race for status and opportunity, whereas Black women dated interracially on campus because of the scarcity of Black men. Black men who were athletes and those coming from predominately White contexts were perceived as the most visible interracial daters and were less likely to have Black friends and engage in Black social life, as April explained to us:

APRIL: I think for sports, Black guys sorta blend. . . . A lot of the White girls will pretty much do a lot to get with them. . . . It's like the Black sports figure kind of ideal.

INTERVIEWER: Does that cause tension among Black women in the Black community?

APRIL: The [Black] girls don't really know them because they don't come to [Black] parties. They're not at any Black parties. They're at the football party, you know?

April, a track star herself, had never dated interracially, and from her point of view, Black women had no other option but to go outside the race because of the lack of suitable Black men, explaining that Black women "will date outside because they have no choice. It's either date outside or don't date at all." She went on to say that Black women who date White men do risk being ostracized by their same-race peers, claiming that "you become the 'Incognegro,' if you date outside the community." Calvin, a second-generation Nigerian student athlete and engineering major, was dating an Asian woman. He explained the gendered complexities of interracial dating from the masculine point of view as follows:

CALVIN: I mean, there is always the whole phenomenon with Black women. Because you know, educated Black men are [hard to find]. And, like, when a Black man goes with a girl of a different race . . . I've been dating my current girlfriend for a month. We been together for like three or four months, but I was in a two-and-a-half-year relationship with another girl and she was also Asian.
INTERVIEWER: So the Black women might not have thought about that too nicely?
CALVIN: Yeah, but every time I pursue it, nothing comes up, so either my reputation oversees it or maybe it just doesn't exist at all.

Calvin's four closest college friends were Asian, Hispanic, White, and Black—the exact configuration of his high school friendship network. During his freshman year, he initially attended meetings of various Black organizations, but his participation waned because of "how serious football was" and how much his parents stressed good grades. Calvin perceived himself as "separate from other Blacks" on campus because "I just don't like being defined."

A number of interviewees from racially segregated backgrounds expressed the strongest disapproval of interracial dating. Darryl was wholly against interracial dating and believed that attitudes about dating relate to an individual's upbringing and socioeconomic origins:

INTERVIEWER: How do you think it's perceived in the Black community?

DARRYL: I think most people are okay with it because of where most people come from. Most people are from communities that don't openly discourage it—that it's okay. I mean, like the community where I'm from, like [laughs] it was made very clear that interracial dating is not—you don't do that. So even Latinos and Blacks. Sometimes it's like, "Oh, why you doing that?" But yeah, it seems to be more accepted than I expected it to be.

Darryl perceived a large intraracial class divide among Black students at his university beyond dating patterns. He argued that his wealthier Black peers were more "assimilationist" in their beliefs relative to "poor" individuals like himself.

Where Darryl expressed his own disapproval of interracial dating, others from segregated backgrounds instead experienced that disapproval. Karen, who also had limited prior contact with White or Asian peers because they were not present in her neighborhood or school, nonetheless had a White college boyfriend, a relationship her mother strongly opposed:

My mother actually had a conversation with him about why she doesn't think we should be dating. . . . My mom was really more concerned [because] she doesn't want me to marry and have children with a White guy. Just because she feels like, how am I going to uplift the Black race if I do that? I'm like, "What are you talking about?" I'm like, "The same way I would have if I had all Black children!"

Neither of Karen's parents had completed college, and she described her family as working-class and "Afrocentric in their mindset."

Brian, a second-generation Jamaican, actually referenced Julie's (described below) relationship as unacceptable and said that he disapproved of interracial dating, informing us that she "would probably lose friends over that." In his view, interracial relationships were undesirable because Black and White people "don't come from similar socioeconomic backgrounds." He contended that Black-Latino relationships were more common because of their shared (presumably disadvantaged) socioeconomic origins.

Julie grew up in a working-class, Black neighborhood, and the majority of her friends from high school and college were Black. Nevertheless, she was in a long-term relationship with a White man; she thought he was acceptable because he had attended a historically Black institution on a basketball scholarship. Still, she was uneasy about having a White boyfriend. After listing all the Black organizations that she participated in, Julie admitted,

> I think it was also an effort on my part to be part of the Black community because my boyfriend was White and I noticed people would see us together. I didn't want to be seen as somebody who would be the kind to turn their back on their race. It was a conscious effort on my part to be part of the Black community.

Following Julie's story of trying to offset her romantic relationship by joining Black organizations to strategically assimilate, we turn now to see how Black diversity affected student decisions to join different extracurricular activities.

Divergent Organizational Affiliations

Finally, table 6.4 examines differences in the likelihood of affiliating with majority-Black and Black-focused organizations across dimensions of Black diversity. As noted earlier, we found that joining Black-focused organizations was much less common than joining majority-Black organizations, and we generally find few departures from this basic pattern. For example, we observe no significant differences in the likelihood of affiliating with Black-focused organizations by racial identification, skin tone, gender, or social class status. The clearest differences in the propensity to join race-themed organizations are by nativity and generational status, national origin, and childhood experience of segregation. Multigenerational natives are least likely to join race-themed organizations with a membership rate of 18.2 percent, compared to rates of 26.9 percent for first-generation immigrants and 25.8 percent for second-generation immigrants. Among respondents born abroad, those from "other" regions (neither African nor Caribbean nor American) displayed the lowest average membership in Black-focused organizations (18.0 percent); those from the Caribbean evinced the highest membership rate (32.7 percent), with Africans falling in between (21.1 percent).

The greatest divergence in affiliation with Black-focused groups occurred with respect to the prior experience of segregation. At one extreme are Black respondents from predominantly White schools and neighborhoods, only 16.1 percent of whom joined such an organization. At the other end of the continuum are Black respondents who grew up in segregated schools and neighborhoods, 26 percent of whom joined Black-focused organizations. In between are those from racially mixed schools and neighborhoods

TABLE 6.4. Organizational memberships of Black NLSF respondents by dimensions of Black diversity

Dimension of diversity	Member of majority-Black organization	Member of Black-themed organization
Racial identification		
Monoracial	61.5%**	20.8%
Mixed race	44.6	18.5
Nativity and generation		
Multigenerational native	60.7$^+$	18.2*
Second-generation immigrant	59.9	25.8
First-generation immigrant	50.9	26.9
Region of origin		
USA	60.7*	18.2**
African immigrant	54.4	21.1
Caribbean immigrant	57.7	32.7
Other immigrant	39.8	18.0
Skin tone		
Light	50.2*	16.1
Medium	61.3	21.1
Dark	62.3	23.3
Gender		
Female	61.9*	21.5
Male	53.2	18.6
Parental education		
No college	62.8	20.7
College degree	57.6	19.5
Advanced degree	56.8	21.0
Experience of segregation		
Predominantly White	50.9***	16.1*
Integrated neighborhood and school	61.6	22.0
Predominantly minority	68.8	26.4
Minority neighborhood/White school	55.4	17.4

$^+$ p < 0.10; * p < 0.05; ** p < 0.01; *** p < 0.001

(22.0 percent) and those who lived in segregated neighborhoods but attended White schools (17.4 percent).

Turning to the share of students who affiliated with majority-Black campus organizations, we observe no significant differences by socioeconomic status but substantial differences by racial identification and prior experience of segregation. Just over 60 percent of monoracial respondents reported membership in a majority-Black organization, compared to 44.6 percent of mixed-race respondents. Likewise, the share joining Black-majority organizations was 68.8 percent among respondents from segregated schools and neighborhoods, nearly 20 percent higher than respondents from predominantly White neighborhoods and schools (50.9 percent). The corresponding figures were 55.4 percent for those who lived in segregated minority neighborhoods but attended majority-White schools and 61.6 percent for those from racially mixed environments.

Our interview data confirm that mixed-race students were generally less interested in joining majority-Black organizations, as were respondents from predominantly White schools and neighborhoods. Jacob played varsity soccer and the guitar in a jazz band; for him, a typical weekend involved attending White fraternity parties with his Korean American girlfriend. Before college, Jacob attended an elite private day school with few Black students, and with his Irish American father and Cape Verdean mother, he insisted throughout the interview that he was not Black and did not have much in common with his Black college peers.

> INTERVIEWER: So you didn't really do any "Black-oriented" activities?
> JACOB: No, I've never done that stuff.
> INTERVIEWER: Why not?
> JACOB: It just doesn't appeal to me because I don't feel like I am Black, you know? If I went to a Black-oriented thing, I would feel like something that doesn't really apply necessarily, you know? I feel like I'm a fusion. I'm a different thing.
> INTERVIEWER: But you could also say, well, "I'm half-Black"?
> JACOB: Yeah, but for example, Black people wouldn't think of me as Black. White people wouldn't think of me as White. They would think of me as ethnic or something.
> INTERVIEWER: Why wouldn't Black people think you're Black?
> JACOB: Because I don't look Black. I look like something else.
> INTERVIEWER: But you just don't feel like you would connect that way?
> JACOB: I don't think so.

Megan, a senior whose mother is Black and father is White, also sees herself as an "outsider to the Black community" and said that she checks "all that apply" when classifying herself racially on forms. On campus, she did not participate in Black activities or Black-themed clubs. Instead, she served on the board of the mixed-race student association, rowed for the university's crew team, and joined the most elite White sorority on campus. Although Megan listed three close Black girlfriends (all of whom were also on the crew team), she had an Asian American boyfriend and did not feel "comfortable" in all-Black settings. Coming from an affluent family, she felt that many of her Black peers were not sufficiently knowledgeable of upper-class White manners and mores, and she felt that they looked upon her disparagingly as "the Black girl who hangs out with White people."

Sadie, the daughter of a White mother and Panamanian father, had just a hint of brown to her skin and relaxed hair that belied her Black heritage. With European, African, and Native American ancestry, she customarily checks "Other" on forms, explaining that "as much as I think that I am Black, I am also other things and I've never been a part of the Black circuit." During her freshman year, Sadie joined a Black dance troupe, but she didn't know much about "Black culture," and her Black women peers often excluded her from social events.

> SADIE: When I first joined [the dance troupe], I didn't think it would be a problem, but like I didn't get invited out as much. Like, they'd all be talking about where they were going, and . . . it was not addressed to me. I don't know if it is that I actually got left out or that I felt left out because I'm not part of that culture. . . . I went to private White schools, so, you know, I didn't know about that stuff. So I couldn't necessarily relate to what they were doing. I would need to learn it, but I guess I didn't make an effort. But I guess I didn't make the proper effort to learn it.
>
> INTERVIEWER: So what was different about what they were doing compared to what you were doing?
>
> SADIE: It was just the way that people interacted with each other. I don't really know, but if you watched the way my dance group interacted versus my sorority, they're very different.

During her sophomore year, Sadie joined an elite White sorority and quit the dance troupe, telling us that she did not "feel pressure" to join Black organizations because "no one knows what my racial background is." She insisted that her "comfort level is definitely greater with White people" because she "spent the majority of her life around White people" and not around Black people.

Not all mixed-race students feel this way, though. Some adopt an exclusively Black identity, and their racial attitudes and experiences tend to mirror those of monoracial, multigenerational natives. They generally expressed greater closeness to Black people than White people, opposed interracial dating, and were embedded within exclusively Black friendship networks. Unlike the mixed-race interviewees quoted above, these students tended to have working-class origins and grew up in concentrated minority or racially mixed environments.

For instance, although Erica's father was Black, he left the family when she was young. She and her Italian American mother lived in a Black, working-class neighborhood where she attended a racially mixed high school and developed a strong Black identity. Erica met most of her close friends as a result of living in her university's Black-affinity dorm and was heavily involved in Black-focused extracurricular activities. As she explained,

> It is important for me to have an active voice in the things which most impact my life. . . . I'm a Black student at [name of university] and I'm a Black student in the [name of city] community . . . and I'm the product of public schools and grew up in an area that is predominately Black.

At the time of her interview, Erica was involved in seven campus organizations, five of them Black-oriented. The other two groups included a community service project for low-income children and a university advisory board, on which she represented Black interests on campus.

Immigrant origins were also associated with less involvement with majority-Black organizations. Although immigrant-origin Black respondents were less likely to join predominantly Black groups or clubs, they were *more* likely to participate in extracurricular activities that were Black focused, particularly if they were of Caribbean origin. Although Ashley had become a U.S. citizen just before we met her, she identified herself as "Caribbean American" and served as president of the Caribbean Student Association. When asked why she decided to participate in that organization, she stated, simply, "because I wanted to meet other Caribbeans," explaining that it welcomed "all Black Caribbeans." She chose not to join the Black Student Union (BSU) because she believed they were "too militant."

There were many more Caribbean-themed groups than African groups on the campuses where we did our interviews. In addition to umbrella groups for all students of Caribbean origin, there were dance groups, performing arts organizations, and clubs that focused on specific ethnicities, such as the Haitian Association. Calvin, a second-generation Nigerian, decided against joining the Pan-African Association because he did not feel close to first-generation Africans, preferring to self-identify as "African American" rather than "African." He went on to discuss the wide variety of Black affinity groups on his campus:

There is even a direct quote [from the Pan-African Association] that would say, "Oh the BSU, that's for African Americans—that's not for us." They have their own separate organization. I believe it's called [name of African Association]. Typically, a person who is an international student wouldn't go to the BSU immediately because there are all these distinctions. If you are born in America, you go here. If you were born in Africa, you go here. If you were born in the Caribbean, you go here.

Among our interviewees, only one second-generation African student participated in the Pan-African Association. Yolanda joined because she "had never been around so many African people" and wanted to learn from those "born and raised in Africa, being second-generation, as I am." Unlike most second-generation immigrants, she identified as "African" not "African American."

Proud of her Trinidadian and Belizean ancestry, Madison was part of several Black-affinity groups, including the Black Women's Association, the High Steppers Club, and the Caribbean Association, which she described as "more ethnically" than racially focused. Her primary motivation to join the Caribbean Association was to experience "the dynamics between someone who's actually lived there their whole life, as opposed to me, who's only been there for summers." Madison opted not to join the BSU because she felt that it focused on issues she had already explored at her elite all-girls high school in Manhattan.

Although social class clearly shaped Madison's decisions about which clubs to join, socioeconomic status generally had little influence on the organizational affiliations mentioned by interviewees, affecting mostly working-class students who reported that athletics, work, and family commitments made it difficult to regularly participate in campus activities. Brad, a mixed-race junior, participated in no extracurricular activities because he worked more than forty hours a week at two jobs: as a server in the university dining hall and as a bartender at a local nightclub.

INTERVIEWER: And what about the on-campus organizations activities you've been involved in? What have you done?
BRAD: Nothing.
INTERVIEWER: What about like any reasons why you decided not to join any organizations, or do any extracurriculars?
BRAD: I had jobs.

Although Brad enjoyed a very generous scholarship, his family could not provide any financial assistance. His mother worked sporadically as a day care provider back in the Bronx, and his African father was not in the picture, so Brad worked to fill in the gaps.

Football limited Thomas's extracurricular involvement. He was recruited to his university to play football and accepted under its early decision program.

INTERVIEWER: What kinds of campus activities/organizations are you involved in?

THOMAS: Football. I wish I could do more, but football takes up too much time and doesn't really allow me to do more.

In addition to the elite status of the institution, Thomas came to his university because of the financial aid package they offered, telling us that "it was a very important part of my decision to come here. Most of my tuition is paid for through grants from the school," but he also worked part time on campus to earn spending money.

Interviewees at both universities reported that the BSU (also known as the Black Student League) was the largest Black-oriented group on campus, describing its membership as predominately multigenerational native Black students. Interviewees who regularly participated in the BSU viewed themselves as the "Black leaders" on campus. The BSU and its related programs provided a support system and a setting where Black students could engage with a critical mass of same-race peers. According to James, the union at his institution was popular with Black students because of its "catchall" focus and "political mission":

The Black Student League is pretty popular because—I think its leadership is really big. They are really gung-ho about the mission of the Black Student League. . . . It tries to better the Black experience at [name of university].

Despite his enthusiasm for the Black Student League, James said that his energies were focused more on developing his career prospects in business and that he was a dedicated member of a Black business club. James explained that Black students like himself belonged to this club as a way of cultivating their professional interests. James grew up in an affluent New England suburb and graduated from an elite prep school.

A majority of both survey and interview respondents found themselves gravitating toward majority-Black extracurricular groups, often specifically race-themed or race-focused organizations. These social groups provided a resource, a refuge, and a sense of purpose for Black students. Many interviewees who were not part of majority-Black organizations made it clear that this was not a conscious decision; rather, it was a consequence of the competing demands of employment or athletics. For others, the lack of involvement in Black organizations reflected a sense of alienation or "mismatch" after growing up in mostly White settings, or the perception that the organizations were "too militant" for them.

Campus Racial Climate

One's experience of race is not only about one's own background, identity, and social connections but also the context in which these elements of sociality occur. Here, we move beyond individual ties to friends, romantic partners, and organizations to consider the general state of race relations on campus and views about the institution's efforts to promote campus diversity. During their junior year, respondents were asked to share their perception of the overall degree of racial separation on campus, and as seniors, they were asked to assess the relative visibility of different racial groups on campus as well as the intensity and quality of interactions with them.

Campus Race Relations

Table 6.5 summarizes the foregoing evaluations, beginning in the top panel with respondents' rankings of the visibility of Black, White, Latino, and Asian students on campus on a 0 (not visible at all) to 10 (extremely visible) scale. Given the demographics of most institutions, it is not surprising that respondents rated White people the most visible on campus, with an average score of 9.1, followed by Asian (7.0), Black (6.5), and Latino people (4.6). These numerical ratings from the survey are generally consistent with what our interviewees told us. For example, when asked to describe what kind of people he noticed while walking down the main pedestrian pathway through campus, James volunteered that "ethnically, it's going to be mostly White, maybe 6 or 7 percent Black, [and] a decent Asian population."

In James's statement, White people clearly dominate, followed by Asians if we assume that "decent" refers to a quantity greater than the single-digit percentages he assigned to the prevalence of Black pedestrians on the walkway. Latinos were not mentioned and, by implication, were largely invisible to him. Although Julie avoided mentioning her own group, she nonetheless ranked the other groups in the same order as James. In her mind's eye, she saw "mostly White people, a lot of Asian people—a lot of East Asian people and also a lot

TABLE 6.5. Perceptions of campus racial climate among Black NLSF respondents

Racial climate indicator	Mean/%
Racial group visibility (0–10)	
Black students	6.5
White students	9.1
Latino students	4.6
Asian students	7.0
Intensity of interaction (0–10)	
Black students	8.5
White students	8.1
Latino students	5.7
Asian Students	5.4
Quality of interaction (0–10)	
With Whites	5.1
With Latinos	6.9
With Asians	4.8
Degree of racial separation on campus (0–4)	3.3
Institutional commitment to diversity	
Too little	52.1%
Just right	35.6
Too much	12.4

of Southeast Asian people as well, from India—[and] there is a small Latino population."

Interaction intensity was also assessed on a 0–10 scale where 0 indicated "no interaction at all" and 10 indicated "a great deal of interaction." If interpersonal contacts on campus were random, we would expect interaction intensities to follow the rank order shown in the first panel: White people first, followed in order by Asian, Black, and Latino. In fact, the observed order of interaction frequencies is quite different. As shown in the second panel of table 6.5, other Black people rank first with an average intensity rating of 8.5, followed by Whites at 8.1, Latinos at 5.7, and Asians at 5.4. This nonrandom ordering of interaction intensities indicates that relatively powerful social processes must be operating to boost the same-race interaction intensities so far above what the small Black percentage on most campuses would predict, and these same processes also functioned to raise the intensity of interaction with Latinos and lower the intensity of interaction with Asians.

One of our interviewees, Devon, a sophomore when we spoke with him, offered his theory of what these structured social processes might be:

I think when it comes down to it, like anywhere, there's always going to be the groups that stick together. Like, the Blacks will stick together, the Asians will stick together. . . . I think people are more comfortable being around people that they know and they feel comfortable with.

Although Devon's "stick together" model of interpersonal behavior might explain the high intensity of same-race interactions among Black students, it does not necessarily address the depressed intensity of Black-Asian interactions, the elevated intensity of Black-Latino interactions, or even the high intensity of Black-White interactions.

Devon himself alluded to this contradiction when he noted that unlike at his high school, where "Black kids really didn't associate with the White kids," he saw less Black-White separation on his university's campus. When asked why he thought that was, he responded, "Because here you might see Black kids talking to White kids, like hanging out with them, not necessarily going to parties, like in classes and stuff." Julie likewise attributed the relative intensity of Black-White interactions to the classroom setting, observing that "when it comes to classes and things, people do interact in class." Still, many interviewees agreed that racial divides remained large on campus, especially between Black and White people. Classroom interaction typically did not lead to more sustained or meaningful interactions after class. Interviewees also rarely spoke about cross-racial interactions between themselves and other non-White racial and ethnic groups. To them, the campus racial divide was more of a "Black-White" issue.

In addition to assessing the intensity of intergroup interactions on campus, survey respondents were also asked to rate the *quality* of their relations with different group members using a 0 (very poor) to 10 (excellent) scale, and these ratings shed light on the social processes responsible for the socially structured interaction intensities. The third panel of table 6.5 reports on the quality of respondents' interactions with non-Black people. As can be seen, the quality of interactions with Latinos was rated highest at 6.9, followed at some distance by interactions with White people (5.1) and finally Asian community members (4.8). These numbers suggest that despite the overrepresentation of Asians on most elite campuses, relations with Asian peers on campus were perceived to be of such low quality that Black students avoided contact with them. In contrast, interactions with Latinos are perceived to be of much higher quality, causing them to be sought out. Although interactions with White people were also perceived to be of low quality, frequent interactions with them cannot be avoided given their numerical dominance among students, faculty members, and administrators.

As mentioned above, during their junior year, respondents were asked to rate the degree of racial separation on campus, in this case on a 0–4 scale where 0 indicated "very little," 1 indicated "slight," 2 indicated "some," 3 indicated "substantial, and 4 indicated "very substantial." The average rating given by Black students was 3.3, roughly three-tenths of the psychological distance between "substantial" and "very substantial." Very clearly, then, Black students attending selective colleges and universities in the early twenty-first century perceived substantial racial separation on their campuses.

Finally, in their senior year, NLSF respondents were asked to rate their institution's commitment to racial and ethnic diversity on campus as "way too little," "somewhat too little," "just enough," "somewhat too much," or "way too much." The bottom panel of table 6.5 summarizes their responses, collapsing these five descriptors into three broad categories, revealing that a little more than half (52.1 percent) of respondents believe their institutions were insufficiently committed to the cultivation of racial and ethnic diversity. A little over one-third (35.6 percent) of survey respondents thought the level of institutional commitment was just right, and just 12.4 percent said it was too much.

Despite the fact that a majority of survey respondents wanted more institutional commitment to diversity, the interviewees we spoke to at length also put the burden of making diversity happen on themselves and their peers. When asked about his institution's efforts to diversify, Ervin, who had a diverse network of Black, White, and Asian friends, waived off the query, saying that "besides letting in who they should admit, I don't really know—I don't know what else they could do." Although Karen also wanted her university to do more to promote diversity, she also recognized that social dynamics could be challenging and that universities could do only so much to encourage more meaningful interracial interactions on campus.

> INTERVIEWER: Do you think the administration and the faculty here make an effort to promote racial diversity?
>
> KAREN: Yeah, I think more with time, they are. I think some students take issue with there not being more interactions. So there's always sort of talk about more of what we could do.
>
> INTERVIEWER: How do you think things could be improved?
>
> KAREN: [Long pause]. I don't know. You can't throw the content of diversity in people's faces. You can't force diverse people to interact.

It's not like you're not going to get diverse experiences, diverse opinions, diverse whatever from your organizations, be they race related or religion related or not. Certainly, my freshman year, I was eating with a much more diverse group than I'm eating with now. But, then, yeah, I think it's more of an issue junior and senior year [when] some [groups] are more diverse than others.

Even though Karen described herself as "extremely sociable," she admitted she was a bit intimidated by the size of the White student body when she first arrived on campus. Although she initially made a concerted effort to socialize with non-Black students, specific racial incidents made her uncomfortable, and over time, her social network narrowed to become exclusively Black.

Disappointment in Campus Race Relations

To this point, we have documented significant and often stark differences in the friendship networks, dating practices, and organizational affiliations exhibited by different subsets of Black students. Yet, when we disaggregated the ratings of group visibility along the various dimensions of Black diversity, we encountered only four statistically significant differences. Given the relative lack of statistically significant differences between Black respondents in how they rated different group visibilities, racial separation, and the quality of intergroup relations on campus, we do not present full tables of cross-tabulations for these outcomes and instead focus only on statistically meaningful differentials.

Black visibility was greatest for light-skinned respondents at 6.8 and least for dark-skinned respondents at 6.2, with medium-toned respondents falling in between at 6.6. In other words, the perceived visibility of Black people on campus rose as the observer's skin color lightened. Turning to the perceived visibility of racial outgroups, White people were rated as more visible by Black women (9.2) than Black men (8.9), and White visibility generally increased as parental education rose, going from 8.9 among respondents whose parents had not completed college to 9.1 among those whose parents were college graduates, and reaching 9.3 among those whose parents held advanced degrees. The perceived visibility of Asians also varied by parental education, being 7.3 among respondents whose parents held an advanced degree compared with 6.8 among those whose parents had not completed college and 6.6 among those whose parents held a college degree (6.6). Thus, it was Black students from the best educated families who were most attuned to the position of White and Asian students on campus.

Overall, we found considerable consensus that racial separation was substantial or very substantial with an overall rating of around 3.3. This was the view for all Black respondents except those who lived in segregated minority neighborhoods but attended predominantly White schools. On average, they rated racial separation to be 9 percent higher at 3.6, meaning they leaned toward perceiving campus racial separation as "very substantial." It thus seems that the contrast between living in segregated neighborhoods and attending majority-White schools highlighted the salience of racial separation in the minds of respondents.

We also observe a paucity of significant differences among Black students with respect to the perceived quality of intergroup relations. Differences emerged only for specific immigrant-origin groups and were only marginally significant. With a mean quality rating of 5.1, Caribbean-origin students rated relations with White students to be slightly better than those with origins in Africa (4.7) or other world regions (4.5). Caribbean immigrants also rated their relations with Asians (5.2) as better than those of African origin (4.7) and ancestry in other regions (4.2). One of our interviewees, Ann, shed light on the relatively low quality of relations with Asians experienced by immigrants from Africa and other locations in the African diaspora.

Of Nigerian and Taiwanese descent, she grew up in Taiwan and spoke Mandarin fluently. Although Ann identified as "mixed," she had dark skin and kinky hair. When she got to campus, she joined activities that matched her identities, seeking to affiliate with the African, Chinese, and Black student associations. Although she got along well in the African and Black student associations, she was not embraced by the Asian association:

> It didn't work so well on the Asian side of things. I looked more different than they did. So whenever I tried to go to their events, they'd be like, "What is she doing here? Why is she here?" But you know, culturally, I have more in common with them than I do with Black students here.

Ann went on to explain that she felt more welcomed by Black peers on campus because they "have seen a lot more heterogeneity than the Asian community has. So I think that's the difference that makes me welcomed in the Black community." Back home in Taiwan, Ann attended a small, international school where she was readily accepted for who she was.

In table 6.6, we examine intragroup differences with respect to the intensity of interactions with different groups. The most salient differences in Black interaction intensities occurred with respect to their relations with other Black students.

TABLE 6.6. Intensity of interaction with people from different racial groups for Black NLSF respondents by dimensions of Black diversity

	Intensity of interaction with:			
Dimension of diversity	Whites	Blacks	Latinos	Asians
Racial identification				
Monoracial	8.1	8.6***	5.7	5.3
Mixed race	8.4	7.7	5.5	5.5
Nativity and generation				
Multigenerational native	8.2*	8.6*	5.6	5.2**
Second-generation immigrant	7.5	8.6	5.8	5.3
First-generation immigrant	8.2	8.1	5.9	5.9
Region of origin				
African immigrant	8.2	8.2+	5.7	6.3**
Caribbean immigrant	7.9	8.3	6.0	5.4
Other immigrant	7.6	8.3	5.7	5.5
Skin tone				
Light	8.3	8.1**	5.5	5.2
Medium	7.9	8.7	5.6	5.3
Dark	8.2	8.6	6.0	5.4
Gender				
Female	8.1	8.6*	5.7	5.4
Male	8.1	8.3	5.6	5.4
Parental education				
No college	8.0+	8.8**	5.7	5.3
College degree	8.1	8.4	5.6	5.3
Advanced degree	8.3	8.3	5.6	5.5
Experience of segregation				
Predominantly White	8.5**	8.0***	5.5	5.4
Integrated neighborhood and school	7.9	8.7	5.6	5.3
Predominantly minority	7.9	8.8	5.8	5.4
Minority neighborhood/White school	8.0	8.8	6.1	5.3

$+ p < 0.10; * p < 0.05; ** p < 0.01; *** p < 0.001$

Looking at the top two panels, we see that the intensity of within-group interaction was greater for monoracial respondents (8.6) than mixed-race respondents (7.7), as well as for native and second-generation immigrants (8.6) compared to first-generation immigrants (8.1). Turning to skin tone, we find that the intensity of within-group interaction was greater for dark-skinned respondents (8.6) and those with medium skin tones (8.7) compared to light-skinned respondents (8.1).

Moving down the table, we see that interactions with other Black people were also more intense for women (8.6) than men (8.3), and greater for those with non-college-educated parents (8.8) than for those whose parents had completed college (8.4) or held an advanced degree (8.3). Finally, the intensity of same-group interaction was considerably greater among respondents who grew up in racially mixed schools and neighborhoods (8.7) and segregated neighborhoods and schools (8.8) than for those from predominantly White neighborhoods and schools (8.0).

In sum, the intensity of Black-on-Black interactions is greatest for native-born, monoracial, dark-skinned respondents who grew up in segregated circumstances with less educated parents. Among those who fit this profile, the intensity of same-race interactions was additionally greater for women than men. The intensity of within-group interactions was lowest for men of mixed race and of immigrant origin with well-educated parents who grew up in predominantly White neighborhoods and schools. However, less intense intragroup interaction does not necessarily imply higher intensities of interaction with other groups. We do not observe any significant dimensional differences in the intensity of interaction with Latinos, for example.

The intensity of Black interactions with White people *is* greater, however, for respondents from predominantly White schools and neighborhoods (8.5) compared to those from other neighborhoods (around 7.9 or 8.0). Black-White interaction intensity is also greater for first-generation immigrants and multigenerational natives (8.2) than for second-generation immigrants (7.5), as well as for respondents whose parents held an advanced degree (8.3) compared to those whose parents held no degree (8.0) or just an undergraduate college degree (8.1). First-generation immigrants also report more intense interaction with Asians (5.9) than either multigenerational natives (5.2) or second-generation immigrants (5.3), and interactions with Asians are especially intense among those with immigrant origins in Africa (6.3).

In his interview with us, Darryl talked at some length about his interactions with Black, White, and Asian students on campus. In general, he thought that White students were too quick to judge Black peers for not wanting to integrate:

> I mean, there are a lot of feelings of self-segregation on campus. A lot of White people accuse Blacks of that, which is always interesting because some Blacks are always quick to argue, "Well, y'all don't say anything when the football players eat together, or when the lacrosse players eat together or the sorority girls eat together, but it's because you can all see that we have Black faces that you're gonna label that as segregation.

Darryl perceived an especially acute split between Asians and everyone else, which was new to him even though he had attended an elite boarding school.

> I remember we [one guy] was at the gym waiting to play basketball, me and this White guy, I don't know him, he asks me if there was another game going on, and I was like, "You can check over there." And I saw him snicker, and he looked over and he was like, "Yeah, those are the Asian guys and you can't play with them. If there is a group of Chinese or Korean guys, or basically any East Asian guys playing, nobody else can play with them. They find a court to the farthest, to the back end, they play by themselves." I never see East Asians mingling much, and though it's interesting, it's not discussed. [In] the Black community, everything that we do is chastised. If you have more than five Black guys on a court, they assume that the Black men got together, but it's the assumption that's dangerous—that we have to be self-segregated somehow.

Not surprisingly, Darryl found the racial climate at his university to be hostile and "not what I thought it would be." Specifically, he criticized White students for denying that there are racial issues on campus:

> The majority [of White students] tend to believe that we don't really have a race problem and the people that play the race card are like being too dramatic and aren't being realistic. That is of the things, such as class and culture that, um, create the disparities.

Throughout his interview, Darryl readily discussed the problems he had fitting in on a wealthy White campus as a "poor Black man."

Table 6.7 concludes our analysis of campus race relations by examining how perceptions about how institutional commitment to diversity varies among Black respondents. The share of respondents who thought that their college or university was doing too little to promote racial and ethnic diversity was greater for women compared to men (54.1 percent versus 48.3 percent) and for those with medium or dark skin tones (52.5 percent and 58.1 percent) compared to light skin tones (44.7 percent). Support for the belief that one's college or university is doing too little to promote diversity falls with rising parental education, dropping from 53.6 percent to 52.6 percent to 50.5 percent as the category shifts from no college, to college degree, to advanced degree, though this differential is only marginally statistically significant ($p < 0.10$).

TABLE 6.7. Perceived institutional commitment to diversity for Black NLSF respondents by dimensions of Black diversity

Dimension of diversity	Institutional commitment to diversity		
	Too little	Just right	Too much
Racial identification			
Monoracial	53.6%	35.0%	11.4%
Mixed race	44.0	38.6	17.4
Nativity and generation			
Multigenerational native	51.7	36.6	11.7
Second generation immigrant	50.1	34.6	15.4
First generation immigrant	59.4	29.1	11.5
Region of origin			
African immigrant	50.0	33.9	16.1
Caribbean immigrant	55.7	31.0	13.3
Other immigrant	50.5	36.6	13.0
Skin tone			
Light	44.7*	39.5*	15.7*
Medium	52.5	35.1	12.4
Dark	58.1	32.8	9.2
Gender			
Female	54.1*	34.5*	11.5*
Male	48.3	37.7	14.0
Parental education			
No college	53.6+	34.4+	12.0+
College degree	52.6	31.3	16.1
Advanced degree	50.5	39.9	9.6
Experience of segregation			
Predominantly White	51.5*	36.0*	12.5*
Integrated neighborhood and school	51.5	37.4	11.1
Predominantly minority	50.7	33.6	15.6
Minority neighborhood/White school	59.6	32.9	7.5

+ $p < 0.10$; * $p < 0.05$; ** $p < 0.01$; *** $p < 0.001$

Black students who lived in segregated minority neighborhoods but attended White schools were the most critical of their institutions' commitments to diversity, again suggesting that experiencing the stark contrast between minority and White settings on a daily basis somehow underscored the salience of race in students' minds, though it also may be a comparison to elite high schools that were either more progressive or more active in manipulating student social experiences compared to colleges. Whereas 59.6 percent of those who lived in segregated neighborhoods while attending White schools said their institution was doing too little to promote diversity, the figure was only 50.7 percent among those from segregated schools and neighborhoods and just 51.5 percent among those who grew up in either White or racially mixed settings.

Conclusion

Attending college at a selective residential institution of higher education offers an opportunity for social exploration and self-discovery for most students. Graduation speeches often reminisce about late-night conversations, the formation of bonds that last a lifetime, and experiences that profoundly shape their perceptions and beliefs. Even though residential colleges lack the rigorous rules and rituals of military and mental institutions, they are an example of what Goffman (1961) calls total institutions, social settings that redefine the individual as a member of a new community with a new worldview shaped by that membership. Until recently, the unspoken assumption about Black students at selective colleges and universities was that their academic socialization constituted a universal experience characterized by common challenges and pitfalls shared by all.

Our analysis of NLSF survey data reveals that racially mixed light-skinned students with well-educated parents who grew up in predominantly White schools and neighborhoods have very different college experiences compared to monoracial, multigenerational students from segregated schools and neighborhoods whose parents did not finish college. We also find that social experiences on campus are qualitatively different for Black men and Black women. These conclusions, derived from our interpretation of descriptive univariate tabulations, hold up well under multivariate analysis, except that skin tone and parental education turn out to have no independent influence on campus social outcomes once racial identification, gender, prior segregation, and other background factors are taken into account.

Compared to their monoracial peers, mixed-race students report having more White friends and fewer Black friends, and they are more likely to date interracially, especially with White partners (see appendix tables A6.1 and A6.2). Black men exhibit exactly the same pattern of sociality, making gender a key factor conditioning Black sociality on campus. Mixed-race and Black men also report less intense interactions with other Black students. The tendency to have more White and fewer Black friends is reinforced for those who grew up in predominantly White schools and neighborhoods. Students of immigrant origin, especially from the Caribbean, also have more White and fewer Black friends on campus. Despite these differences between monoracial and mixed-race students, however, the peer groups of students in the latter category *did* become Blacker in the transition from high school to college.

Multivariate analyses also indicate that membership in majority-Black campus organizations is linked to immigrant generation and gender, with second-generation immigrants and men being significantly less likely to join such organizations compared to first-generation immigrants, multigenerational natives, and women (see appendix table A6.3). Although univariate tabulations suggest that membership in majority-Black organizations also differs by racial identification, skin tone, parental education, and prior experience of segregation, these differences failed to emerge in the multivariate models. Consistent with our simple descriptive results, however, membership in Black-themed organizations is significantly and positively predicted by origins in the Caribbean and negatively predicted by having grown up in White schools and neighborhoods.

Also as in the descriptive results, the multivariate analyses uncovered few significant differences among Black students in how they perceived the relative visibility of White and Black people on campus, the degree of racial separation they witnessed at their institutions, and their estimation of the overall quality of campus intergroup relations. Although Black men perceive White people to be less visible on campus than Black women (appendix table 6.4), we discern no other significant differences across Black subgroups in their ratings of the quality of interactions with White people or the degree of racial separation on campus (appendix table 6.5). With respect to perceptions about institutional commitment to campus diversity, only Black students with college-educated parents stood out, and they perceived their schools to be *too* committed to diversity as a goal (appendix table 6.6).

As expected, the social experiences of Black students at Howard University proved to be quite different from those at predominantly White institutions (see appendix tables A6.1–A6.6). In the multivariate models, they unsurprisingly report having fewer White friends and more Black friends. They also perceive Black students to be highly visible and White students as much less visible, report intense interactions with Black students and weak interactions with White students, and rate the quality of interactions with Black students high and White students low. Although these findings are not very informative about what are obvious features of social life on a predominantly Black campus, controlling for attendance at Howard in the multivariate models ensures that patterns of sociality indicated by other coefficients are not affected by the distinctive collegiate experiences of students at a historically Black college and university.

Although skin tone and parental education statistically have no independent effects once the other factors are taken into account, in their interviews mixed-race students did recognize that light skin tones, affluent origins, and familiarity with White social spaces did make it easier for them to interact with diverse others on a predominantly White campus. Mixed-race students generally confronted the challenges of elite college life without apprehension and were able to acquire what Bourdieu (1977) would call the *habitus* of elite White academia with relative ease. Their acclimation to college life was less strategic than other Black students in that they socialized with friends and partners who already shared their class and racial backgrounds, privileged life experiences, and comfort with White society.

Many observers from across the political spectrum worry that selective colleges and universities are segregated socially due to institutional inaction, Black self-segregation, White racial insensitivities, or some combination of these factors. In this chapter, however, we found relatively high rates of interpersonal interaction, mostly with same-race friends and romantic partners but also with diverse peers. Although the majority of Black respondents thought their institutions were not committed enough to diversity, it was only a slim majority and roughly one in ten thought that their institution was overly focused on diversity.

Their own social circles demonstrate that this fear of social segregation is misguided. Nearly all of our respondents reported having at least a few same-race friends and dates; however, those with mixed-race, immigrant, and affluent backgrounds who originated in White schools and neighborhoods tended to have fewer Black friends and romantic partners in college, though typically more than they had in high school. Our interviews generally revealed dating and romance to be topics of intense thought, self-reflection, and frustration and fraught with a multitude of interpersonal, political, and emotional risks. Skin color stratification heavily influenced the frequency of interracial dating and partnering, especially with White partners. The likelihood of forming a romantic attachment to a White person was strongly associated with racial identification, skin tone, nativity status, gender, social class, and prior experience with segregation. Fortunately, interviewees who dated interracially reported few negative reactions from social others, though there were significant differences in the frequency of such reactions by racial identification, skin tone, and socioeconomic status characteristics.

Despite these promising signs of social integration and racial equanimity, our respondents rated the quality of their interactions with White and Asian peers relatively poorly. Moreover, even though the *frequency* of interaction with different groups tended to vary by the now-familiar dimensions of Black diversity, the *quality* of those interactions did not. Respondents consistently rated the quality of their interactions with White and Asian peers as low, and interviews suggest that it was their unpleasant social experiences that drove them toward initially unplanned and undesired monoracial social networks on campus.

7

Downsides of Upward Mobility

I mean, the fact is, that being African American automatically kind of puts a little damper [on Black students]—people have this preconception, even if sometimes they've shaken it. But when it comes to society, it's just the way things are. People just think African Americans aren't as smart as other races, and you just have to deal with it, you know?

CALVIN, SECOND-GENERATION NIGERIAN AMERICAN

THE ACQUISITION of a degree from a prestigious college or university represents a critical step for students seeking to enter the Black professional class. Earning a degree from an Ivy League university, a selective liberal arts college, or a flagship state university opens up significant opportunities for socioeconomic mobility and personal gratification. Appreciating these possibilities, Black students work hard in anticipation of the gains that are expected to follow: admission to a nationally ranked medical, law, business, or graduate school; access to a prestigious, high-paying job; greater status, wealth, and respect; and perhaps even a position of leadership in business, philanthropy, public administration, or politics.

Although membership in America's professional elite has its rewards, it also has costs. In this chapter, we consider some of the downsides of college as a pathway for upward mobility among aspiring young Black students. The potential costs incurred on the way to graduation include exposure to White racial hostility on campus, encounters with own-group class resentment, the stress of performance at an elite academic institution, pressures stemming from parental expectations, the accumulation of debt, and feelings of alienation from communities of origin. In addition, for those Black students whose ties extend back to friends and relatives living in very disadvantaged neighborhoods, there is the ongoing risk of experiencing trauma within one's social network. Ultimately, of course, the cumulative burden of these costs can take a toll on students' mental health.

Exposure to Racial Hostility

Despite the Black student diversity we have documented to this point, Brown and Jones (2015:186) argue that a process of "ethnoracialization" serves to unify African Americans in a common worldview within a "structure of institutional power relations" that compels young Blacks to engage in "the discursive reinterpretation of group meanings and boundaries." Shared phenotypical characteristics differentiate Black students from their White and Asian peers, making them keenly aware of how others view them. This resulting "two-ness" noted by Du Bois (1903) leads students to expend considerable psychological energy contemplating the meaning of Blackness (see Torres and Charles 2004). Common exposure to racial prejudice and discrimination also serves to blur the boundaries between Black and other non-White groups that share similar experiences of exclusion and marginalization, potentially creating broader panethnic solidarities (Moore 2008; Tovar and Feliciano 2009; Greer 2013; Smith 2014; Thornton, Taylor, and Chatters 2014; Reyes 2017). As our interviewee Denise candidly put it, "Being Black is the link. I mean, yes, we do have our own intraracial issues, class, things like that, but for the most part, okay, you're Black; you're a sister or brother, you know?"

Scholars have identified "strategic assimilation" as a key mechanism by which high-status Blacks seek to avoid rejection by less socioeconomically advantaged same-race peers (Lacy 2004; Moore 2008). Hiding interracial dating while pointedly attending Black-oriented events is emblematic of this strategy. The enactment of a symbolic Blackness also enables aspiring members of the twenty-first-century Black elite to maneuver within a milieu of White privilege that otherwise tends to reproduce racial and class inequalities (Moore 2008). For these students, fluency in the finer points of Black urban culture signifies racial solidarity and allegiance in the face of White racism and can offer a protective psychosocial buffer for those seeking to achieve success in an often hostile White world (see Moore 2008; Torres 2009; Martin 2010; Rollock et al. 2011; Carter 2012; Lofton and Davis 2015; Wallace 2017). Cultural capital is by definition culturally dependent. Cultural knowledge that is useful in a Black context is not necessarily useful in a White context, and vice versa. Students who straddle the Black and White worlds therefore deploy Black cultural signifiers in Black settings to indicate solidarity and belonging while withholding them in White settings where they would not necessarily be understood or appreciated. Having certified their membership in the Black community, however, they are then free to cultivate a knowledge of White signifiers for use in the predominantly White settings on campus without feeling disloyal to the group.

Strategic assimilation, however, is not without its downsides. Lacy (2004) argues that privileged African Americans, in particular, devote considerable mental effort and emotional energy to cultivating, maintaining, and policing racial identities. Although the acquisition of a college degree brings material rewards, it also entails exposure to a variety of "achievement-oriented stressors" that affect all students but are intensified for Blacks trying to navigate a largely (often elite) White world (Parham 1989). How students manage these stressors depends on their social, economic, and demographic origins as well as their prior social experiences within White and Black social settings. Despite a general awareness of differences in identity formation and behavior among African Americans, few studies have examined the heterogeneity of Black psychosocial responses to life at selective academic institutions (Johnson 2019).

The principal driver of ethnoracialization for college students is exposure to common experiences of racial prejudice and discrimination on campus. However, as Jack (2019) demonstrates ethnographically—and as prior chapters have confirmed—young Black adults arrive at selective colleges and universities with varying degrees of prior exposure to White environments and, by extension, different experiences and understandings of what it means to be Black within White spaces. Yet, less is known about how Black students differ in their exposure to discriminatory treatment on campus and how they interpret it. We do not know, for example, whether discriminatory episodes are defining moments for those who experience them or simply aggravations that are brushed aside, or the degree to which encounters with racial prejudice on campus influence perceptions about acceptance or exclusion at the institution (e.g., Chavous and Leath 2017).

These issues are important because exposure to a hostile or unwelcoming social environment carries the potential not only to undermine academic performance but also to influence which subjects are studied, which professions are pursued, which political views are expressed, and how Black students situate themselves in U.S. society generally. Research shows that student retention at selective schools is negatively affected by perceptions of the campus racial climate as hostile, isolating, and unwelcoming (Massey and Probasco 2010), and exposure to prejudice and discrimination on campus can have lasting, long-term effects on those seeking to enter the Black professional class (see Feagin, Vera, and Imani 1996; Solórzano, Ceja, and Yosso 2000; Allen, Dawson, and Brown 1989; Willie 2003; Griffin et al. 2011; Strayhorn 2011; Johnson 2019).

Our in-depth interviews uncovered a number of public and private incidents in which respondents confronted explicit prejudice and racism. One very public incident took place at a local business on the border of the institution's campus. In that instance, a White retail employee was accused of committing a racist act against a Black student. Interviewees reported a number of other racial incidents both on and off the school's campus, including racial slurs made by White men to Black women students at an honor society induction ceremony, the chilling effects of a White student government candidate who posed in blackface, a swim team party where White members dressed as Black gang members, catcalls and racial epithets directed at Black women by White fraternity brothers, and the frequent questioning of Black men by police both on and off campus. On top of that, interviewees at both institutions—men and women—underscored the importance of always carrying university identification to be able to validate their presence on campus to non-Black members of the college and wider communities.

Not everyone experienced such prejudicial acts, of course, but many drew from such experiences in discussing the campus racial climate, one of whom was April:

> INTERVIEWER: Have you experienced racism and or prejudice since you've been here?
>
> APRIL: Yes, I would say so—at the bookstore. . . . I had an orgo chemistry book that I was returning, and they had mispackaged it, and I was like, "Well, I need to return the book." I was told I would be able to . . . and [the store employee] was like, "I will call the police." He's just flipping out. . . . The staff at the bookstore had to go through sensitivity course training. . . . He was like, "You know what I think? I think you're lying." I was like, "Look, I have my receipt here. I'm trying to return the book. It's a week into class. I just dropped the class. I'm not premed anymore. . . . I'm not lying to you." He was like, "If you don't leave now, I'm going to have to throw you out," and I'm like, "What are you talking about?"

This experience made April rather pessimistic about the university's commitment to diversity. In her view, race relations on campus and in the broader community were "not good" due to entrenched stereotypes and systemic racism.

To gauge whether experiences like April's are common, we turn to our survey data. During each of their first two years of college, respondents were asked a series of questions about how often they experienced different forms of racial hostility on campus. These included being made to feel racially uncomfortable or self-conscious by classmates, professors, and staff; being made to feel unwelcome while "just walking across campus"; overhearing derogatory racial remarks from students, professors, and college staff members; and experiencing racial harassment from police, professors, or others in the campus community. For each type of prejudice reported, respondents assessed the frequency of occurrence using a scale that ranged from 0 to 4 (never, rarely, sometimes, often, very often). The resulting data are summarized in table 7.1.

The first column shows the percentage of Black respondents who *ever* experienced each of eleven types of racial hostility listed in the table during their first two years of college. Incidents of racial hostility stemmed most frequently from interactions with other students. More than three-quarters of the National Longitudinal Survey of Freshmen (NLSF) respondents (78.4 percent) said they had been made to feel uncomfortable or self-conscious by classmates at some point as freshmen or sophomores; nearly as many (72.3 percent) overheard students making derogatory remarks about African Americans. Only slightly fewer respondents (69.5 percent) reported feelings of discomfort or self-consciousness while walking across campus, confirming the negative effects of social isolation on predominantly White campuses noted earlier by Benjamin (2005). Since White students dominate the campuses and classrooms in our study, the foregoing responses suggest they are the principal source of racial discomfort, though by no means the only source.

Faculty members appear to be the next most important source of racial harassment and prejudice on campus. Just over half of all respondents (53.4 percent) reported that a professor had at some point made them feel uncomfortable or self-conscious because of their race; 36.6 percent said a faculty member had unfairly discouraged them from a course of study; 23.4 percent said a professor had given them an unfair grade; and 19.6 percent said that an instructor had inappropriately discouraged them from speaking in class. Although these are subjective assessments that cannot be independently verified, one must remember the sociological truism that "if [people] define situations as real, they are real in their consequences" (Thomas and Thomas 1928:571). Even if faculty members are not

TABLE 7.1. Perceptions of racial prejudice experienced on campus by Black NLSF respondents

	Percent ever experienced	Frequency of experience
Made to feel uncomfortable or self-conscious by:		
Classmates	78.4%	0.99
Professors	53.4	0.51
Just walking around campus	69.5	0.88
Heard derogatory racial remarks from:		
Students	72.3%	0.83
Professors	21.9	0.17
Staff or others	43.4	0.26
Experienced harassment from:		
Campus police asking for ID (except at entrances)	24.5%	0.25
Professor who discouraged speaking in class	19.6	0.18
Professor who gave unfair grade	23.4	0.21
Professor discouraged a course of study	36.6	0.34
Other harassment on campus	43.4	0.38
Total	1,039	

intending to communicate prejudice, the Thomas theorem recognizes that the effects on Black students are likely the same as if they were. This point is important because racial bias is often unconscious and expressed without awareness. Implicit biases are implanted in people's social cognition as a result of years of experience and socialization in a society still rife with negative racial stereotypes and prejudices (see Eberhardt 2019).

Beyond students and professors, some 43.4 percent of respondents reported that a staff member or some other figure on campus had made derogatory racial remarks, and roughly one-quarter (24.5 percent) reported being asked for identification by the campus police. The latter form of harassment was highly gendered, however. Whereas only 17.7 percent of Black women had been asked to present ID, the figure was 37.3 percent for Black men. This finding is consistent with sociological research on how Black men at predominately White colleges and universities and in society at large are often surveilled by Whites in line with the pernicious stereotypes of Black criminality and violence (see Russell-Brown 1998; Harper 2015; Boyd and Mitchell 2018).

The second column of table 7.1 presents the average frequency of racially hostile experiences coded on the aforementioned 0–4 scale. After two years on campus, the mean frequency of being made to feel uncomfortable or self-conscious by classmates was 0.99, a value that corresponds roughly to "rarely" on the scale. The mean frequency rating for being made to feel uncomfortable for walking around campus was 0.88 and that for hearing derogatory remarks from other students was 0.83. Thus, although harassment from other students was the most common form of hostility reported, on average it seemed to be a relatively rare occurrence.

Other forms of harassment varied between "never" and a position half the distance up the continuum toward "rarely." The ratings ranged from 0.17 for hearing derogatory remarks from a professor to 0.51 for being made to feel uncomfortable by a professor. In between were ratings for being discouraged by a professor from undertaking a course of study (0.34), hearing derogatory remarks from staff members or others on campus (0.26), being asked for identification by the campus police (0.25), and being given an unfair grade by a professor (0.21). Despite these low-frequency ratings, only 21.6 percent of respondents said they had *never* experienced *any* form of racial hostility on campus. Across all categories, the mean number of hostile incidents experienced was approximately five (4.98), meaning that the average student had experienced around five expressions of racial hostility.

To examine whether perceptions of racial hostility vary across the different subgroups of Black student diversity, we turn to the data in table 7.2. The first column shows the number of different kinds of racial hostility experienced by the average respondent during the first two years of college (with a possible range 0–11). The second column displays the total number of hostile experiences accumulated across all eleven categories of prejudice over this period (possible range 0–44). In both sets of numbers, we see the largest discrepancies in exposure to prejudice by racial identity, skin tone, prior experience of segregation, and gender. Respondents reported few differences in exposure to racial hostility by nativity, generation, or region of origin.

Unsurprisingly, given what we have seen to this point, both the mean number of kinds of hostility experienced and the total frequency of their occurrence were significantly greater for monoracial, dark-skinned young men from segregated backgrounds. Whereas monoracial respondents reported experiencing an average of 3.95 kinds of racial hostility with a mean frequency of 5.14 occurrences, the respective values for those of mixed race were 3.49 types of hostility ($p < 0.05$) and 4.18 incidents ($p < 0.01$). In terms of skin tone, the mean types of hostile experiences rose from 3.59 to 3.87 to 4.15 going from light to medium to dark skin tones ($p < 0.05$), and the mean total frequency of occurrences rose from 4.39 to 5.04 to 5.41 across the same categories ($p < 0.01$).

TABLE 7.2. On-campus expressions of racial hostility experienced by Black NLSF respondents by dimensions of Black diversity

Dimensions of Diversity	Mean hostile experiences (0–11)	Mean frequency of hostile occurrence (0–44)
Racial identification		
Monoracial	3.95*	5.14**
Mixed race	3.49	4.18
Nativity and generation		
Multigenerational native	3.88	5.02
Second-generation immigrant	3.85	4.80
First-generation immigrant	3.92	4.92
Region of origin		
USA	4.88	5.02
African immigrant	3.68	5.35
Caribbean immigrant	4.16	4.57
Other immigrant	3.87	4.90
Skin tone		
Light	3.59**	4.39**
Medium	3.87	5.04
Dark	4.15	5.41
Gender		
Female	3.81	4.82+
Male	4.00	5.27
Parental education		
No degree	3.98	5.22
College degree	3.81	4.80
Advanced degree	3.85	4.95
Experience of segregation		
Predominantly White	3.52***	4.22**
Racially mixed	4.07	5.30
Predominantly minority	3.92	5.32
Minority neighborhood/White school	4.46	6.06
Total	1,039	

+ p < 0.10; * p < 0.05; ** p < 0.01; *** p < 0.001

We also observe strong differences in exposure to racial hostility by prior experience with school and neighborhood segregation. Students who came of age in White residential and educational settings reported encountering only 3.52 kinds of prejudice, whereas those growing up in segregated neighborhoods but attending White schools reported 4.46. Those coming from racially mixed and predominantly minority upbringings fell in between with values of 4.07 and 3.92, respectively ($p < 0.001$). We observe the same pattern with respect to the frequency of racially hostile incidents, which stood at 4.22 for those coming from predominantly White schools and neighborhoods and 6.06 for those who grew up in segregated minority neighborhoods but attended White schools. Again, the values were similar for respondents from racially mixed and segregated backgrounds, falling in between the former extremes at 5.30 and 5.32, respectively. In terms of gender, Black men on average reported 5.27 racially hostile experiences compared to 4.82 for Black women ($p < 0.10$).

As in the prior chapter, these results underscore the intersectional nature of Black experiences on campus, with exposure to racial hostility varying by identity, skin tone, prior segregation, and gender. Before turning to the interview data, we note that survey respondents were also asked about exposure to *intraracial* harassment. In data not shown here, we found that nearly one-third of Black respondents (31.5 percent) reported receiving negative treatment from other Black students for associating with non-Blacks on campus. Interestingly, negative treatment was more common for respondents from racially mixed environments (37.2 percent) and who grew up in segregated neighborhoods but attended White schools (33.7 percent) than for those who grew up either in predominantly White (27.5 percent) or predominantly minority (29.5 percent) settings.

The foregoing results thus offer somewhat of a "good news/bad news" story. The good news is that negative racial episodes occur infrequently—on average somewhere between "never" and "rarely." The bad news is that a sizable majority of Black college students report at least one negative experience on campus and the typical student reported a total of about five such experiences, most often at the hands of other students and to a lesser extent (in descending order) from professors, campus police officers, and other college staff members. These results, of course, refer to respondents' *own* experiences of prejudice and exclude racially hostile treatment they may have witnessed being visited on other Black students or workers.

Although reports of overt hostility may have been rare, racial prejudice remained a constant threat to students who told us that even the *possibility* of encountering prejudice could spoil social interactions on campus. Monoracial respondents, in particular, viewed the college milieu as considerably less welcoming than their mixed-race peers. Although some said they had experienced *overt* maltreatment because of their skin color, most said the racism they faced was "more subtle" and "less flagrant." For example, when asked if she had personally experienced racism or prejudice on campus, Nia, a monoracial junior, answered that it was "hard to say," but as the only Black person in her majority-White singing group during freshman year, she felt distinctly out of place:

> INTERVIEWER: Have you personally experienced racism or prejudice since you've been here?
>
> NIA: Nothing is coming to mind . . . , but it's kind of hard to believe. . . . At the time, I don't think I knew that it was [racist]. People have made little comments, like the [name of singing group] said certain things and I'd be like, okay. Like they would say, I don't even know, stuff that I feel like come from hip-hop culture or something like that. They'll all laugh at it, like okay, you know?

Shana, a freshman and also monoracial, came from an integrated, middle-class background, and she was surprised to learn how insulated some of her White peers had been prior to college. Lack of interracial contact and experience, not overt prejudice, she believed was most commonplace:

> INTERVIEWER: So do you think that there's a lot of racism and/or prejudice here?
>
> SHANA: I don't think it's a lot. . . . [T]he first day I got to campus, there was a girl—she told me this—I was in her [orientation] group. I was the first Black girl she had actually ever talked to. She's from Texas and she's Jewish. She was like, "You know, you're the first Black girl I've actually liked to talk to and wanted to be friends with." I was like, "Really?"
>
> INTERVIEWER: Were you surprised when she said that?
>
> SHANA: I really was. I know some people are like that. . . . I don't think they're necessarily racist or prejudiced. I think people are adapting, I would say. Racism and prejudice definitely exist, but I don't think the majority of people are [racist].

Growing up in a racially diverse New Jersey suburb and attending large, public high school, Shana was used to diversity, and at college, her peer network included Black, White, and Asian friends. She also participated in several Black-oriented organizations on campus.

Although Bob, a sophomore, told us he personally had not experienced any racism or prejudice on campus, he agreed with Shana that a lack of interracial contact spurred individuals to act in close-minded ways:

> I think there is a lot of prejudice—probably stemming from ignorance, you know, from kids coming from different backgrounds. So if you come from

a background where you've never been in a racially heterogeneous [environment], if you come from a very racially homogenous background, you know, um, you're probably not gonna quite have the sensitivity or level of education or awareness. I haven't felt uncomfortable over anything.

Of Ghanaian descent, Bob had attended an elite midwestern boarding school, and both of his parents had professional careers and lived in an affluent Atlanta suburb. His closest college friends were an even mix of affluent Whites and Blacks.

In contrast, Tia reported experiencing much more overt racism during her time at college. Walking on campus one night, she was called a "Black bitch" by a White fraternity brother. Although she blamed the incident on his extreme inebriation, she felt that the alcohol simply gave him the license to say what he really felt:

> TIA: Like I've seen some crazy, crazy things at [name of university]. I've been called, like, a Black bitch . . . by some drunken frat boys. I was going across the road to [name of Black dorm], and he was walking from probably one of the parties that is on [name of street] or whatever. It was like a Thursday night, Friday night. He just started screaming it out loud, like, "You Black bitch! You Black bitch!" I forget what fraternity it was now, but they were all wearing the same paraphernalia and they had these girls with them and one of the [White] girls who, I guess, wasn't drunk, said, "I'm so sorry. He's so drunk," and I was just so angry.
> INTERVIEWER: Did you say anything back?
> TIA: I think I might have said, like, "Fuck you." You know what I mean? And I could tell he was drunk and [he] probably would not be saying that normally. But that's what they say, alcohol brings the worst out in you. . . . It brings your true feelings out.

Although Tia reported this rather shocking incident of overt hostility from a White peer, many of our in-depth interviewees described persistent but unspoken and more subtle forms of prejudice that the quantitative survey might not have captured (see Byrd 2017). Black men felt particular discomfort "just walking around campus" because they sensed that Whites perceived them as threatening. Troy was sensitive to how his presence on campus was perceived, especially by White women:

> You get the vibes a lot of White students feel uncomfortable around you. I mean especially walking down [main campus thoroughfare] at night. Many

times, many [White] girls pull over and stop, so, I mean, that everybody does that. That's just across the board. But in recognizing that, I know sometimes I might do something extra to alleviate that fear for them. I know if I'm walking past and I'm coming behind you, I'm gonna move to the side so you can [pass] because I know they're probably scared.

Richard likewise sometimes found himself feeling a bit uncomfortable and felt "awkward" in his interactions with White classmates:

It just feels awkward sometimes. Like, interacting with classmates, how they might not talk to you after class. You see them in [the campus center] and you're like, "Hey!" And they just walk past.

He thought that the university administration was especially biased against Black men. As an active member of a Black men's group on campus, Richard was dismayed that the Black women's group received more funding for its events. He was also troubled by a recent dodgeball tournament in which the Black men's group was pitted against a team from Campus Safety. It was only after someone said something that team pairings were changed.

RICHARD: This is sad. We had the dodgeball tournament a couple of weeks ago and they broke up the different groups into different match-ups. And they had [name of Black men's group] going against [Campus] Safety for the first round. I'm like, "That's kind of weird, right [laughs]?" So they changed it initially. They changed it, and then they had all the Black groups, the three Black groups that were in the tournament, playing at the same time. So it was little stuff like that might pop up randomly.

INTERVIEWER: So do you think you've personally experienced racism or prejudice since you've been here?

RICHARD: I don't think I've experienced something that [] could [be] blatant. . . . Maybe the little things I've said already, it might make me question it, but it's not blatant enough.

Richard was of West Indian descent and self-identified as "Black." He said he had limited exposure to Whites before coming to college and rarely left campus because of concern about how he'd be treated as a Black man in the public realm.

Interviewees of racially mixed origins and those who grew up in White settings were less likely to report hostile acts and to perceive the racial climate either as neutral or more welcoming than monoracial interviewees. For example, Mark, a freshman who identified as mixed race, grew up in an affluent White suburb with his African American mother and White father and attended a private school where he socialized exclusively with Whites. In his view, the campus racial environment was benign:

> I would say the [race] relations are fairly good. I don't think there's a lot of tension that I can feel. It seems like people interact more or less freely. I don't get a sense that there's any undercurrent or anything.

He told us that he had "never" experienced any racism or prejudice either on or off campus and felt the broader campus environment was "welcoming" to him, likely because "people guess I'm Hispanic before they would guess that I'm Black or White." At the time we spoke with Mark, he told us he had White roommates and friends and was not involved in Black life on campus.

When asked how she was doing on campus, Emily, who identified as mixed race, opined that "on the whole, I think it's a pretty good experience." She described a sense of "racial awareness" that brought different racial and ethnic groups together into various campus organizations.

> EMILY: I haven't encountered any racism.
> INTERVIEWER: Do you think that students from different racial and ethnic backgrounds get along here, then?
> EMILY: Yeah, I think they get along to the extent that race wouldn't be a means of treating someone better or worse.

Emily's closest college friends were White, Black, and mixed-race students from predominately White backgrounds like herself. She revealed that she felt "more comfortable with Black students who feel comfortable with White people." Emily described her Black peers from segregated minority backgrounds as "ethnocentric," whereas she said that her friends "shy away from the stereotypes about light skin color being better in the Black community."

Jake, a junior, who was notably light skinned, reported that it was Blacks, not Whites, who were unwelcoming to him and he saw them as being primarily responsible for poor relationships between racial groups on campus:

> INTERVIEWER: In terms of the racial climate here, how would you describe it? Is it different than you thought it would be before you got here?
> JAKE: No, it is the same as it was in high school: the Black kids, the White kids, the Black kids not trying to hang out with White kids. Expected.

INTERVIEWER: Um, the racial climate here, do you ever feel like there's any kind of animosity?

JAKE: Yeah, from the Black kids.

INTERVIEWER: What about the other groups, like Latinos or Asians and all them?

JAKE: They're kinda just hanging out. . . . That really doesn't affect me.

Jake went on to describe an incident that occurred at a local deli where he and his Black friend were chastised by Black women for "laughing" at their discussion about "something racist" that occurred on campus.

JAKE: Some Black girls were going on about something racist, someone being racist, and my friend started laughing. And they're standing right there, and I just started shaking my head. I was just standing there in a yellow polo shirt and they were like, "Oh, look at these guys, like, look at these kids: they think that, they think that like, they don't have Black skin, like, like they have no respect for themselves, like I'm Nigerian, I'm from Africa."

INTERVIEWER: What did your friend, your Black friend say?

JAKE: I mean, he feels the same way I do about that shit.

INTERVIEWER: Does he come from a similar background as you?

JAKE: Yeah, he comes from . . . he's from Queens, but he went to a private school in Manhattan. But he's from Queens, so it's not like he could avoid Black people.

Jake was a history major and also earning a certificate in African American studies. He had been recruited to his university for both football and track. Although he identified as racially "mixed and biracial," he explained that "experience in the world has made me think I'm White." He didn't know any of his Black relatives or even where his father lived. Although his views were extreme relative to other self-identified mixed-race interviewees, other mixed-race Blacks similarly perceived their monoracial college peers to be "self-segregating" and unwelcoming toward people like them because of their mixed origins and more privileged upbringings.

In sum, our data indicate that light-skinned Blacks who self-identify as mixed or mixed race perceive the least racial hostility on campus, a finding that may be tied to the reality that their lighter skin tone provokes less of a reaction compared to dark-skinned students, both native and immigrant. As our interviewee Darryl put it, "The darker your skin is, the more trouble you're gonna have." As we come to learn in the next chapter, however, immigrant-origin Black students espoused a more assimilationist philosophy than did multigenerational natives, in addition to harboring less nationalist Black sentiment. Nonetheless, these two groups have nearly identically negative perceptions of the campus racial climate—and similarly dark skin tones.

The Weight of Performance Burdens

All students attending selective colleges and universities likely feel pressure to achieve academically. The pressure stems from a variety of sources including concerns about the need to prepare adequately for graduate or professional school, worries about gaining the right job skills, anxieties about how other students perceive them, qualms about disappointing a professor, fears of not meeting parental expectations, and feelings of guilt about the financial sacrifices families were making to get them into and through college. These sorts of pressures can create psychological performance burdens that undermine academic achievement.

In addition to the pressures of college attendance common to all students, Black students face additional burdens stemming from their membership in a stigmatized social group. Whenever Black students are called on to perform academically, they face the possibility of confirming the canard of Black intellectual inferiority, yielding a condition known as stereotype threat (Steele 1997). This performance burden is likely to be especially acute at selective institutions, where admissions criteria are strict, the Black presence is small, and affirmative action is alleged by critics to result in lower standards for minority students, putting Black students in an uncomfortable spotlight (Bowen and Bok 1998; Massey et al. 2003; Charles et al. 2009; Owens and Massey 2011). Black students need not believe the canard of intellectual inferiority for stereotype threat to occur; they only need to know that it exists and that some students, professors, and administrators likely believe it.

Analysis of interview and focus-group data gathered among Black and White students by Torres and Charles (2004) found evidence that White students do indeed have doubts about Black intelligence and tend to be critical of affirmative action. They also found that Black students were quite aware of these attitudes. As a result, the burden of "representing the race" was a theme commonly expressed by Black students, who felt a special obligation constantly to prove themselves academically. Indeed, survey data from the NLSF has confirmed the existence of the phenomenon of *stereotype externalization* wherein Black students *expect* that racial others will evaluate them negatively on the basis of invidious stereotypes (Massey and Fischer 2005; Charles et al. 2009). In addition, studies have also identified a process of *stereotype internalization* in which Black students at some level *do* have doubts about their own group's intellectual abilities (see Steele and Aronson 1995; Owens and Massey 2011; Inzlicht and Schmader 2012).

Both the externalization and internalization of negative stereotypes serve to undermine Black students' academic performance by increasing the performance burden, a psychological weight that is heightened by the awareness that many Whites believe that affirmative action policies unfairly allow academically unqualified minorities to enter selective institutions (Steele and Aronson 1995; Crocker, Major, and Steele 1998; Nussbaum and Steele 2007; Marx and Goff 2006; Fischer and Massey 2007; Massey and Mooney 2007; Charles et al. 2009; Owens and Lynch 2012). The Black students most at risk of experiencing stereotype threat are those who embrace an exclusively "American" identity and who tend to have internalized many of the negative stereotypes prevalent in American popular culture (Benjamin 2005; Fischer and Massey 2007; Charles et al. 2009). Also at greater risk are students who are sensitive to faculty perceptions and unsure of their own abilities. Massey et al. (2003:195–196) found that 9 percent of Black students evinced these traits and were between 11 percent and 23 percent more likely to fail a course in their first semester of college than their same-race peers who did not fulfill these criteria.

The dynamics of performance burden came up in our interview with Calvin, a senior who fully expected others to judge him through a stereotypical lens:

> I mean, the fact is, that being African American automatically kind of puts a little damper [on Black students]—people have this preconception, even if sometimes they've shaken it. But when it comes to society, it's just the way things are. People just think African Americans aren't as smart as other races, and you just have to deal with it, you know? And it's like the opposite with Asians. If you're Asian, they automatically think you're brilliant.

An engineering major and football player, Calvin felt like he had "proven himself" academically and told us that "nobody can say anything about my abilities." However, he still found it tough to battle against racialized perceptions.

Drawing on our survey data, here we consider responses to six items designed to capture the performance burdens associated with stereotype externalization. The items ask respondents to rate on a 0 to 10 scale the degree to which they believe that instructors will think less of them if they have difficulty

TABLE 7.3. Race-based and family-based performance burdens experienced by Black NLSF respondents

	Freshman year	Senior year	Overall
Race-based performance burden			
If instructors know difficulty, reflects negatively on race	1.85	2.63	2.24
If students know difficulty, reflects negatively on race	2.22	3.50	2.86
When R excels, reflects positively on race	6.86	7.56	7.21
When R performs poorly, reflects negatively on race	5.80	6.88	6.34
Do not want to look foolish	5.57	7.38	6.48
People will look down on race	4.34	5.87	5.11
Overall Race-Based Performance Burden	4.44	5.64	5.04
Family-based performance burden			
Importance of making parents proud	8.31	—	8.31
Importance of not embarrassing parents	6.43	—	6.43
Importance of family's sacrifice for education	7.04	—	7.04
Importance to parents of attending college	6.61	—	6.61
Importance to parents of working hard in college	9.20	—	9.20
Importance to parents of getting good grades in college	8.60	—	8.60
Importance to parents of graduating from college	9.48	—	9.48
Importance to parents of graduate/professional school	6.31	—	6.31
Importance to parents of studying something practical	6.37	—	6.37
Overall Family-Based Performance Burden	7.59	—	7.59
Total		1,039	

in class; that students will look down on them if they perform poorly in class; that their own performance reflects positively on African Americans as a group; that their own individual performance reflects negatively on their race; that they are concerned about appearing foolish or stupid; and whether they believe that others look down on African Americans if they do not perform well academically. These items were administered to students in both the freshman and senior years, and mean values for each item are presented in the top panel of table 7.3, along with average values for the two years combined. Cronbach alpha coefficients were computed to judge the reliability of the two summed indexes, which equaled 0.66 in the freshman year, 0.70 in the senior year, and 0.70 for the two years combined.

In every case, the performance burden was greater in the senior than the freshman year, indicating that pressures to perform academically actually *increased* over time spent in college. Other studies have also shown that the Black performance burden increases over time in mostly White professional work settings (e.g., Roberson and Kulik 2007; Emerson and Murphy 2014;

Travis, Thorpe-Moscon, and McCluney 2016). Across all items, the average performance burden rose from a value of 4.44 in the freshman year of college to 5.64 in the senior year of college, an increase of 27 percent. The largest increases were observed for burdens associated with not wanting to look foolish in front of others (with the average rating going up by 1.81 points, going from 5.57 to 7.38), people looking down on the race if they did poorly (up 1.53 points, from 4.34 to 5.87), and feeling that they would reflect negatively on the race if they showed difficulty in class (up 1.28 points, from 2.22 to 3.50).

Looking at the two-year averages, we see that the greatest burdens were associated with wanting to excel in order to reflect positively on the Black race (7.21), not wanting to look foolish personally (6.48), and fear that performing poorly will reflect negatively on the race (6.34). Less burdensome were concerns about experiencing difficulty before instructors (2.24) and/or other students (2.86). Overall, the two-year index combined across all items equaled a value of 5.04, confirming a fundamental tenet of the stereotype threat hypothesis: that Black students view their academic performance as "representing the race," thereby creating a palpable "threat in the air" (see Steele 1997), one that unfortunately appears to increase over time.

As Trenton, who grew up in an affluent mid-Atlantic suburb with mostly White friends and attended an elite private school, told us,

> I think in the back of my mind I know that I always need to be trying my best because I am always representing Black people, especially when I am the token Black person. In my group of friends, I am most of their [only] Black friend. So I am the experience that they have. I am the face that is put forward.

Denise relayed the tensions she felt as one of the few Blacks in her classes, noting a direct correlation between minority status and achievement at her university:

> If you're the only Black person in a White class and you're feeling completely uncomfortable, being in the class since you need it, you're forcing yourself to go, your grades are gonna reflect that because there are so many other tensions weighing on your shoulder so it's gonna influence your being here. . . . It's distracting your ability to succeed.

Denise would not disclose her GPA to us because she felt that it was not an accurate representation of her abilities. She was disappointed in herself and felt that she was not working up to her potential.

Karen, a senior, was also concerned about how her instructors viewed her and her Black classmates in science courses, telling us that

I stand out in the classes. . . . I'm almost always the only Black person. I'm almost always the only person of color. So I stand out. . . . I do feel like sometimes people might expect less of me. In one of my courses, our TA [teaching assistant] was specifically reaching out to me and my lab partner—who is also Black. I wasn't sure if it was based on a previous performance or if he just felt like we just might need a little bit more help. . . . Here's one of those specific incidents when I felt like someone wasn't taking me seriously as an academic. Ultimately, my goal in terms of going to grad school is to publish papers, do research, affect policy, etc., etc.

Karen and her lab partner both ended up dropping the class. As a biology major with an African American studies minor, Karen was struggling to raise her science grades.

As noted earlier, stereotype threat is not the only source of performance burden. Another important source of external pressure comes from the expectations of family members and students' perceptions of family expectations— whether real or imagined—especially from parents (again, recall the Thomas theorem). Here, we use the stereotype threat framework as a jumping-off point to consider this burden by asking students to rate on a 0 to 10 scale how important it was for them to make their parents proud, not embarrass their parents, and to make good on the sacrifices family were making for their education. We also asked them to assess how important it was to their parents that they attend college, work hard in college, get good grades in college, graduate from college, attend graduate or professional school, and to study something that was practical (see the bottom panel of table 7.3).

Respondents were told that 0 indicates "not at all important" while 10 indicates "extremely important." The overall average rating was 7.59 with a Cronbach's alpha of 0.80. The fact that the average family-based performance burden score was so high (2.55 points greater than the race-based stereotype threat score) and that two of the scale's items had average ratings in excess of 9.0 indicates the extent of the pressure Black respondents felt to fulfill familial expectations. Whereas the race-based stereotype threat burden rating for individual items ranged from 1.85 to 7.56, the family-based rating ranged from 6.31 to 9.48, with the latter score indicating the perceived importance to parents not simply of attending college but of graduating with a college degree. Close behind was the perceived importance to parents of working hard in college, with a rating of 9.20. Respondents also felt rather strong pressures from parents to get good grades (8.60) and to make their parents proud (8.31). Whereas the race-based performance burden is abstract, implicit, and context specific, familial and parental pressures are directly stated, explicit, ever present, and thus more palpable.

Table 7.4 draws on the summed indexes from the prior table to examine how both race-based and family-based performance burdens vary across the underlying dimensions of Black diversity. Prior work has shown that race-based performance burdens varied by skin tone, racial identification, nativity, and prior experience of segregation (Massey and Owens 2014). Here, we find that both types of performance burdens were felt more intensely by monoracial students and those with dark skin tones than by mixed-race students or those with light skin tones. For example, compared to mixed-race students, those who identified as monoracial reported higher levels of both race-based and family-based performance burdens. Skin tone differences follow a similar pattern, even though they are somewhat smaller. Students with dark skin tones reported feeling more intense race-based pressures than those with light skin tones (with respective ratings of 5.11 and 4.87, $p < 0.10$). They also reported greater family-based pressures (7.71 versus 7.36, $p < 0.001$).

Immigrant-origin Black students generally report a greater performance burden than multigenerational natives, especially those with roots in Africa. Their index values were 5.39 on the race-based and 8.18 on the family-based scales ($p < 0.10$ and $p < 0.001$, respectively). Close behind were respondents of Caribbean origin, with values of 5.08 and 7.92. In contrast, the respective values for multigenerational natives were significantly lower at just 4.95 for the race-based index and 7.45 for the family-based index. The index values for Black students of "other" immigrant origins were closer to those of multigenerational natives with values of 4.96 and 7.64.

With respect to class background, both family- and race-based performance burdens rose as status increased. Whereas the race-based performance index stood at 5.12 for students whose parents held an advanced degree, it was just 4.88 for those whose parents held a college degree and 4.97 for those whose parents never completed college ($p < 0.05$). Likewise, the respective family-based burden index rose from 7.46 to 7.50 to 7.76 for those whose parents lacked a degree, held a college degree, and possessed an advanced degree ($p < 0.05$).

Although we found no significant differences in race-based burdens by prior experience of segregation, we did uncover significant differences with

TABLE 7.4. Race-based and family-based performance burdens experienced by dimensions of Black diversity

Dimensions of diversity	Race-based performance burden	Family-based performance burden
Racial identity		
Monoracial	5.06**	7.67***
Mixed race	4.73	7.18
Nativity and generation		
Multigenerational native	4.95+	7.45***
Second-generation immigrant	5.14	8.04
First-generation immigrant	5.18	7.92
Region of origin		
USA	4.95+	7.45***
Africa	5.39	8.18
Caribbean immigrant	5.08	7.92
Other	4.96	7.64
Skin tone		
Light	4.87+	7.36*
Medium	5.01	7.63
Dark	5.11	7.71
Gender		
Female	5.02	7.63
Male	5.06	7.53
Parental education		
No degree	4.97*	7.46*
College degree	4.88	7.50
Advanced degree	5.12	7.76
Experience of segregation		
Predominantly White	4.93	7.63*
Racially mixed	5.00	7.65
Predominantly minority	5.01	7.36
Minority neighborhood/ White school	5.29	7.78
Total	1,039	

$^+$ p < 0.10; * p < 0.05; ** p < 0.01; *** p < 0.001

respect to family-based pressures. The family-based performance burden was greatest for those who lived in segregated neighborhoods but attended White schools (7.78) and least for those who came of age in segregated schools and neighborhoods (7.36), with students from predominantly White and racially mixed backgrounds falling in between with respective scores of 7.63 and 7.65. We observe no significant differences in the performance burdens experienced by Black men and Black women.

In their interviews, both multigenerational natives and second-generation immigrants recognized that Blackness marked them as collectively disadvantaged and stigmatized, with most seeing it as the primary characteristic by which they were defined on campus. Moreover, compared to mixed-race students, students with a monoracial identity more frequently used terms such as *we* and *us* when discussing their personal experiences with other Blacks they encountered, both on and off campus. For example, when asked what he thought it meant to be Black at his university, James explained that for him, it was about "representing the Black race" in a favorable light and being willing to take on that burden:

> I think you have a tremendous opportunity at one of the best schools in the country. There are a lot of people that you can meet. There are a lot of things you can learn. . . . [But] you definitely have more weight on your shoulders than the White students in that you're *representing your race* [his emphasis]. Every time you take [a] class, let's say you are *the* Black student in class—anything I do in life where I am one of the only Black people—generally, that tends to be academically or professionally related—I am going to be representing my race. . . . So obviously, you know, you have that added pressure to be successful.

Destiny echoed James's sentiments, telling us explicitly that she worried how she would be perceived in class if she did not do well:

> Sometimes I do [feel pressure]. Actually, if I feel, for example, I don't do well on something—a test or something. For example, there was a study group for math. At a point, well, I felt that I'm the only Black person here, and if I don't do well on this problem set, or if I don't do well on the midterm or final, I'd look bad. Like, I'm representing my race. Sometimes I did feel that and it did actually make me work harder—sometimes.

Despite his Ghanaian origins, Ervin knew that Whites did not necessarily differentiate him from other Black students, and he felt the burden of representing the race as well:

INTERVIEWER: It is something like you feel like you have to "represent" in a way? Or is it more about you as an individual?
ERVIN: Yeah, I definitely feel like, not so much me as an individual but me sort of representing me, sort of providing. . . . Yeah, it's definitely me taking the race as like a condition upon myself. I've heard like, the

kids like me who are second-generation immigrant kids, we all do very well in high school and we don't really have a problem. That's what I've heard. . . . Like, they're filling up more spots with people like me. I mean, I felt the pressures of an African American kid just 'cause when people see me, they don't think I'm African. It's just I'm Black, so I've definitely felt the pressure.

Ervin's parents emigrated to the United States with professional occupations, and Ervin self-identified as "African." Despite worrying about his 2.9 GPA, Ervin was about to declare a double major in chemistry and music at the end of his sophomore year.

Several interviewees invoked W. E. B. Du Bois's (Du Bois 1899:396) assertion that "all the better classes of Negroes should recognize their duty toward the masses." Troy, who came from a "strict" household and identified as "Black, African American, and Ghanaian," equated being Black at his university as being "a diamond in the rough" and went so far as to make a direct reference to Du Bois's notion of Blacks in the Talented Tenth and their obligation to represent the race at elite institutions:

Being Black at [name of university] means you probably are *a diamond in the rough* [emphasis in original]. It's somewhat being looked at as the one that made it out of your community. Like all the Black people who came here, they made it—the diamond. Like Du Bois used to like to say the Talented Tenth. I look at it as a lot of White students look at you that way. I mean, even [compared to] some other Black students, we all realize the majority of us [aren't] here.

In addition to feeling an obligation to represent the race for its own sake, interviewees also understood the power of racial stereotypes in affecting their performance, noting that instructors' and students' negative stereotypes about people of African origin likely affected perceptions of them as individuals. Although they generally perceived themselves as "different" from their monoracial peers, mixed-race interviewees nonetheless acknowledged that the same negative racial stereotypes applied to them. As Peter, a foreign-born student of mixed Nigerian and Welsh background, who participated in one of the mixed-race focus groups shared,

If an event takes place against a Black person on this campus, the assumption . . . would be that the people with a Black face on this campus would take a personal offense to such an event—a personal event—they [other mixed-race students like himself] could see themselves in those circumstances.

Although the parents of multigenerational native Black students were involved in the college application process, they tended to stay out of final decision making and put comparably less pressure on their children to select an elite school, an experience that was more common among the sons and daughters of immigrant parents. Among our interviewees, immigrant-origin Blacks were not only the most concerned with how others viewed them, but they were also most preoccupied with how family members perceived their academic achievements. They often spoke of the sacrifices their parents were making to send them to college and of how their performance collectively reflected not just on themselves as individuals but on their family as well (see Clerge 2014).

Given these circumstances, immigrant-origin students were unusually driven and highly motivated to do well in school. They generally saw high academic achievement as the critical ticket to getting ahead. Brian, of Jamaican descent, faced the pressures head-on, often worrying whether his 3.6 GPA was "good enough" for him to succeed in business. He explicitly recognized that Blacks had to perform better academically in order to disprove the racial stereotype about not being as qualified as Whites:

> Whereas the Black person, oh, he's an affirmative action case, that's why he got a 3.0. So it's important for that Black person to have that 3.5 and the 3.7 where I don't necessarily think it's as important for the White person. I don't know. That's what I think. It's a deep, heavy subject.

Brian revealed that he chose an "easy" major because he was so concerned with getting good grades, telling us,

> Academically, I've taken a lot of easy classes [so] that I can just make a good GPA. And I've never really taken any classes I really like want to learn about because I have to make a good GPA.

Although Brian's mother had an advanced degree and had previously worked in government, he was receiving nearly full financial aid but still had to work several hours a week at a work-study job. Brian described his Jamaican-born mother as "gung-ho" about his education and asserted that he had always "worked harder than the average student." His mother "definitely made a lot of sacrifices [while he was] growing up" and she "wanted to give me the best."

In selecting an "easier" liberal arts track, Brian was unlike many of his immigrant peers who choose professionally oriented majors because they feel compelled to study something "practical," often at their parents' urging. Greg, a second-generation immigrant, believed that having a business degree would provide better career options and a higher salary than if he had gone to a less prestigious school than the Ivy League institution he attended. He stated,

> Because I'm at [name of university] and I guess in my mind I know . . . I'm in a really good position to have money in the future . . . I've come to the fact that okay, I'm gonna have money but . . . I don't need to work my ass off and become really rich. I can concentrate on other things while being comfortable. But whereas if I had only gone to [name of less competitive university], I'd be saying I have to work my ass off, I've got to get a good job and try to be rich. But whereas I'm here, you know what I'm saying, I'm gonna be comfortable.

In part, Greg was reacting to the situation of his parents, who struggled financially after moving to the United States. His father had been out of work as an accountant because his foreign CPA degree did not meet U.S. standards and licensing requirements.

Olivia also stressed the importance of Black students majoring in something practical and useful to help pay off college loans, a reality she believed most White students did not have to deal with:

> A lot of my Black friends say they can't afford to go have fun here. They really have to get an education and use it. . . . It's not a place to find yourself; it's time to make a move and get out. . . . Pick a career and start doing things for yourself and start paying back your loans. There's no time for switching majors. . . . I feel like a lot of White students can afford to spend an extra year here or just switched their majors a couple of times. Financially, they have that option and it's not just seen as *you need to come out of here with something solid to work with* [emphasis added].

Ironically, this desideratum did not really apply to her, as her parents were both well-paid physicians, and Olivia, a senior when we spoke to her, had been accepted to a prestigious law school and planned to enter the corporate world after acquiring her JD.

Respondents' social class backgrounds are modestly associated with their experiences of race- and family-based performance burdens, though maybe not in the ways that some might have anticipated. As we have seen, both race- and family-based burdens are greatest for Black students whose parents held an advanced degree. It could be that respondents whose parents had less education received greater financial aid, thus requiring fewer sacrifices by their parents. In addition, lower status parents might assign less importance on going to graduate or professional school, compared to those whose parents have a college or advanced degree, for whom a college education was much more salient as a marker of success.

Finally, respondents with the most divergent experiences of childhood segregation (i.e., those growing up in segregated minority neighborhoods while attending a predominantly White high school) experienced the greatest race- and family-based performance burdens (though only the family-based performance differentials were statistically significant). This pattern mirrors the earlier finding that performance burdens increase over time and suggests that exposure to high-status White peers in both high school and college exacerbates the performance burdens experienced by Black students (see Massey and Fischer 2005; Massey and Owens 2014).

Comments from our in-depth interviews reveal how both forms of performance burden powerfully shape Black students' motivations and self-perceptions. Harrison, for example, was a legacy student at his university (where both his mother and father had received advanced degrees), but his family was far from wealthy. Living in a predominantly Black New Jersey suburb, he recognized the sacrifices his parents were making to ensure his education. Harrison had graduated from a costly private high school with a 3.9 GPA having completed numerous honors and Advanced Placement (AP) courses, which put a strain on the family budget. As he explained, "Because now my mom's working, we have a decent income. But they sacrificed a lot financially to send us there." Moreover, even though his parents did not pressure him to attend their alma mater, Harrison felt that "[because] they went here, you know, that was an influence because my mom got her PhD here, so I was here a lot as a kid. I was here at the library and stuff."

A junior, Harrison was completing a premed track and felt special pressure to succeed in his largely White, molecular biology courses:

I feel the discomfort. When you're in a [study group] and you're the only person of color. . . . I feel frustrated because, of course, people are going to try and project on us—all people of color, just in general, in these science classes. I don't know if there's any faculty [of color] in my department. When I was looking for a supervisor, there were no people of color beyond

Asians. So when I sit in a lab meeting or any sort of class, I can't *not* be conscious of the fact that I might be the first person of color that some of these people have ever interacted with at this academic level.

Despite these worries, Harrison was dead set on earning an MD/PhD and becoming a medical researcher.

Julie, a first-generation college student, also talked about the sacrifices her parents made for her education and believed that mediocre academic performance for her was simply not an option:

> I was sitting in class today and there were these [White] guys, no, they were actually Asians, but like people talk about, "Oh, I'm not going to class today; I just don't feel like it." I know I have those times, but I know I'd always feel really bad about it because my parents struggled for me to be here. Why am I throwing this [sacrifice] away by not going to class?

Julie was in a highly competitive business program and had a GPA of 3.26 at the end of her junior year. She underscored the importance of making good on her family's investment in her future, telling us that

> I know for me, going to college is very, very important because there are a lot of people in my family who haven't and who never did and I'm one of the firsts.

Neither of her parents had a college degree at the time we met Julie, but her mother was taking courses to complete her bachelor's degree.

After graduating from boarding school, Darryl decided that he had to "do something that really made noise." Darryl believed that family and peers from his segregated neighborhood had never recognized his potential, so he chose to enroll at the "most" prestigious institution he got into:

> I'm the first person to ever go to college in my family. So I wanted to do something that really made noise. My family's always written me off as like the inferior one, and even when I went to boarding school, a lot of my family speculated that it was like, by chance, and I didn't really deserve to be there. So for me, it was like if I get into an Ivy League school, I can shut up all of the naysayers. Turns out that's not true, but what can you do [laughing]?

Darryl "hated" being at his university but insisted that he needed to attend the best "namesake school" because he did not feel that he would work as hard at a school that aligned more with his social interests.

I never worked hard at school in general, so why put myself in a situation where I know I'm gonna have a lot of fun and neglect school? I sorta set myself up to go to [name of university] because it would be the lesser of two evils for me. Like I wouldn't have fun, but that's a good thing. 'Cause I would be able to go to class . . . I did the same thing here anyway.

Because he failed two classes in his sophomore year for lack of attendance, however, Darryl had to take a leave of absence for a year. Darryl was fatigued by racial stereotypes about affirmative action and implicit notions of Black inferiority. Over time, he felt more and more pressure to succeed in order to make a way forward for other low-income Blacks.

I'm sure people will see me in my sweatpants and my do-rag and you know all that music I might listen to and be like, oh that's just another kid that they pulled out the ghetto and probably didn't have a very good SAT score. I'm sure of it, but yeah, I realized that regardless of what I do, I can't really change their minds. Like I don't want to try to, I don't want to try to uplift the Black race, I want to try to uplift people like me.

Darryl was president of the Black Student Union and was heavily involved in several Black organizations. He struggled to maintain a 2.4 GPA and was majoring in history with an African American studies minor.

Moving Up but Not Necessarily Moving On

In their discussions of Black racial identity, recall that Jessica and Mia made compelling critiques of how the perceived "right" and "authentic" ways of being Black were policed on campus. Although Mia focused her criticism on the Black community she encountered on campus, Jessica's critique was broader—she felt African Americans generally too often bought into a "media-based" definition of Blackness that she found both outdated *and* inaccurate. Although the Black students we interviewed generally felt they had the flexibility to embrace different ways of being Black, a broader question for us was whether this perception is a privilege that comes with elite status or more a universal viewpoint that the media and sociologists have neglected. Despite being widely debunked in the research literature, the idea that academic achievement somehow "whitens" young Blacks and brands them as inauthentic sellouts to their peers somehow remains powerful in the public imagination (Fryer and Torelli 2005; Buck 2010; Christie 2010; Harris 2011).

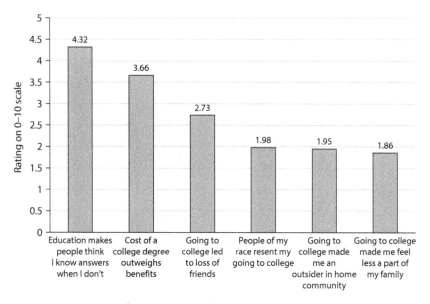

FIGURE 7.1. Degree of agreement with indicators of disconnection and alienation for Black respondents to the NLSF

In this section, we explore the psychosocial consequences of educational success for Black students, focusing particularly on those who come from more segregated neighborhoods and less privileged family circumstances. Among these students, we sought to detect any feelings of alienation that might arise as a result of their being at an elite academic institution, something that is often outside the experience of their friends, relatives, and acquaintances (Lee and Kramer 2013). Specifically, we asked respondents to respond to a series of six items describing the potential emotional costs of their success in attending a selective college or university: "Going to college has made me feel less a part of my family"; "Going to college has made me an outsider in my home community"; "My education makes people think I have answers when I don't"; "People of my race resent my going to college"; "Going to college has led to the loss of some of my friends"; and "Sometimes I think the cost of a college degree outweighs the benefits."

Respondents were asked to rate each item on a scale from 0 to 10, ranging from complete disagreement to complete agreement. Figure 7.1 presents the results in rank order of agreement. We observe the highest level of agreement to the item about education making people think students have answers when they do not; however, with an average rating of only 4.32 out of a possible 10, responses to this item do not yield very much evidence of sharp feelings of

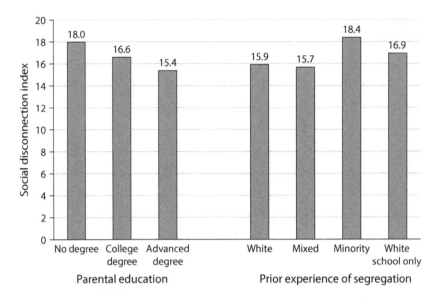

FIGURE 7.2. Feelings of social disconnection and alienation stemming from
gaining a college education

discomfort vis-à-vis others concerning respondents' educational achievements. Likewise, there was little second-guessing of the value of a college education. Agreement with the item about the costs outweighing the benefits of
college averaged only 3.66. We uncovered even less evidence of disconnection
from the broader Black community. Agreement with the statement that going
to college led to a loss of friends was only 2.73, and ratings for the statements
about experiencing resentment, alienation from the community, and being
less a part of families clustered around a value of just 1.9.

To create an overall index of social disconnection, we summed the agreement ratings across all six items to generate a scale that in theory ranged from
0 to 60, but in practice, the scores went from 0 to 57 and averaged 16.5 with a
Cronbach's alpha of 0.94. The fact that the maximum observed score was 57
compared to a mean of just 16.5 suggests that the distribution has a long upper
tail and that at least some students did experience a strong sense of disconnection from their social origins. However, when we computed averages across
the various Black subgroups, we found significant differences ($p < 0.05$) along
only two dimensions: parental education and prior segregation. These scale
ratings are shown in figure 7.2.

The fact that we observe no statistically significant differences by racial
identification, nativity, generation, region of origin, skin tone, or gender

suggest that the origins of any feelings of estrangement, to the extent that they existed among respondents, stemmed not from tensions along the lines of race or gender but instead from cleavages associated with social class (as measured by parental education and prior experiences of segregation). With a score of 18.0, students whose parents were not college graduates felt the greatest sense of disconnection. In contrast, the score of 16.6 among those with college-educated parents was very close to the overall mean value of 16.5, and the score of 15.4 among those whose parents held an advanced degree was well below the mean. Likewise, those who grew up in White or racially mixed neighborhoods, which generally are characterized by higher levels of employment, income, and home ownership than predominantly minority neighborhoods, displayed social disconnection scores below the mean value.

The scale score was 15.9 for Black students who grew up in White schools and neighborhoods and 15.7 for those who arose in racially mixed circumstances; however, for those who came of age in minority-dominant schools and neighborhoods, the social disconnection score was 18.4, the highest of any subgroup. The sense of disconnection was partially mitigated if students from segregated neighborhoods managed to attend a White school, but their score of 16.9 was still significantly above that of students growing up in White schools and neighborhoods. These results are consistent with Tyson, Darity, and Castellino's (2005) assertion that the derogation of educational achievement as "acting White" is a cultural adaptation to localized structural inequalities.

Social disconnection is thus felt most acutely among those for whom a college degree signifies a wide gap in knowledge and experience relative to their less educated parents and people in the poor minority neighborhoods from which they came. For these students, their status as the "successful" member of the family may bring weighty expectations of resource provision, problem solving, and other forms of assistance. Or perhaps the contrast between the privileged circumstances they experience at college and the more disadvantaged circumstances of their families and former neighborhoods can be alienating, though the average score for students from those neighborhoods is still indicative of relatively little social disconnection from going to elite, predominantly White college and universities.

Stress in Social Networks

College, as most any student will tell you, is stressful. Beyond the typical stressors of moving away from home, making new friends, and performing well in a competitive and rarefied academic setting, Black students experience other race-specific stressors. We have already mentioned stereotype threat, but there are others to consider. In their study of race-related stress at historically Black and majority-White institutions, Greer and Chwalisz (2007) found that Black students' stress levels rose year by year on predominantly White campuses. As a result, Black juniors and seniors reported higher levels of stress and more negative perceptions of the campus climate than freshmen and sophomores, consistent with our own findings that the performance burden for Black students increases over time (see also Chavous et al. 2018).

Unfortunately, on-campus experiences are not the only source of stress for Black students at elite colleges and universities; to a greater extent than other students, they are also exposed to stresses emanating from deleterious life events that occur to friends and family members in their social networks. This phenomenon arises because the social networks of Black students often connect them to friends and relatives living in very disadvantaged and quite dangerous neighborhoods (Brown et al. 2011). Exposure to events such as job loss, reduced earnings, eviction, sickness, death, marital dissolution, unplanned pregnancy, and crime victimization are not randomly distributed across residential areas but instead concentrate in poor, racially segregated portions of the urban (and also rural) landscapes (see Massey and Denton 1993; Peterson and Krivo 2010; Sampson 2012; Sharkey 2013; Desmond 2016).

The image of college as an idyllic escape into the life of the mind, away from the harsh realities of the real world, may be true for students from elite socioeconomic backgrounds (Arnett 2016), but as one moves down the status and residential hierarchies, stressful life events tend to proliferate even as the emotional and material resources available to cope with stress grow scarcer. Because residential segregation acts to concentrate poverty spatially within Black neighborhoods (and hence also public schools), students coming from a segregated background experience an elevated risk of experiencing stressful life events. Charles et al. (2009) found, for example, that Black NLSF respondents from segregated schools and neighborhoods experienced 60 percent more life stress during their first two years of college than Whites. In contrast, those coming from integrated or White settings experienced only 9 percent more stress (see also Peterson and Krivo 2010; Massey et al. 2003).

Earlier, we documented the diverse neighborhood and school experiences reported both by our survey and interview respondents. Mixed-race, light-skinned, second-generation immigrant respondents grew up in comparatively Whiter precollege environments and were exposed to significantly less social disorder and violence than other Black subgroups (see tables 3.2 and 3.3).

These students also experience less of what Torres (2009) and Jack (2014) call "culture shock" upon arrival on campus. They also tend to view the campus climate as more open and tolerant than their peers from segregated origins (see Johnson 2019); these same respondents were also more likely to come from higher status households with parents working in professional occupations.

During each year of college, we asked NLSF respondents whether any member of their immediate family, a close relative, or close friend had experienced any of a series of potentially stressful life events. The list of events varied from year to year, but fourteen stressful life events were consistent across all waves of the survey. The most common stressor was the death of a close family member, which afflicted more than two-thirds of all respondents (68.7 percent). An additional quarter (25.2 percent) reported the death of a close friend, and more than one-fifth (21.0 percent) experienced the death of an extended family member. Well over one-third of respondents (37.2 percent) reported a serious illness or disability in the family, and 28.8 percent experienced parental job loss.

Slightly fewer (26.7 percent) reported that a family member had been the victim of a crime or had gotten in trouble with the law (24.1 percent). Fluctuating around a frequency of 10 percent were events such as parental separation or divorce (12.2 percent), familial entry onto public assistance (11.8 percent), and respondent illness (9.9 percent). Less frequent were the events such as having a family member enter into rehab (7.5 percent), an unwed sister becoming pregnant (6.7 percent), a sibling dropping out of school (6.5 percent), and a family member becoming homeless (5.3 percent).

The first column of table 7.5 presents the mean number of such stressful life events experienced by members of respondents' social networks, classified by the dimensions of Black diversity. The second column presents an index created by weighting each event by the severity of its stress on a 0 to 100 scale adapted from Hobson et al.'s (1998) updating of the classic Holmes-Rahe stress scale. At the top of the scale, we find the death of a close friend or family member with a scale value of 82, and at the bottom, we encounter having a sibling dropping out of school with a score of 26. In between are other stressful events such as parental divorce or separation (73), respondent illness (53), parental job loss (47), familial serious illness or disability (44), familial entry into public assistance or rehab (44), unwed pregnancy of a sister (40), familial crime victimization or legal entanglement (37), and familial homelessness (30).

TABLE 7.5. Stressful life events experienced by family members of Black NLSF respondents classified by dimensions of Black diversity

Dimensions of diversity	Mean number of stressful life events	Mean stressful life events weighted score
Racial identification		
Monoracial	4.7	276.1
Mixed race	4.8	272.7
Nativity and generation		
Multigenerational native	4.8	283.3[+]
Second-generation immigrant	4.8	272.7
First-generation immigrant	4.2	246.1
Region of origin		
USA	4.8	283.3*
African immigrant	4.4	261.0
Caribbean immigrant	4.2	240.8
Other immigrant	4.8	285.0
Skin tone		
Light	4.8	272.7
Medium	4.6	269.8
Dark	5.0	288.7
Gender		
Female	4.7	273.8
Male	4.9	278.9
Parental education		
No degree	6.0***	336.3***
College degree	4.3	251.2
Advanced degree	4.2	249.5
Experience of segregation		
Predominantly White	4.1*	239.0**
Racially mixed	4.8	287.0
Predominantly minority	5.2	302.2
Minority neighborhood/White school	5.4	312.9
Average	4.7	275.6
Total		1,039

[+] $p < 0.10$; * $p < 0.05$; ** $p < 0.01$; *** $p < 0.001$

These results provide insight into the kinds of external pressures that can distract and derail the plans of Black college students as they pursue educational attainment and occupational mobility. Looking down the first column, we observe no significant differentials in the number of stressful events within respondents' social networks by racial identification, nativity, generation, region, skin tone, or gender. However, the number of stressful events varied significantly with level of parental education ($p < 0.001$). Those with non-college-educated parents experienced an average of 6.0 stressful events among their circle of family and friends compared with 4.3 among those with college-educated parents and 4.2 among those whose parents held an advanced degree. In addition, the frequency of stressful events rose as exposure to segregation increased ($p < 0.05$), being least for students who grew up in majority-White schools and neighborhoods (4.1) and rising to respective values of 4.8 and 5.2 for those coming from racially mixed and predominantly minority backgrounds. The number of events tops out at 5.4 among those who came from segregated neighborhoods but attended White schools, indicating that access to a White school does not provide refuge from stressors present in poor minority neighborhoods, even though some of their close friends attend those elite schools compared to peers whose high school friends were all from segregated schools.

The second column showing the weighted stress scores generally replicates the findings of the first column, though with larger levels of statistical significance and bigger differences along the continuum of segregation ($p < 0.01$). Whereas the mean stress scale stood at 239.0 for respondents coming from predominantly White schools and neighborhoods, it was 312.9 for those who lived in minority neighborhoods and attended a White school. In between were Black students from racially mixed schools and neighborhoods (287.0) and predominantly minority schools and neighborhoods (302.2).

As before, exposure to stress within social networks also declined with parental education, being greatest for those whose parents lacked a college degree (336.3), less for those whose parents had completed college (251.2), and least for those whose parents held an advanced degree (249.5). Taking account of the relative stress of the events also produces a significant difference in exposure by region of origin, with multigenerational Black respondents displaying a significantly higher index value (283.3) than immigrants either from Africa (261.0) or the Caribbean (240.8).

Although we did not ask interviewees directly about the stressful circumstances experienced by people in their social networks, several interviewees from working-class families and segregated environments did spontaneously mention family misfortunes and how they interfered with their lives on campus. Darryl, for example, detailed his concerns about his "little sisters" back home in their disadvantaged Bronx neighborhood. He was especially concerned that his thirteen-year-old sister might be affected by gang activities (his other sister was only eight years old). Many of Darryl's family members had ties to the notorious Bloods Gang, and he wanted to protect his sisters and mother from the violence and criminal activity potentially introduced into their lives. He explained how such family-based stresses affected him:

> It's more than your intellectual ability that's going to show on your GPA. It's going to be a lot of circumstances you deal with. I have to deal with a lot of family matters that would distract me and a lot of financial matters. But in retrospect, [I see that] the stress that I deal with might have distracted from my abilities in the classroom.

Darryl explained that schoolwork at his elite boarding school was actually more difficult than his first semester of coursework at college, but nonetheless, "family issues and drama were a distraction" as his sisters grew older. Darryl's father had a long history of selling drugs, and his mother earned only the minimum wage working as a nursing aide. To supplement his family's income during his leave of absence from the university, Darryl worked three jobs while he looked after his two younger sisters. Darryl's oldest sister (twenty-five years old) had dropped out of high school in the ninth grade to have a baby, and he did not want this to happen to his younger sisters.

> I was in the Bronx the entire time. . . . My biggest pride of taking time off [was that] my little sister's GPA was like 78 when I got there [and] like 86, 87 when I left. But it was my biggest concern that I would miss out on my little sister's growth and I wasn't aware that she was struggling in school. My mother keeps her home every Friday because there's no after-school program and she can't pick her up and you know and things like that. Fortunately, I had a car so I was able to drive her to school, and she had a lot of issues with schoolwork that my mother and older sister couldn't help her with 'cause they weren't educated and I was able to show her the ropes.

Darryl worked thirty to thirty-five hours a week as a building supervisor and a cashier at his university to make ends meet. He also went home regularly to check on his mother and sisters.

Kareem dealt with similar stressors. His mother had a GED, and his father's whereabouts were unknown. Growing up, half siblings were in and out of the house, and his mother relied on him to help her with everything from watching his youngest siblings to balancing the checkbook. Kareem's neighborhood was rife with gangs and drugs, and even when he was away in the safety of an elite boarding school, he worried about the well-being of his family. His mother often pressured him to come home to deal with problematic issues, and at the time of his interview, she had recently split from her live-in boyfriend with whom she shared an eight-month-old baby. He worried about them even though his mother had recently gotten a better-paying job. Kareem got a full ride from his university along with spending money for books and supplies. His stipend had recently been increased because his mother was hospitalized after the birth of his sister and was unable to contribute anything to his college expenses.

Stress and Mental Health

The cumulative effect of the foregoing stressors—experiencing racial hostility on campus, the pressure of performing academically in the face of negative stereotyping, living up to lofty parental expectations, accumulating ever larger amounts of college debt, feeling alienated from communities and families of origin, and experiencing stressful events within social networks—have clear implications for health (Lovallo 2016). Stereotype threat, especially, has been found to affect both the physical and mental health of African Americans, with well-documented effects on blood pressure, anxiety, depression, and memory (Verplanken, Jetten, and Knippenberg 1996; Blascovich et al. 2001; Inzlicht and Schmader 2012; Inzlicht and Kang 2010; Williams and Mohammed 2013; Aronson et al. 2013).

College presidents have recently recognized poor mental health to be a growing issue for students at their institutions (Chessman and Taylor 2019). Whereas Lipson, Lattie, and Eisenberg (2019) showed that mental health issues have increased for all college students, they found that access to treatment was less common for Black than White students (Lipson et al. 2018). Although measuring physical health of our respondents was beyond the scope of the survey, in order to assess their mental health, we asked a series of nineteen questions developed by Radloff (1977) to capture the frequency of depressive symptoms experienced during the past week. Most of the items asked about the frequency of negative emotions or behaviors, but in order to avoid acquiescence bias, some of the items were worded to indicate positive emotions and behaviors (see Sudman and Bradburn 1982); these items were then reverse coded such that higher numbers always reflect worse mental health.

The first column of table 7.6 lists the items in descending order of the percentage who said they had *ever* experienced the mental health symptom while at college. In addition, respondents were asked to rate how often the symptoms recurred, with the response options being "never," "rarely," "sometimes," and

TABLE 7.6. Symptoms for the Center for Epidemiologic Studies Depression (CES-D) Scale reported by Black NLSF respondents during their junior year to create the CES-D Scale

In the past week, respondent has:	Percent ever experienced	Average score on 0–3 scale
Felt too tired to do things	87.3	1.82
Had trouble keeping focused on tasks	86.6	1.71
Had difficulty getting started on things	82.5	1.62
Was happy (reverse coded to be not happy)	81.2	1.12
Felt sad	79.5	1.21
Talked less than usual	67.0	1.09
Was bothered by things that usually don't bother me	66.6	1.09
Felt lonely	65.9	1.06
Enjoyed life (reverse coded to did not enjoy life)	65.5	0.91
Felt hopeful regarding future (reverse coded to not hopeful)	64.9	0.96
Thought people were unfriendly	57.4	0.81
Felt disliked by people	54.1	0.72
Felt depressed	52.2	0.82
Didn't feel like eating or had poor appetite	49.3	0.85
Felt as good as others (reverse coded not as good)	47.2	0.69
Felt just as good as other people (reverse coded)	47.2	0.69
Couldn't shake off the blues even with help from others	45.0	0.75
Felt fearful	44.6	0.69
Thought life had been a failure	19.6	0.26
Felt life was not worth living	10.7	0.14
Average	59.3	0.96
Total	1,039	

"often or all the time," coded 0 to 3 and shown in the second column. The top three items in the ranking indicate the degree to which respondents felt preoccupied and listless (being "too tired to do things," having "trouble keeping focused on tasks," and having "difficulty getting started on things"). The share ever experiencing any of these systems ranged from 82.5 percent to 87.3 percent, indicating a significant potential for influence on students' mental health.

The next seven items indicate a set of bleak emotions in which respondents reported feeling ("unhappy," "sad," "lonely," and "unhopeful") as well as moody behaviors (talking "less than usual," being "bothered by things that usually didn't bother me," and not "enjoying life"). The percentage ever experiencing these symptoms ranged from 64.9 percent to 81.2 percent. The next two items indicate feelings of alienation and social disconnection (thinking "people were unfriendly" and feeling "disliked by people"). The respective shares ever experiencing these feelings were 57.4 percent and

54.1 percent. Finally, the bottom-ranked items capture concrete manifestations of low self-worth and disappointment, such as feeling "depressed" (with 52.2 percent reporting this symptom), having a "poor appetite" (49.3 percent), feeling "not as good as others" (47.2 percent), not being able to "shake off the blues" (45.0 percent), feeling "fearful (44.6 percent), thinking "life had been a failure" (19.6 percent), and feeling that "life was not worth living" (10.7 percent).

When the scale scores presented in the right-hand column are summed, they yield a reliable index known as the Center for Epidemiologic Studies Depression (CES-D) scale, with a possible range of 0 to 57, a mean of 18.7, and a Cronbach's alpha of 0.83. Although researchers debate about which threshold index value indicates an elevated risk of depression, values above 19 are generally considered to reveal at least a "moderate risk of depression." The share of Black respondents with a score above this threshold is 47.2 percent, indicating a fairly widespread prevalence of this risk. Table 7.7 presents mean CES-D scores and the share assumed to be at moderate risk of depression across the various dimensions of Black diversity.

Although we observe no significant differences in mental health by racial identity, skin tone, or socioeconomic status, we do see significant differentials by nativity and gender, with the risk of depression being greatest for Black students of immigrant origin and women. Whereas multigenerational natives displayed a mean CES-D score of 17.7, the values were 20.0 for second-generation immigrants and 19.5 for first-generation immigrants ($p < 0.01$). We see the same pattern looking at the percentage displaying a moderate risk of depression, which is 42.1 percent for native-origin African Americans compared with 53.8 percent among second-generation immigrants and 54.3 percent among first-generation immigrants. With respect to region, we see few differences between students originating in Africa, the Caribbean, and other regions—the principal difference is between Black students who are multigenerational natives and those of immigrant origin, regardless of region or generation. We also observe a marginally significant increase in the CES-D score as the prior experience of segregation goes from predominantly White circumstances (17.7) to racially mixed (18.2) and predominantly minority circumstances (18.6). Those living in minority neighborhoods but attending White schools were highest at 20.3, with more than half being at least at moderate risk of depression.

The native-foreign gap in the risk of depression should not be terribly surprising given the data we have presented to this point. In chapter 4, we saw

TABLE 7.7. Mean CES-D scores and percentage at moderate risk of depression among Black NLSF respondents by dimensions of Black diversity

Dimensions of diversity	Mean CES-D score 0–57	% at Moderate Risk of depression
Racial identification		
Monoracial	18.3	45.7
Mixed race	18.4	43.0
Nativity and generation		
Multigenerational native	17.7**	42.1**
Second-generation immigrant	20.0	53.8
First-generation immigrant	19.5	54.3
Region of origin		
USA	17.7**	42.1**
African immigrant	21.0	55.5
Caribbean immigrant	18.9	52.3
Other immigrant	20.5	56.1
Skin tone		
Light	18.7	45.5
Medium	18.2	44.9
Dark	18.2	45.7
Gender		
Female	19.0***	49.0*
Male	17.0	38.4
Parental education		
No degree	19.1	49.4
College degree	17.5	40.4
Advanced degree	18.4	46.0
Experience of segregation		
Predominantly White	17.7+	42.6
Racially mixed	18.2	44.8
Predominantly minority	18.6	47.0
Minority neighborhood/White school	20.3	52.9
Average	18.7	47.2
Total	1,039	

$^{+}$p < 0.10; *p < 0.05; **p < 0.01; ***p < 0.001

that academic achievement was a paramount concern for Black respondents of immigrant origin, and results presented in this chapter revealed very strong family-based performance burdens on the children of immigrants. On top of these individual and familial circumstances, Black students of immigrant origin displayed the highest SAT scores, the greatest human capital endowments, and were disproportionately likely to attend the most selective academic institutions, all of which contributed to Brian, a junior of Jamaican origin, viewing college as a "humbling" experience. When asked how adjusting to college life had gone for him, he replied,

> Like pretty much like the whole thing where, you know, like everyone from their high school class is like the valedictorian and like they made like straight As and all that stuff. And then you come to like a place and everyone's like doing like eight thousand things more than you. That's very like difficult, very humbling. It's probably like the most humbling experience I've ever had, and it's been pretty tough.

Coming from a family headed by Jamaican immigrants who spoke Patois in the home, Brian had gone to a top public high school in Florida where he achieved all A's but which did not prepare him for the competitive environment he encountered on campus.

Since high school, Brian has sought to prepare himself socially for life on an elite campus. At his predominantly White high school, for example, his close friends include eight White young men and two Black men, and at college he told us that he "strategically" sought to befriend "a bunch of different people from different groups" so that "no one could identify me with any group." As he put it,

> I did it on purpose. I didn't want to, like, have to deal with—because I knew that I wasn't gonna be able to come here and just have totally Black friends. I knew I wasn't gonna want to come here and have totally all White friends. I made a conscious effort to do my very best not to associate with any one group.

Brian grew up around "a lot of, you know, White people" and said, "I don't really have any desire to, like, be around only Black people." Still, he worried about being "labeled" by his Black peers as not being "loyal to the race" and "being respected less" for interacting with Whites. Ironically, despite his efforts to prepare socially for interacting with diverse races, Brian closely monitored how he interacted with his same-race peers from working-class backgrounds who enacted a Black identity dissimilar to his own and often patrolled the boundaries of racial group membership and legitimacy. With only about five hundred Black students on campus, Brian called his social interactions with White students his "little secret."

Greg, of Ghanaian ancestry, was also concerned about the difficulty of being accepted by his Black peers on campus. He told us about how hard some

second-generation Black immigrant students had to work to be accepted by
their multigenerational African American peers:

> In [my] household, we spoke proper English, and I'm aware of my racial
> identity to the extent that there's racism and discrimination. But I come to
> [name of university], and I'm like . . . This is weird for me, right? Isn't it?
> 'Cause I don't speak any Black slang.

He felt there was a "learning curve" for those who were not familiar with certain aspects of Black American culture and that "you have to learn from others
around you" and "to be able to fake it" to prove racial authenticity. Greg contends that Blacks must actively seek out same-race allegiances because of what
he sees as the extreme degree of racial and ethnic segregation on campus and
the importance of "being conscious of your racial identity." At the same time,
he nevertheless concluded that "you have to condition yourself because
you . . . you can't be Black with all White friends and constantly feel alienated.
You have to I guess sacrifice, or just pacify yourself to assimilate," which for
him meant choosing to be with White students exclusively.

Our findings correspond with those of Johnson (2019) in his qualitative
study of Black and Latino engineering students at an elite university who
hailed from majority-White schools and neighborhoods. Unlike their previously segregated same-race peers, Johnson's respondents from White backgrounds were "culturally flexible" and had "multiple cultural competencies to
straddle White-dominant and same-race peers or co-ethnic peer networks"
(Johnson 2019:10; also see Carter 2012). Thus, in addition to pressures stemming from high personal aspirations for academic achievement, heavy family
expectations for educational success, and the race-based performance burdens
that face all Black students, many immigrant-origin Blacks also had to deal
with the pressures of trying to understand and keep up with the norms of
African American culture.

The other salient dimension of difference with respect to mental health we
uncovered was gender, consistent with research on gender and depression that
has documented a persistent gender gap in CES-D scores, though not necessarily to the same degree as observed here (Platt et al. 2020). As shown in
table 7.7, by a statistically significant margin, Black women are at much greater
risk of depression than Black men. In addition to all the normal stresses of
being a student at a selective academic institution and the additional pressures
of being Black in a largely White environment, women had to deal with the
intersectional disadvantages of dating within a racialized romantic scene characterized by a highly imbalanced sex ratio. Whereas the CES-D score for Black

women was 19 (the threshold for moderate risk), it was just 17 for Black men. Likewise, whereas only 38.4 percent of Black men displayed a score indicating a moderate risk of depression, the figure was 49 percent for Black women.

In addition to the foregoing stresses, Black women from immigrant families also experienced difficulties fitting in with multigenerational African Americans. Yolanda, for example, who was born in the United States to parents from Sierra Leone, had adjusted well to the elite boarding school she attended but found the "social scene" and "racial atmosphere" on campus to be alienating. She didn't like the fact that many Black students lived in a Black-themed dorm and was concerned about what they thought of her because she didn't live there or attend its events:

> There's so many groups of like Black cliques, and I don't know . . . There are groups of like White cliques, too [pause]. I don't know, if they see you in a clique, that's not all or at least mostly Black people, it's just like, the looks are just kind of like, "Oh, what's she doing?"

Yolanda spent a lot of time studying and earned high grades, but when she socialized, she mostly sought out other second-generation peers with "direct ties from Africa." She was frustrated by having to explain herself to other Black students who "don't know that I'm African." She felt that native-origin Blacks dominated the Black social scene and that "it was a big deal to show that you're of African ancestry." However, she was not impressed to "see them trying so hard to show they're 'African culturally' and go back to our roots and stuff."

Nia, a second-generation Jamaican, also commented on the stress of having to choose between "acting Black" or "assimilating into White culture." She had graduated from a private day school where she had exclusively White and Asian friends, but at college, all her friends were Black. By her sophomore year, she found herself participating in all-Black activities because she found it "really difficult to go back and forth" between the White and Black social worlds on campus. When asked how she has adjusted to college life, Nia stated,

> I used to cry a lot. I used to call my friends a lot. I used to sleep a lot. Like instead of going to lunch in the dining hall, I would come back to my room and I would sleep that half hour. It's not borderline depression, but I know that sleeping a lot is a symptom of depression. I'm very shy. I'm very quiet, and I didn't want to take myself out of that comfort zone. I hadn't had to make new friends really for thirteen years. I was kind of an introvert. Now I had to come here and get to know people, and it was really, really hard for me to do.

Although a number of our interviewees often spoke about issues of anxiety and depression, they rarely mentioned seeking professional attention for these challenges. Overall, there was a keen focus among all interviewees, regardless of background, on "fitting in" with same-race peers while still attempting to retain other key aspects of their social identities (see Torres and Massey 2012). The stresses of managing this duality did not decrease over time but instead remained a constant as these upwardly mobile Black students struggled to achieve at a high level and comport themselves with dignity in often conflicting race- and class-based contexts. Those challenges can have substantial effects on students' mental health and the need for psychological support is not easily met or even acknowledged on campus.

Student Loan Debt

One of the most significant trends in American education over the past generation is the explosive growth of college student debt (e.g., Watson 2018; Strassmann 2019; U.S. Federal Reserve 2019). Concurrently, debate rages over the amount and effect of debt on students' collegiate experiences, outcomes, and postgraduation trajectories. Research documents a large gap in college debt incurred by Black students compared to White students, with negative consequences for rates of Black retention and levels of integration on campus, as well as significant postcollege effects on rates of marriage, employment levels, and childbearing patterns (Johnson, Van Ostern, and White 2012; Baum et al. 2015; Huelsman 2015; Quadlin and Rudel 2015; Addo, Houle, and Simon 2016; Min and Taylor 2018). Whereas the prior sections of this chapter look at negative experiences on campus, here we turn briefly to the economic cost of attending selective colleges for Black students to see how these burdens may affect respondents' expectations and worries for their future.

Overall, one in three Black students graduates from college in debt, compared to one in five White students, with the interracial debt gap ranging from $5,000 to $10,000 (Baum et al. 2015; Addo, Houle, and Simon 2016; Seamster and Charron-Chénier 2017). Nationwide, the amount of student debt varies considerably across institutions, with the burden being greater for students at for-profit colleges and less prestigious institutions, schools that are less well resourced than those represented in the NLSF and where students all too often run up large debts without earning a degree (Goldrick-Rab 2016).

Consistent with national trends, most Black NLSF respondents relied on loans to help pay for their studies (Center for Responsible Lending 2019). Indeed, as shown in figure 7.3, we see that only 26.6 percent had *not* accumulated debt by the end of their senior year. Among the nearly three-quarters of those

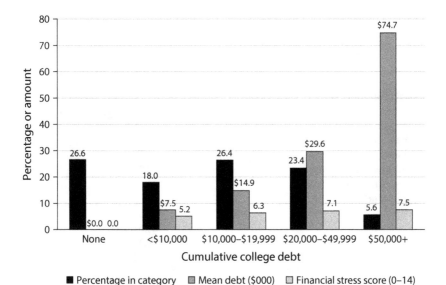

FIGURE 7.3. Indebtedness and financial stress reported by Black NLSF respondents
at the end of college

students who were indebted, the mean amount owed was around $21,500, with
18.0 percent owing under $10,000, 26.4 percent owing between $10,000 and
$20,000, 23.4 percent owing between $20,000 and $50,000, and 5.6 percent
owing in excess of $50,000. Among those in the lowest debt category (under
$10,000), the amount owed averaged around $7,500. In the next category upward
($15,000–$20,000), the amount owed rose to $14,900, and in the next-to-
highest category ($20,000–$50,000), it reached $29,600. Whereas the amount
of debt doubled across each of the foregoing three categories, in the final category
top-coded at $50,000, it increased by a factor of 2.5 to reach $74,700.

Among those Black NLSF students who were poised to graduate with college debt, only 20.9 percent expected any help paying it down. When we asked
those with outstanding debt how concerned they were about the amount
owed, 44.0 percent said they were somewhat concerned, 20.2 percent reported
they were very concerned, and 10.1 percent said they were extremely concerned. Only one-quarter of those with debts (25.1 percent) said they were not
concerned at all. We then asked these same students to rate on a 0 to 10 scale
the degree to which the size of their debt affected their planning for life after
college, yielding a mean rating of 4.94.

After coding the responses to the first question 0 to 4 moving from not
concerned at all to extremely concerned, we combined responses to the two

TABLE 7.8. Cumulative debt held by various subgroups of Black NLSF respondents at the end of college

	Graduated with debt	Mean amount of debt, if had debt	Mean overall financial stress
Racial identification			
Monoracial	77.2%	$21,062*	6.31
Mixed race	78.0	25,382	6.65
Nativity and generation			
Multigenerational native	75.6%	$21,580	6.36
2nd generation immigrant	83.5	19,971	7.18
1st generation immigrant	78.8	23,195	6.01
Region of origin			
USA	75.6%+	$21,580	6.36
Caribbean	83.9	23,648	6.53
Africa	78.3	19,349	5.91
Other	83.6	23,242	6.73
Skin tone			
Light	71.9%+	$23,095	6.83
Medium	77.1	21,017	6.15
Dark	82.6	21,956	6.36
Gender			
Female	76.9%	$22,115	6.45
Male	78.1	21,103	6.20
Parental education			
No college	80.6%*	$20,672	6.71
College degree	79.9	21,677	6.44
Advanced degree	72.7	22,795	6.00
Experience of segregation			
Predominantly White	75.6%	$22,069	6.08
Racially mixed	77.9	22,579	6.64
Predominantly minority	77.4	19,721	6.20
Minority neighborhood/ White school	80.1	20,053	6.86
N		1,039	

$^+$p < 0.10; *p < 0.05; **p < 0.01; ***p < 0.001

items to create an index that ranged from 0 to 14, yielding a measure of student financial stress that averaged 6.36 with a Cronbach's alpha of 0.72. As shown in the lightest gray bar of figure 7.3, financial stress rose steadily across levels of indebtedness, climbing from 5.2 among those with debts under $10,000 to 7.5 among those with debts in excess of $50,000. In between, the scores were 6.32 for those owing $10,000–$20,000 and 7.09 for those owing $20,000–$50,000 (7.09). As shown in the third column of table 7.8, however, when we examined financial stress across the different dimensions of Black diversity, we found no significant differences between Black subgroups with respect to financial stress.

In fact, we found few significant differences across the dimensions of Black diversity, either with respect to the likelihood of being indebted or the amount owed. With respect to the amount owed, the only significant difference was between monoracial respondents, whose debt average $21,062, and mixed-race respondents, who owed $25,382. However, the share of students in each group who were indebted was about the same (77.2 percent versus 78.0 percent). The likelihood of graduating in debt *did* vary significantly by socioeconomic status, rising from 72.7 percent among students whose parents held advanced degrees, to 79.9 percent among those whose parents held college degrees, to 80.6 percent among those whose parents never completed college ($p < 0.05$).

Beyond this class differential, we found only two other marginally significant differences ($p < 0.10$) in the likelihood of graduating with debt. Whereas 71.9 percent for students with light skin tones were indebted upon graduation, the figure was 77.1 percent for those with medium skin tones and 82.6 percent for those with dark skin tones. Whereas the share indebted was 75.6 percent among multigenerational Americans, it was 83.9 percent among those from the Caribbean and 78.3 percent among those from Africa. Nonetheless, despite these small differences, in the end, no Black subgroup was under any more financial stress than any other subgroup.

Conclusion

This chapter explored the psychic and experiential downsides of life for Black students on elite college campuses. Despite the racial commonalities they share, we found differences that were often subtle but at times stark in how they experienced some of the downsides of life on the campus of a selective academic institution. The downsides of an elite education for Black students include exposure to racial prejudice and hostility on campus, as well as the psychological pressures of performing academically under the shadow of stereotype threat and high family expectations. In addition, life on a relatively safe and secure college campus does not eliminate student's exposure to stressful life events occurring within their family and friendship, and Black students may also experience a sense of loss and alienation from their families and communities. As the majority of Black students in our sample took out loans to finance their educations, debt represents yet another cost of an elite education.

Finally, the cumulative influence of the foregoing costs and stresses increase the risk of experiencing depression and other mental health issues.

The descriptive data marshaled in this chapter reveal that experiences of racial prejudice on campus were more common and occurred with higher frequency among dark-skinned monoracial students who grew up in segregated circumstances. These students also experience greater race- and family-based pressures for academic performance burdens. In the multivariate models shown in appendix A, however, the effects of racial identification, skin tone, and racial segregation largely disappear, and what emerges as a powerful predictor of experiencing racial hostility was a critical correlate of growing up under conditions of racial segregation: exposure to social disorder and violence (see appendix table A7.1).

We saw in chapter 3 that exposure to disorder and violence rose dramatically as one shifted from predominantly White to racially mixed to predominantly minority schools and neighborhoods (see figure 3.4). We conjecture here that growing up in a violent and socially disordered neighborhood renders Black students more sensitive to instances of racial prejudice. Indeed, looking back on the multivariate models from earlier chapters, we see that the Total Disorder-Violence Index strongly and negatively predicts closeness to Whites and strongly and positively predicts the perception of Whites as prone to discrimination (see appendix table A4.3). In addition, the index positively predicts viewing racial diversity as an important criterion in deciding where to attend college (appendix table A5.5) and the view that the student's institution is doing too little to promote diversity (appendix table A6.6). Given the foregoing relationships, it is not surprising that the index negatively predicts the number of White friends on campus (appendix table A6.1).

Although the descriptive data suggested that mixed-race, light-skinned students with less educated parents experienced lower race- and family-based performance burdens, the differentials were not large in substantive terms and these relationships failed to emerge in the multivariate models we estimated (appendix table A7.2). The descriptive tabulations also indicated that performance burdens varied by nativity, generation, and regional origin, and it was these effects that prevailed in the models. They showed African-origin students to experience a greater race-based performance burden and first- and second-generation immigrants to experience greater family-based burdens.

In assessing the financial burden of accumulated debt and the sense of loss or alienation created by going away to an exclusive college, we found few differences across the various dimensions of Black diversity, either in the descriptive tables or the multivariate analyses (appendix tables A7.4 and A7.5). The descriptive data suggested stressful life events within students' social networks varied by nativity, parental education and prior experience of segregation. Although multivariate models showed stressful life events within respondents' social networks were less frequent and less severe for students with college-educated parents, they revealed no significant differences by nativity or segregation (appendix table A7.3). Again, however, we found strong effects associated with the level of disorder and violence within the students' home neighborhoods and schools. As the level of disorder and violence rose, the number of stressful events and the severity-weighted stress index both increased sharply.

In our descriptive results, vulnerability to depression was not predicted by exposure to disorder and violence but was instead associated closely with immigrant origins and gender (appendix table A7.6). This finding was confirmed in the multivariate models, which showed Black women to have significantly greater CES-D scores than Black men and second-generation immigrants to be more vulnerable to depression than either natives or first-generation immigrants. The sons and daughters of college-educated parents also exhibited lower CES-D scores. Thus, among the Black college students in our sample, second-generation women with non-college-educated parents were most vulnerable to depression.

In this chapter, the sociological concepts of strategic assimilation and Black habitus proved useful in trying to understand the multidimensionality of Black students' experiences and the complex intraracial divides that play out on elite campuses (Lofton and Davis 2015). Like the "minority culture of mobility" described by Neckerman, Carter, and Lee (1999), the concept of strategic assimilation recognizes how expectations and norms that are race-, class-, and family specific can both differentially prepare Black students for interactions with White students and distance Black students from one another, thereby undermining the prospects both for social integration and academic achievement as they seek success in American society through higher education.

Scholars posit strategic assimilation as a distinctly middle-class strategy that stems from a "lack of consensus . . . with respect to defining and theorizing Blackness" and the failure to acknowledge intraracial diversity with respect to "social, economic, political, and cultural differences" (Martin 2010:235). Given conceptualizations of Blackness in the United States that are uncritically tethered to presumptions of economic disadvantage—and the implicit association of Whiteness with economic advantage—a certain level of intra-group tension perhaps becomes inevitable among aspiring Black students attending selective colleges and universities, where their presence is relatively recent and their numbers still quite small.

Whatever their particular origins, the pressures of trying to "fit in" on campus can extract a psychic toll on Black students with significant potential to increase stress, undermine emotional well-being, and hinder academic performance (see Torres and Massey 2012). In the twenty-first century, Black identity is a contested concept, rendering intra- and interracial interactions fraught in the "post-integration generation" (Simpson 1998). Those from predominately White, racially integrated, and higher status backgrounds often find that "acting Black" in this collegiate milieu is constraining, static, and out of step with the experiences they bring to campus. Nonetheless, they assert a Black identity that remains important to their self-conceptualization and feel connected to the larger Black community, even as they embrace elements of structural assimilation into mainstream society.

Although elite college campuses are often portrayed as "ivory towers" that stand apart from the "real world" where normal people make hard decisions about jobs, bills, relationships, and child-rearing, this idyllic image is far from accurate for Black students who must juggle multiple pressures stemming from experiences of prejudice, stereotype threat, family expectations, debt, alienation, and stressful life events, all while negotiating the dilemmas of group identity and allegiance in a racially stratified society. Although the collegiate setting may provide something of a buffer from some of these stressors, they inevitably penetrate the hallowed halls of academia to make social integration and academic achievement on campus more challenging for Black students and can harm their mental health, though they often do not seek treatment (Lipson et al. 2018). Today, there is an increasing demand for colleges and universities to hire mental health counseling staff trained to work with students of color to help remedy that gap. Nonetheless, aspiring Black students persist and, as the next chapter demonstrates, emerge with a shared racial worldview informed by the highs and the lows of seeking to become part of the new Black elite.

8

Emerging Elite Identities

Contemporary Blackness is an appreciation of one's cultural heritage. It's
about rising above whatever obstacles have come before you, like getting past,
like okay, racism happened, so what, it's time to do something about it rather
than just bitch and complain for the next hundred years.

VERONICA, SECOND-GENERATION HAITIAN AMERICAN

THE FINAL WAVE of the National Longitudinal Survey of Freshmen (NLSF)
was administered in the spring of 2003 when most of our students were looking forward to graduation and making plans for life after college. Many were
also reflecting on how college had changed them and their views of the world.
For Black students, four years with a critical mass of well-educated same-race
peers provided a fertile context for contemplating the meaning of race and the
nature of Blackness. In this chapter, we draw on data from the final two waves
of the NLSF to assess changes in Black students' racial identities and attitudes
since they arrived on campus. We then undertake a more in-depth analysis of
the structure of Black racial identity using Sellers and colleagues' (1997) Multidimensional Inventory of Black Identity (MIBI).

Our analysis reveals the emergence of a distinct identity configuration
among elite Black students early in the twenty-first century, one characterized
by a strengthening consensus about Black self-identification, most commonly
in combination with an equally valued "American" identity but increasingly as
an unhyphenated construct. Student racial attitudes also displayed a remarkable convergence on commonly held views with respect to perceptions about
social distance, stereotyping, discrimination, and racial stratification. At the
same time, however, students also moved away from a shared sense of common fate with all Black Americans. The share of students perceiving "a lot" of

common fate identity fell sharply over four years of college while the share perceiving "little or no" shared fate markedly increased. This pattern of change suggests a growing belief among high-achieving students that they constitute a distinct group set apart from their same-race counterparts who do not attend selective postsecondary institutions.

Despite the consensus on the importance of a Black identity, our multidimensional analysis revealed a split among students on the meaning and importance of Blackness. Although all students shared an assimilationist ideology that favored integration within mainstream society, they differed significantly on other dimensions of Black identity. Monoracial, dark-skinned students who grew up in minority-dominant or racially mixed contexts perceived Blackness to be quite central to their identities and expressed rather strong support for cultural nationalism. In contrast, mixed-race, light-skinned students who grew up in White social settings viewed Blackness as less central to their identity and expressed less support for cultural nationalism. Although support for political nationalism was weak in both sets of students, it was stronger among monoracial, dark-skinned students who grew up in segregated or racially mixed circumstances. On issues related to Black identity, the views of students who attended White schools but lived in segregated neighborhoods were generally closer to those coming of age in minority schools and neighborhoods.

Forging an Elite Black Identity

Pierre Bourdieu compared elite education in France to Maxwell's demon, a famous thought experiment in physics in which a hypothetical demon sorts molecules into two separate chambers according to their temperature, cold or hot, thereby violating the second law of thermodynamics. To Bourdieu (1998), the French educational system was the social equivalent of Maxwell's demon. It selects students who fit a certain worldview, or habitus, to enter and receive credentials from elite universities. Although the French like to think of their educational system as a meritocracy, students chosen to attend France's grandes écoles to a significant degree already fit into the elite social world they are entering. They likely read the same newspapers, were educated in the same canon of classic works, knew about the same foods and wines, and consumed the same emblems of high culture. Even if they did not yet have access to the financial capital of France's elite, students entering the grandes écoles had already acquired many of its tastes and customs, yielding a valuable stock of cultural capital that would serve them well in their academic and professional careers.

In the United States, Cookson and Persell's (1985) classic study of elite boarding schools likewise saw them not simply as providing academic credentials but also serving as a mechanism for elite socialization. In these schools, new generations of students were trained to perceive themselves as worthy of the power and prestige they would enjoy as adults. Khan (2011) similarly showed how students at one elite boarding school came to see themselves as deserving of status and influence, not because of their lineage (often including multiple generations of elite prep school alumni) but because of the intense work they put into their rigorous studies, thus rendering them "meritorious." As in France, a firm belief in meritocracy deeply informed their view not only of the educational system but also of their position within it.

In many ways, elite colleges and universities perform the same function as France's grandes écoles. However, as we have seen, many Black students do not come from privileged backgrounds that lend themselves to easy socialization as professionals. In chapter 4, we saw how parental involvement in the cultivation of human capital, cultural capital, and social capital varied widely depending on factors such as racial identity, nativity, skin tone, class status, and segregation. As a result, Black students on average differ from White students with respect to their opinions, attitudes, and sensibilities. They upset the logic of Maxwell's demon because they were selected to diversify the historic character of students at their institutions. Whereas selective colleges and universities evolved to socialize privileged White students into the habitus of the nation's educated elite, here we ask what happens to the heterogeneous population of Black students as they proceed through four years at a selective college or university. Having described who these students were when they entered college and how they differentially experienced campus life, here we adopt a longitudinal perspective, considering how they have changed and who they have become.

As they approached graduation, Black students had spent considerable time away from their families and friends, embedded within peer networks that in some cases were Whiter and in other cases Blacker than those they knew in high school. As they approached the end of their senior year, we therefore revisited the issue of racial identity. Given their diverse origins and varied on-campus experiences, we are interested in how college might have changed their racial attitudes and beliefs after four years of contact with elite White students and ongoing interaction with Black intellectual peers.

Chavous et al. (2018) argue that college strongly influences the construction of racial identity during key phases of social and emotional development that unfold between the ages of eighteen and twenty-two. Our qualitative data generally confirm this view. Interviewees readily acknowledged that their racial identities had changed, especially for mixed-race students who had grown up in predominately White or racially mixed circumstances. Many of these students arrived on campus intent on making Black friends and immersing themselves in a Black social world that had eluded them before college. Other students entered with varying degrees of curiosity and no small amount of apprehension about interacting with privileged Whites for the first time—and both sets of students talked a lot about race.

Earlier, we saw that as freshmen, Black survey respondents overwhelmingly favored a "hyphenated identity," one that regarded Black and American identities as equally important, with small shares favoring either an exclusively Black or solely an American identity. Over the course of their college careers, however, respondents appeared to shift away from adherence to an American identity and moved toward a Black identity. As shown on the left side of figure 8.1, among seniors, the share self-identifying solely as American dropped by 2.4 percentage points to 7.4 percent while the percentage favoring a hyphenated Black and American identity fell by 7.5 points to 63.9 percent. In contrast, the share choosing an exclusive Black identity markedly rose by 10.1 points to 28.7 percent. These shifts were highly significant statistically ($p < 0.001$).

Insights into the reasons for this shift come from our in-depth interviews. Jessica, for example, told us that before arriving on campus she identified as "racially mixed" rather than Black, in keeping with the diverse West Coast environment where she grew up. Her closest friends saw themselves as mixed as well, and it was common among her high school peers to recognize different ethnic and racial identities even within the same family. However, she found that college was quite different. Not only did she discover that she "looked Black," but she went on to explain how she became heavily involved in Black activities on campus, forging close ties to monoracial Black peers who did not necessarily recognize the complexity of her origins:

> At home, there's just a lot of other mixed people that I'm close to, that I'm friends with. All of our family friends have mixed kids, so it's just the norm. . . . Even just at my high school, there were a lot of us. In the Bay Area, there's a lot of mixed people whereas at [name of university], there

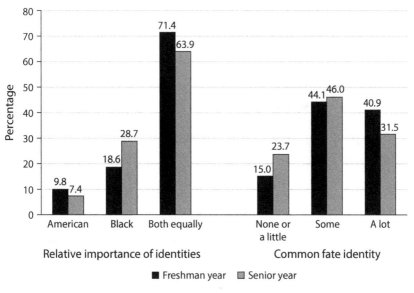

FIGURE 8.1. Changes in the strength of Black versus American identity and individual versus group fate during college

aren't very many. It's just really not as acceptable as a way to identify, and it doesn't have the same kind of meanings, I think, as it does when I'm at home.

When asked why identifying as mixed was less acceptable for her as a college senior than it was as a freshman, she answered,

I think because there's less people that are mixed [on campus] so there's different kinds of connotations and less understanding of what somebody might be meaning when they're saying that. And, also, I guess just because I associate with mostly Black people.

As a senior, Jessica was double-majoring in English and Africana studies and was involved in a research project with two Black professors. Although her father was Black, she grew up with her White mother and twin brother in a racially diverse area of Northern California. Consequently, she did not see her newly acquired Black identity as "homegrown," explaining that "we didn't grow up listening to gospel or being around Black people. . . . No Black church, no Black music." At college, she had come to see herself as "Black" and not "biracial" because she felt accepted by Black people on campus and "that's where I've found my home."

Carl also found the experience of being Black on an elite, predominately White campus to be galvanizing, telling us that "I feel like the experiences that result from having dark skin at [name of university] bring us somewhat closer together." Likewise, Olivia chose to downplay the West Indian and African origins she proudly espoused at the beginning of college. Her overarching concern was to find Black friends and to distance herself from the awkwardness she always felt at her overwhelmingly White high school. To ensure that she was "not ostracized or isolated from the Black community," she chose to live in a dorm that celebrated Black culture during her freshman and sophomore years. As she put it:

> I think [name of dorm] did a lot for my sense of self as a Black person, being more aware of it and then being proud of it. Before, I had always, I mean I always considered myself Black, but I'm not sure if I associated certain ties to it. When I got to [name of university], I think [Black-theme dorm] fostered that in me.

As a senior in college, Olivia had no White friends and was a leader in several Black campus organizations.

Paradoxically, these shifts in racial identity did not yield a concomitant increase in a sense of a shared fate with other African Americans. Instead, respondents' experiences on campus appear to have *reduced* the degree of their adherence to a common fate identity, challenging Dawson's (2001) view that racial group interests serve as proxies for individual interests. As shown on the right side of figure 8.1, between the freshman and senor years, the share saying that what happens to African Americans affected them "none or a little" rose from 15.0 percent to 23.7 percent (an increase of 8.7 points) while the percentage answering "a lot" fell from 40.9 percent to 31.5 percent (a drop of 9.4 points). As was the case with Black versus American identity, these shifts were highly significant statistically ($p < 0.001$).

Despite the upward shift in Black racial identification and the downward shift in common fate identity among Black respondents, we found few differences in the degree of change across the dimensions of Black diversity—so little change, in fact, that we opted not to present any dimensional data on these topics here. What we observed across all Black subgroups was a common pattern of change: a modest but significant shift away from self-identification as "American" and a sharper shift toward allegiance to a solitary "Black" identity, moves that were accompanied by a decline in the degree to which students felt they shared a common fate with Black people generally. Despite the formation of a stronger Black identity, as prospective graduates of prestigious

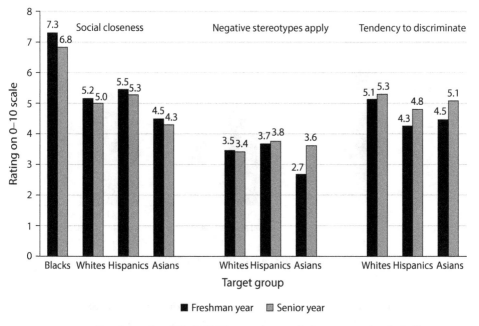

FIGURE 8.2. Racial attitudes of Black NLSF respondents at the beginning and end of college

academic institutions, students appear to have come to perceive themselves as standing apart from and not burdened with the same risks as less educated Black Americans. The seemingly paradoxical combination of a strengthened Black identity and a weaker common fate identity suggests the emergence of not simply a Black identity but an *elite* Black identity.

Converging Racial Attitudes

When we examined students' perceptions about social closeness, stereotyping, and the propensity of others to discriminate, we found relatively little change in average ratings over four years of college. As indicated in figure 8.2, when asked to rate their perceived closeness to various groups as seniors, the mean ratings dropped only slightly from the freshman year, declining by an average of about 0.2 points on a 0 to 10 scale. Likewise, changes in the average rating of outgroups according to negative stereotypes were small, with an average increase toward negativity around 0.3 points on a 0 to 7 scale. Finally, the average change in the perceived tendency for outgroups to discriminate was only slightly larger, with an increase of 0.5 points on the 0 to 10 scale.

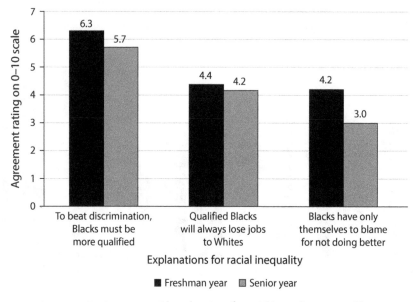

FIGURE 8.3. Agreement with explanations for racial inequality expressed by
Black NLSF respondents at the beginning and end of college

As shown in figure 8.3, we observe a similar pattern of modest change when considering students' agreement with various explanations for Black socioeconomic disadvantage. Support for the view that Blacks have to be more qualified to overcome discrimination dropped by 0.6 points on the 0 to 10 scale of agreement. Support for the precept that Blacks will always lose jobs to equally qualified Whites declined by 0.2 points. The exception that proves the rule is that support for the view that Blacks have only themselves to blame for their lack of success and should just try harder, which was low to begin with, dropped by highly significant 1.2 points to just 3.0 on the 0 to 10 scale ($p < 0.001$). Due to their coursework and experiences on an elite White campus, Black students apparently came to appreciate more fully the structural barriers to racial advancement in American society. As Aaron noted, "Black people at this school, you know, because they're educated, tend to be pretty socially aware. They're aware of continued racism and stuff like that."

The relative lack of change in students' racial attitudes nonetheless belies considerable underlying movement in individual ratings over time. Close inspection of the data revealed a remarkable pattern of convergence in Black students' attitudes, with significant shifts from the extremes of the original distribution toward the center. Table 8.1 illustrates this fact by deconstructing

TABLE 8.1. Change in racial attitudes during college among Black NLSF respondents

	Fall 1999 Wave 1 mean	Spring 2003 Wave 5 mean	Pattern of change Wave 1 to Wave 5		
			Started college at mean	Started college below the mean	Started college above the mean
Social closeness					
Black people	7.29	6.83	+0.66	+1.55***	−2.60***
White people	5.15	5.02	+0.34	+1.99***	−2.57***
Hispanics	5.46	5.28	+0.13	+2.29***	−2.44***
Asians	4.50	4.31	+0.28	+2.34***	−2.78***
Racial stereotyping					
White people	3.46	3.42	+0.12	+1.37***	−2.00***
Hispanics	3.66	3.76	+0.10	+1.10***	−0.91***
Asians	2.68	3.61	+0.81	+2.85***	−0.56***
Discrimination					
White people	5.13	5.30	+0.14	+1.93***	−2.39***
Hispanics	4.25	4.80	+0.10	+2.22***	−1.30***
Asians	4.46	5.08	+0.30	+2.64***	−1.75***
Explanations for Black disadvantage					
To beat discrimination, be more qualified	6.29	5.71	+0.79	+3.31***	−3.18***
Qualified Black people always lose jobs to White people	4.37	4.17	+0.03	+2.32***	−2.71***
Black people have only themselves to blame	4.21	3.00	+1.40	+1.95***	−5.05***

⁺ p < 0.10; * p < 0.05; ** p < 0.01; *** p < 0.001

the change in average values (shown in the two left-hand columns) into three categories (shown in the three right-hand columns): those where the initial freshman rating was near the middle of the distribution (within one standard deviation above or below the mean), those initially at the lower end of the distribution (at least one standard deviation below the mean), and those initially at the upper end of the distribution (at least one standard deviation above the mean).

The top panel of table 8.1 presents this analysis for perceptions of social closeness to the nation's four broad racial-ethnic groups. The third column shows that changes in feelings of social closeness among respondents whose freshman responses were close to the mean were slight, with no significant differences in ratings between the first and final wave of the survey. In contrast, the fourth column reveals that students who began with ratings below the mean moved significantly upward between the two dates. In contrast, the final column shows that respondents who began with ratings above the mean moved significantly downward ($p < 0.001$). The data thus indicate a significant and powerful convergence in perceptions of closeness with respect to America's principal ethnoracial populations.

We see very much the same pattern of convergence in the other attitudinal measures: no change in ratings that were near the freshman mean, significant upward shifts in ratings that began at the lower part of the freshman distribution, and significant downward shifts in those that began in the upper segmented of the distribution. The one exception to the foregoing pattern of change, as already noted, is observed in the final line of the table. Not only did a consensus emerge that Blacks were not themselves to blame for not doing better in life and just had to work harder, but the average agreement with this sentiment significantly dropped (going from 4.21 to 3.0). This pattern of change reflected a huge drop in agreement among those with initially higher scores compared to much smaller increases among those with initial scores that were below or close to the average.

The survey data thus reveal a clear and consistent convergence in racial attitudes toward commonly shared views over time. Students moved away from expressing either a mainstream American identity or a mixed Black and American identity and moved toward greater adherence to an unhyphenated Black identity. The diverse origins and experiences of elite Black students underscored subtle but meaningful differences in racial identities and attitudes expressed as freshmen, but these differences dissipated over the course of four years of socialization at selective institutions of higher education, yielding a remarkable consensus on racial identity and attitudes by the spring of their senior year.

The Dimensions of Black Identity

Research has found that Black identity is complex and reflects sentiments arrayed along several underlying dimensions. As a result, findings based on single attitudinal measures fail to capture the nuances of racial self-identification in contemporary American society. In an effort to address this shortcoming, we now revisit the issue of racial identity using the MIBI. The MIBI was designed by the social psychologist Robert Sellers and colleagues (1997:805) in an effort to reconcile apparent "inconsistencies in the research literature on racial identity." It is grounded in social identity theory (Stryker and Burke 2000), which posits that every person has multiple ranked identities (by race, gender, ethnicity, class, etc.) and that within each person's identity hierarchy, some identities are more salient than others (see also Tajfel and Turner 1986; Fogg-Davis 2001).

The MIBI lets Black respondents indicate what racial group membership means to them personally without presuming a single, uniform identity derived from a shared, normative conceptualization of Blackness (Cross 1971, 1991). Instead, individuals first state the importance of race in their own lives and then articulate its relevance with respect to other dimensions. The junior-year wave of the NLSF included items from three subscales of the MIBI: racial centrality, assimilationist ideology, and nationalist ideology. For each subscale, respondents were asked to rate the strength of their agreement with a set of statements on a 0 (no agreement) to 10 (complete agreement) scale.

Within each subscale, scores are averaged to create a summary measure that also ranges from 0 to 10. Individual items from the inventory and their mean values are reported in table 8.2, along the mean value for each subscale. For example, the Racial Centrality Subscale seeks to assess the degree to which respondents "normatively define [themselves] with regard to race." It is based on eight items quantifying the degree to which an assertion of a Black identity is a core aspect of one's self-concept (Sellers et al. 1997:806). Scores on the eight items ranged from 4.5 to 7.9 with a mean scale value of 6.5 and Cronbach's reliability alpha index of 0.763, suggesting that Blackness is quite central within students' identity configuration.

Ideology is another key component of racial identity and it entails meanings ascribed to Black identity that define appropriate attitudes and behaviors for Black individuals. Here, we focus on two subscales, the assimilationist and the nationalist, but further divide the latter into separate cultural and political components. The Assimilationist Ideology Subscale is constructed from nine items that emphasize similarities between Black Americans and the rest of U.S. society and stress the importance of cross-racial interactions and cooperation. Average scores across the nine items ranged from 5.1 to 9.1 with an overall mean of 6.9 and a Cronbach's alpha of 0.707, suggesting a rather assimilationist stance.

Following Charles et al. (2015), we divided items in the nationalist inventory into separate categories focusing on different forms of nationalist sentiment: cultural and political. Among NLSF respondents, Charles and colleagues found these two scales to be more internally consistent than the overall nationalist subscale. The Cultural Nationalist Subscale is derived from

TABLE 8.2. Subscales from the Multidimensional Inventory of Black Identity

	Score
Racial centrality	
Being Black affects how I feel about myself	5.6
Being Black is an important part of my self-image	7.9
My destiny is tied to the destiny of other Black people	4.5
Being Black is important to the kind of person I am	6.7
Being Black provides a sense of belonging	7.1
I have a strong attachment to other Black people	7.3
Being Black reflects who I am	7.4
Being Black is a major factor in social relationships	5.5
Mean Racial Centrality	6.5
Assimilationist ideology	
Should not espouse Black separatism	6.3
More Black people in mainstream is a sign of progress	6.4
Attending White schools teaches how to interact with White people	5.1
Black people should be full members of the American political system	7.8
Black people should work within the system to achieve goals	7.5
Black people should strive to integrate all segregated institutions	7.4
Black people should feel free to interact socially with White people	9.1
Black people should view themselves first and foremost as Americans	5.9
Plight of Black people improves when Black people hold important positions	6.8
Mean Assimilationist Ideology	6.9
Nationalist ideology—Cultural	
Black people should surround children with Black art, music, books	7.9
Black people should shop at Black stores	6.9
Black people should know African American history	8.6
Mean Cultural Nationalism	7.8
Nationalist ideology—Political	
Black people should not intermarry racially	2.0
Black people should adopt Afrocentric values	3.8
Black people should attend Black schools	3.2
Black people should organize a separate political force	3.2
Black people can never live in harmony with White people	2.9
Black people cannot trust White people	2.3
Mean Political Nationalism	2.9
N	1,039

agreement ratings on three statements focusing on the preservation and extension of Black culture: the desirability of exposing children to Black cultural artifacts, knowing Black history, and buying from Black-owned businesses. As shown in the third panel, adherence to Black cultural nationalism is quite strong among our respondents, with mean ratings on the items ranging from

6.9 to 8.6 and averaging 7.8 with a Cronbach's alpha of 0.690. In contrast, mean ratings across the six items in the Political Nationalist Subscale are much lower, ranging from 2.0 to 3.8 and averaging only 2.9 with an alpha of 0.719, indicating less support for political as opposed to cultural nationalism.

Sellers et al. (1997) offer an example of how the centrality, assimilationist, and nationalist scales together capture the nuances of Black racial identity in ways that a single unidimensional scale cannot. Whereas both Martin Luther King Jr. and Malcolm X would presumably score high on the racial centrality scale, we would expect King to score high on the assimilationist scale but low on the nationalist scale, but we would expect the opposite profile for Malcom X. Much the same contrast also would be predicted for the historical rivals W. E. B. Du Bois and Booker T. Washington. In the words of Sellers et al. (1998:32), "Although other aspects of African American racial identity are important predictors of different phenomena, it is clear that, without a dimension like ideology, one's view of individual African American's racial identity would be overly simplistic."

Results in table 8.2 confirm that "being Black" is quite central to the identities of Black NLSF respondents, with a centrality index of 6.5. However, contrary to common characterizations of African Americans as being either assimilationist or nationalist in their ideology, we find that elite Black students at the dawn of the twenty-first century exhibited both assimilationist and nationalist tendencies but were far more supportive of cultural nationalism (index value 7.8) than political nationalism (index value 2.9). This configuration of ideological sentiments was also in evidence among our interviewees. As Veronica, a second-generation Haitian woman, poignantly put it,

> Contemporary Blackness is an appreciation of one's cultural heritage. It's about rising above whatever obstacles have come before you, like getting past, like okay, racism happened, so what, it's time to do something about it rather than just bitch and complain for the next hundred years.

For her part, Francheska, a mixed-race woman of Haitian and Croatian heritage, condoned cultural nationalism but vehemently opposed a separatist, political ideology, telling us with reference to militant nationalists,

> They want to celebrate their culture, but they want to embrace it to the point that they exclude everything else and try to exist in a culture but not remember that they're also part of a bigger society, you know?

Thus, both survey respondents and the in-depth interviewees articulate the importance of Blackness to their self-identities and support both Black pride

TABLE 8.3. Adherence to different dimensions of Black identity derived from the Multidimensional Inventory of Black Identity for Black NLSF respondents

	Racial centrality	Assimilationist ideology	Political nationalism	Cultural nationalism
Racial identification				
Monoracial	6.7***	6.8+	3.0***	7.9***
Multiracial	5.3	7.1	2.4	6.7
Nativity and generation				
Multigenerational native	6.6**	6.9+	2.9	7.9*
Second–generation immigrant	6.1	7.1	3.1	7.6
First–generation immigrant	6.2	7.1	2.9	7.5
Region of origin				
USA	6.6*	6.9	2.9	7.9**
African	6.1	7.0	3.1	7.3
Caribbean	6.2	7.1	2.8	7.8
Other	6.0	7.3	3.3	7.4
Skin tone				
Light	5.9***	7.1+	2.6	7.2***
Medium	6.6	6.9	3.0	8.0
Dark	6.6	6.9	2.8	7.9
Gender				
Female	6.6	6.9	2.8	7.9**
Male	6.4	7.0	2.9	7.5
Parental education				
No degree	6.8+	6.8	3.0	8.0
College degree	6.3	7.0	2.8	7.6
Advanced degree	6.5	6.9	2.9	7.8
Experience of segregation				
Predominantly White	6.1***	7.1	2.7*	7.4***
Racially mixed	6.5	7.0	3.0	7.8
Predominantly minority	6.8	6.8	3.1	8.1
Minority neighborhood/ White school	6.7	6.8	3.2	7.9
N		1,039		

+ $p < 0.10$; * $p < 0.05$; ** $p < 0.01$; *** $p < 0.001$

and assimilation into the mainstream of American life but generally reject exclusionary nationalism.

Table 8.3 examines differences in the structure of Black racial identity across the various dimensions of diversity. As one might expect given the results presented so far, the degree of commitment to the various dimensions of Black identity differs depending on respondents' racial identification and origins.

For example, race is significantly less central for mixed-race respondents (5.3) compared with their monoracial peers (6.7). Mixed-race respondents are also more assimilationist than monoracial students (7.1 versus 6.8), less culturally nationalist (6.7 versus 7.9), and less politically nationalist (2.4 versus 3.0).

Given these findings, it is hardly surprising that the Racial Centrality Index is also significantly lower for light-skinned respondents (5.9) compared to those with medium and dark skin tones (6.6 in each case). Respondents with light skin tones were also less committed to cultural nationalism (7.2) than medium- (8.0) and dark-skinned (7.9) students. They also were marginally more assimilationist (7.1 versus 6.9 for both medium- and dark-skinned students). Racial centrality also tends to be lower among immigrant-origin Blacks, with respective means of 6.2 and 6.1 for those in the first and second generations, compared with 6.6 for multigenerational natives. We observe no differences by region of origin, however.

Immigrant respondents also tend to be marginally more assimilationist (7.1) than multigenerational natives (6.9) and less culturally nationalist as well, with average scores of 7.5 (in the first generation) and 7.6 (in the second generation), compared with a mean of 7.9 for multigenerational natives. Finally, race is less central among students who grew up in predominantly White (6.1) and racially mixed (6.5) environments, compared to those who came from segregated neighborhoods, with little difference depending on whether they attended White schools (6.7) or minority-dominant schools (6.8).

Black students who came of age in predominantly White schools and neighborhoods are also less politically nationalist (2.7) than those from racially mixed neighborhoods (3.0), minority neighborhoods (3.1), and those who came from minority neighborhoods but attended White schools (3.2). Black students who grew up in predominantly White environments were also much less culturally nationalist, with an average rating of 7.4 compared to 8.1 for those from predominantly minority schools and neighborhoods and 7.9 for those who came from segregated neighborhoods but attended White schools. Among those from racially mixed schools and neighborhoods, the index of cultural nationalism stood at 7.8.

In sum, racial segregation during childhood intensifies the centrality of race and adherence to nationalist ideological perspectives. Given the selectivity of our sample, it is perhaps unsurprising that we observe no meaningful differences in adherence to an ideology of mainstream assimilation. Attending a selective college or university is itself an indicator of desire to integrate within U.S. society. Differences across the remaining dimensions of Black diversity (gender and class) were generally muted. Black women respondents were more culturally nationalist than Black men, with a scale score of 7.9 versus 7.5 ($p < 0.01$) and the centrality of Black identity was marginally greater ($p < 0.10$) among students whose parents did not complete college (6.8) compared to those whose parents were either college educated (6.3) or held an advanced degree (6.5).

Despite the increasing allegiance to Black identity documented earlier, the foregoing results suggest a significant split in the dimensional structure of Black racial identity. Light-skinned, mixed-race Black students and those who came of age in White schools and neighborhoods report Blackness to be less central to their identity and are less politically and culturally nationalistic compared to darker skinned monoracial students from racially mixed or minority-dominant schools and neighborhoods. This contrast is also apparent in the qualitative data.

Aaron, for example, a middle-class student from Canada with a Black mother and a White father (both U.S. citizens), grew up around other racial minorities but in situations where Whites always dominated. As a result, Aaron had no Black friends before college and, possibly for this reason, felt that Black American students were a bit too concerned with racial issues and excessively "Afrocentric," consistent with Benjamin's (2005) finding that young people in the post–civil rights generation are less connected to that identity.

> I'm not really about curing all the world's woes or anything like that. . . . I'm just trying to be who I am. You know? Being very individualistic, let's put it that way, rather than selfish: individualistic. So it's kind of hard— sometimes you find yourself in a position where people, Black people at this school anyway . . . there's just a point where they're talking about racism or segregation or something like that [and] sometimes I find myself in the situation where I'm just kind of like, "All right." You know what I mean? There's more things to talk about than this.

Although the divides are generally not as large, we observe a similar set of differences between immigrant-origin Blacks and multigenerational natives, with the former exhibiting an identity configuration in which Blackness was less central, assimilationist sentiments were stronger, and cultural nationalism weaker. Because recent Black immigrants, especially Africans, are a highly selected group who typically come to the United States with the instrumental goals of acquiring an education, getting a good job, and achieving economic mobility, assimilationist sentiments are not unexpected. Immigrants come to the United States to advance in U.S. society, not reject it.

When asked what it meant to be a Black person at her selective university, Ashley—the Jamaican immigrant we referenced earlier—told us that "in my opinion, it's just that you are student of a darker hue," suggesting that for her, race was only skin deep—not particularly central and not tied to any kind of nationalist agenda. When asked if she had anything to add, she replied, "No, I don't think so." However, she went on to say that many of her multigenerational native-born peers had a "chip on their shoulder" and were too quick to "blame Whites for their problems," illustrating the case with one of her classmates:

> This one particular [Black] guy in the class was just like, you know, he just had this humongous chip on his shoulder. Like, you know, if I go out and I'm in a suit and I won't get a cab because . . . all they see is a Black man and they don't wanna stop, you know? And while that may be true . . . we're just like, get over it and move on.

As previously noted, second-generation immigrant interviewees often place more emphasis on an ethnic than a racial identity. Eugena, of Nigerian origin, offers a good example of how ethnicity can overshadow racial identity among immigrant-origin Black young adults. When asked whether it was important for Blacks to join race-based organizations, Eugena initially responded with a simple "no." After a moment of additional thought, however, she agreed that doing so was sometimes appropriate—but "only if you feel a really strong affinity or if it's a large part of the way you identify yourself." She told us that in her case, it was not "important to how I define myself, because [being Nigerian] affects the way I speak at home, the food I eat, and most of the people I know outside of school. It's like a whole aspect of my life that is defined by the fact that I am Nigerian."

Conclusion

The foregoing divisions in the structure of Black identity continue a long-running debate among Black intellectuals over the issue of whether the educated Black elite serves as a vanguard for racial advancement, as Du Bois (1903) argued in his essay on the Talented Tenth, or whether they are just materially selfish individuals concerned mainly with their own social mobility rather than "advancing the race," as Frazier (1957) argued in *The Black Bourgeoisie*. As we have seen, however, quantitative results reveal no strong class differences in the expression of Black identity compared to the other dimensions of

Black diversity, a finding supported by our qualitative data as well. Again as Denise explained, "Yes, being Black is the link. I mean yes, we do have our own [intraracial] issues, class, things like that, but for the most part, okay, you're Black, so you're a sister or brother, you know?"

Our analysis nonetheless reveals important differences in the expression of Black identity along its separate dimensions, and several interviewees expressed a need for Black Americans to adopt a more expansive view of what it means to be "authentically Black" in the twenty-first century. Some interviewees, such as racially mixed Jessica, expressed disappointment in the degree to which Black identity was policed by some monoracial native Blacks on campus:

> I feel it's a small, very vocal group of people that feel they have given themselves the power of defining what Black is . . . kind of basing it on these 1960s models of Blackness. And not even 1960s, because I think it's something that the media has come to represent.

Mia, a second-generation Ghanaian woman, also asserted the need for a more inclusive understanding of Black identity, telling us that in her opinion,

> I guess it's just having an idea of your identity and how your experience is shaped—I don't know, like a general understanding of what the common tie of Blackness is. And an understanding that though there is a common tie, we all have different experiences that cause us to define our Blackness differently. And within having that understanding requires us to have a larger responsibility to our community. So on campus, I mean as much as I complain about it, I think it's necessary to have a BSU [Black Student Union] and to be like, "Okay, we're here to accept all forms of Blackness no matter how you define it." But it also means you have more of a responsibility to the community because we do have a large Black community [on campus].

The final part of Mia's statement is especially telling. Many interviewees described the BSU, Black-themed housing, and Black affinity groups as divisive and problematic. However, later in their interviews, they did acknowledge that although they themselves might not need or want such programs, others might. Likewise, many of the more outspoken advocates of Afrocentric programs also reported White friends and did not question the authenticity of racial identities expressed by Black peers who chose not to be involved with the BSU and other Black organizations on campus.

These more flexible and varied articulations of Black identity are a relatively new phenomenon in American society. Until recently, immigrant and mixed-race Blacks were a smaller presence and considerably less visible, yielding a historically specific, homogenized, and monolithic definition of Blackness in America (Cornell and Hartmann 1998; Eggerling-Boeck 2002). However, it should not be surprising at this historical juncture—with the Black population becoming increasingly diverse through immigration, intermarriage, and upward social mobility—that the content of Black identity is being contested and redefined by younger generations of Black Americans and that these new expressions of Blackness are highly gendered (Collins and Bilge 2016).

The tensions arising from the diversity that underlies Black solidarity in the twenty-first century were mentioned by several of our interviewees. When asked whether she thought the Black student community on campus was tightly knit, Agnes, a second-generation student whose parents emigrated from Belize, replied, "No, not at all." When asked why not, she went on to explain:

> There's a lot of cliques within the Black community. There's cliques based on ethnicity. Not so much, though. I guess it's like, "We're Nigerian and we're this." There's cliques based on like I want to say class standing. There's cliques based on social background. People who are from the inner city hang out a lot. And there's cliques based on like where you live.

Crystal, a mixed-race student who lived with her upper-middle-class White grandparents while attending a predominantly White high school, appreciated the racial solidarity that existed on campus but also noted certain gender-related tensions.

> CRYSTAL: When you're thrust into an environment like this, where you're really, really in the minority, and especially people who come from neighborhoods where Black people aren't the minority, then I think you do flock into groups where you have an obvious visual—you can see another person and say, "Oh, I already have something in common with you. You look like me." Like, I think a lot of people think it makes it easier to make friends with someone or start off a conversation.
>
> INTERVIEWER: How do you think Black students here view you or perceive you?

CRYSTAL: So, with Black women, that's one of the reasons I kind of left the [Campus Association of Black Women] because for some reason, in my opinion, in my experience, I've experienced a lot of Black women who aren't the fondest of mixed Black and White women. So I kind of felt that on campus here, a lot of the full-Black women haven't really been the most open to me.

INTERVIEWER: So they're not as nice as they could be?

CRYSTAL: Some of them. I do have a lot of full-Black friends, which is good. But then, full-Black men, which may be one of the reasons full-Black women don't necessarily like me, of course, I have so many guy friends that are Black.

Jessica, a racially mixed junior, felt that as long as she self-identified as "Black" and not "mixed," she would be accepted by Black students; however, if she said that she was mixed, she would be less accepted. Although Jessica strongly supported Black solidarity, she nonetheless felt certain strains in dealing with other Black students owing to her class and racial origins.

JESSICA: We're using our power. All Black people need to stick together. But it's more than that and it's less than that—because so many people aren't necessarily politically active.

INTERVIEWER: People are just talking about it?

JESSICA: Yeah. It's just like, he doesn't want to be Black. She doesn't want to be Black. She wants to be White. It's really annoying. I think there's a lot more to it than just that. . . . You have to make choices to live in [a predominantly White dorm] or to join a Black organization or to have a White best friend or something. And if you do something like that, then people will take issue with them. And so, kind of the more involved with the White community you get, the more suspicious you become. . . . So the people who are like, We need change. We need change. This is what Black is. We need to all come together and fight. And if you're not part of us, you're the enemy.

Jessica then went on to elaborate, telling us that

Being Black is difficult anyways because there are just so many contradictory expectations that you're supposed to be down and still part of the community but kind of realistically maybe your family isn't from that kind of background, so what does down and being a part of the community mean to you? Does it mean pretending like you were poor once? Or does it really mean kind of proclaiming this middle classness—which would then say you're White?

Adam, of mixed White and African parentage and upper middle class in terms of socioeconomic status, felt tensions arising from differences between immigrant-origin students and natives as well as from regional differences among immigrants.

I think that's because in the Black community in general, that's how it is. I mean, you have divisions. There's always been conflict between the Caribbean American community and the Black American community that has descended from slaves. Same with the African community. I mean, I have friends from Africa, I mean, even on [ ] campus, a lot of the African students that I know that are from the continent, they don't necessarily interact too much with the Black American community. So I've noticed divisions. I think that's even in the greater society.

Chris, of White, West Indian, middle-class origins, was philosophical in emphasizing Black solidarity but tempering it with realism about the prospects for unity on questions of identity.

I see a good amount of solidarity among Black American students here. I mean, I don't really think you can expect, you can't expect one voice, you know? That's impossible. If you have that many, I mean, it's not that many students, but you know, you have a hundred students, there's no way you can have one voice. You know? Everybody has different opinions. And I don't think it's necessary you know, because you have one thing in common. Fine. You're all Black. You do share certain experiences, but in other ways, it's different. For everybody, it's different. They come from different places. So I don't see how you can really . . . I think there is a community, but within any community, you can't expect everybody to be the same, you know? And agree. But I think I do see there being a community, there being support, you know, solidarity.

Ultimately, the data presented in this chapter suggest that Black students simultaneously entertain a diversity of thought about racial identity at the micro level of the individual while simultaneously becoming more unified at the macro level in terms of group consciousness. At least among the educated elite students, a firm Black identity and a solid identification with Blackness seem to coexist alongside the great diversity that is now characteristic of young Black people today, though at times that coexistence may be a bit uneasy. Nonetheless, the capacity of well-educated Black students to find unity in diversity helps us understand the expansion of racial solidarities in an era of growing panethnicity, putting into sharper focus the surge in support for the Black Lives Matter movement in 2020.

9

Leaks in the Pipeline

You are given this very special gift, opportunity to be here, and you have to make sure you're working all the time. So you need to work really hard so you can use it and be thankful for it.

IZZY, SECOND-GENERATION MIXED-RACE DOMINICAN

IN POPULAR CULTURE and the public's imagination, college consists of four years at a single residential campus that offers the "best years" of a student's life. The reality, however, is that for the majority of students in the United States, college is not four full-time years, it is not residential, and whether it is the best years of one's life is a matter of considerable debate (Armstrong and Hamilton 2013; Goldrick-Rab 2016). The popular image of a bucolic campus and a carefree existence is built on the stereotypical experience of students at selective colleges and universities, such as those in the NLSF, which can boast graduation rates of 90 percent and above. Nationwide, however, the data reveal that compared to Whites and Asians, Black and Hispanic college students are more likely to take time off, to transfer between schools, to delay graduation, and not complete college at all.

According to the U.S. National Center for Educational Statistics (2020b), out of the cohort of freshmen who entered four-year academic institutions in 2010, only 45 percent of White students and 50 percent of Asian students graduated within four years, compared to 21 percent of Black students and 32 percent of Hispanics. After six years, the White and Asian rates rose to 64 percent and 74 percent, respectively, while the Black and Hispanic rates reached only 40 percent and 54 percent, respectively. Among educational researchers, the flow of students from primary school, into middle school and high school, to college and beyond is commonly referred to as the educational "pipeline" (DeSousa 2001; Yosso 2005; Blockett et al. 2016). Continuing the metaphor, exits by students from the pipeline before final graduation are considered to be "leaks" (James et al. 2012). Here, we undertake a systematic analysis of leaks in the Black student pipeline, even at some of the most selective institutions of American higher education, assessing the academic progress and graduation prospects for Black students in the National Longitudinal Survey of Freshmen (NLSF) four and six years after starting college.

Swimming Upstream

The low graduation rates cited above suggest that many, if not most, students in the later passages of the educational pipeline encounter significant countercurrents as they attempt to move ahead. More importantly for our work here, these opposing currents are not the same for all students. Indeed, the racial differentials are such that Wilkins (2008) has described the struggle of students of color to graduate as "swimming upstream." The top panel of table 9.1 draws on data obtained from National Student Clearinghouse Research Center (2020)—appended to the NLSF data set by Massey and Probasco (2010)—to assess graduation rates for Black survey respondents four and six years after their entry as freshmen. Overall, some 57.3 percent of Black NLSF students graduated at the four-year mark, with another 22 percent after six years, bringing the total share up to 79.3 percent. In some of the nation's most elite institutions of higher education, therefore, which pride themselves on high completion rates, more than one-fifth of Black students still had not graduated six years after their original enrollment.

These students clearly must have been swimming against rather strong countercurrents. This conjecture is bolstered by the fraction of students who reported transferring institutions or taking time off from their studies, a phenomenon labeled stopping out in the jargon of educational researchers (Horn and Carroll 1998). As seen in the second panel of table 9.1, some 13.7 percent of Black NLSF respondents had stopped out over the four years they were followed, a fraction representing one-third of all those who had not graduated on time and two-thirds of those still without a degree after six years. In order to assess the nature of the countercurrents faced by Black students, the third panel lists the reasons given by students to explain their stopping out in descending order of frequency.

With relative frequencies of 52.9 percent and 49.0 percent, the top two reasons were high cost and excessive financial debt. These findings are consistent with prior work by Goldrick-Rab (2016) and others who argue that the "real

TABLE 9.1. Collegiate educational outcomes for Black NLSF respondents

Characteristic	Outcome
Percent graduating	
After four years	57.3%
After six years	22.0
Persistence	
Transferred or took time off	13.7%
Reasons for transfer or time off	
High cost	52.9%
Too much debt	49.0
Lack of interest	43.1
Lack of effort	39.2
Poor grades	39.2
Family responsibilities	33.3
Campus racial climate	21.6
Poor teaching	19.6
Family unsupportive	19.6
Not enough credits	17.6
Classes too large	13.7
Course too difficult	9.8
Did not fit in	9.8
Friends unsupportive	9.8
Lack of friends	5.9
Major course of study	
Preprofessional	26.6%
STEM	31.2
Social Sciences	35.6
Humanities	23.4
Multiple majors	21.1
Grades	
Mean GPA in major (first listed)	2.68
Mean GPA in major (second listed)	2.90
Mean overall GPA	2.83
N	1,039

challenge" for many college students is finding the money needed both to survive and thrive as a student (see also Dowd, Cheslock, and Melguizo 2008; Armstrong and Hamilton 2013; Kelly and Goldrick-Rab 2014; Kelchen, Goldrick-Rab, and Hosch 2017). Financial struggles compel many students to transfer to another, less expensive institution, even if it means moving away from a more prestigious and highly regarded institution, and sometimes the stop-out prevents them from graduating entirely (Horn and Carroll 1998).

In their article "Priced Out?" Jones-White et al. (2014) found that the challenge of covering the cost of college attendance is a hard reality for many working-class and middle-class students who are, for a variety of reasons, reluctant to accumulate thousands of dollars in debt in order to secure a four-year degree. Among Black students at selective colleges and universities, research finds that financial concerns, coupled with negative appraisals of the campus racial climate, are key reasons for lower rates of college persistence and delays in graduation (Milem, Chang, and Lising 2005; Yosso et al. 2009).

Moving down the list of reasons for stopping out, the next two items pertain to problems of motivation: a lack of interest (43.1 percent) and a lack of effort (39.2 percent). Next on the list are poor grades, which were cited as a reason by exactly the same share of respondents as mentioned lack of effort (39.2 percent). Family responsibilities were cited as an important reason by one-third of all respondents and another 19.6 percent mentioned a lack of family support. More than one-fifth of all students (21.6 percent) mentioned the hostile racial climate on campus as a reason for stopping out. Less prevalent reasons included insufficient course credits (17.6 percent), excessively large classes (13.7 percent), and finding college courses to be too difficult (9.8 percent). A few students mentioned social issues as important considerations, saying that they did not fit in on campus (9.8 percent), had unsupportive friends (9.8 percent), or lacked friends entirely (5.9 percent).

The foregoing reasons for not persisting in college are not mutually exclusive, of course, and the modal number of reasons cited as somewhat or very important was three, with a mean of 7.5 and a range of 0 to 12; and multiple reasons for stopping out were often mentioned by our interviewees. Both Darryl and Richard had to leave their respective universities for a year because their GPAs fell below the required threshold of 2.0, an outcome reported by 2.5 percent of Black respondents in the NLSF. However, Darryl and Richard had other issues to deal with besides their grades. Darryl, for example, worried about his family members' safety in the drug- and crime-infested Bronx neighborhood where they lived, and he spent his year away from school taking care of his siblings and working to help support his family.

When he returned to campus as a junior, Darryl said that despite feeling "like one of the sharpest students in class," his grades "didn't reflect his intelligence" because he was "distracted by family and financial matters." In addition, he told us that he never really liked being on campus because he "always felt misunderstood." He failed three classes in one semester for reasons of poor attendance and reported that his "urban attire" (baggy jeans, hoodies, and do-rags) did not fit in with the "preppy" look of other students on the bucolic campus.

Darryl also perceived the campus racial climate to be hostile, and he reported feeling especially disconnected not from White students but from middle-class Black students, finding them "even more pretentious" than his White classmates:

> The Black students here seem to be afraid of a Black community. . . . A lot of people are middle class and they're trying to run away from being, being capsuled into being Black and they want to simply be American. So their idea of being American and not simply being considered Black at [name of university] is to branch out and not associate themselves with Blacks. One girl said, "If a Black person waves to me, I'm not gonna wave back because I feel like he's only waving because I'm Black." . . . I feel like even . . . if you cut yourself off from the Black community, you're cutting yourself off from things you could be learning.

Darryl went on to report that he was "frustrated" by what he perceived to be an absence of "a unified Black front" to which he could relate. He recognized that his heavy involvement in Black-specific clubs and activities detracted from his studies but said he harbored "a Malcolm X sentiment," confiding to us that he did not approve of Black peers "integrating with Whites" and "assimilating" to get ahead. He told us that he knew five other Black young men students with similar attitudes who had either dropped out or taken time off; they all came from poor, racially segregated circumstances like his.

For his part, Richard returned to his working-class, majority-Black hometown in New Jersey after failing to meet the grade point requirement. While he was away from campus, he took courses at a nearby state university while working and spending time with his mother. Richard attributed his academic struggles to a lack of academic preparation, noting that his high school was ranked as one of the worst in New Jersey. He also mentioned the "culture shock" he experienced during his freshman year when he had to interact socially with Whites for the first time in his life (all four of his roommates were White). He also had difficulty facing up to the reality that his initial choice of engineering as a major was just too hard for him.

During his first two years of college, Richard constantly felt "stressed" as he failed courses and struggled to find a social niche. He knew his mother was disappointed in him and she kept pushing him "to work up to his potential." However, no one in his family had ever gone to college, and both she and he lacked a reference point or role model that could help him succeed academically. Richard knew several other Black students who also had to take time off, but said that "you don't hear about it much because people don't want to talk about it." As he went on to explain, "I mean it's [name of university], so you figure people are pretty on-point with their stuff. You'd figure at least—because even if they're not, you're not going to hear about it." Although Richard held leadership positions in three of the six Black organizations on campus, he felt the Black community was not "tightly knit."

> I guess if you don't go to BSU meetings, you're not considered "Black," and people might wonder, oh, they don't like Black people. . . . They say there's a type of student that hangs out more with Black people, but I don't necessarily see it like that. . . . They, like, force it to create some idea of their idea of what Blackness is.

Richard did not feel like he had to prove his Blackness to anyone, but he did feel the intraracial climate on campus caused many Black students to feel this pressure.

Coming from the "90 percent Black bubble" of his home community, Richard perceived interracial interactions on campus to be difficult because of the "ignorance" of White students about Black issues and the conditions they endured in their home communities. He often felt uncomfortable in class and recalled several incidents where he had unsuccessfully tried to interact with his White classmates but was "dissed." During the second semester of his junior year, Richard changed his major to English "because I like to write." He had two close Black friends who were also students in that department. Nonetheless, he remained "stressed" about passing his classes.

Like Darryl, Richard received a full scholarship from his university that included a stipend for food and other incidentals. Nonetheless, he had felt he had to work to help support his family, and his work-study job was in Africana studies where he liked the fact that he "could interact with Black faculty members." By working there, he came to feel more comfortable on a campus where he otherwise struggled to fit in. For Richard, college was a constant struggle both academically and socially. The only respite was when he socialized with his few Black friends and spent time in Africana studies, where he always found same-race peers and faculty hanging around.

Although most NLSF respondents took courses in African American/ Africana studies programs or departments, few actually completed a major in such studies or in related areas of the humanities. In fact, as shown in the fourth panel of table 9.1, humanities majors were the least common with just 23.4 percent of respondents selecting this option. That low figure was not due to a large number majoring in preprofessional programs (26.6 percent). Instead, it reflected the fact that nearly one-third of all respondents majored in science, technology, engineering, and mathematics (STEM) fields (31.2 percent) and more than one-third (35.6 percent) majored in one of the social sciences, with 21.1 percent of students reporting more than one major.

In the bottom panel of the table, we see that respondents earned grades in the B/B– range on average, with a mean GPA of 2.83. The average GPA was even lower in the first or only major (2.68) and only slightly higher in the second major among those declaring multiple majors (2.90). These B/B– grades occurred despite the significant amount of effort that students reported putting into their studies (see Charles et al. 2009). When we asked respondents to rate their academic effort on a 0 to 10 scale going from no effort to maximum effort, the average score was 7.57.

Among our interviewees, a commonly expressed sentiment was the strong desire to study something "practical," acquiring skills and a degree that would help pave their way toward financial success and upward mobility in the "real world." Among those in the qualitative sample, 32 percent reported a preprofessional course of study (i.e., business, engineering, architecture, law, nursing, premed, etc.), a figure slightly lower than the 36 percent of respondents who reported a social science major but nearly triple the share majoring in the humanities (13 percent). Sixteen percent of interviewees double-majored, almost exclusively in a preprofessional field, whereas just 8 percent chose a STEM field as an additional major.

Many interviewees saw a preprofessional major as essential for their future financial success and a necessary first step on the road to membership in the Black professional class. Often, this choice came in response to pressure from their parents, as Tia explained:

TIA: It seems like people are pushed into these sorts of preprofessional majors by parents. . . .
INTERVIEWER: Are you talking about like doctors, lawyers, kind of thing?
TIA: Right, exactly. And they take these courses that they don't really want to take and aren't really good at and take them anyway.
INTERVIEWER: Because of family pressure?
TIA: Right, exactly, family pressures, even society pressures, you know what I mean? Like you go to college, right, to make money.

Tia was not in a preprofessional program herself, instead double-majoring in Africana studies and English. At the time of her interview, she had a 3.5 GPA and was applying to graduate school in English.

Eugene elected to major in political science because he felt he would get a better job out of college than if he had majored in Africana studies. He chose to minor in Africana studies instead, telling us "it was more so from a practical standpoint—that it would be hard as hell to get a job as an Af-Am major, more than it would be as a political science major." Eugene was part of the subset of interviewees who either majored or minored in a subject related to race or ethnicity. Others revealed that they had chosen similar majors or minors because the topic was of interest to them as Black people and relevant to their life experiences, though they were also quite conscious of career options.

James, a multigenerational native, was headed for a career in business. He grew up in an affluent household and was the son of a marketing executive and stay-at-home mom. During his time at college, James had become very involved in campus politics as vice president of the school's Black Business Student Organization. His position in the group required him to put together a résumé for distribution to recruiters at top firms. James explained that the organization is among the most popular organizations for Black students at his university because of its career focus:

> I think [name of organization] [is popular] just because people want to get jobs. . . . It's going to be popular. Today, as a matter of fact, I'm sending a résumé to AOL/Time Warner. So after I'm done here, I'm going to go home, make sure everybody's résumé is okay and send them out. It's popular because people realize, "Hey, I might be able to get a good job."

As a Black man, James felt compelled to increase the presence of African Americans in the corporate world, telling us,

> JAMES: Now Black people are legitimately becoming leaders. The AOL/Time Warner CEO is Black. The American Express CEO is Black. Colin Powell is the secretary of state. You have powerful Black people. . . . And now we have to keep pushing forward. A lot is expected of us.
> INTERVIEWER: By whom?
> JAMES: I think by ourselves, by the older generations, and by the younger generations. A lot—I'm—a lot more is expected of me than my father, definitely. That's because of where his generation is. . . . They were striving for equality.

Jay, a mixed-race engineering and computer science major, explained that there were no other Black sophomores in his major.

INTERVIEWER: And far as your major goes—it's computer science and engineering, right?

JAY: Right.

INTERVIEWER: So there are other Black people in that major, right?

JAY: No, they're not, not in my grade. . . . Yeah, everybody dropped out.

INTERVIEWER: They dropped out. What happened? It was too hard?

JAY: Yeah. There are—there used to be three or four, but they dropped out.

INTERVIEWER: So, in your classes, are there other Black students in your classes?

JAY: There's another Black girl I've met that actually lives on the floor below me. She's not really from here. She's from Nigeria, but she lived in Switzerland, so she speaks French. And she told me she doesn't identify with the NSBE [National Society of Black Engineers] thing as well with African Americans. Now I do hang out with her; I do have somebody to study with.

Alex was an engineering major who wanted to minor in Spanish but could not afford to stay an extra semester or two to fulfill the necessary requirements.

I was going to minor in Spanish, but I'd have to be here for five or six years because of the requirements of engineering. It's very rigid, so I can't really devote other time to other credits—not six years, maybe five, and a summer course or something.

From Boston, Alex received a prestigious scholarship from a university trustee in second grade, guaranteeing full-paid college tuition as long as he graduated high school in good standing. Alex received no financial aid from his university as a result, and he described his family as "middle class." Both parents had mid-level management positions and held master's degrees. At the midpoint of his sophomore year, however, Alex's GPA was only in the C range at 2.4.

Divergent Graduation Rates

Table 9.2 examines how the college academic performance of Black students varies across the different dimensions of Black diversity. The indicators we consider include the share transferring or taking time off, the earned grade point average (GPA), and both four- and six-year graduation rates. Across all

TABLE 9.2. Collegiate educational outcomes by dimensions of diversity among Black NLSF respondents

Dimensions of Diversity	Transferred or took time off	GPA	Four-year graduation	Six-year graduation
Racial identification				
Monoracial	13.4%	2.81$^+$	57.9%	79.8%
Mixed race	15.4	2.91	54.2	76.5
Nativity and generation				
Multigenerational native	15.0%	2.81	55.1%*	78.6%
Second-generation immigrant	9.4	2.91	67.0	83.3
First-generation immigrant	12.5	2.86	54.5	77.3
Region of origin				
USA	15.0%$^+$	2.81	55.1%**	78.6%
Africa	6.7	2.85	64.1	82.6
Caribbean	11.6	2.88	67.8	83.9
Other	13.9	2.93	45.5	70.5
Skin tone				
Light	15.5%	2.87	59.4%	79.7%
Medium	14.9	2.81	54.9	78.3
Dark	9.9	2.82	59.6	80.9
Gender				
Female	11.8%$^+$	2.83	62.4%***	82.8%***
Male	17.4	2.83	47.7	72.7
Parental education				
No college degree	19.4%**	2.77*	49.1%**	72.4%***
College degree	13.2	2.78	59.9	82.4
Advanced degree	9.9	2.90	61.3	82.1
Experience of segregation				
Predominantly White	11.2%*	2.91**	62.7%***	84.4%***
Racially mixed	12.2	2.80	58.0	78.8
Segregated minority	17.9	2.74	46.5	72.2
White school only	18.0	2.86	60.8	79.4
N		1,039		

$^+$ p < 0.10; * p < 0.05; ** p < 0.01; *** p < 0.001

four outcomes, we observe a significant differential by parental education, demonstrating the clear existence of class advantages in transferring valuable human, social, and cultural capital between generations. Moving up the categories of parental education, the percentage of students who stopped out fell from 19.4 percent among those whose parents lacked a college degree, to 13.2 percent among those whose parents held a college degree, to 9.9 percent among those whose parents held an advanced degree ($p < 0.01$).

Although grade performance did increase with parental education, no sub-group of students displayed much distinction, with GPA remaining in the B/B– range, on average. It climbed only from 2.77 to 2.78 to 2.90 across the three educational categories ($p < 0.05$). Class differentials are even greater with respect to on-time college graduation. Less than half of all students whose parents lacked a college degree (49.1 percent) graduated after four years, compared to 59.9 percent among those with college-educated parents and 61.3 percent whose parents held an advanced degree. After six years, the graduation rate had risen in all categories, but the differentials remained. Whereas the graduation rate was 72.4 percent for students with non-college-educated parents, it was 82.4 percent among those whose parents held a college degree, about the same as among students whose parents held an advanced degree (82.1 percent).

Along the dimension of segregation, we see that students who grew up in predominantly White schools and neighborhoods consistently enjoyed the greatest academic success, whereas those coming up in segregated, predominantly minority schools and neighborhoods evinced the least success, with students from racially mixed schools and neighborhoods falling in between. Only 11.2 percent of students growing up in White circumstances stopped out of college, but the figures were 17.9 percent among those arising in segregated conditions and 12.2 percent among those from racially mixed settings ($p < 0.05$). In contrast, GPA steadily fell as segregation rose, dropping from 2.91 among students coming up in White circumstances to 2.80 among those from mixed circumstances and reaching a low of 2.74 among those from segregated circumstances ($p < 0.01$). As with parental education, the dimensional differentials were sharper with respect to graduation rates. Whereas 62.7 percent of students from White circumstances graduated after four years and 84.4 percent did so after six years, the respective figures for students from segregated circumstances were 46.5 percent and 72.2 percent. Once again, students from racially mixed schools and neighborhoods fell in between with respective values of 58.0 percent and 78.8 percent.

Students who lived in segregated minority neighborhoods but attended White schools achieved academic outcomes that were only slightly lower than those observed for students who grew up in neighborhoods and schools that were both predominantly White. Their GPA, for example, was 2.86 compared to a value of 2.91 for students arising in White circumstances. Likewise, the respective graduation rates were 60.8 percent and 62.7 percent after four years, and 79.4 percent versus 84.4 percent after six years of college. With respect to stopping out of college, those who lived in segregated neighborhoods but at-tended White schools displayed a rate of 18.0 percent compared to 11.2 percent among those whose educational and residential contexts were both White.

As the patriarchal constraints on women have declined over time, Black women have come to both outnumber and outperform Black men in the edu-cational sphere, throughout the developed world (Pekkarinen 2012; Van Hek, Kraaykamp, and Wolbers 2016). As of 2018, among U.S. college enrollees, women outnumbered men 56.5 percent to 43.5 percent (U.S. National Center for Educational Statistics 2020c) and among Americans age twenty-five and older, 35.8 percent of women held a four-year college degree compared to just 34.6 percent of men (U.S. Census Bureau 2020).

This gender imbalance also prevails among NLSF respondents, with the skew being especially extreme for Black students. When they entered as fresh-men, the ratio of women to men was 1.12 for Whites, 1.18 for Hispanics, and 1.25 for Asians but 2.05 for Blacks (Massey et al. 2003). At the beginning of their college careers, in other words, Black women outnumbered Black men by a ratio of 2:1, 67 percent to 33 percent. Moreover, as shown in table 9.2, the Black gender imbalance grew worse over time. After four years, 17.4 percent of Black men had transferred or taken time off compared to 11.8 percent of Black women. Likewise, the four-year graduation rate was 62.4 percent for Black women but just 47.7 percent for Black men, nearly a 15-point gap. Although the gap nar-rowed to around 10 points by the six-year mark, Black women graduates still outnumbered Black men graduates 82.8 percent to 72.7 percent. The only aca-demic indicator showing gender parity was GPA, which stood at 2.83 for both Black men and Black women.

We observe no significant differences in academic achievement among Black students with respect to racial identification or skin tone, with the mar-ginal exception of GPA, which was 2.91 for mixed-race students and 2.81 for monoracial students ($p < 0.10$). However, the four-year graduation rate differs significantly by nativity and generation, as high as 67.0 percent for second-generation immigrants compared with 54.5 percent among first-generation immigrants and 55.1 percent for multigenerational natives ($p < 0.05$). With respect to region of immigrant origin, students of Caribbean and African ancestry graduated at significantly higher rates than students from other world regions, with rates of 67.8 percent and 64.1 percent among the former and only 45.5 percent among the latter ($p < 0.01$). The share transferring or taking time off was marginally lower for Africans (6.7 percent) than for Caribbeans (11.6 percent) and students of other regional origins (13.9 percent).

In sum, although by senior year Black students had grown more similar to one another in terms of racial identity (shifting toward stronger self-identification as Black), as well as racial attitudes (converging on common viewpoints) and their sense of shared racial fate (which weakened), after four years of college, their academic and professional futures had diverged, with different rates of college persistence and graduation (and hence future mobility prospects) varying significantly by social class, gender, nativity, regional origin, and prior segregation. In the next section, we consider the degree to which the dimensional differences in attitudes, identities, and other factors documented to this point might help to explain differences in the likelihood of college persistence and graduation.

Explaining the Dimensional Gaps

Prior chapters have described significant patterns of variation in outcomes across six salient dimensions of Black diversity. The dimensions include racial identification, skin tone, gender, class, nativity, generation, regional origins, and prior segregation in schools and neighborhoods, which also brought about differences in exposure to conditions of disorder and violence. The outcomes explored so far include racial identities and attitudes, parental child-rearing practices, parental capital cultivation efforts, factors important in college decision making, campus social experiences, and the downside costs of attending a selective, expensive, and competitive academic institution.

In order to explore whether dimensional differences on these outcomes might explain observed differences in college persistence and graduation, we undertook a two-step analysis: we first estimated logistic regression models to predict the likelihood of transferring institutions or taking time off, and then we moved on to estimate models predicting the likelihood of graduation contingent on having experienced a transfer or time off. At each step, we estimate a basic model that predicts outcomes from each student's dimensional characteristics plus controls for family background. We then estimate a full model that adds in the variables prior chapters have shown to be associated with dimensional differences.

The first exercise enables us to assess how each dimension independently influences the likelihood of stopping out or graduating from college, controlling for the influence of all other dimensions. The second operation enables us to consider the degree to which conditions associated with the various dimensions explain away any differences between them uncovered in the first step. Table 9.3 begins the analysis by showing basic and full logistic regression models that predict the likelihood of transferring institutions or taking time off from college.

When indicators for all dimensions are simultaneously included in the model with basic controls for family background, we see that only one variable significantly predicts the likelihood of stopping out: exposure to disorder and violence ($p < 0.05$). This finding would seem to imply that significant differences in the odds of stopping out by parental education and racial segregation uncovered in table 9.2 are attributable to differential rates of exposure to disorder and violence by class and segregation, which is consistent with the reports of several interviewees. However, the model chi-square indicates that the dimensional indicators entered together do not constitute a statistically significant prediction model, weakening this possible interpretation.

Adding in the correlates of dimensional status actually *reduces* the fit of the model, and after wiping out the significance of the disorder-violence index yields only one marginally significant positive coefficient—that for membership in a Black-themed group or organization ($p < 0.10$). This finding is consistent with Tinto's (1993) view that social attachments within the college milieu rather than academic performance increase college persistence. However, when we estimated a simple logistic regression containing only the disorder-violence index and the Black-themed membership indicator, neither coefficient proved statistically significant, leading us to conclude that none of the dimensions or dimensional correlates are important in predicting the likelihood of stopping out in a multivariate context. This conclusion leads us to rely more on the simple univariate tabulations in table 9.1 as a basis for understanding the risks of transferring or taking time off for Black students.

Table 9.4 repeats the two-step estimation strategy to predict graduation after four and six years of college in separate bivariate logistic regressions. As shown in the left-hand columns, the model chi-square is once again not significant in either of the basic models and few of the individual coefficients are statistically significant either. In the four-year model, the coefficient for attendance at Howard University is significant and positive at the 0.05 level and mixed racial identification is significant and positive at the 0.10 level, suggesting that on-time graduation is most likely for mixed-race students and for students at Howard.

In the six-year model, however, Howard attendance loses significance, the mixed-race indicator weakens to clear insignificance, being a second-generation

TABLE 9.3. Logit regression models predicting the likelihood of transferring or taking time off from college: Black respondents to the NLSF

	Basic model	Full model
DIMENSIONS OF DIVERSITY		
Racial identification		
Monoracial (Ref)	—	—
Mixed race	−0.057	0.102
Nativity and generation		
Multigenerational native (Ref)	—	—
First-generation immigrant	−0.076	−0.172
Second-generation immigrant	−0.042	0.188
Skin tone		
Light (Ref)	—	—
Medium	0.151	0.076
Dark	−0.040	0.139
Gender		
Female (Ref)	—	—
Male	−0.146	−0.018
Parental education		
No degree (Ref)	—	—
College degree	0.023	0.079
Advanced degree	0.012	−0.222
Experience of segregation		
Predominantly White	0.181	0.080
Racially mixed	0.018	0.004
Predominantly minority (Ref)	—	—
Minority neighborhood/White school	−0.220	−0.217
Total disorder-violence index	0.016*	0.010
CONTROLS FOR UPBRINGING		
Family background		
Ever single-parent household	−0.033	0.066
Mother always worked full time	−0.036	−0.074
Parents own home	−0.080	−0.049
Mean household income	0.002	0.001
Parental disciplinary style		
Intellectual independence index	—	0.001
Strict discipline index	—	−0.023
Shame and guilt index	—	0.000
Capital cultivation effort		
Human capital index	—	0.023
Cultural capital index	—	−0.004
Social capital index	—	0.010
IDENTITY/ATTITUDE CONTROLS		
Racial identity at Wave 5		
Black and American (Ref)	—	—
Just Black		0.002
Just American		0.056

(continued)

TABLE 9.3. (*continued*)

	Basic model	Full model
Common fate identity at Wave 5		
None or a little (Ref)	—	—
Some	—	0.062
A lot	—	−0.265
Attitudinal indexes at Wave 5		
Closeness to Whites	—	0.100
White propensity to discriminate	—	0.016
Belief that Blacks should try harder	—	−0.061
Belief that Blacks must be more qualified	—	−0.003
Important factors in choosing college		
School prestige	—	0.068
Academic support index	—	−0.039
Financial support	—	0.026
Social life	—	0.008
Racial diversity	—	0.023
CAMPUS SOCIALITY CONTROLS		
Campus social experiences		
Number of White friends	—	−0.079
Number of Black friends	—	−0.030
Ever Dated Outside Group	—	−0.049
Ever dated White partner	—	−0.028
In majority-Black group	—	−0.130
In Black-themed group	—	−0.273[+]
Visibility of Black students	—	−0.040
Visibility of White students	—	0.078
Intensity of interaction with Whites	—	−0.058
Intensity of interaction with Blacks	—	0.059
Quality of interaction with Whites	—	0.058
Campus racial separation index	—	0.014
Institutional commitment to diversity		
Just right (Ref)		
Too little	—	0.182
Too much	—	−0.236
COST OF MOBILITY CONTROLS		
Mean frequency of prejudice	—	−0.004
Race-based performance burden	—	−0.041
Family-based performance burden	—	−0.041
Weighted stressful events score	—	0.000
Depression score	—	0.276
Total debt	—	0.000
ATTENDED HBCU		
Went to Howard	−0.189	−0.128
Log-likelihood chi-squared	65.506	50.311

[+] p < 0.10; [*] p < 0.05

TABLE 9.4. Logit regression models predicting the likelihood of graduation from college in four or six years: Black respondents to the NLSF

	Basic models		Full models	
	Graduated in four years	Graduated in six years	Graduated in four years	Graduated in six years
DIVERSITY INDICATORS				
Racial identification				
Monoracial (Ref)	—	—	—	—
Mixed race	0.219+	0.145	0.308*	0.342
Nativity and generation				
Multigenerational native (Ref)	—	—	—	—
First-generation immigrant	0.305	0.366	0.400+	0.443
Second-generation immigrant	−0.204	−0.315+	−0.267	−0.338
Skin tone				
Light (Ref)	—	—	—	—
Medium	0.068	0.001	0.193	0.188
Dark	−0.034	−0.107	−0.001	−0.134
Gender				
Female (Ref)	—	—	—	—
Male	0.038	0.131	−0.048	0.135
Parental education				
No degree (Ref)	—	—	—	—
College degree	0.059	0.086	0.131	0.166
Advanced degree	0.009	−0.050	−0.074	−0.278
Experience of segregation				
Predominantly White	−0.082	0.041	−0.157	0.011
Racially mixed	0.064	0.068	0.118	0.131
Predominantly minority (Ref)	—	—	—	—
Minority neighborhood/White school	0.053	0.195	0.013	0.184
Total Disorder-violence index	0.007	0.005	0.017+	0.016
CONTROLS FOR UPBRINGING				
Family Background				
Ever single-parent household	−0.088	−0.068	−0.077	−0.073
Mother worked full time	0.044	0.099	−0.114	−0.257+
Parents own home	0.005	0.106	−0.003	0.122
Mean household income	0.002	−0.001	0.003	−0.001
Parental disciplinary style				
Intellectual independence index	—	—	0.015	0.016
Strict discipline index	—	—	−0.001	0.021
Shame and guilt index	—	—	−0.005	−0.001
ATTITUDE/IDENTITY CONTROLS				
Capital cultivation effort				
Human capital index	—	—	−0.001	−0.009
Cultural capital index	—	—	0.006	0.018
Social capital index	—	—	−0.021	−0.013
Racial identity at Wave 5				
Black and American (Ref)	—	—	—	—
Just Black	—	—	0.107	0.060
Just American	—	—	0.021	0.194

(continued)

TABLE 9.4. (*continued*)

	Basic models		Full models	
	Graduated in four years	Graduated in six years	Graduated in four years	Graduated in six years
Common fate identity at Wave 5				
None or a little (Ref)	—	—	—	—
Some	—	—	−0.136	0.054
A lot	—	—	−0.217	−0.417[+]
Attitudinal indexes at Wave 5				
Closeness to Whites	—	—	0.061	0.149[+]
White propensity to discriminate	—	—	−0.138	0.002
Blacks should try harder	—	—	−0.021	0.005
Blacks must be more qualified	—	—	0.055[+]	0.068
Important factors in choosing college				
School prestige			−0.113[+]	−0.125
Academic support index	—	—	0.006	0.095[+]
Financial support	—	—	0.064[+]	0.027
Social life	—	—	0.013	0.073
Racial diversity	—	—	0.049	0.045
CAMPUS SOCIALITY CONTROLS				
Campus social experiences				
Number of White friends	—	—	0.068	0.053
Number of Black friends	—	—	−0.039	0.003
Ever dated outside group	—	—	−0.095	−0.392
Ever dated White partner	—	—	0.080	0.217
In majority-Black group	—	—	0.151	0.199
In race-themed group	—	—	-0.229[+]	−0.309
Visibility of Black students	—	—	−0.02	0.022
Visibility of White students	—	—	−0.071	−0.155
Intensity of interaction with Whites	—	—	0.092[+]	0.196*
Intensity of interaction with Blacks	—	—	0.075	0.092
Quality of interaction with Whites	—	—	−0.082	−0.109
Campus racial separation index	—	—	0.008	0.078
Institutional commitment to diversity				
Just right (Ref)				
Too little	—	—	−0.297[+]	−0.302
Too much	—	—	0.367	0.032
COST OF MOBILITY CONTROLS				
Mean Frequency of Prejudice	—	—	0.002	0.008
Race-Based Performance Burden	—	—	0.027	0.112
Family-Based Performance Burden	—	—	0.059	−0.049
Weighted Stressful Events Score	—	—	0.000	0.000
Depression Score	—	—	0.040	0.553
Total Debt	—	—	0.000	0.000
Transferred/Took Time Off	—	—	−1.835***	−2.074***
ATTENDED HBCU				
Went to Howard	0.462*	0.118	0.634*	−0.054
Log-likelihood chi-squared	20.717	14.381	303.672***	312.101***

[+] p < 0.10; * p < 0.05; ** p < 0.01; *** p < 0.001

immigrant becomes marginally significant and at the 0.10 level, and the chi-square statistic is even lower than in the four-year model. Thus, neither the four- nor six-year basic model is significant in predicting the likelihood of on-time graduation. Once again, the basic multivariate analysis of graduation rates adds little to our understanding of how the dimensions of Black diversity shape the likelihood of college graduation beyond what we learn from the univariate tabulations in table 9.2.

In contrast, the model chi-squares for the full versions of four- and six-year models shown in right-hand columns are both highly significant ($p < 0.001$). However, this high level of statistical significance is largely attributable to the indicator of taking time off or transferring, It is hardly surprising that those who stop out of college graduate at lower rates than those who do not, whether assessed after four or six years.

In the full four-year model, coefficients for attendance at Howard and racially mixed origins increase in size compared with the basic model and both are significant at the 0.05 level, strengthening the tentative interpretations derived from the basic four-year model. In addition, we detect a number of marginally significant associations ($p < 0.10$). On-time graduation is positively predicted by first-generation immigrant status, exposure to disorder and violence, believing that Blacks must be more qualified than Whites, the relative importance of financial support in college decision making, and the intensity of interaction with Whites. Marginally significant negative associations appear with respect to the importance of school prestige in decision making, membership in a race-themed group, and perceiving the institution to have too little commitment to diversity.

It is not clear how to interpret this congeries of marginal associations and estimates from the full six-year model provide no help in clarifying them. Although the significant association with transferring or taking time off persists to generate a highly significant model chi-square ($p < 0.001$), the significant associations with mixed racial origins and attendance at Howard disappear. The positive effect of intensity of interaction with Whites increases in size and becomes significant ($p < 0.05$), but the other marginal associations from the four-year model disappear and new marginal associations ($p < 0.10$) appear for perceiving lot of common racial fate (negative) and the importance of academic support in college decision making (positive).

Below, we offer a cautious initial interpretation based more on the descriptive tabulations than these weak, mixed, and sometimes contradictory multivariate findings.

Conclusion

We began this chapter by examining rates of college persistence and graduation among Black respondents to the NLSF. This exercise revealed that nearly 14 percent of Black NLSF respondents transferred to a different institution or had taken time off between the first and final survey waves of the survey (in 1999 and 2003). Moreover, around 43 percent of students had not graduated four years after entering as freshmen and around a fifth had not graduated after six years. Grades averaged in the B/B– range, with a mean GPA of 2.83. Transferring institutions or taking time off dramatically reduced the likelihood of graduation both four and six years after entry, but nothing appeared to predict the likelihood of stopping, so how this mediating variable operates to influence college graduation is unclear.

The most common reasons given for stopping out of college were high cost and excessive debt, followed by lack of interest, lack of effort, and poor grades, family responsibilities, and a poor campus racial climate. Although these explanations also came up in our in-depth interviews, in multivariate analyses they were not associated with either stopping out or graduation after four or six years. Neither family-based performance burdens, race-based performance burdens, exposure to racial hostility, stressful events within family networks, nor student debt were statistically significant in predicting the likelihood of either stopping out or graduating.

The descriptive tabulations are more revealing about how stopping out, course grades, and graduation rates are influenced by the dimensions of Black diversity. Parental education, gender, segregation, and to a lesser extent, immigrant origins appear to be central in understanding differences in college persistence and graduation but less important in assessing grade achievement which varies only within a narrow B/B– range. As parental education rises from no college, to college graduate, to advanced postgraduate, graduation rates and grades rise while the likelihood of stopping out falls. As segregation increases, the opposite pattern ensues: grades and graduation rates fall while the likelihood of stopping out rises, outcomes that may be mitigated if students from segregated neighborhoods are able to attend White schools.

Although the multivariate models did not yield significant effects, based solely on descriptive dimensional tabulations, we can construct two contrasting composite student profiles:

(1) The Black students who are most likely to graduate from college on time or in six years are second-generation Black women with

college-educated parents who grew up in White neighborhoods and attended White schools.

(2) Those Black students who are least likely to graduate from college on time or in six years are multigenerational native-born men whose parents never completed college and who grew up living in segregated neighborhoods and attending segregated schools.

In between these two extremes are Black students of whatever nativity, generation, and parental education who lived in racially mixed neighborhoods and attended racially mixed schools, along with those students who lived in segregated neighborhoods but attended White schools, whose outcomes were generally closer to those of students living in White neighborhoods as well as attending White schools.

10

Convergence and Intersectionality in the Black Elite

But I guess to the school, we're united because like we say today if a professor calls someone the N-word, trust me, every Black student would be burning down [the president's] office. We're united in that sense. But we're not united in terms of like everyone is friends. There's cliques.

JESSICA, MIXED-RACE MULTIGENERATIONAL NATIVE

THE BLACK POPULATION of the United States was created by the transatlantic slave trade, which from 1619 to 1865 brought somewhere around six hundred thousand Africans into the territory we now call the United States (Miller and Smith 1997). Although Congress ended the slave trade in 1807, a contraband trade in enslaved Africans continued into the Civil War (Marques 2016). At the time of the first U.S. census in 1790, the Black population of the United States stood at 757,208, and by 1860, it had risen to 4.4 million, 89 percent of whom were enslaved and 92 percent of whom lived in the South (Gibson and Jung 2002). Newly arriving enslaved Africans reflected the continent's rich diversity of regions, cultures, and languages and in most cases could not communicate with one another in their native tongues. Under the harsh conditions of chattel slavery, they developed their own distinctive language, culture, and society.

Although America's Black population originally arose from diverse roots, after the legal end of the slave trade in 1807, it progressively homogenized under a succession of repressive regimes: enslavement through 1865, and then after a brief and tenuous respite during Reconstruction, after 1876 under the brutal strictures of Jim Crow. Until 1900, nine out of ten Black Americans lived in the South and were heavily concentrated in rural areas. The rural South thus constituted the principal context in which Black American identities were made and social relations constructed. Over the next seven decades, however, the Great Migration progressively urbanized and geographically diversified the Black population as rural-origin migrants moved en masse to metropolitan areas outside the South (Wilkerson 2010).

As the Great Migration drew to a close in the 1970s, more than half of all Blacks lived outside the South and two-thirds resided in metropolitan areas. Between 1900 and 1970, discriminatory policies and practices confined the arriving rural migrants to segregated neighborhoods in the nation's cities, and the Black urban ghetto increasingly replaced the rural South as the core structural context for Black socialization, cultural adaptation, and identity formation (Clark 1965; Massey and Denton 1993).

Given this history, circa 1970 America's Black population was overwhelmingly composed of the descendants of enslaved Africans raised under the oppressive conditions of de jure segregation in the South and de facto segregation in the North. Most Black Americans were born and raised within racially endogenous unions, poorly educated in segregated public schools, and whether they were one of the lucky few who could attend an HBCU, were confined by law and custom to the lowest status occupations, except for a small middle class that served an exclusively Black clientele (Lieberson 1980; Massey and Denton 1993; Rothstein 2017). To be sure, centuries of sexual exploitation and scattered consensual interracial unions meant that many, if not most, Black Americans had White family origins as well.

In daily life, however, a Black American's White family relations were rendered irrelevant to most Whites. The "one-drop rule" defined anyone with the tiniest share of African ancestry as legally and socially "Black" and rendered them exploitable, excludable, and all-too-often expendable. Within the Black community itself, the elite consisted of a small insular middle class of disproportionately light-skinned Blacks descended both from free Blacks and those who were enslaved. They were educated principally at historically Black colleges and universities (HBCUs) and created their own world of clubs, churches, and social organizations to serve the Black community and also themselves (Frazier 1957; Graham 1999; Gatewood 2000).

As noted in the chapter 1, America's Black population increasingly diversified after 1970 as rates of intermarriage rose, immigration increased, fertility rates fell, the hegemony of the one-drop rule declined, and the Black middle and upper classes grew in the wake of the civil rights movement. Levels of

Black residential segregation also declined after 1970, albeit slowly and un-evenly across U.S. metropolitan America (Rugh and Massey 2014). As more individuals acknowledged and embraced their multiracial family origins, the U.S. Census Bureau finally began to recognize and enumerate people with multiple mixed-racial origins in 2000 (Parker et al. 2015).

As a result of these trends, the cohort of Black students entering the na-tion's selective colleges and universities at the end of the twentieth century was the most diverse in U.S. history, with unprecedented variation in terms of racial origins, skin tone, nativity, generation, class, and segregation. Draw-ing on data from surveys and interviews fielded in the early years of the twenty-first century, here we have explored the nature of this diversity, marshaling large quantities of data not just to describe the heterogeneity of students aspiring to enter the new Black elite but also to explore how this heterogene-ity differentiates them from one another with respect to identity, attitudes, sociality, and academics. In this final chapter, we review our findings from prior chapters to paint a portrait of the twenty-first century's rising Black professional class. Having done so, we argue that the Black elite, as a slice of Black America, is best understood as an imagined community and not as a monolith and that prior efforts to understand the Black elite fail to adequately engage with the diversity within this subgroup. At the same time, we argue that the experience of entering the adult Black elite via American higher edu-cation creates a shared sense of the challenges and opportunities they face as Black Americans.

Portraits in Diversity

The descriptive tables and figures presented in chapters thus far have shown how the fundamental dimensions of Black diversity are linked to key social and academic outcomes among Black students as they move through their collegiate years. These descriptive analyses, however, did not account for the fact that the dimensions of Black diversity are often closely interrelated, mak-ing it difficult, for example, to separate the influence of skin tone from that of racially mixed parentage. The multivariate analyses included in appendix A and referred to throughout the book were estimated to address this issue by entering all the dimensional indicators simultaneously into a series of regres-sion models, the estimates from which enable us to assess each dimensional trait's *independent* association with outcomes of interest while holding the influence of all other dimensions constant.

In order to interpret the mountain of data created by this effort, here we constructed a series of visual displays designed to summarize the multivariate results presented in the twenty-five tables contained in appendix A. Specifically, we draw on our regression results to create a series of matrices defined by columns indicating the dimensions of Black diversity and rows indicating social and academic outcomes of interest. In these matrices, each cell pertains to an association or relationship between a particular dimensional trait and a specific social or academic outcome. Whenever a coefficient from the relevant regression model is at least marginally statistically significant ($p < 0.10$), we place a plus or a minus in the cell to indicate the direction of the corresponding association. Cells indicating associations that do not reach statistical significance are left blank.

Identity, Attitudes, and Upbringing

In figure 10.1, for example, we present a matrix connecting the dimensions of Black diversity (in columns) to indicators of Black identity, racial attitudes, and parental child-rearing practices (in rows). The data represented in the cells of the matrix are taken from appendix tables A4.1–A4.3 and tables A5.1 and A5.2. In this matrix, column 1 reveals the identities, attitudes, and upbringing that follow from being of mixed racial parentage, and the rectangle outlined at the top of the column summarizes the distinctive identity/attitude profile displayed by mixed-race students as they entered college as first-term freshmen.

Looking at the figure, it is quickly evident that compared to monoracial students, *mixed-race students perceive American identity to be relatively more important and Black identity relatively less important* in the construction of self-identity. Although majorities of both groups see Black and American identities as equally important, among those who depart from this ideal, monoracial students favor a Black identity whereas mixed-race students prefer an American identity, signaling a weaker connection to Blackness as a component of their self-identity. In addition, *mixed-race students are less likely to perceive a lot or even some common racial fate with other Black people.* Moreover, *they perceive themselves to be socially closer to White people and see White people as less discriminatory.*

Since the large majority of mixed-race students are of White and Black parentage, most mixed-race students come to college having had more contact with White people than their monoracial peers as a result of sustained interactions with White members of their extended families. In addition, to the

	Identity (1)	Generation (2)	(3)	Region (4)	(5)	Skin tone (6)	(7)	Gender (8)	Parental education (9)	(10)	Segregation and disorder (11)	(12)	(13)	(14)
	Mixed	First	Second	Caribbean	African	Medium	Dark	Male	College degree	Advanced degree	White school and neighborhood	Mixed school and neighborhood	White school only	Disorder and violence
W1 Solo american identity	+							+					−	
W1 Solo Black identity	−			+										
W1 Some common fate	−													
W1 A lot of common fate	−													
W1 Closeness to Whites	+					−		+			+		+	−
W1 Whites discriminatory	−	−				+		−			+	+	+	+
W1 Blacks should try harder						+	+	+		−				
W1 Blacks more qualified		−				−			−					
Intellectual independence		−	−											
Strict parental discipline	−											+		+
Parental shame and guilt														−
Human capital cultivation		−	−						+	+				
Cultural capital cultivation	+	−	−						+	+				−
Social capital cultivation		−												−

FIGURE 10.1. Schematic depiction of association between dimensions of Black diversity and identity, attitudes, and child-rearing style at college matriculation

extent they grew up having a sustained close relationship with their White parent, they had a unique opportunity to observe and learn about White ways of being. We thus expect mixed-race students to be more comfortable interacting with White students and professors in the predominantly White social spaces that prevail at selective colleges and universities. In this way, they are better prepared socially for life on the campus of a selective academic institution.

Turning to the rectangle at the bottom of column 1, we also see that compared to their monoracial counterparts, *persons of mixed race report experiencing less strict parental discipline growing up*. At the same time, they *experience more parental involvement in the cultivation of cultural capital*. In racially mixed households more than monoracial households, parents appear to assume the role of Maxwell's demon, pushing their offspring toward greater familiarity with the cultural artifacts and practices of America's educated elite, which further demonstrates the need for careful consideration of race along with class in our understanding of parenting culture (Manning 2019).

Columns 2 and 3 reveal the identities, attitudes, and upbringings associated with first- and second-generation immigrant status. The lack of significant relationships in the top third of the columns indicates that the *views of immigrant-origin students with respect to identity, common fate, and closeness to White people are essentially the same as those of multigenerational native students.* In the large rectangle at the bottom, however, we see that *parents of immigrant origin Black students nonetheless practiced a distinctive style of child-rearing.* Specifically, *the foreign-born parents of first- and second-generation immigrant students provided significantly less support for intellectual independence* and *fewer opportunities for their children to cultivate human and cultural capital.* From our interviews, immigrant parents expected their children to dutifully follow family traditions, ethnic customs, and parental dictates, which together compel them to study hard, be respectful, stay out of trouble, and not bring shame on their family or ethnicity.

In addition to these parenting differences, *first-generation immigrants view White people as less discriminatory* compared to multigenerational natives and the native-born children of immigrants. They also *express weaker support for the view that Black people must be more qualified than White people if they wish to get ahead.* As new entrants to American society, immigrants generally arrive with little direct experience of White racial prejudice, likely leading them to discount the power of discrimination and therefore to see little need to compensate for it. As seen in column 5, *Africans report being more socially distant from White Americans than Caribbeans or multigenerational natives and express greater skepticism about the need to overqualify* to achieve success in American society. Students of African origin thus appear to enter college with faith in meritocracy and confidence in their ability to circumvent any racial barriers to advancement through grit and determination.

Turning to second-generation immigrants, we see that *their parents are less involved in the cultivation of <u>any</u> form of capital—human, social, or cultural—* relative to multigenerational natives, again indicating adherence to a child-rearing philosophy Lareau (2003) calls natural growth accomplishment, a style of loving but firm child-rearing that entails providing children with support, care, and limits that allow them to grow up and mature on their own terms. Finally, as shown in column 4, *irrespective of generation, persons of Caribbean origin tend to see a Black identity as more important than students of African or other origins,* though our interviews suggest that their embrace of Blackness often is tied to a specific Caribbean identity.

Columns 6 and 7 indicate that, holding constant the influence of nativity, generation, and region of origin, *skin tone has few independent associations with racial identity, perceptions about common fate, or parental child-rearing practices.* Since darker-skinned students are likely those who bear the brunt of White prejudice, *medium- and dark-skinned students unsurprisingly see Whites as more discriminatory* than those with light skin tones. Perhaps for this reason, *they also agree more strongly that Blacks need to try harder if they wish to get ahead in American society.* These findings reflect the continued reality of skin color stratification in the United States, wherein darker-skinned Blacks experience higher levels of discrimination and exclusion compared to their lighter-skinned counterparts (Monk 2014).

Column 8 suggests that *Black racial identities and attitudes are highly gendered.* In the rectangle outlined in the top half of the column, we see that compared to Black women, *Black men perceive an American identity as relatively more important.* They also see themselves as being *closer to White people* and view *White people as less discriminatory.* At the same time, *Black men more strongly endorse the view that Black people need to try harder in order to get ahead.* Aspiring Black men students thus appear to view U.S. society less harshly than Black women students, who are more alienated from mainstream White socializing on campus. That is, Black women students view American identity as less important, see White people as more distant and discriminatory, and are less willing to buy into the bromide that Black people just need to try harder to get ahead.

The two rectangles in the lower half of columns 9 and 10 capture the fact that the influence of parental education is limited to parental efforts to cultivate human and social capital among offspring and just two racial attitudes. As shown in the bottom rectangle, *parents with college and advanced degrees are significantly more involved in the cultivation of human and cultural capital* than parents who did not graduate from college, suggesting adherence to child-rearing behaviors associated with Lareau's (2003) style of concerted cultivation. In addition, the rectangle outlined toward the middle of columns 9 and 10 reveal that *students with college-educated parents also question the precept that Black people must be more qualified than White people in order to get ahead.* Likewise, *students whose parents held advanced degrees less strongly support the view that Black people should try harder in order to get ahead.*

The foregoing pattern of associations suggests that Black students with well-educated parents (holding college degrees) have some faith in the meritocracy and fairness in U.S. society (Blacks do not need to be more qualified than Whites to advance) but that students with highly educated parents (holding advanced degrees) are more skeptical about the fairness of life in the United States (perceiving that trying harder does not necessarily offer a panacea for overcoming racial barriers to advancement). This U-shaped pattern of skepticism indicates that exposure to racial inequality—either by coming from underresourced families or from seeing one's parents achieve elite levels of education but still suffer racial discrimination—drives students' views of racial inequality in the United States.

Columns 11–13 examine the influence of segregation on social outcomes to reveal only one significant connection to racial identity: *those growing up in racially mixed circumstances are less likely to favor an American identity,* suggesting that within contexts in which significant numbers of White and Black people interact on an ongoing basis, intergroup competition weakens adherence to a free-standing American identity. Likewise, we observe just one association with parental child-rearing practices: *parents who send their children to White schools but live in minority neighborhoods tend to rely on strict discipline,* suggesting a protective stance toward their children, for in addition to removing their children from segregated neighborhood schools, they employ strict discipline to shield them from risks in the segregated neighborhoods they continue to inhabit, a child-rearing strategy also observed by others (see Furstenberg et al. 1999; Amato and Fowler 2002; Dow 2016, 2019; Holt 2020).

The rectangle toward the center of the three columns indicates that the *racial composition of neighborhoods and schools mainly predicts attitudes toward White people.* Relative to Black students who grew up in segregated or racially mixed neighborhoods, *those who attended White-majority schools feel significantly closer to White people.* This outcome prevails irrespective of whether students lived in a White or minority neighborhood while growing up. At the same time, however, _all_ *students exposed to White people (whether in neighborhoods, schools, or both) perceive White people to be more discriminatory.* In other words, the more exposure to White people that Black students have while growing up, the more they perceive White people to be discriminators, even as they also felt closer to them socially. Contact makes one more comfortable around Whites, but as McMillan Cottom (2019:103) notes, it also makes Black people better "know their Whites . . . to be intimate with some white persons but to critically withhold faith in white people categorically."

Apart from differentially exposing students to White people, segregation influences student outcomes to the extent that it is associated with greater exposure to social disorder and violence within schools and neighborhoods. In column 14, we see that *with rising exposure to violence and disorder, perceived social distance from White people increases and the assessment of White people as discriminators steadily rises.* In addition, *strictness of parental discipline also increases as safety and security deteriorates in their children's schools and neighborhoods.* In contrast, *parental reliance on shame and guilt in child-rearing decreases as disorder and violence rise*. Finally, greater exposure to disorder and violence in residential and educational settings is associated with *lower levels of parental involvement in the cultivation of cultural and social capital*.

Segregation thus is rather influential in the formation of racial attitudes and in determining styles of parental child-rearing. Black students who come into contact with White students in their schools and neighborhoods perceive greater closeness to White people as a group but also see them as more discriminatory. To the extent that school and neighborhood segregation entail higher levels of exposure to disorder and violence, the perception of White people as discriminators is reinforced and perceived closeness to White people as a group additionally reduced. Finally, high levels of violence and disorder seemingly push parents toward a protective, inward-looking stance of stern yet caring child-rearing: strict discipline but with less reliance on shame and guilt and fewer efforts to venture outside the confines of the immediate family to facilitate the cultivation of cultural and social capital within the riskier surroundings they inhabit.

Preparation for College

Having documented distinct patterns of dimensional differentiation among Black students with respect to identity, attitudes, and upbringing, we now draw on data from appendix tables A5.3–A5.6 to examine the degree to which Black students are differentially prepared for entry into the sphere of selective higher education. Figure 10.2 presents a matrix defined by rows indicating the kind of schools students attended before college (private religious or private secular versus a public school) and the degree to which prior schooling prepared them academically for elite academia (number of Advanced Placement [AP] credits, difficulty of coursework, high school GPA, and SAT scores). As before, the columns refer to the dimensions of Black diversity.

A quick glance at the matrix reveals that identification as mixed race, immigrant generation, region of foreign origin, and skin tone have almost no bearing on educational preparation. The one outlier in column 5 is that *immigrant-origin students from Africa earned significantly higher grades than other Black students*, a result that reflects the strong selection of African immigrants to the United States on the basis of education (Hamilton 2019). This helps to explain the academic success of the children of African immigrants in college, given that prior work using the National Longitudinal Survey of Freshmen

	Identity (1)	Generation (2)	(3)	Region (4)	(5)	Skin tone (6)	(7)	Gender (8)	Parental education (9)	(10)	Segregation and disorder (11)	(12)	(13)	(14)
	Mixed	First	Second	Caribbean	African	Medium	Dark	Male	College degree	Advanced degree	White school and neighborhood	Mixed school and neighborhood	White school only	Disorder and violence
Private religious school													−	+
Private secular school										+			−	+
AP tests taken										+				−
Course difficulty								+						
GPA					+			−			−	−	−	−
SAT score										+			+	−

FIGURE 10.2. Schematic depiction of associations between the dimensions of Black diversity and academic preparation for college

(NLSF) shows that among college students generally, high school GPA is the strongest single predictor of grades earned in college (Massey and Probasco 2010).

Almost all the significant dimensional associations are found to the right of the matrix in columns 8–14, meaning that differences in academic preparation vary primarily by gender, parental education, and segregation. Compared to Black women, *Black men experienced greater difficulty in their high school course-work and earned lower grades in their courses.* Although we cannot know the source of this gender gap in high school academic preparation, we note both that this is true for all American students, and given the research on high school GPA and college academic achievement, the lower GPA earned by men is certainly not a harbinger of their success in college (see DiPrete and Buch-mann 2013).

Parental education unsurprisingly emerges as a key predictor of schol-arly preparation. Black students with the *best educated* parents enjoyed clear academic advantages over all others. That is, *students whose parents held an advanced degree are more likely to attend a private secular high school, accumu-late more AP credits, and score higher on the SAT* compared to other Black students.

Given the strong association between educational quality and the share of minority students in schools (see Reardon and Owens 2014; Reardon 2016), segregation unsurprisingly emerges as a critical determinant of scholarly prep-aration. Relative to Black students who grew up in minority-dominant neigh-borhoods and schools, those who attended schools that contained at least a plurality of White students earned significantly lower grades. As seen in the rectangle demarcated in the fifth line of columns 11–13, *GPAs were systematically lower for Black students who lived in White neighborhoods and attended White schools, those who lived in minority neighborhoods but attended White schools, and those who came of age in racially mixed neighborhoods and schools* that contained significant numbers of both Black and White people.

These lower GPAs likely reflect exposure to a more demanding and rigorous education in private and magnet schools compared to racially segregated public schools. This interpretation is consistent with the findings contained in the rectangle outlined at the top of columns 12 and 13, which indicates that *Black students who left the public school system for private schools (whether religious or secular) differentially went into White schools rather than racially mixed schools.* Such a move apparently paid off for students in this category, since *Black students from minority neighborhoods who attended White schools scored significantly higher on the SAT* than students from other educational settings, despite earning lower GPAs.

Finally the rectangle in column 14 reveals that the disadvantages of segregation are transmitted in important ways through higher levels of exposure to social disorder and violence. *As the degree of exposure to disorder and violence rises, the number of AP tests taken, GPA, and SAT scores all decline significantly,* underscoring the risks to learning and cognition brought about by high rates of violence in the nation's segregated schools and neighborhoods, even among high-achieving youth headed to selective colleges (see Sampson, Sharkey, and Raudenbush 2008; Sharkey 2010; Sharkey et al. 2012, 2014). Racial segregation concentrates affluence and privilege in certain schools and neighborhoods while intensifying poverty and disadvantage in others to create very unequal social worlds for Blacks and Whites (Massey and Tannen 2016; Massey and Rugh 2021).

Social Life on Campus

As noted in earlier chapters, attending college is an important vehicle for informal socialization as well as formal education. Social interactions on campus are in many ways as important for intellectual development as the skills and knowledge taught in classrooms. Figure 10.3 summarizes associations between the dimensions of Black diversity on student friendships, dating behaviors, organizational memberships, group visibilities, and intergroup interactions, as well as perceptions about the campus racial environment, drawing on information from appendix tables A5.3–A5.6.

	Identity (1)	Generation (2)	(3)	Region (4)	(5)	Skin tone (6)	(7)	Gender (8)	Parental education (9)	(10)	Segregation and disorder (11)	(12)	(13)	(14)
	Mixed	First	Second	Caribbean	African	Medium	Dark	Male	College degree	Advanced degree	White school and neighborhood	Mixed school and neighborhood	White school only	Disorder and violence
Number of White friends	+			+		−	+	+			+			−
Number of Black friends	−	−	−					−			−			+
Ever dated outside group	+							+						
Ever dated White partner	+							+						−
In majority-Black group	−		−					−						
In Black-themed group				+						+	−			
Visibility of Black students						−								
Visibility of White students								−						−
Intensity of interaction: Blacks	−							−			−			
Intensity of interaction: Whites		−									+			
Quality of interaction: Whites														
Racial separation on campus													+	
Diversity effort too little														+
Diversity effort too much								+						

FIGURE 10.3. Schematic depiction of associations between dimensions of
Black diversity and campus social relations

As in figure 10.1, we again observe significant differentiation in the social experiences of Black students along the lines of racial identification, nativity, and generation, often in ways that are consistent with attitudes and identities portrayed in the earlier figure. Recall, for example, that mixed-race students felt closer to Whites, viewed Whites as less discriminatory, evinced a stronger attachment to American identity, and perceived less common racial fate than monoracial Black students. Consistent with this attitudinal profile, in the rectangle shown in column 1 of figure 10.3, we see that *mixed-race students had more White friends and fewer Black friends* than their monoracial peers and were *more likely to date outside the group* and when doing so *were more likely to date Whites.* In addition, mixed-race students *were less likely to join majority-Black organizations on campus* and thus reported *less intense interaction with Blacks* on campus generally.

With respect to nativity and generation, we see in columns 2–5 that *first-generation Black immigrants experience less intense interaction with White peers* while *second-generation immigrants are less likely to join majority-Black organizations; both generations have fewer Black friends on campus.* Although *Caribbean-origin students reported having more White friends, they also were more likely to join a race-themed organization,* consistent with their stronger inclination to embrace their Caribbean Black identity. From our qualitative interviews, we find that Caribbean students typically joined a West Indian Student Association rather than a Black Student Union.

With respect to skin tone, in column 6 we see that *those with medium skin tones had fewer White friends than those with light skin tones* (consistent with their view of Whites as prone to discrimination), and they *also perceived Black students to be less visible on campus*. Somewhat surprisingly, *dark-skinned students unexpectedly reported having more White friends than either medium- or light-skinned students*. Importantly, these skin tone differences persist in our models that control for self-identification as mixed race, immigrant origins, and exposure to segregation and disorder. It is worth noting that dark-skinned respondents reported having only an average of 2.2 White friends out of 10, whereas light-skinned respondents averaged 3.2.

Here, the multivariate analyses indicate that the skin tone gap in the number of White friends is driven by factors *related* to Black respondents' skin tone (class, immigrant origin, etc.), and not skin tone per se. We hypothesize that this unexpected, positive association may be part of an effort by dark-skinned respondents to manage their social standing due to concerns about racism and colorism. It may also reflect their stronger belief that Black people need to try harder to succeed, which may then prompt them to make special efforts to befriend White students as part of a strategy to integrate at college. Tiffany, for example, spoke about making a conscious effort to diversify her friendship network while in college.

Because the Black men in our sample generally support the view that Black people need to try harder, favor an American identity, and perceive White people to be socially closer and less discriminatory than women students, it is not surprising in column 8 that they also *report having more White friends and fewer Black friends* on campus compared with Black women. They are also *more likely to date outside the group and to date White partners when doing so*. Black men are similarly *less likely to join majority-Black groups and report less intense interactions with Black peers* on campus. Interestingly, *Black men students perceive White students as being less visible on campus* than Black women students do, which could mean that White students do not loom as large in Black mens' daily consciousness given the closeness they perceive toward White peers and their tendency to see White people as less discriminatory.

Of all the dimensions of Black diversity considered in figure 10.3, parental education displays the fewest associations with social life on campus. Perusing columns 9 and 10, we see that class background has no independent influence on the number of White or Black friends, intergroup dating, membership in majority-Black organizations, the perceived visibility of Black and White students, or the intensity and quality of interactions with members of either group. The only significant associations that emerge concern institutional efforts to promote diversity and membership in Black-themed organizations. *Black students with college-educated parents are more likely to state that their college or university puts too much effort into promoting diversity,* suggesting a confidence in their ability to gain entry based solely on their achievements. *Students whose parents hold advanced degrees are more likely to join a Black-themed organization on campus,* indicating that students coming from the most elite educational background are more interested than others in joining Black-themed campus organizations.

In contrast to the sparse associations between class origin and sociality on campus, segregation displays multiple connections to social outcomes, as shown in column 11. These connections suggest a distinctive pattern of campus sociality among those students who grew up in predominantly White contexts. As one might expect, *students who grew up in White schools and neighborhoods report having more White friends and fewer Black friends* on campus. They also report that they *engage in more intense interactions with the former and less intense interactions with the latter.* Finally, those coming of age in White social environments are also *less likely than other Black students to join a Black-themed organization* on campus.

Black students who lived in segregated neighborhoods but attended predominantly White schools perceived racial separation on campus to be greater than other Black students, underscoring how daily exposure to the racial dichotomies characteristic of social life in the United States heighten awareness of the racial cleavages that continue to exist in twenty-first-century America, a tendency also noted by Shedd (2015). They may also be comparing the selective college experience—where students come from all over the United States—to their private high school setting, which might have seemed less segregated than college to their younger selves. Whereas Black students who grew up entirely in White settings are comfortable occupying the White social spaces they encounter in college, those who experienced the split existence of living in segregated neighborhoods while attending White high schools appear to be more sensitive and attuned to racial divisions on campus.

Students who grow up in segregated schools and neighborhoods are exposed to higher levels of disorder and violence than most Americans, and for this reason, they generally display a pattern of social behavior opposite to those who arose exclusively in White schools and neighborhoods. Column 14 indicates that *as levels of school and neighborhood violence rise, the number of White friends on campus decreases, the number of Black friends increases, and the intensity of interaction with White people drops, the likelihood of dating White partners declines, and the visibility of White students on campus decreases.* Exposure to violent and disordered social contexts through childhood and adolescence thus seems to translate into a more racially isolated social life on campus.

The Costs of an Elite Education

The downsides of attending a selective institution of higher education are listed in rows down the side of the matrix shown in figure 10.4 using data from appendix tables A7.1–A7.6. Associations in the cells created by cross-tabulating these rows with the dimensions of diversity in the columns reveal that the costs of an elite education are not borne equally by all Black students. Exposure to racial hostility on campus, for example, does not vary by racial identification, generation, region, skin tone, gender, or parental education. Instead, as seen in the rectangle highlighted in columns 12 and 13, *the burden of racial hostility falls principally on students who grew up in racially mixed schools and neighborhoods and those who grew up in minority neighborhoods but attended White schools.*

Mixed neighborhoods are generally less affluent than White neighborhoods and the schools serving them tend to be less well resourced than predominantly White schools (Reardon and Owens 2014; Owens 2020). In such settings, relatively large contingents of White and Black students encounter each other on a daily basis in an environment of relative scarcity, leading to intergroup tensions. Likewise, Black students living in minority neighborhoods while attending White schools tend to be at magnet academies or prep schools that are generally well resourced and cater principally to upper-class Whites, compelling them to confront the savage inequalities dividing Black and White America and sensitizing them to the daunting racial cleavages that persist in American society (Shedd 2015). Thus, as a result of their prior experience in mixed settings, both sets of students may be more attuned to racial hostility and discrimination.

In contrast, Black students who grew up entirely in minority schools and neighborhoods interacted with few White people on a day-to-day basis and thus had little direct experience with White hostility, leaving them less sensitive to potential racial slights and snubs on campus. For their part, Black

	Identity	Generation		Region		Skin tone		Gender	Parental education		Segregation and disorder			
	(1)	(2)	(3)	(4)	(5)	(6)	(7)	(8)	(9)	(10)	(11)	(12)	(13)	(14)
	Mixed	First	Second	Caribbean	African	Medium	Dark	Male	College degree	Advanced degree	White school and neighbor-hood	Mixed school and neighbor-hood	White school only	Disorder and violence
Incidents of racial hostility												+	+	+
Frequency of racial hostility												+		+
Racial performance burden					+									+
Family performance burden	−	+	+				+							
Stressful life events									−					+
Stressful events score									−					+
Sense of loss			+							−				+
Accumulated debt														
Depression index			+					−	−					+

FIGURE 10.4. Schematic depiction of associations between dimensions of Black diversity and the costs of an elite college education

students who grew up entirely in White and typically more affluent settings were used to being around White peers and inhabiting White social spaces. They often came from more advantaged families and were thus more confident being in privileged settings. Even though they saw White people as discriminatory, they also felt closer to them and as we have seen, had more White friends and more intense interactions with them, rendering them less sensitive to racial bias.

Since Black students who grew up in more segregated settings generally experience greater exposure to social disorder and violence during their formative years (see Peterson and Krivo 2010), they are also more likely to exhibit the negative outcomes that follow from such exposure, as suggested by the string of pluses in the long rectangle outlined in column 14. Moving down the column, we see that *Black students coming from disordered and violent neighborhoods experience a higher racial performance burden, more stressful life events, more severe stresses, a greater sense of loss and alienation on campus, and a higher likelihood of depression.* Thus, among all the downsides of elite education considered here, exposure to disorder and violence has the most deleterious set of influences across the greatest number of outcomes. In addition to increasing stress and stereotype threat, it also appears to trigger a form of survivor's remorse for having left underresourced neighborhoods and schools for idyllic, wealthy campuses while continuing to have to manage and deal with the havoc that disorder and violence can cause for one's family and friends back home.

In many ways, Darryl exemplifies the challenges faced by Black students on elite White campuses who grew up in poor, segregated, and very disadvantaged neighborhoods. He told us that "because there aren't very many people like me at institutions like [name of prep school], being Black and poor, you know usually being poor will finish it off for you . . . so I was usually misunderstood." He felt White peers did not like him and that the Black community at [name of university] was "superficial," "pretentious," and "bourgie." He stopped going to class in his sophomore year and had to take a year off to work and take classes before he could return. He came back but still hated the Black community and felt that he did not fit in as a poor Black kid with a hip-hop style and had only a few Black friends from similar backgrounds as his. His sentiments are summed up in the following exchange:

> INTERVIEWER: Okay, um, what was it like here when you first got here as a freshman?
>
> DARRYL: Um, hated it. 'Cause it had all of the negatives I didn't like about [name of prep school] as in the superficiality and people being pretentious and the culture that I refused to be a part of because I just, I didn't prefer it and um, people not really getting the chance to know me. My roommates didn't speak to me the entire year, and I had three roommates.
>
> INTERVIEWER: Why? What do you think?
>
> DARRYL: Well, I half-joke that throughout my first winter there, I wore what a normal Bronx kid would wear, which would be a black hoodie with a black ski mask 'cause it was cold: black gloves and a black hat. And for them, I looked like a Black guy with a bunch of black on, so I'm gonna rob them. You know, so people were intimidated by that and I always wore my do-rag which people usually associate with the penitentiary. . . . So my attire gave off the impression that I was up to no good. And I usually wore my headphones because I was accustomed to wearing, listening to my CDs throughout the day, so there are a lot of barriers between myself and the predominant culture.
>
> INTERVIEWER: What about the Black students?
>
> DARRYL: Even more pretentious than the White students. Less friendly. The Black students here seem to be afraid of a Black community.

Turning to immigrant-origin students, we see in columns 2–5 that *racial performance burdens are greater for students of African than Caribbean origin and multigenerational natives.* Moreover, compared to multigenerational natives, *family performance burdens are greater for first- and second-generation immigrants, as well as among students with dark skin tones,* as shown in the cell outlined in the third row of column 7. In contrast, as shown in column 1, *students of mixed racial parentage experience lower family pressures to perform academically.* It appears that non-Black origins on one side of the family serve to make mixed-race students feel less need to "represent the race" for their family members when called on to perform academically at college.

In column 9, we see that *stressful life events are less numerous and less severe for students with college-educated parents,* and column 10 shows that *those whose parents hold an advanced degree experience less sense of loss as a result of attending a selective school,* once again underscoring the advantages of higher class-status origins. As shown in column 3, *second-generation immigrants experience a greater sense of loss and are also more vulnerable to depression* whereas *men are less likely to report signs of depression than women* (see column 8). In contrast, *students whose parents are college educated experience a lower risk of depression* (see column 9).

In sum, with respect to the downsides of an elite education, results indicate that exposure to incidents of racial hostility is greatest for students from racially mixed neighborhoods and schools, who live in segregated neighborhoods but attend White schools, and those who arise in disordered and violent contexts. Racial performance burdens are more likely for students of African immigrant origin and those originating in violent schools and neighborhoods, whereas family performance burdens are greatest for dark-skinned first- and second-generation immigrants and least for mixed-race students. Experiencing negative life events within social networks is least likely for Black students with college-educated parents and most likely for those coming out of disordered and violent neighborhoods.

Converging Identities and Attitudes

Finally, in the matrix depicted in figure 10.5, the rows indicate racial identities and attitudes reported by students in their fourth year of college, along with indicators defined by the Multidimensional Inventory of Black Identity (MIBI) administered in the third year (Sellers et al. 1997). Cross-tabulation of these row outcomes with the dimensions of Black diversity shown in the columns yields cells filled with directional signs corresponding to significant relationships found in appendix tables A8.1–A8.4. Recall that our analyses in chapter 8 showed a shift toward stronger self-identification as Black combined with less sense of a common racial fate and a convergence of racial attitudes.

	Identity (1)	Generation (2)	(3)	Region (4)	(5)	Skin tone (6)	(7)	Gender (8)	Parental education (9)	(10)	Segregation and disorder (11)	(12)	(13)	(14)
	Mixed	First	Second	Caribbean	African	Medium	Dark	Male	College degree	Advanced degree	White school and neighborhood	Mixed school and neighborhood	White school only	Disorder and violence
W5 Solo American identity	+							+						
W5 Solo Black Identity														+
W5 Some common fate			+											
W5 A lot of common fate	−							−						
W5 Closeness to Whites	+	−						+						−
W5 Whites discriminatory														
W5 Blacks should try harder								+						
W5 Blacks more qualified				+	+				−					
Racial centrality	−	−	−	−	−				−					+
Assimilationist index														−
Cultural nationalist index	−						+	+						+
Political nationalist index	−													+

FIGURE 10.5. Schematic depiction of associations between the dimensions of Black diversity and late college racial identity.

Typically, social science focuses on the statistically significant associations between variables to identify how specific backgrounds are associated with racial attitudes. Here, however, we note the move *away* from statistical significance as the more meaningful shift. Overall, of the twenty-nine significant associations between our dimensions of diversity and racial attitudes and identities observed in figure 10.1, only nine remain in figure 10.5 while nineteen disappear and one switches sign. Only three newly significant associations appear. In other words, the relationship between one's origins and one's racial attitudes and identity weakens over the course of four years of college, suggesting that the collegiate experience changes how young Black adults understand themselves and their place in the racial order of society.

The resulting convergence of racial identities and attitudes is characterized by consistent associations between racial identity and attitudes, on the one hand, and mixed-race identification, gender, and exposure to disorder and violence, on the other hand. After four years of college, the dimensions of identity, gender, and neighborhood disorder and violence are practically alone in structuring any intraracial differences in racial identities and attitudes among our respondents, though even their influence has weakened over the course of four years of elite higher education.

As seen in column 1, *mixed-racial origins continue to be associated with seeing American identity as more important, as well as a lower likelihood of perceiving a lot of common racial fate and greater closeness to White people.* However, earlier associations with the importance of Black identity, the perception of a common racial fate, and seeing Whites as discriminatory have gone away. Although some of the differences between mixed-race and monoracial students may have moderated, however, the former's support for a Black identity in opposition to Whites still continues clearly weaker, a view backed up by new data created by the addition of the MIBI measures, which reveal that *among mixed-race students, racial centrality is lower and both cultural and political nationalism are weaker than for monoracial students.*

Although the perception of Whites as more discriminatory by first-generation immigrants persists from freshman to senior year, their stronger agreement with the view that Blacks need to be better qualified than Whites to get ahead does not. At the same time, looking at column 3, we see that *second-generation immigrants have come to perceive more common racial fate* and as shown in columns 4 and 5, *students of both Caribbean and African origin now more strongly support the view that Black people need to be more qualified than White people to get ahead.* At the same time, however, *these national origins predict a lower centrality of race in the construction of self-identity.* Finally, as shown in columns 2 and 3, first- and second-generation immigrants report lower racial centrality compared with multigenerational natives.

With respect to gender influences, the data in column 8 show that *relative to Black women, Black men continue to more strongly favor a solitary American identity, perceive greater closeness to White people, and more strongly endorse the view that Black people should try harder.* However, *the negative association between gender and one's perception of White people as discriminatory has disappeared while Black men now are more likely than Black women to perceive "a lot" of common fate identity.* On the MIBI indexes, *Black men are more positively disposed toward cultural nationalism than women,* and as shown in column 7, *the same is true for dark-skinned students compared to those with medium and light skin tones.* Thus, after several years of college experience, identity continues to be gendered, with Black men leaning more strongly toward an American identity, perceiving less common racial fate, feeling closer to White people, seeing White people as less discriminatory, and supporting cultural naturalism to a greater degree than Black women.

Although columns 9 and 10 indicate *Black students with college-educated parents continue to support less strongly the view that Black people need to be more qualified than White people,* those with parents holding advanced degrees no longer less strongly support the view that Black people should try harder.

Finally, as columns 11–13 reveal, earlier associations between neighborhood racial composition and identities and attitudes have completely disappeared, but column 14 shows *greater exposure to social disorder and violence in neighborhoods continues to be associated with lower perceived closeness to White people and stronger perceptions of White people as discriminatory.* In addition, *exposure to disorder and violence now predicts adherence to a solitary Black identity,* and consistent with this finding, we also learn that *exposure to disorder and violence also serves to increase the centrality of Black identity while rendering Black students less assimilationist and more nationalist in both politics and culture.* These findings underscore the powerful effect of childhood segregation—via greater exposure to disorder and violence—in molding Black attitudes and identities even after years of immersion in elite higher education.

Manifold Intersectionalities

The concept of intersectionality was originally developed by Crenshaw (1989) to recognize the fact that the experience of Blackness is not uniform but is instead defined by the intersection of race and gender, creating different experiences for Black men and Black women. Over the years, the concept has been broadened by Crenshaw and others to incorporate multiple intersections between race and other dimensions of difference (see Crenshaw 1991; McCall 2005; Weldon 2008; Collins 2019; Norwood 2021). In the words of Collins and Bilge (2016:8), "using intersectionality as an analytic lens highlights the multiple nature of individual identities and how varying combinations of class, gender, race, sexuality, and citizenship categories differentially position each individual."

Our analyses here strongly support this viewpoint, suggesting that in the early twenty-first century, after decades of sustained immigration from Africa and the Caribbean, rising class stratification, increasing rates of intermarriage, and uneven declines in residential segregation, the concept of intersectionality indeed encompasses more than just gender. As we have shown, racial identities, attitudes, upbringing, social relations, and academic performance differ not only along the lines of gender but also by racial identification, nativity, generation, region of origin, parental education, and segregation. What we have learned about these manifold intersections is summarized in table 10.1, which synthesizes the information compiled in figures 10.1–10.5 and elsewhere. Here, we draw on this table to offer a composite sketch of how the experience of Blackness is defined by the intersection of race with the different dimensions of Black diversity we have identified.

TABLE 10.1. Summary profile of students' traits and characteristics associated with the dimensions of Black diversity

Racial identification

Compared to monoracial students, those of mixed race:
- Perceive an American identity to be more important (freshman and senior years)
- Perceive a Black identity to be less important (freshman year only)
- Are less likely to perceive some common racial fate (freshman year only)
- Are less likely to perceive a lot of common racial fate (freshman and senior years)
- Perceive race as less central to their identity (on the MIBI)
- Express less Black cultural nationalism (on the MIBI)
- Express less Black political nationalism (on the MIBI)
- Perceive greater social closeness to White people (freshmen and senior years)
- Perceive White people to be less discriminatory (freshman year only)
- Have parents who relied less on strict discipline in child-rearing
- Have parents who were more involved in cultivating cultural capital growing up
- Have more White friends and fewer Black friends on campus
- Are more likely to date outside the group and when doing so, to date White partners
- Are less likely to join majority-Black organizations on campus
- Experience less intense interaction with other Black students on campus
- Experience a lower family performance burden

Immigrant origins

Compared to native-origin Black peers, first- and second-generation Black immigrants:
- Perceive race as less central to their identity (on the MIBI)
- Have parents who provided less support for intellectual independence growing up
- Have parents who were less involved in cultivating human and social capital growing up
- Have fewer Black friends on campus
- Experience a greater family performance burden

Compared to native-origin Black peers, first- but not second-generation immigrants:
- Perceive White people to be less discriminatory (freshman and senior years)
- Believe less strongly that Black people must be more qualified than White people to get ahead (freshman year only)
- Experience less intense interaction with White students on campus

Compared to native-origin Black peers, second- but not first-generation immigrants:
- Are more likely to perceive some common racial fate (senior year only)
- Have parents who were less involved in cultivating human, social, and cultural capital
- Are less likely to join majority-Black organizations on campus
- Experience a greater sense of loss as a result of attending a selective institution
- Have a higher risk of depression

Region of origin

With respect to regional origins of first- and second-generation immigrants, those with African roots:
- Perceive less closeness to White people than Caribbean or native-origin students (freshman year only)
- Feel more strongly that Black people need to be more qualified than White people to get ahead (senior year only and a switch from feeling less strongly as freshmen)
- Earned a higher GPA in high school than Caribbean or native-origin students
- Experience a greater racial performance burden than Caribbean or native-origin students

(continued)

TABLE 10.1. (*continued*)

Region of origin

With respect to regional origins of first- and second-generation immigrants, those with Caribbean roots:

    -See Black identity as more important than Africans or native-origin students (freshman year only)

    -Feel more strongly that Black people need to be more qualified than White people in order to get ahead (senior year only)

    -Have more White friends on campus than Africans or native-origin students

    -Are more likely to join a race-themed organization than Africans or native-origin students

Skin tone

Compared to light-skinned students, those with medium skin tones:

    -Perceive White people to be more discriminatory (freshman year only)

    -Believe more strongly that Black people must try harder in order to get ahead (freshman year)

    -Have fewer White friends

    -Perceive Black students to be less visible on campus

Compared to light-skinned students, those with dark skin tones:

    -Believe more strongly that Black people must try harder in order to get ahead (freshman year)

    -Have more White friends

    -Experience a higher family performance burden

Gender

Compared to Black males, Black females:

    -Perceive an American identity to be less important (freshman and senior years)

    -Perceive less social closeness to White people (freshman and senior years)

    -View White people to be more discriminatory (freshman year only)

    -Believe less strongly that Black people must try harder in order to get ahead (freshman and senior years)

    -Experienced less difficulty in their high school coursework

    -Earned a higher GPA in high school

    -Have fewer White friends and more Black friends

    -Are less likely to date outside the group and less likely to date White partners when doing so

    -Are more likely to join majority-Black groups and have more intense interactions with Black students

    -Perceive White students to be more visible on campus

    -Have a higher risk of depression

Parental education

Compared to students with noncollege-educated parents, those whose parents hold a college degree:

    -Believe less strongly that Black people must be more qualified to get ahead (freshman and senior years)

    -Have parents who are more involved in cultivating both human and cultural capital

    -Are more likely to believe that their institution puts too much effort into promoting diversity

    -Experience fewer and less severe stressful life events in their social networks

    -Have a lower risk of depression

Compared to students with noncollege-educated parents, those whose parents hold an advanced degree:

    -Believe less strongly that Black people must work harder to get ahead (freshman year only)

    -Have parents who were more involved in cultivating human and cultural capital

    -Were more likely to attend a private secular high school

    -Earned more AP credits in high school and scored higher on the SAT

    -Are more likely to join a Black-themed organization on campus

    -Experience a lower sense of loss as a result of attending a selective school

Neighborhood and school segregation

Compared to students who grew up in minority-dominant schools and neighborhoods, those from racially mixed schools and neighborhoods:

-Perceive an American identity to be more important (freshman year only)
-Perceive White people to be more discriminatory (freshman year only)
-Earned lower GPAs in high school
-Experienced a greater number and variety of racially hostile incidents on campus

Compared to students who grew up in minority-dominant schools and neighborhoods, those from White schools and neighborhoods:

-Perceive greater closeness to White people (freshman year only)
-Perceive White people to be more discriminatory (freshman year only)
-Had parents who tended to rely on strict discipline in child-rearing
-Earned lower GPAs in high school
-Have more White friends and fewer Black friends on campus
-Experience more intense interactions with White students on campus
-Experience less intense interactions with Black students on campus
-Are less likely to join a Black-themed organization on campus

Compared to students who grew up in minority-dominant schools and neighborhoods, those who attended White schools while living in minority neighborhoods:

-Perceive greater closeness to White people (freshman year only)
-Perceive White people to be more discriminatory (freshman year only)
-Had parents who tended to rely on strict discipline in child-rearing
-Earned lower GPAs in high school but scored higher on the SAT
-Perceive greater racial separation on campus
-Experience a greater variety of racially hostile incidents on campus

Exposure to disorder and violence

As exposure to violence and disorder rises:

-The perception of American identity to be more important increases (senior year only)
-Perceived social closeness to White people declines (freshman and senior years)
-The perception of White people as discriminatory increases (freshman year only)
-Strictness of parental discipline in child-rearing rises
-Parental reliance on shame and guilt in child-rearing falls
-Parental involvement in the cultivation of cultural and social capital declines
-GPAs, AP credits, and SAT scores decline
-The number of White friends on campus decreases
-The number of Black friends on campus increases
-The intensity of interaction with White students declines
-The likelihood of dating a White student decreases
-The visibility of White people on campus declines
-The racial performance burden increases
-The number of stressful events within students' social networks increases
-The sense of loss from attending a selective school increases
-The risk of depression increases

The Intersection of Race and Identity

Having one Black and one non-Black parent necessarily complicates the construction of Black identity, especially when one parent is White, a category that historically was manufactured by Whites to stand in contrast to Blackness (Painter 2010). Those individuals who have one White and one Black parent are faced with a choice as they approach adulthood. Based on their phenotype, in most cases they will be seen in American society as Black, and one choice is simply to accept this designation and identify themselves as such. Alternatively, they may choose to present themselves to the world as biracial, multiracial, or mixed, contesting society's usual taxonomic inclinations. Recognizing the rise of mixed-race people as a visible segment of the U.S. population, the U.S. census first recognized multiracial origins as a response to the race question in 2000 (Parker et al. 2015). Since that date, a growing share of Americans have exercised this option not only on censuses and surveys but also in daily life (Rockquemore and Brunsma 2007; Spencer 2011). Whatever their choice, young people of mixed parentage must confront the duality bequeathed to them by their parents, and this cannot help but influence the decisions they make.

Our analysis suggests that *racially mixed origins are most consequential for the construction of Black identity, the formation of racial attitudes, and the organization of social behavior.* Self-identification as mixed race implicitly acknowledges a non-Black contribution to racial identity, and our data consequently indicate that mixed-race students perceive Black identity to be less important and an American identity more important to their self-perceptions. Although we observe some movement toward a stronger embrace of Blackness during the college years, as seniors, persons of mixed race are still less likely to perceive a common racial fate and continue to view an American identity as more important than monoracial students. As juniors, they also score lower on indexes measuring the centrality of race to their self-identity and are less supportive of Black nationalist sentiments, either cultural or political.

Growing up, mixed-race students tend to be raised under a looser, less strict disciplinary regime than monoracial students, as parents who are of different races are almost by definition more tolerant and open-minded than average. Parents of mixed-race students thus deploy a strategy of *concerted cultivation* in child-rearing and are actively involved in the transfer of elite cultural capital to their children, taking them to museums, science centers, plays, concerts, and other venues for the display of high-status culture (Lareau 2003). As a result of their upbringing and origins, mixed-race students experience fewer family-based performance burdens as college students. As both freshmen and seniors, they perceive greater closeness to White people and have more White friends and fewer Black friends than monoracial students. Mixed-race students also report interacting less intensively with other Blacks on campus and are less likely to join majority-Black campus organizations.

Given these differences in interracial exposure, mixed-race students are far more likely to date non-Black partners, and when doing so, they are more likely to date White partners. Although as freshmen they perceive White people to be less discriminatory, by senior year they have come to adopt the monoracial perspective of White people as tending to discriminate. This shift does not seem to undermine their greater comfort in White social spaces, however, giving them a clear advantage over those monoracial students who are less prepared to navigate the uncharted waters of selective higher education. Like the students who make it into France's *grandes écoles* that Bourdieu (1998) studied, they have already mastered the cultural repertoires and social skills needed to move without friction through the social currents of elite academia.

The Intersection of Race and Skin Tone

Among Black college students surveyed by the NLSF, 25 percent displayed a light skin tone, 26 percent a dark skin tone, and 49 percent a medium skin tone. Unfortunately, skin color still has social and economic consequences in the United States, for society continues to be stratified socially and economically on the basis of skin color (Monk 2014). Colorism remains alive and well (Hunter 2007) and the persistence of skin color discrimination is well documented (Hall 2010; Hersch 2011; Monk 2015, 2018; Quillian et al. 2017; Quillian, Lee, and Honoré 2020). Although identification as mixed-race is associated with lighter skin tones, the two dimensions are not coterminous. Indeed, among Black NLSF respondents, 53 percent of those rated as having a light skin tone self-identified as monoracial.

Given the realities of color prejudice and skin tone discrimination, the experiences of light- and dark-skinned individuals can be expected to diverge as they move through American society, including on college campuses. Compared to light-skinned students, those with dark skin tones perceive White people as more discriminatory and, consistent with this perception, when they arrive on campus as freshmen, they believe that Black people must work harder if they wish to move ahead socially and economically. Those with medium skin tones report having fewer White friends and perceive Black people to be less visible on campus, while those with dark skin tones experience greater family pressures to achieve academically, yielding a greater performance burden that exacerbates vulnerability to stereotype threat.

The Intersection of Race and Immigrant Origins

Immigration is always a selective process, and the Black immigrants who arrive in the United States are not a random sample of their origin nations. Voluntary immigrants are positively selected on traits such as ambition, determination, and a willingness to take risks. In addition, those who make it through the screening process imposed by U.S. immigration laws are selected on the basis of class, with occupational statuses and education levels well above the average in their home countries (Hamilton 2019). In contrast, involuntary immigrants such as refugees and asylum seekers are less selected with respect to personal attributes such as ambition and determination and are admitted to the United States through a separate track that does not select on the basis of class, introducing significant heterogeneity into the Black immigrant population.

Nonetheless, NLSF respondents have been filtered through selective college admissions systems and are not representative of Black immigrants generally. Among immigrant-origin students in our sample, three-quarters come from just eight nations, five in the Caribbean (Jamaica, Trinidad, Guyana, Barbados, and Haiti) and three in Africa (Nigeria, Ghana, and Kenya), none of which send significant numbers of involuntary migrants to the United States. Although Haiti is a poor country prone to political violence, natural disasters, and poverty, only 2.4 percent of refugees or asylees entering the United States between 2009 and 2018 were from Haiti (U.S. Office of Immigration Statistics 2019). Origins in refugee-sending countries such as Ethiopia, Liberia, Libya, Rwanda, Sierra Leone, Somalia, Sudan, and Uganda together constitute less than 5 percent of immigrant-origin Black students in the NLSF. Thus, the large majority are likely positively selected with respect to personal traits and socioeconomic status.

In addition to being positively selected, immigrants arriving from Africa and the Caribbean generally came of age in Black-majority societies, giving them little direct experience with White prejudice, discrimination, and political domination. They also bring with them their national and ethnic cultures, which in African nations tend to be patriarchal (Gordon 1996) and in the

Caribbean more matrifocal (Barrow 1996; Smith 1996). No matter what their origin, they not only have less knowledge of White society and its racism, they also have less knowledge of Black American culture and its social mores.

As a result of immigration's intrinsic nature and selectivity, students of immigrant and native origin arrive on campus with different upbringings, attitudes, and identities, and at college, they experience divergent social and academic outcomes. Having been socialized in a foreign culture and society, first-generation immigrant students simultaneously report interacting less intensely with White peers and having fewer Black friends. Moreover, being less familiar with race relations in the United States, both first- and second-generation Black immigrants perceive race to be less central to their identity than native-origin Black students. In addition, although they were raised by foreign-born parents who provided less support for intellectual independence and were less involved in the cultivation of human and social capital, most immigrant-origin students are nonetheless subject to very high expectations for academic achievement, and consequently, they experience weightier family-based performance burdens. Arising from a highly selective process such as immigration has its academic benefits, but it also has its costs.

Around two-thirds of foreign-origin Black students in the NLSF sample were second-generation immigrants who were born and raised in the United States, with the remainder coming from abroad with their parents but growing up mostly in the United States. In addition to having parents who are less involved in the cultivation of human and social capital, the parents of first-generation immigrants are also less involved in the cultivation of cultural capital. Despite the lack of parental involvement in their academic preparation, however, first-generation students appear to benefit from immigrant optimism, perceiving White people to be less discriminatory and evincing less support for the view that Black people must be more qualified than White peers to get ahead in American society. As already noted, however, due to their foreign roots they also have less intense interactions with White people and are probably less aware of White proclivities for prejudice and discrimination.

Compared to their first-generation peers, second-generation immigrants experience a greater sense of loss in moving away from their families and communities to enter the privileged confines of a selective college or university. When combined with the high family-based performance burdens they share with first-generation immigrants, this sense of loss puts them at higher risk of depression. Living up to high parental expectations in order to realize the

American dream by attending a selective academic institution clearly comes at a cost for the native-born children of Black immigrants.

The Intersection of Race and Gender

The different experiences of race and racism created by the intersection of race and gender were pointed out some time ago (see Crenshaw 1989), and our data confirm the salience of this intersectionality among Black students attending selective colleges and universities. As with racism and colorism, sexism and misogyny have not disappeared from American society. Indeed, in the era of "me too," issues related to the treatment of women on campus have become more salient (Giesler 2019) and instances of date rape and sexual harassment are increasingly being brought to light (Hirsch and Khan 2020). *Given the centrality of gender as a political issue among college students, we unsurprisingly detect a clear divergence in the social and academic experiences of the young Black men and women we surveyed.*

As freshmen, Black women see American identity as less important than Black men, perceive greater social distance from White people, see White people as more discriminatory, and give less credence to the view that Black people must try harder to get ahead in society. Moreover, with the exception of seeing White people as more discriminatory, they hold on to these views throughout their college careers, affirming them as both freshmen and seniors. Compared to Black men, Black women report having fewer White friends and more Black friends on campus. They are also more likely to join majority-Black campus organizations, report more intense interactions with other Black students on campus, and are painfully aware of the greater visibility enjoyed by White students on campus, particularly White women.

In addition, Black women are far less likely than Black men to date interracially and are especially unlikely to go out with White partners, tendencies that reduce the size of a dating pool already constricted by the highly skewed sex ratios that prevail on the campuses of selective academic institutions. In their in-depth interviews, Black women expressed considerable frustration, resentment, and no small amount of bitterness about the campus dating scene. In the end, Black women report being more alienated from White students and from White society generally and experience a higher risk of depression. Thus, they appear to be less prepared attitudinally to enter the White social world prevailing at selective institutions and at college they are more estranged from White people than are Black men.

In contrast, Black women arrive on campus better prepared academically for study at a selective institution of higher education than Black men. As high school students, they earned higher grades and experienced less difficulty with their coursework. Accordingly, at college they were less likely to stop out and more likely than Black men to complete an on-time degree, a gender gap that continues to prevail six years out from enrollment. The greater academic success of Black women compared to Black men likely exacerbates the tensions already present between them because of their demographic imbalance in the Black student population, As we have seen, in our sample, the six-year graduation rate was 83 percent for Black women and 72 percent for Black men, but nationally, the respective rates are only 44 percent and 34 percent (U.S. National Center for Educational Statistics 2020b).

The Intersection of Race and Parental Education

Our indicator of social class status is parental education. Defined broadly, education begins in early childhood (Heckman 2011; García et al. 2020) and much of it occurs in the home before formal schooling begins and during summer vacations (Alexander, Entwisle, and Olson 2014). *The fact that learning depends heavily on the intellectual environment created in the home by parents puts first-generation Black college students at a distinct disadvantage relative to those with college-educated parents, channeling them into divergent academic streams.* As with financial capital, human capital is passed from parents to children and accumulates across generations, making college attendance much more of a leap for students whose parents never completed a college degree, especially when the jump is likely from a failing or middling high school to a selective college campus (Ward, Siegel, and Davenport 2012).

Our data clearly show that Black students whose parents hold either a four-year or an advanced degree are more involved in cultivating their children's human and cultural capital during childhood and adolescence, giving Black children of well-educated parents a significant head start in acquiring the cognitive, social, and cultural skills that support later learning in college. As freshmen, Black students with college-educated parents enter college with greater faith in the meritocratic nature of U.S. society, being more skeptical than students with less-educated parents of the view that Black people need to be more qualified than White people to get ahead. Students whose parents hold an advanced degree are also less sympathetic to the view that Black people have to work harder if they want to advance, a pattern also documented by Welburn

(2016). Students with college-educated parents report experiencing fewer and less stressful events in their social networks, and as a consequence, they experience a lower risk of depression than Black students whose parents never completed college. Coming from a privileged scholastic background, these Black students are more likely to believe their own institution puts too much effort into promoting diversity on campus.

Of course, Black students whose parents hold advanced degrees are in the best position to compete academically at selective academic institutions. They are more likely to have attended a private secular high school where they earned more AP credits than other Black students and also scored higher on the SAT. Given their superior academic preparation, extensive social ties to college-educated people, and cultural familiarity with the college milieu, they are less likely to experience a sense of loss in moving from home into the competitive academics characteristic of selective institutions. For these students, attending a selective college or university is an expectation, not a shock. These scholarly advantages do not preclude an embrace of Blackness on campus, however, for as college students, these Black students are also more likely to seek out and join Black-themed organizations.

The Intersection of Race and Segregation

As of 2010, one-third of all Black urbanites lived in hypersegregated metropolitan areas characterized by a high degree of segregation across multiple geographic dimensions simultaneously, and another 21 percent lived in areas that were highly segregated (with a dissimilarity index of 60 or above), meaning that more than half of metropolitan Black residents grow up under conditions of high or intense residential segregation (Massey and Tannen 2015). As noted earlier, poverty and all of its negative correlates tend to become more spatially concentrated in Black neighborhoods as residential segregation rises (Massey and Denton 1993; Quillian 2012). As poverty and its sequelae become geographically concentrated in Black neighborhoods, they also become more concentrated within the public schools that serve them (Fahle et al. 2020). The interplay of school and neighborhood segregation thus yields a very disadvantaged educational environment that compounds the disadvantage that many Blacks already experience in their neighborhoods (Massey and Brodmann 2014; Owens 2020).

Among NLSF respondents, about one-third grew up in predominantly White neighborhoods, one-third came from racially mixed neighborhoods, and one-third arose in predominantly minority neighborhoods. Among the latter, a few were able to escape the disadvantages of neighborhood public education by attending selective magnet schools or a private academy. We expect that the differential exposure of Black students to the "savage inequalities" of American education noted by Kozol (1991) channel them into very divergent academic currents of higher education. *Compared to Black students growing up in minority-dominant schools and neighborhoods, those coming of age in predominantly White residential and educational settings experience a very different pattern of socialization and education that leaves them far better prepared for collegiate social and academic life.*

Their parents rely on strict discipline in child-rearing and they arrive on campus perceiving a greater closeness to White people and go on to have more White friends and fewer Black friends on campus. In addition to this difference in the number of White and Black friends, the interaction intensity with White peers is greater and with Black peers low compared to Black students from segregated schools and neighborhoods. After arriving on campus, students coming out of White residential and educational settings are also less likely to join Black-themed campus organizations.

Black students coming out of predominantly White contexts are thus more comfortable in the predominantly White social and academic settings they encounter upon arriving on campus. This comfort, however, does not blind them to the reality of White racism, for as a result of their prior experience with White people, they come to college perceiving them to be more discriminatory than do Black students who grew up entirely in minority settings where they had little contact with White people. Although students from White schools and neighborhoods earn lower grades, this outcome likely reflects the more competitive environment and rigorous curriculums they encounter at their schools, which leave them not only better socially prepared but also better academically prepared for success in higher education.

The small segment of Black students who live in minority neighborhoods but attend White schools earn lower grades in high school but score higher on the SAT than Black students from other educational backgrounds, confirming the academic advantages of attending a more privileged White high school. These students also arrive on campus more socially prepared, perceiving greater closeness to White people even though, like others exposed to White people while growing up, they perceive them to be discriminators. As with the parents of students living in White neighborhoods and attending White schools, their parents similarly rely on strict discipline in child-rearing.

Although escaping a segregated neighborhood to attend a White school may better prepare Black students for the social and academic milieu of selective higher education, it also appears to sensitize them to racial inequality, for these students also perceive greater racial separation at college and report experiencing a greater number and variety of hostile racial incidents on campus. Students coming out of racially mixed schools and neighborhoods similarly encounter a greater number and variety of racial incidents on campus and likewise perceive White people to be more discriminatory; however, unlike others who encounter White students at school, they do not perceive White people to be socially closer, though they do perceive an American identity to be more important compared with students originating entirely in segregated circumstances.

The Intersection of Race and Exposure to Violence

Of all the correlates of the concentrated poverty created by racial segregation, perhaps the most important is the intensification of exposure to social disorder and violence (Peterson and Krivo 2010), for such exposure has been found to have powerful negative social, psychological, and cognitive consequences for human development and well-being (Sharkey 2018). It comes as no surprise, therefore, *that differential exposure to disorder and violence among Black students while growing up creates strong divergences in college, beginning with academics.* NLSF data reveal that as exposure to disorder and violence within schools and neighborhoods rises, the number of AP credits, GPAs, and SAT scores decline and parental involvement in the cultivation of cultural and social capital declines.

Socially, rising exposure to disorder and violence is associated with greater parental reliance on strict discipline in child-rearing and less reliance on shame and guilt, as parents lovingly but firmly try to protect their children from their risky and dangerous surroundings (see Furstenberg et al. 1999; Dow 2016, 2019; Holt 2020). Greater exposure to disorder and violence also reduces social closeness with Whites while reinforcing the perception of White people as discriminatory, leading to fewer White friends, less intense interactions with White peers, and a lower likelihood of dating them. In contrast, as exposure to disorder and violence increase, the number of Black friends rises and White peers become less visible. In addition, students coming out of disordered and violent settings experience more stressful events within their social networks, bear a heavier racial performance burden, and suffer a greater sense of loss in moving from risky schools and neighborhoods to the safety of an elite college campus. As exposure to disorder and violence increases, these stresses accumulate and the risk of depression correspondingly rises.

Intersectionality in the New Black Elite

Since the term was first introduced by Crenshaw in 1989, intersectionality has expanded beyond the nexus of race and gender to consider multiple intersections and their implications for the well-being of different subsets of the Black population as they navigate a racially stratified society. Our goal here has been to do intersectionality justice by moving beyond the cliché of the race-versus-class debate. What we find is that although race and class certainly shape the perspectives and experiences of the Black intellectual elite that coalesced around the turn of the twenty-first century, by themselves they are inadequate to understand the complexities and subtleties of the contemporary Black experience. At the end of the day, the Black professional class does end up agreeing on a common set of attitudes and values, but they take a variety of different paths to get there.

The Future of the Black Elite

The profiles we have constructed here suggest that today's Black leadership class is far more diverse than generally appreciated and that this diversity matters for how its members fit within the nation's broader social, economic, and political elite. Continuing the metaphor of the flow of students into and through college as a river (introduced by Bowen and Bok in 1998 and continued in prior books using the NLSF), we have presented evidence to show how membership in the Black racial category interacts with gender, parentage, nativity, skin tone, class, and segregation to generate divergent currents in the stream of Black students flowing toward graduation. Some of the currents are rapid, propelling students forward to an on-time graduation and entry into the nation's professional class. Other currents are slower, hampered by institutional transfers and time taken off from studies due to financial difficulties, poor grade performance, mental health challenges, or family issues that delay graduation. Still other currents become "leaks" in the pipeline of higher education, and some never graduate at all. Far too many young Black Americans never even get to college, much less attend a selective institution, given the structural constraints on Black educational achievement and social mobility that still characterize American society.

As a result, the demographic currents flowing into America's Black population today are not equally reflected in the Black elite graduating from the nation's top colleges and universities. The Black graduates are disproportionately women, first- and second-generation immigrants, mixed-race students, and persons who grew up in predominantly White neighborhoods and attended privileged schools. This partly reflects the admissions policies and practices pursued by elite colleges and universities, where well-meaning "diversity initiatives" all too often focus on Blackness to the exclusion of class, racial origins, nativity, generation, or segregation. In doing so, they create cohorts of students (and future leaders) that underrepresent the majority of Black people in the United States.

This gap between the composition of the Black leadership class and the larger Black population in the United States is problematic both for the Black community and for the nation as a whole, contributing to intragroup schisms with respect to political ideology, values, and goals, a problem long acknowledged by Black scholars (see Frazier 1957; Cohen 1999; Benjamin 2005; Robinson 2016). As we have seen, the homogenizing experience of exposure to an elite education is associated with a convergence of attitudes and identities as members of the new Black elite come to recognize themselves as exceptions; however, this very fact nonetheless creates gaps between their interests and worldviews and those of the broader Black population. To be truly effective, leaders should reflect the people they represent, knowing their life experiences and understanding their hopes and aspirations as well as their discontents and disappointments. In the end, a racialized noblesse oblige is still a noblesse oblige.

Some progress toward democratizing entry into the Black professional elite can be made by reforming college admission procedures to take into account other dimensions of diversity besides race alone, and after admission by providing greater support for students who cannot benefit from the advantages of immigrant selectivity, multiracial origins, light skin tones, well-educated parents, and prior access to advantaged schools and neighborhoods. However, although reforms within the system of higher education may improve outcomes for those passing through the rarified confines of academia, they do not address the categorical mechanisms of racial inequality that pervade the rest of American society. Therefore, as Black immigration continues, rates of intermarriage rise, and class differentials widen, the mismatch between the Black elite and the masses will not only persist but also grow unless two structural pillars of racial stratification are eliminated.

The first is the racialized system of criminal justice that was systematically constructed in the service of the twin "wars" on crime and drugs (Western 2006; Alexander 2010). During the 1980s and 1990s, the United States constructed a rapacious carceral system that imprisons a far higher fraction of its population than any other nation, the weight of which falls very disproportionately on Black men (Davis 2017). Their rate of incarceration is four times that of White men (Carson 2020) and the lifetime risk of incarceration for a Black man in the United States is 32 percent compared to 6 percent for White men (Bonczar 2003).

The end result is a formidable school-to-prison pipeline that funnels far more Black men into prison than into college (Alexander 2010), which goes a long way toward explaining the 2:1 ratio of women to men in our survey of elite college students. Even among those Black Americans who are never incarcerated, exposure to crime and violence in their daily lives—and to excessive police violence in their communities—has been shown to undermine academic achievement in powerful ways, rendering Black students less likely to be able to enter, attend, and graduate from institutions of higher education with a college degree, increasingly the ticket to entry into the professional class (Sharkey et al. 2012, 2014; Ang 2020).

The second pillar of racial inequality in the United States is racial residential segregation, which Pettigrew (1979) long ago identified as the "linchpin" in the nation's system of racial stratification. In hypersegregated metropolitan areas such as Chicago, New York, Philadelphia, and eighteen others, spatial isolation not only builds poverty and its correlates into the neighborhoods inhabited by Black Americans, but it also concentrates deprivation and disorder within the public schools they attend (Reardon and Owens 2014; Urban Institute 2018). In doing so, it perpetuates the transmission of Black disadvantage throughout the life cycle and across generations (Sharkey 2013).

Residential segregation also makes the exclusion and exploitation of Black Americans easy and efficient (Charles 2003; Massey 2020). Segregation made it simple to bring the full power of a militarized police force and a predatory prosecutorial system to bear on Black Americans in ways that left privileged White people unscathed, unconcerned, and unaware. The punitive actions and repressive policies that are routinely inflicted on Black people would not last long if they were unleashed on Whites. In addition, because segregation clusters people together in space, one can disinvest in Black people simply by disinvesting in a place. As a result of systematic disinvestment in Black neighborhoods, a huge wealth gap persists even as the Black-White earnings gap has narrowed since the civil rights era. The most common means of wealth accumulation for American families is through homeownership and the equity it creates, a form of wealth accumulation that continues to be a primary site of racial discrimination, exploitation, and profiteering (Massey and Rugh 2018; Choi et al. 2019; Taylor 2019; Quillian, Lee, and Honoré 2020).

Throughout this book, we have sought to reveal not only the varied origins of today's Black elite but also to show that the salient axes of Black diversity are meaningful and impactful among our respondents. We hope that future research on race will continue to follow the recent trend of examining not only interracial divides but also the intraracial differences that shape Black attitudes, identities, and experiences (Davenport 2016; Clerge 2019; Jack 2019). Our finding of a convergence in Black attitudes and identities suggest that differences do not necessarily constitute divides and that people can indeed come together in ways that respect but are not paralyzed by intragroup differences. The new generation of the Black elite has seen triumph and defeat and the emergence of new opportunities coupled with resurgent racism. As we conclude this book during a global pandemic, a presidential election, and antiracism protests met with White vigilantism, cautious optimism may be what we need.

Multivariate Models of Student Outcomes

TABLE A4.1. Predicting most important identity (multinomial logit model)

Characteristic	Most important identity		
	Both Black and American (Ref)	Black only	American only
DIMENSIONS OF DIVERSITY			
Racial identification			
Monoracial (Ref)		—	—
Mixed race		−0.305+	0.321*
Nativity and generation			
Multigenerational native (Ref)			
Second-generation immigrant			
First-generation immigrant			
Region of origin			
USA (Ref)			
Africa		0.338	0.226
Caribbean		0.498*	−0.030
Other		−0.961+	0.049
Skin tone			
Light (Ref)		—	—
Medium		0.111	−0.118
Dark		0.144	0.139
Gender			
Female (Ref)		—	—
Male		−0.098	0.468***
Parental education			
No college degree (Ref)		—	—
College degree		0.019	0.211
Advanced degree		0.107	−0.400
Experience of segregation			
Predominantly White		−0.171	−0.182
Racially mixed		−0.132	−0.518*
Predominantly minority (Ref)		—	—
Minority neighborhood/White school		0.161	0.217
Neighborhood disadvantage			
Total disorder/violence index		0.010	−0.046
CONTROLS			
Ever in single-parent household		0.044	−0.012
Mother always worked full time		−0.139	−0.044
Parents own home		−0.112	−0.044
Mean annual income		0.002	0.003
Respondent attended Howard		0.133	0.079***
Log-likelihood χ^2		95.082	95.082

+ $p < 0.10$; * $p < 0.05$; ** $p < 0.01$; *** $p < 0.001$

TABLE A4.2. Predicting sense of common fate identity (multinomial logit model)

Characteristic	None or a Little (Ref)	Some	A lot
		What Happens to Blacks Affects Respondent	
DIMENSIONS OF DIVERSITY			
Racial identification			
Monoracial (Ref)		—	—
Mixed race		−0.259⁺	−0.469**
Nativity and generation			
Multigenerational native (Ref)		—	—
Second-generation immigrant		−0.304	0.133
First-generation immigrant		0.350	−0.035
Region of origin			
USA (Ref)			
Africa			
Caribbean			
Other			
Skin tone			
Light (Ref)		—	—
Medium		−0.087	−0.033
Dark		0.046	0.066
Gender			
Female (Ref)		—	—
Male		−0.014	−0.127
Parental education			
No college degree (Ref)		—	—
College degree		−0.130	−0.173
Advanced degree		−0.047	0.099
Experience of segregation			
Predominantly White		−0.019	−0.023
Racially mixed		0.115	0.023
Predominantly minority (Ref)		—	—
Minority neighborhood/White school		0.212	0.415
Neighborhood disadvantage			
Total disorder/Violence index		−0.007	0.012
CONTROLS			
Ever in single-parent household		0.095	0.126
Mother always worked full time		−0.063	−0.063
Parents own home		−0.113	−0.147
Mean annual income		0.003	0.001
Respondent attended Howard		0.654*	0.666*
Log-Likelihood χ^2		55.897	55.897

⁺p < 0.10; * p < 0.05; ** p < 0.01; *** p < 0.001

TABLE A4.3. Predicting selected measures of racial attitudes (OLS regression models)

Characteristic	Closeness to Whites	White propensity to discriminate	Belief that Blacks should try harder	Belief that Blacks must be more qualified
DIMENSIONS OF DIVERSITY				
Racial identification				
Monoracial (Ref)	—	—	—	—
Mixed Race	0.955***	−0.247*	0.218	−0.487
Nativity and generation				
Multigenerational native (Ref)	—	—	—	
Second-generation immigrant	−0.128	0.061	0.188	
First-generation immigrant	0.056	−0.357**	0.356	
Region of origin				
USA (Ref)				—
Africa				−0.861*
Caribbean				0.281
Other				0.436
Skin tone				
Light (Ref)	—	—	—	—
Medium	−0.245	0.201*	0.411[+]	0.123
Dark	0.113	0.18	0.492[+]	0.740*
Gender				
Female (Ref)	—	—	—	—
Male	0.455***	−0.327***	0.437*	0.262
Parental education				
No college degree (Ref)	—	—	—	—
College degree	−0.116	−0.134	−0.369	−0.453[+]
Advanced degree	−0.158	−0.050	−0.931***	−0.269
Experience of segregation				
Predominantly White	0.394*	0.377***	−0.536	0.201
Racially mixed	0.084	0.238*	0.016	0.096
Predominantly minority (Ref)	—	—	—	—
Minority neighborhood/ White school	0.741**	0.307*	−0.500	0.318
Neighborhood disadvantage				
Total disorder/Violence index	−0.038***	0.02***	0.011	0.004
CONTROLS				
Ever in single-parent household	−0.176	0.106	−0.225	−0.583**
Mother always worked full time	−0.097	0.069	−0.224	−0.280
Parents own home	0.065	0.076	0.281	0.008
Mean annual income	0.000	0.000	−0.001	0.001
Respondent attended Howard	−0.758**	0.514**	0.591	1.258**
R-Squared	0.127	0.100	0.062	0.044

[+] $p < 0.10$; * $p < 0.05$; ** $p < 0.01$; *** $p < 0.001$

TABLE A5.1. Predicting parental disciplinary style (OLS regression models)

Characteristic	Parental cultivation of intellectual independence index	Strictness of parental discipline index	Parental use of shame and guilt index
DIMENSIONS OF DIVERSITY			
Racial identification			
Monoracial (Ref)	—	—	—
Mixed race	0.381	−1.420	−0.162
Nativity and generation			
Multigenerational native (Ref)	—	—	—
Second-generation immigrant	−1.273[+]	−0.012	−0.585
First-generation immigrant	−2.242*	0.105	−1.066
Region of origin			
USA (Ref)			
Africa			
Caribbean			
Other			
Skin tone			
Light (Ref)	—	—	—
Medium	0.070	0.954	0.295
Dark	−0.471	0.950	0.803
Gender			
Female (Ref)	—	—	—
Male	−0.591	0.384	−0.511
Parental education			
No college degree (Ref)	—	—	—
College degree	0.874	0.814	−0.074
Advanced degree	0.831	0.545	0.334
Experience of segregation			
Predominantly White	0.855	1.271[+]	−0.158
Racially mixed	0.651	1.056	−0.352
Predominantly minority (Ref)	—	—	—
Minority neighborhood/White school	0.984	−1.977	−0.578
Neighborhood disadvantage			
Total disorder/Violence index	−0.022	0.063*	−0.043*
CONTROLS			
Ever in single-parent household	0.795	0.921	0.368
Mother always worked full time	−0.351	0.690	0.010
Parents own home	0.302	0.337	−0.959[+]
Mean annual income	−0.004	−0.005	−0.006
Respondent attended Howard	−0.391	1.723	−0.349
R-Squared	0.039	0.052	0.042

[+] $p < 0.10$; * $p < 0.05$; ** $p < 0.01$; *** $p < 0.001$

Note: Generational status results driven by Caribbean origins.

TABLE A5.2. Predicting parental capital cultivation efforts (OLS regression models)

Characteristic	Human capital cultivation index	Cultural capital cultivation index	Social capital cultivation index
DIMENSIONS OF DIVERSITY			
Racial identification			
Monoracial (Ref)	—	—	—
Mixed race	−0.189	1.338*	−0.035
Nativity and generation			
Multigenerational native (Ref)	—	—	—
Second-generation immigrant	−1.691+	−0.923+	−0.952*
First-generation immigrant	−2.733+	−2.652***	−0.443
Region of origin			
USA (Ref)			
Africa			
Caribbean			
Other			
Skin tone			
Light (Ref)	—	—	—
Medium	0.178	−0.639	−0.313
Dark	0.851	−0.585	−0.715
Gender			
Female (Ref)	—	—	—
Male	−2.977**	−1.964***	−0.207
Parental education			
No college degree (Ref)	—	—	—
College degree	2.909*	1.165*	0.117
Advanced degree	3.852**	2.324***	−0.136
Experience of segregation			
Predominantly White	0.761	0.111	0.304
Racially mixed	0.137	−0.217	0.384
Predominantly minority (Ref)	—	—	—
Minority neighborhood/White school	1.028	1.214	0.376
Neighborhood disadvantage			
Total disorder/Violence index	0.003	−0.085***	−0.039*
CONTROLS			
Ever in single-parent household	−3.618**	−0.253	−0.365
Mother always worked full time	1.083	−0.133	0.49+
Parents own home	1.412	0.590	0.141
Mean annual income	0.013	0.012*	0.002
Respondent attended Howard	2.288	0.346	0.011
R-Squared	0.115	0.160	0.057

+ $p < 0.10$; * $p < 0.05$; ** $p < 0.01$; *** $p < 0.001$

TABLE A5.3. Predicting type of high school attended (multinomial logit model)

Characteristic	Public High school (Ref)	Private religious school	Private nonreligious school
DIMENSIONS OF DIVERSITY			
Racial identification			
Monoracial (Ref)		—	—
Mixed race		−0.221	−0.103
Nativity and generation			
Multigenerational native (Ref)		—	—
Second-generation immigrant		0.164	0.122
First-generation immigrant		0.208	0.042
Region of origin			
USA (Ref)			
Africa			
Caribbean			
Other			
Skin tone			
Light (Ref)		—	—
Medium		0.140	−0.046
Dark		−0.409*	−0.076
Gender			
Female (Ref)		—	—
Male		0.117	−0.046
Parental education			
No college degree (Ref)		—	—
College degree		0.186	0.146
Advanced degree		0.084	0.310*
Experience of segregation			
Predominantly White		−0.186	0.095
Racially mixed		−0.933***	−0.843***
Predominantly minority (Ref)		—	—
Minority neighborhood/White school		1.872***	2.643***
Neighborhood disadvantage			
Total disorder/Violence index		−0.015	−0.016
CONTROLS			
Ever in single-parent household		−0.135	0.103
Mother always worked full time		0.241*	0.128
Parents own home		−0.153	−0.354**
Mean annual income		0.003	0.003
Respondent attended Howard		−0.546+	−0.869*
Log-Likelihood χ^2		274.196	274.196

$^{+}p < 0.10$; $^{*}p < 0.05$; $^{**}p < 0.01$; $^{***}p < 0.001$

TABLE A5.4. Predicting level of academic preparation for college (OLS regression models)

Characteristic	Number of AP Tests Taken	High School Course Difficulty	Grade Point Average	SAT Score
DIMENSIONS OF DIVERSITY				
Racial identification				
Monoracial (Ref)	—	—	—	—
Mixed race	0.039	0.015	0.005	18.476
Nativity and generation				
Multigenerational native (Ref)	—	—		—
Second-generation immigrant	0.256	0.182		21.333
First-generation immigrant	0.122	0.300		−0.975
Region of origin				
USA (Ref)			—	
Africa			0.138**	
Caribbean			0.024	
Other			0.018	
Skin tone				
Light (Ref)	—	—	—	—
Medium	−0.163	−0.205	0.013	−30.823*
Dark	−0.210	0.047	−0.011	−33.023+
Gender				
Female (Ref)	—	—	—	—
Male	−0.200	0.221+	−0.092***	−3.107
Parental education				
No college degree (Ref)	—	—	—	—
College degree	0.259	−0.064	0.043	14.363
Advanced degree	0.483*	0.022	0.031	33.252*
Experience of segregation				
Predominantly White	−0.010	0.224	−0.079*	48.532**
Racially mixed	0.154	0.001	−0.091**	20.891
Predominantly minority (Ref)	—	—	—	—
Minority neighborhood/White school	−0.017	0.370+	−0.154***	62.318**
Neighborhood disadvantage				
Total disorder/Violence index	−0.012*	0.002	−0.003*	−1.734**
CONTROLS				
Ever in single-parent household	−0.016	−0.052	−0.014	4.630
Mother always worked full time	−0.156	0.213+	−0.018	−10.200
Parents own home	0.547***	−0.097	0.046	3.472
Mean annual income	0.000	0.002	0.000	0.117
Respondent attended Howard	−1.605***	−0.411+	−0.147**	−83.585**
R-Squared	0.080	0.036	0.068	0.118

$^+ p < 0.10$; $^* p < 0.05$; $^{**} p < 0.01$; $^{***} p < 0.001^*$

TABLE A5.5. Predicting importance of selected factors in college decision making (OLS regression models)

Characteristic	School prestige index	Academic support index	Financial support index
DIMENSIONS OF DIVERSITY			
Racial identification			
Monoracial (Ref)	—	—	—
Mixed	−0.236	−0.403	−0.340
Nativity and generation			
Multigenerational native	—	—	
Second-Generation Immigrant	0.223	0.007	
First-Generation Immigrant	0.011	−0.100	
Region of origin			
USA			—
Africa			0.008
Caribbean			0.689**
Other			−0.869+
Skin tone			
Light	—	—	—
Medium	0.305+	0.448+	−0.310
Dark	0.297+	0.869**	−0.402
Gender			
Female	—	—	—
Male	−0.274*	−0.522**	−0.405*
Parental education			
No college degree (Ref)	—	—	—
College degree	−0.021	0.081	−0.204
Advanced degree	−0.163	−0.329	−0.277
Experience of segregation			
Predominantly White	−0.059	−0.486+	−0.341
Racially mixed	−0.089	−0.110	−0.116
Predominantly minority	—	—	—
Minority neighborhood/White school	−0.056	−0.058	0.154
Neighborhood disadvantage			
Total disorder/Violence index	0.001	0.017*	0.024**
CONTROLS			
Ever in single-parent household	−0.214+	−0.154	0.262
Mother always worked full time	0.037	−0.097	0.391*
Parents own home	−0.012	−0.097	−0.004
Mean annual income	0.001	−0.003	−0.016***
Respondent attended Howard	0.573+	−1.092**	−0.508
R-Squared	0.030	0.062	0.180

+ p < 0.10; * p < 0.05; ** p < 0.01; *** p < 0.001

TABLE A5.6. Predicting importance of selected factors in college decision making (OLS regression models)

Characteristic	Social life index	Racial diversity index	Number of college applications
DIMENSIONS OF DIVERSITY			
Racial identification			
Monoracial (Ref)	—	—	—
Mixed	0.097	−1.652***	−0.221
Nativity and generation			
Multigenerational native	—	—	—
Second-generation immigrant	−0.052	−0.057	0.645+
First-generation immigrant	−0.123	−0.340	1.301**
Region of origin			
USA			
Africa			
Caribbean			
Other			
Skin tone			
Light	—	—	—
Medium	0.003	−0.133	−0.063
Dark	0.324	0.043	0.083
Gender			
Female	—	—	—
Male	0.058	−0.839***	−0.373
Parental wducation			
No college degree (Ref)	—	—	—
College degree	0.062	0.308	−0.299
Advanced degree	0.244	0.428+	0.222
Experience of segregation			
Predominantly White	0.685**	0.161	−0.133
Racially mixed	0.230	0.284	−0.222
Predominantly minority	—	—	—
Minority neighborhood/White school	0.693*	0.966**	0.254
Neighborhood disadvantage			
Total disorder/Violence index	0.007	0.033***	0.013
CONTROLS			
Ever in single-parent household	−0.315+	−0.156	0.410
Mother always worked full time	0.407*	0.242	0.156
Parents own home	−0.016	−0.020	−0.377
Mean annual income	−0.001	0.002	−0.001
Respondent attended Howard	1.225*	1.990***	−1.152*
R-Squared	0.037	0.115	0.064

$^+ p < 0.10$; $^* p < 0.05$; $^{**} p < 0.01$; $^{***} p < 0.001$

TABLE A6.1. Predicting Black and White friendships (OLS regression models)

Characteristic	Number of White friends	Number of Black friends
DIMENSIONS OF DIVERSITY		
Racial identification		
Monoracial (Ref)	—	—
Mixed race	1.291**	−1.830***
Nativity and generation		
Multigenerational native		—
Second-generation immigrant		−1.185***
First-generation immigrant		−0.986***
Region of origin		
USA	—	
Africa	0.112	
Caribbean	0.706**	
Other	−0.287	
Skin tone		
Light	—	—
Medium	−0.443*	0.458+
Dark	−0.328	0.285
Gender		
Female	—	—
Male	0.735***	−0.871***
Parental education		
No college degree (Ref)	—	—
College degree	−0.101	0.319
Advanced degree	0.200	0.002
Experience of segregation		
Predominantly White	0.680**	−0.669+
Racially mixed	0.254	−0.064
Predominantly minority	—	—
Minority neighborhood/White school	0.364	0.077
Neighborhood disadvantage		
Total disorder/Violence index	−0.033***	0.034*
CONTROLS		
Ever in single-parent household	−0.029	0.167
Mother always worked full time	−0.063	0.287
Parents own home	0.078	−0.361
Mean annual income	0.005	0.002
Respondent attended Howard	−2.074***	3.500***
R-Squared	0.176	0.213

$^+ p < 0.10$; $^* p < 0.05$; $^{**} p < 0.01$; $^{***} p < 0.001$

TABLE A6.2. Predicting intergroup dating behavior (simple logit models)

Characteristic	Ever dated outside group	Ever dated White person
DIMENSIONS OF DIVERSITY		
Racial identification		
Monoracial (Ref)	—	
Mixed	0. 258***	0.552**
Nativity and generation		
Multigenerational native		
Second-generation immigrant	0.112	−0.123
First-generation immigrant	0.141	0.336
Region of origin		
USA		
Africa		
Caribbean		
Other		
Skin tone		
Light	—	
Medium	0.153	0.079
Dark	−0.116	−0.125
Gender		
Female	—	
Male	0.453***	0.412***
Parental education		
No college degree (Ref)	—	
College degree	−0.042	−0.130
Advanced degree	0.075	0.118
Experience of segregation		
Predominantly White	0.139	0.226
Racially mixed	0.047	−0.025
Predominantly minority	—	—
Minority neighborhood/White school	0.013	0.229
Neighborhood disadvantage		
Total disorder/Violence index	−0.004	−0.022**
CONTROLS		
Ever in single-parent household	0.055	0.005
Mother always worked full time	−0.194*	−0.125
Parents own home	0.036	0.046
Mean annual income	0.000	0.000
Respondent attended Howard	−0.324	−0.116
Log-likelihood χ2	126.376	124.222

$^+ p < 0.10;$ $^* p < 0.05;$ $^{**} p < 0.01;$ $^{***} p < 0.001$

TABLE A6.3. Predicting organizational memberships (simple logit models)

Characteristic	In majority-Black group	In race-themed group
DIMENSIONS OF DIVERSITY		
Racial identification		
Monoracial (Ref)	—	—
Mixed race	−0.295**	0.101
Nativity and generation		
Multigenerational native	—	
Second-generation immigrant	−0.257**	
First-generation immigrant	0.113	
Region of origin		
USA		—
Africa		−0.310
Caribbean		0.505*
Other		−0.057
Skin tone		
Light	—	—
Medium	0.001	0.053
Dark	0.168	0.152
Gender		
Female	—	—
Male	−0.258***	−0.044
Parental education		
No college degree (Ref)	—	—
College degree	0.024	−0.105
Advanced degree	−0.027	0.238[+]
Experience of segregation		
Predominantly White	−0.122	−0.367*
Racially mixed	−0.01	−0.123
Predominantly minority	—	—
Minority neighborhood/White school	−0.079	−0.084
Neighborhood disadvantage		
Total disorder/Violence index	0.008	−0.004
CONTROLS		
Ever in single-parent household	−0.017	−0.073
Mother always worked full time	−0.121[+]	−0.065
Parents own home	0.016	−0.008
Mean annual income	0.001	−0.002
Respondent attended Howard	0.325*	−0.153
Log-Likelihood χ2	61.123	45.425

[+] $p < 0.10$; * $p < 0.05$; ** $p < 0.01$; *** $p < 0.001$

TABLE A6.4. Predicting group visibilities on campus (OLS regression models)

Characteristic	Visibility of Blacks on campus	Visibility of Whites on campus
DIMENSIONS OF DIVERSITY		
Racial identification		
Monoracial (Ref)	—	—
Mixed eace	−0.042	−0.140
Nativity and generation		
Multigenerational native	—	—
Second-generation immigrant	−0.255	0.005
First-generation immigrant	−0.169	0.239
Region of origin		
USA		
Africa		
Caribbean		
Other		
Skin tone		
Light	—	—
Medium	−0.469+	−0.081
Dark	−0.542	0.014
Gender		
Female	—	—
Male	−0.041	−0.421**
Parental education		
No college degree (Ref)	—	—
College degree	0.109	−0.048
Advanced degree	−0.118	0.180
Experience of segregation		
Predominantly White	−0.153	−0.033
Racially mixed	−0.282	0.024
Predominantly minority	—	—
Minority neighborhood/White school	−0.449	0.009
Neighborhood disadvantage		
Total disorder/Violence index	−0.011	0.017*
CONTROLS		
Ever in single-parent household	−0.185	0.329+
Mother always worked full time	0.010	0.131
Parents own home	0.236	0.021
Mean annual income	0.000	−0.001
Respondent attended Howard	2.8530***	−5.111***
R-squared	0.070	0.274

+ p < 0.10; * p < 0.05; ** p < 0.01; *** p < 0.001

TABLE A6.5. Predicting intergroup interactions (OLS regression models)

Characteristic	Intensity of interactions with Blacks	Intensity of interactions with Whites	Quality of interaction with Whites	Racial separation on campus
DIMENSIONS OF DIVERSITY				
Racial identification				
Monoracial (Ref)	—	—	—	—
Mixed race	−0.756**	0.329	0.190	−0.028
Nativity and generation				
Multigenerational native	—	—	—	—
Second-generation immigrant	−0.309	−0.063	−0.283	0.013
First-generation immigrant	−0.013	−0.727*	−0.198	0.135
Region of origin				
USA				
Africa				
Caribbean				
Other				
Skin tone				
Light	—	—	—	—
Medium	0.236	−0.098	−0.105	0.032
Dark	0.232	0.224	−0.119	−0.005
Gender				
Female	—	—	—	—
Male	−0.413	0.006	0.185	−0.116
Parental education				
No college degree (Ref)	—			—
College degree	−0.302	−0.073	−0.188	−0.069
Advanced degree	−0.260	0.057	−0.146	0.012
Experience of segregation				
Predominantly White	−0.352+	0.429+	−0.148	−0.035
Racially mixed	0.010	0.013	0.078	0.056
Predominantly minority	—			—
Minority neighborhood/White school	0.016	0.044	0.157	0.262+
Neighborhood disadvantage				
Total disorder/Violence index	0.001	−0.020**	−0.012	0.002
CONTROLS				
Ever in single-parent household	−0.063	−0.075	0.141	0.286*
Mother always worked full time	0.087	0.144	0.114	−0.087
Parents own home	−0.269	−0.098	−0.087	0.088
Mean annual income	0.002	−0.001	0.002	0.001
Respondent attended Howard	1.056*	−1.955***	0.985**	−1.373***
R-squared	0.082	0.095	0.027	0.093

+ p < 0.10; * p < 0.05; ** p < 0.01; *** p < 0.001

TABLE A6.6. Predicting perceived institutional commitment to diversity
(multinomial logit model)

Characteristic	Just right (Ref)	Too little	Too much
DIMENSIONS OF DIVERSITY			
Racial identification			
Monoracial (Ref)		—	—
Mixed race		−0.070	0.154
Nativity and generation			
Multigenerational native			
Second-generation immigrant		−0.117	0.192
First-generation immigrant		0.190	−0.075
Region of origin			
USA			
Africa			
Caribbean			
Other			
Skin tone			
Light		—	—
Medium		0.107	0.120
Dark		0.113	−0.196
Gender			
Female		—	—
Male		−0.138+	0.061
Parental education			
No college degree (Ref)		—	—
College degree		0.142	0.436*
Advanced degree		−0.122	−0.264
Experience of segregation			
Predominantly White		0.093	0.111
Racially mixed		−0.001	−0.070
Predominantly minority		—	—
Minority neighborhood/White school		0.0708	−0.559
Neighborhood disadvantage			
Total disorder/Violence index		0.012+	−0.006
CONTROLS			
Ever in single-parent household		0.017	−0.019
Mother always worked full time		−0.068	−0.150
Parents own home		0.012	0.229+
Mean annual income		−0.001	−0.002
Respondent attended Howard		−0.308	−0.348
Log-likelihood χ2		68.937	68.937

+ p < 0.10; * p < 0.05; ** p < 0.01; *** p < 0.001

TABLE A7.1. Predicting perceptions of racial prejudice on campus (OLS regression models)

Characteristic	Mean incidents of prejudice	Mean frequency of prejudice
DIMENSIONS OF DIVERSITY		
Racial identification		
Monoracial (Ref)	—	—
Mixed race	−1.028	−0.037
Nativity and generation		
Multigenerational native	—	—
Second-generation immigrant	0.636	0.029
First-generation immigrant	0.101	0.000
Region of origin		
USA		
Africa		
Caribbean		
Other		
Skin tone		
Light	—	—
Medium	0.469	0.002
Dark	0.682	0.005
Gender		
Female	—	—
Male	−0.025	−0.008
Parental education		
No college degree (Ref)	—	—
College degree	−0.104	−0.001
Advanced degree	0.978	0.042
Experience of segregation		
Predominantly White	−1.000	−0.045
Racially mixed	1.937*	0.064[+]
Predominantly minority	—	—
Minority neighborhood/White school	2.378[+]	0.078
Neighborhood disadvantage		
Total disorder/Violence index	0.239***	0.008***
CONTROLS		
Ever in single-parent household	0.811	0.030
Mother always worked full time	−0.595	−0.019
Parents own home	−0.189	−0.009
Mean annual income	0.015	0.002*
Respondent attended Howard	−10.873***	−0.385***
R-squared	0.126	0.112

[+] $p < 0.10$; * $p < 0.05$; ** $p < 0.01$; *** $p < 0.001$

TABLE A7.2. Predicting race-based and family-based performance burdens
(OLS regression models)

Characteristic	Race-based performance burden	Family-based performance burden
DIMENSIONS OF DIVERSITY		
Racial identification		
Monoracial (Ref)	—	—
Mixed	−0.176	−0.489*
Nativity and generation		
Multigenerational native		—
Second-generation immigrant		0.392*
First-generation immigrant		0.517*
Region of origin		
USA	—	
Africa	0.372*	
Caribbean	0.199	
Other	0.127	
Skin tone		
Light	—	—
Medium	0.043	0.024
Dark	0.089	0.436*
Gender		
Female	—	—
Male	−0.016	−0.075
Parental education		
No college degree (Ref)	—	—
College degree	−0.065	−0.081
Advanced degree	0.092	0.255
Experience of segregation		
Predominantly White	−0.144	0.063
Racially mixed	−0.031	0.115
Predominantly minority	—	—
Minority neighborhood/White school	0.179	0.408
Neighborhood disadvantage		
Total disorder/Violence index	−0.302	0.239
CONTROLS		
Ever in single-parent household	0.150	0.071
Mother always worked full time	−0.121	0.291*
Parents own home	0.010	0.115
Mean annual income	0.002*	0.002
Respondent attended Howard	−0.302	−0.239
R-squared	0.046	0.115

$^+ p < 0.10$; $^* p < 0.05$; $^{**} p < 0.01$; $^{***} p < 0.001$

Note: For Family-Based Performance Burden, Region of Origin also significant, with Africa = 0.600*, Caribbean = 0.502*, and Other = 0.319 ns, and other coefficients largely unchanged.

TABLE A7.3. Predicting stressful life events in respondent social networks
(OLS regression models)

Characteristic	Mean number of stressful life events	Weighted stressful life events score
DIMENSIONS OF DIVERSITY		
Racial identification		
Monoracial (Ref)	—	—
Mixed Race	0.203	6.522
Nativity and generation		
Multigenerational nNative	—	—
Second-generation immigrant	−0.272	−13.244
First-generation immigrant	0.082	−8.559
Region of origin		
USA		
Africa		
Caribbean		
Other		
Skin tone		
Light	—	—
Medium	−0.014	2.155
Dark	−0.110	1.097
Gender		
Female	—	—
Male	0.047	3.406
Parental education		
No college degree (Ref)	—	—
College degree	−0.605+	−33.703+
Advanced degree	−0.358	−17.563
Experience of segregation		
Predominantly White	0.222	5.150
Racially mixed	0.242	8.964
Predominantly minority	—	—
Minority neighborhood/White school	0.357	19.945
Neighborhood disadvantage		
Total disorder/Violence index	0.074***	3.150***
CONTROLS		
Ever in single-parent household	0.914**	32.464*
Mother always worked full time	−0.631*	−27.523*
Parents own home	−0.466	−18.028
Mean annual income	−0.005	−0.218
Respondent attended Howard	−0.391	−15.959
R-squared	0.115	0.090

+ $p < 0.10$; * $p < 0.05$; ** $p < 0.01$; *** $p < 0.001$

TABLE A7.4. Predicting sense of loss and stopping out of college (OLS and logit model)

Characteristic	Sense of loss index (OLS)	Transferred or took time off (Logit)
DIMENSIONS OF DIVERSITY		
Racial identification		
Monoracial (Ref)	—	—
Mixed race	0.464	0.038
Nativity and generation		
Multigenerational native	—	—
Second-generation immigrant	2.553*	0.132
First-generation immigrant	1.799	−0.170
Region of origin		
USA		
Africa		
Caribbean		
Other		
Skin tone		
Light	—	—
Medium	0.153	0.050
Dark	−0.234	0.106
Gender		
Female	—	—
Male	1.100	−0.099
Parental education		
No college degree (ref)	—	—
College degree	−0.974	0.061
Advanced degree	−2.175+	−0.194
Experience of segregation		
Predominantly White	−1.673	0.069
Racially mixed	−1.979	−0.028
Predominantly minority	—	—
Minority neighborhood/White school	−0.160	−0.115
Neighborhood disadvantage		
Total disorder/Violence index	0.105**	0.007
CONTROLS		
Ever in single-parent household	0.191	0.029
Mother always worked full time	−0.460	0.079
Parents own home	0.204	−0.044
Mean annual income	−0.007	0.001
Respondent attended Howard	−2.114	−0.221
R-Squared/Log-Likelihood χ^2	0.061	7.362

$^+ p < 0.10; \; ^* p < 0.05; \; ^{**} p < 0.01; \; ^{***} p < 0.001$

TABLE A7.5. Predicting total accumulated student debt (OLS regression model)

Characteristic	Total Accumulated Debt (Dollars)
DIMENSIONS OF DIVERSITY	
Racial identification	
Monoracial (Ref)	—
Mixed race	2,649.12
Nativity and generation	
Multigenerational native	—
Second-generation immigrant	1,067.91
First-generation immigrant	−1,032.83
Region of origin	
USA	
Africa	
Caribbean	
Other	
Skin tone	
Light	—
Medium	−136.13
Dark	3,103.30
Gender	
Female	—
Male	−210.33
Parental education	
No college degree (Ref)	—
College degree	2,593.98
Advanced degree	52.59
Experience of segregation	
Predominantly White	2,046.72
Racially mixed	3,868.20
Predominantly minority	—
Minority neighborhood/White school	7,599.34
Neighborhood disadvantage	
Total disorder/Violence index	144.90
CONTROLS	
Ever in single-parent household	1,648.45
Mother always worked full time	2,977.62
Parents own home	2,321.69
Mean annual income	0.74
Respondent attended Howard	3,450.01
R-squared	0.031

$+ p < 0.10$; $^{*} p < 0.05$; $^{**} p < 0.01$; $^{***} p < 0.001$

TABLE A7.6. Center for Epidemiologic Studies Depression Index score
(OLS regression model)

Characteristic	CES-D Depression Index Score
DIMENSIONS OF DIVERSITY	
Racial identification	
Monoracial (Ref)	—
Mixed race	0.013
Nativity and generation	
Multigenerational native	—
Second-generation immigrant	0.113**
First-generation immigrant	0.061
Region of origin	
USA	
Africa	
Caribbean	
Other	
Skin tone	
Light	—
Medium	−0.016
Dark	−0.042
Gender	
Female	—
Male	−0.084**
Parental education	
No college degree (Ref)	—
College degree	−0.088*
Advanced degree	−0.044
Experience of segregation	
Predominantly White	−0.040
Racially mixed	−0.001
Predominantly minority	—
Minority neighborhood/White school	0.071
Neighborhood disadvantage	
Total disorder/Violence index	0.003+
CONTROLS	
Ever in single-parent household	0.021
Mother always worked full time	−0.070*
Parents own home	−0.013
Mean annual income	0.000
Respondent attended Howard	−0.110+
R-squared	0.054

+ p < 0.10; * p < 0.05; ** p < 0.01; *** p < 0.001

Note: Region of Origin Coefficients: Africa = 0.114*, Caribbean = 0.019 (ns), and Other = 0.120+. Other coefficients are largely unchanged.

TABLE A8.1. Predicting most important identity in the senior year (multinomial logit model)

Characteristic	Black and American (Ref)	Black only	American only
DIMENSIONS OF DIVERSITY			
Racial identification			
Monoracial (Ref)		—	—
Mixed		−0.057	0.311+
Nativity and generation			
Multigenerational native (Ref)		—	—
Second-generation immigrant		−0.042	−0.122
First-generation immigrant		−0.076	0.078
Region of origin			
USA (Ref)			
Africa			
Caribbean			
Other			
Skin tone			
Light (Ref)		—	—
Medium		0.151	−0.033
Dark		−0.040	−0.288
Gender			
Female (Ref)		—	—
Male		−0.146	0.399*
Parental education			
No college degree (Ref)		—	—
College degree		0.023	−0.003
Advanced degree		0.012	−0.047
Experience of segregation			
Predominantly White		0.181	0.032
Racially mixed		0.018	−0.102
Predominantly minority (Ref)		—	—
Minority neighborhood/White school		−0.220	0.261
Neighborhood disadvantage			
Total disorder/Violence index		0.016*	−0.004
CONTROLS			
Ever in single-parent household		−0.033	−0.105
Mother always worked full time		−0.036	−0.119
Parents own home		−0.080	−0.109
Mean annual income		0.002	0.003
Respondent attended Howard		−0.189	−0.127
Log-likelihood χ^2		65.506	65.506

+ $p < 0.10$; * $p < 0.05$; ** $p < 0.01$; *** $p < 0.001$

TABLE A8.2. Predicting common fate identity in the senior year (multinomial logit model)

Characteristic	None or a little (Ref)	Some	A lot
DIMENSIONS OF DIVERSITY			
Racial identification			
Monoracial (Ref)		—	—
Mixed race		−0.109	−0.266[+]
Nativity and generation			
Multigenerational native (Ref)		—	—
Second-generation immigrant		0.033	0.292[+]
First-generation immigrant		0.035	−0.158
Region of origin			
USA (Ref)			
Africa			
Caribbean			
Other			
Skin tone			
Light (Ref)		—	—
Medium		0.039	0.055
Dark		0.018	0.013
Gender			
Female (Ref)		—	—
Male		−0.109	−0.182*
Parental education			
No college degree (Ref)		—	—
College degree		−0.040	−0.184
Advanced degree		0.138	0.190
Experience of segregation			
Predominantly White		0.043	−0.089
Racially mixed		−0.117	0.040
Predominantly minority (Ref)		—	—
Minority neighborhood/White school		0.226	0.028
Neighborhood disadvantage			
Total disorder/Violence index		0.005	0.007
CONTROLS			
Ever in single-parent household		0.029	0.008
Mother always worked full time		0.152*	−0.035
Parents own home		0.015	−0.039
Mean annual income		0.002	0.002
Respondent attended Howard		−0.135	0.137
Log-likelihood χ^2		38.545	38.545

[+] $p < 0.10$; * $p < 0.05$; ** $p < 0.01$; *** $p < 0.001$

APPENDIX A   375

TABLE A8.3. Predicting racial attitudes in the senior year (OLS regression models)

Characteristic	Closeness to Whites	White propensity to discriminate	Belief that Blacks should try harder	Belief that Blacks must be more qualified
DIMENSIONS OF DIVERSITY				
Racial identification				
Monoracial (Ref)	—	—	—	—
Mixed race	0.547*	−0.123	0.138	−0.276
Nativity and generation				
Multigenerational native (Ref)	—	—	—	
Second-generation immigrant	−0.141	−0.039	−0.219	
First-generation immigrant	−0.068	−0.070[+]	0.223	
Region of origin				
USA (Ref)				—
Africa				0.806[+]
Caribbean				0.784*
Other				−0.130
Skin tone				
Light (Ref)	—	—	—	—
Medium	−0.293	0.210	0.057	−0.002
Dark	0.119	0.130	−0.191	−0.063
Gender				
Female (Ref)	—	—	—	—
Male	0.456**	−0.150	0.817***	0.292
Parental education				
No college degree (Ref)	—	—	—	—
College degree	−0.027	0.077	0.073	−0.531[+]
Advanced degree	0.035	0.054	−0.159	−0.486
Experience of segregation				
Predominantly White	0.182	−0.087	−0.127	−0.017
Racially mixed	0.190	−0.048	−0.204	−0.008
Predominantly minority (Ref)	—	—	—	—
Minority neighborhood/ White school	0.259	0.078	0.377	0.042
Neighborhood disadvantage				
Total disorder/Violence index	−0.018*	0.009	−0.002	0.009
CONTROLS				
Ever in single-parent household	−0.034	0.007	0.310	−0.025
Mother always worked full time	−0.072	−0.029	0.039	−0.374
Parents own home	0.160	−0.122	0.272	−0.104
Mean annual income	0.001	0.002[+]	−0.001	0.006*
Respondent attended Howard	−0.449	0.335	0.755	0.654
R-squared	0.057	0.034	0.035	0.037

[+] $p < 0.10$; * $p < 0.05$; ** $p < 0.01$; *** $p < 0.001$

TABLE A8.4. Predicting the dimensional indexes of Black identity (OLS regression models)

Characteristic	Racial centrality	Assimilationist ideology	Cultural nationalism	Political nationalism
DIMENSIONS OF DIVERSITY				
Racial identification				
Monoracial (Ref)	—	—	—	—
Mixed race	−1.057***	0.094	−0.940***	−0.464*
Nativity and generation				
Multigenerational native (Ref)	—	—		—
Second-generation immigrant	−0.363*	0.172		0.125
First-generation immigrant	−0.472*	0.225		0.171
Region of origin				
USA (Ref)			—	
Africa			−0.785***	
Caribbean			−0.194	
Other			−0.094	
Skin tone				
Light (Ref)	—	—	—	—
Medium	0.263⁺	−0.151	0.237	0.170
Dark	0.233	−0.133	0.372⁺	−0.057
Gender				
Female (Ref)	—	—	—	—
Male	−0.166	0.167	−0.404**	0.010
Parental education				
No college degree (Ref)	—	—	—	—
College degree	−0.414**	0.020	−0.186	−0.137
Advanced degree	−0.041	−0.140	0.151	0.000
Experience of segregation				
Predominantly White	−0.204	0.047	−0.197	−0.228
Racially mixed	−0.062	0.044	−0.110	−0.041
Predominantly minority (Ref)	—	—	—	—
Minority neighborhood/ White school	0.004	−0.069	−0.136	0.008
Neighborhood disadvantage				
Total disorder/Violence index	0.009⁺	−0.015**	0.015**	0.009⁺
CONTROLS				
Ever in single-parent household	−0.041	−0.084	−0.125	0.142
Mother always worked full time	0.192	0.003	0.129	−0.052
Parents own home	−0.140	0.291*	−0.103	−0.117
Mean annual income	0.001	0.000	0.000	0.001
Respondent attended Howard	0.044	−0.163	0.696*	0.543*
R-squared	0.111	0.043	0.116	0.040

⁺ $p < 0.10$; * $p < 0.05$; ** $p < 0.01$; *** $p < 0.001$

TABLE A9.1. Predicting college persistence, GPA, and graduation (OLS and logit models)

Characteristic	Transferred or took time off (Logit)	Grade point average (OLS)	Graduated in four years (Logit)	Graduated in six years (Logit)
DIMENSIONS OF DIVERSITY				
Racial identification				
Monoracial (Ref)	—	—	—	—
Mixed race	−0.057	0.061	0.219*	0.145
Nativity and generation				
Multigenerational native (Ref)	—	—		—
Second-generation immigrant	−0.076	0.030	−0.204	−0.315
First-generation immigrant	−0.072	0.028	0.305	0.366
Region of origin				
USA (Ref)				
Africa				
Caribbean				
Other				
Skin tone				
Light (Ref)	—	—	—	—
Medium	0.151	0.012	0.068	0.001
Dark	−0.040	−0.021	−0.034	−0.107
Gender				
Female (Ref)	—	—	—	—
Male	−0.146	−0.050	0.038	0.131
Parental education				
No college degree (Ref)	—	—	—	—
College degree	0.023	−0.011	0.059	0.086
Advanced degree	0.012	0.027	0.009	−0.050
Experience of segregation				
Predominantly White	0.181	0.045	−0.082	0.041
Racially mixed	0.018	−0.007	0.064	0.068
Predominantly minority (Ref)	—	—	—	—
Minority neighborhood/ White school	−0.220	0.007	0.053	0.195
Neighborhood disadvantage				
Total disorder/Violence index	0.016*	0.000	0.007	0.005
CONTROLS				
Ever in single-parent household	−0.033	−0.014	−0.088	−0.068
Mother always worked full time	−0.036	−0.009	0.044	0.099
Parents own home	−0.080	−0.004	0.005	0.106
Mean annual income	0.002	0.001	0.002	−0.001
Respondent attended Howard	−0.189	0.063	0.462*	0.118
R-squared or Log-likelihood χ^2	65.506	0.035	20.717	14.381

$^+$p < 0.10; * p < 0.05; ** p < 0.01; *** p < 0.001

APPENDIX B

Interview Guide

PERCEPTIONS OF RACE AND RACIAL
IDENTITY FORMATION

Lead in:

My name is Kim Torres and I am a Research Associate here at [official name of university] developing an in-depth, interview-based study of Black and White students' experiences at predominantly White colleges and universities. I am contacting you because I would like to talk with you about your experiences here at [school's short name]. I am specifically interested in (1) understanding factors leading to your decision to apply to and attend [institution name], (2) what your social and academic experiences have been like since you have been here, (3) your feelings about the racial climate and [institution name], (4) relevant issues regarding the way you believe race impacts on students' experiences here, and (5) your attitudes and opinions about race and the formation of racial identity in contemporary America. This research is connected with research I am doing on the National Longitudinal Study of Freshmen (NLSF) with Professors Douglas Massey and Camille Charles. Dr. Massey is Professor of Sociology and Public Affairs at Princeton and Dr. Charles is Professor of Sociology and Africana Studies at the University of Pennsylvania.

Of course, everything you tell me will be kept confidential. In order to do that, I request that each participant pick a pseudonym. That way, no one except me will know your true identity. If I would like to use any of the information from our conversation, I will always ask your permission before doing so. I understand that your time is valuable. I would like to meet with you for approximately 1.5 to 2 hours. If you like, we can schedule one meeting and finish the entire interview then; or if you prefer, we can break the interview into two parts—each one hour long. I really appreciate your time and participation for this study.

So that I can better concentrate on what you are saying, I'd like to tape-record our conversation. However, if you would prefer that I take notes instead, that is fine, too. Also, if you would like me to turn off the tape recorder for any reason at any time during our conversation, please say so. All identifying information will be taken off the tape when it is transcribed, and nobody but me and my research assistant will know your true identity.

Do you have any questions?

Okay, let's start.

Section I. Introduction

For Everyone:

To begin, would you mind telling me a little bit about yourself? (Probe for class year, age, major, ethnic/racial composition, family, and national origins)

Family and national origins (i.e., Were both your parents born in the United States? What are their racial/national origins?)

Section II. Family Background

Now, if you could tell me a little bit about your family . . . (i.e., family structure, parents' professions and education, number of siblings and siblings' ages, religious background)

Growing up, did you live with both your parents? (If not, who did you grow up with? Are your parents married?)

What do your parents do for a living? (i.e., present and past jobs/careers. How long have they been at their respective jobs?)

What is your mom's highest level of education? What is your dad's highest level of education? (e.g., type of degree, training and experience, and where attended)

Do you have any brothers? Sisters? If so, how many siblings do you have and what are their ages?

(For siblings >18 years old, probe for whether or not attended college/post-secondary training. If any of siblings are currently enrolled in college, ask for name of college and type of degree they are going for.)

How would you classify your family's social class background when you were growing up? (Give your opinion of your family's social class status.)

Section III. Community and Neighborhood

Now could you tell me a little bit about the community and neighborhood that you grew up in? (i.e., state, region of country, length of time living there, racial/ethnic background, social class of neighborhood/surrounding community)

Where did you spend the majority of your childhood? Is that different from where you're living now? (If you lived in more than one place, provide information about each community/neighborhood lived in until start of college.)

What kinds of jobs/professions do your neighbors and the people who live in your neighborhood and surrounding community have?

How would you classify the social class background of the people who live in your neighborhood and surrounding community? What makes you say that? (What are your opinions about the social class status of neighborhood and community?)

Section IV. High School

Where did you go to high school? Was your school public, private, or religiously affiliated? How many years did you go there for? (If more than one high school, provide specifics of each.)

Approximately how many students attended your high school?

What were the students like who went to your high school? (i.e., race and class background of the students)

Roughly, what percentage of the students at your high school were White/Black/Latino/Asian/Other? Do you think your high school was racially diverse?

Was the racial composition of your high school similar to the racial composition of the middle and elementary schools you attended? If not, how were they different?

What kinds of classes did you take in high school? Did your high school offer advanced placement and honors classes? How many (if any) Honors/APs did you take? Which AP classes did you take? How many AP exams (and which ones were they) did you score at least 4 or higher on?

Were there students of color in your classes? In a typical class, how many Black students were in your classes? (What was the average size of a typical high school class that you were in?) What about other racial and ethnic groups?

What was your GPA when you graduated from high school? Do you think you were a good student? Why/Why not? Do you think that your high school prepared you well for [institution name]? Do you think your grades accurately represented your abilities? (Why/Why not?)

Of your high school friends, how many went to college? Are they attending schools similar to [institution name]? In general, what kinds of colleges/universities did students from your high school end up at?

How many close friends did you have in high school? How would you describe the racial/ethnic backgrounds of your close high school friends? That is, how many of your high school friends were Black/White/Latino/Asian/Other? (Note: "Friends" as defined by those you felt "closest" to and socialized with regularly outside of class.)

Name three things that you especially liked about your high school. Now, if you could, name three things that you did not like about your high school. (Describe the quality of academic and social experiences.)

On a scale of 1 to 10 (ten being the highest), how would you rate your high school experience overall? Academically? Socially?

Section V. College Decision Making

What colleges and universities did you apply to besides [institution name]?

How many of these colleges and universities accepted you for admission? (Please list the schools that they were accepted to.)

What are the primary factors that convinced you to apply to [institution name]? (Reasons such as school prestige, financial aid, region of country, school environment, family motivation, type of student body, athletics, academic rigor)

So if you were going to list the three most important factors that contributed to your college decision-making process—as far as the colleges that you decided to apply to—what would those factors be?

What are the primary factors that actually convinced you to enroll at [institution name]? So if you were going to list the three most important factors that contributed to your decision to enroll here, what would they be?

Section VI. Adjusting to College Life

What was it like for you when you first came to [institution name]? (Your initial social and academic experiences)

What was your first impression of [institution name]? (Probe for impressions about student body and social experiences.)

Now can you tell me about three things that surprised you the most when you first came here? Why do you think you were so surprised by these things?

What did you most like about coming to [institution name]? What did you least like about [institution name] when you first got here? Have your opinions changed since you've been here? Why/Why not?

How have you found it adjusting to college life? Have there been times when you have felt uncomfortable/out of place? If so, can you describe a specific incident/occasion that you felt uncomfortable/out of place since you have been here? Have you become more comfortable since you have been here? Why/Why not? What was the hardest part to adjusting to college life?

Did you (do you) ever talk to your friends about the difficulties of adjusting to college? If so, specifically what did you (do you) talk about?

Have you noticed friends/associates who may have had a more difficult time adjusting to college? Why do you think some students have a harder time adjusting to [institution name] than others?

How would you describe the student body at [institution name]? (Your impressions of racial, class backgrounds of students)

Are [institution name]'s students similar to students that attended your high school and/or lived in your community? (Ask for pertinent similarities/differences.)

What is your GPA at [institution name] thus far?

Do you consider your performance to be on par to others around you? (Why/Why not?)

Do you ever feel like you (as a Black student) have to work "extra" hard to prove to your professors, friends, and classmates that you are as qualified to be here? If so, can you describe a specific occasion when you felt this way?

What are your opinions about affirmative action and other race-sensitive admissions policies? Do you think affirmative action is a good/bad policy to have at a place like [institution name]? What makes you say that?

Section VII. Socializing, Campus Activities, and Race Relations

What kinds of campus activities/organizations are you involved in? What influenced your decision to join or partake in these activities/organizations? Is it important for you to participate in activities that are oriented toward your racial/ethnic group?

What kinds of social activities do you do on the weekends? Describe a typical weekend.

Do you attend parties where drinking is a main contributing element for socializing? What are the main elements of the parties/social events that you go to? Is there dancing? Drinking? Smoking? Talking?

What is your general impression of how students socialize at [institution name]? Do students from different racial and ethnic backgrounds hang out together? What about the people that you hang out with? If your opinion is that students of different racial and ethnic backgrounds do not socialize together, why do you think that is so?

Would you say that most of your college friends are from your same racial/ethnic/cultural background? How about your five closest friends? How many of them are Black/White/Latino/Asian/Other? Are any of them biracial/multiracial?

Please list the primary ways that you have met your college friends.

Do you think that students from different racial/ethnic backgrounds have different ways of socializing? (Why/Why not?) If so, list three differences in how Blacks and Whites socialize on campus.

Do you think there is much social separation between students from different racial/ethnic backgrounds at [institution name]? Why/Why not?

Do you think it is difficult to meet students from different racial/ethnic backgrounds? What makes it easy/difficult?

How would you describe the racial/ethnic backgrounds of the students who live in your residence hall/dorm? Did you want to live with students of your own racial/ethnic/cultural background?

For Black/Multiracial Students:

What kinds of resources/activities are there for Black students at [institution name]? Are you involved in any of these? Are some of these organizations/activities more popular than others? What makes them more or less popular, do you think? What affected your decision to partake in some of these organizations/activities?

Do you think that having on-campus living arrangements for Black/Latin/Asian, etc. students would be a good idea to have at [institution name]? Would you like to live in one at [institution name]?

In your opinion, do you think that Black students at [institution name] are tightly knit? Why/Why not? Do you think race brings people closer together here?

Section VIII. Perceptions of the Racial Climate

How would you describe the racial climate at [institution name]? Is it different from how you envisioned it before you enrolled here? If so, how?

Do you think there is a lot of racism and/or prejudice here? Why/Why not?

Have you personally experienced racism and/or prejudice since you have been here?

If so, describe an occasion when you think you personally experienced racism.

Do you think students from different racial/ethnic backgrounds get along here? Have there been any incidents that lead you to believe that students may not be getting along?

How do you think you are perceived by Black students at [institution name]? Do you think that you are easily accepted by other Black students? What makes you say that? (Please provide specifics.)

Do you feel close to other Black students at [institution name]? Yes/No? Biracial/Multiracial students? Do you think you are accepted more by Black students, White students, or other biracial/multiracial students? What makes you say that? Does that hold true for when you are not on campus as well? How so?

Have you seen any conflicts within the Black community at [institution name] about race issues?

Have you seen any conflicts within the White community at [institution name] about race issues?

Do students of different racial/ethnic/cultural backgrounds date each other here? If so, is it common for Black students to date White students? Are Black males more likely to date White females, or vice versa? How is interracial dating perceived by the Black student community (White student community)? Biracials/Multiracials?

What do you think it means to be Black (and a Black man) at [institution name]? What do you think it means to be White at [institution name]? What do you think it means to be biracial/multiracial at [institution name]?

Do students from different racial/ethnic backgrounds talk together about the racial climate on campus? Do they talk about issues related to race and racial identity at all? If so, what do they talk about?

Do you wish that you could socialize more with students from different racial/ethnic backgrounds? What do you think is the biggest barrier to socializing with students from different racial/ethnic backgrounds? What about biracial/multiracial students?

How do you think one's racial/ethnic background figures into one's experiences at [institution name]?

What is your major? Are there few/some/quite a few Black and other students of color in your major? Was your decision to major in _____ affected by the racial diversity of the students in that major?

Section IX. Race Attitudes in Contemporary America

What do you think it means to be Black (to be a Black man) in contemporary America? What do you think it means to be White? Describe for me an average Black person living in America today. White person? (Probe for gender, racial, class, etc. differences.)

What do you think are some of the most popular stereotypes about Black people? What about White people? Have your opinions of Black/White people changed since you've been at [institution name]? Why/Why not?

How do racial stereotypes/perceptions about Black people affect Black/biracial/multiracial people at [institution name] and beyond? (Probe for which stereotypes are most salient as well.)

How would you describe race relations today? As far as your everyday (not on-campus and away from the community) experiences, do you notice differences in the ways Blacks and Whites are treated? Ways that they get along? (Provide specifics.)

Does social class factor into how Blacks and Whites get along today? If so, how?

What role do you think ethnicity plays in your life? Do you think ethnicity is important to how you define yourself? Why/Why not? For Black/multiracial students: How does your ethnicity differentiate you from other Black/multiracial students here?

Section X. Culture Shock
[Only Implemented at Urban Ivy]

Have you ever heard the term *culture shock* before? If yes, when did you hear the term before and in what context?

How would you define the term *culture shock*?

Do you think you have ever experienced culture shock? If so, when do you think you experienced culture shock?

Did you experience culture shock when you first came to [institution name]? (Probe for whether respondent is still experiencing culture shock.)

Have you heard your friends talk about culture shock since you have been at [institution name]? If so, how have they used the term? (If no longer experiencing culture shock, probe for ways in which he/she was able to "get over it.")

Why do you think some students experience culture shock and others do not?

What kind of impact do you think culture shock has on your experience (or other Black students' experiences) at [institution name]?

What do you think are some of the "symptoms" or "telltale" signs that somebody is experiencing culture shock?

Section XI. Social Class

How important do you think social class factors into students' experiences here?

Do you think that it is easier to fit in if you are from a wealthier background? Do students talk about social class? If so, how do they talk about social class and in what context is it discussed?

Are you receiving financial aid right now? Have you received financial aid at [institution name] since you have been enrolled here? How much of your tuition is paid through scholarships? Loans? Other types of funding? (Please provide a specific breakdown of [institution name] grants, loans, scholarships, work study, family contribution, student contribution, etc.)

Do you have a campus job? If so, how many hours a week do you work? Is that part of your financial aid package at [institution name]?

Section XII. Conclusion

And, last, how would you rate your college experience overall? (On a scale of 1–10) Academically? Socially? What makes you give those ratings?

Thank you for your participation. It is greatly appreciated. Is there anything else that you would like to add?

If there's anything else you would like to talk about, please feel free to contact me via email or phone. [Email and phone numbers given]

Table of Qualitative Sample of Black Students Interviewed in Conjunction with the National Longitudinal Survey of Freshmen

TABLE C1. Characteristics of qualitative sample of Black students interviewed in conjunction with the NLSF

Name	Year	Nativity	Race	Country or region
Men (N = 40)				
Thomas	JR	Native	Mono	USA
Carl	SR	Native	Mono	USA
Chris	JR	Native	Mono	USA
Darryl	JR	Native	Mono	USA
Jeff	SR	Native	Mono	USA
Trenton	SO	Native	Mono	USA
Richard*	JR	2nd gen	Mono	Jamaica
Ervin	FR	2nd gen	Mono	Ghana
Calvin	SR	2nd gen	Mono	Nigeria
Bob	SO	2nd gen	Mono	Ghana
Tim*	FR	2nd gen	Mono	Kenya
Doug*	SO	Int.	Mono	Ghana
Albert	SR	2nd gen	Mono	Jamaica/Trinidad
Brian	JR	2nd gen	Mono	Jamaica
Devon	SO	2nd gen	Mono	Jamaica/Barbados
Eugene	JR	Native	Mono	USA
James	JR	Native	Mono	USA
Sean	FR	Native	Mono	USA
Greg*	SO	2nd gen	Mono	Ghana
George*	SR	1st gen	Mono	Trinidad/Guyana
John	JR	2nd gen	Mono	Bermuda/Jamaica
LJ	JR	2nd gen	Mono	Jamaica

Notes: Richard should be a senior but took a leave of absence; Tim had a scholarship; Doug is international, lived and attended school in Ghana and self-identified class status is for Ghana; Greg was born in England and had working-class Whites in his high school; George was born in Canada and had other Black immigrants in his neighborhood.

Neighborhood racial composition	High school racial composition	High school type	Self-reported social class status
< 30% Black	< 30% Black	Private	Middle
< 30% Black	< 30% Black	Private	Upper middle
> 70% Black	Mixed B/L	Public	Working
> 70% Black	< 30% Black	Boarding/P4P	Poor
50-50 B/W	50-50 B/W	Public	Lower middle
Integrated	< 30% Black	Private	Middle
> 70% Black	> 70% Black	Public	Working/Poor
< 30% Black	< 30% Black	Public	Upper middle
> 70% Black	< 30% Black	Private/P4P	
< 30% Black	< 30% Black	Boarding	Upper middle
> 70% Black	< 30% Black	Private	Lower middle
> 70% Black	> 70% Black	Boarding	Middle
> 70% Black	Mixed	Public	Upper
< 30% Black	< 30% Black	Public	Lower middle
< 30% Black	< 30% Black	Public	Upper middle
> 70% Black	Mixed B/W	Public charter	Lower middle
< 30% Black	< 30% Black	Private	Upper
> 70% Black	> 70% Black	Public charter	Lower middle
> 70% Black	< 30% Black	Public	Lower middle
Mixed	< 30% Black	Public/Private	Middle
< 30% Black	< 30% Black	Private	Middle
> 70% Black	> 70% Black	Public	Working

TABLE C1. Characteristics of qualitative sample of Black students interviewed in conjunction with the NLSF (*continued*)

Name	Year	Nativity	Race	Country or region
Malik	SR	2nd gen	Mono	Ghana
Mikal	SR	2nd gen	Mono	Sierra Leone
Troy	SR	2nd gen	Mono	Ghana
Andrew	FR	Native	Mixed/W	USA
Bruce*	SO	Native	Mixed	USA
Harrison	SR	Native	Mixed/W	USA
Jake	JR	Native	Mixed/W	USA
Mark	FR	Native	Mixed/W	USA
Kareem*	FR	2nd gen	Mixed	Barbados
Aaron	JR		Mixed/W	Canada
Adam	JR	2nd gen	Mixed/W	Algeria
Alex	SO	2nd gen	Mixed/W	Nigeria
Blaise	JR	Native	Mixed/W	USA
Brad	JR	2nd gen	Mixed/W	Morocco
Christian*	JR	Int.	Mixed/W	Cape Verde
Chris	SR	2nd gen	Mixed/W	Dominica
Jacob*	SR	Native	Mixed/W	USA
Jay	SO	Int.	Mixed/W	Belgium/Rwanda

Notes: Bruce's non-Black parent is Filipino and Italian; Kareem's non-Black parent is Puerto Rican and Barbadian; Christian's self-identified class status is for Cape Verde; Jacob's mom is second-generation Cape Verde and father is Irish.

Neighborhood racial composition	High school racial composition	High school type	Self-reported social class status
< 30% Black	< 30% Black	Public	Upper Middle
> 70% Black	> 70% Black	Public	Middle
> 70% Black	> 70% Black	Parochial	Poor
> 70% Black	> 70% Black	Public	Working
< 30% Black	< 30% Black	Private	Upper middle
> 70% Black	< 30% Black	Private	Middle
< 30% Black	< 30% Black	Boarding	Upper middle
< 30% Black	< 30% Black	Private	Upper middle
> 70% Black	< 30% Black	Boarding/ABC	Poor
Mixed/W	< 30% Black	Public	Middle
Mixed	< 30% Black	Public	Upper middle
Mixed	Mixed	Public	Middle
< 30% Black	< 30% Black	Public magnet	Upper middle
> 70% Black	Mixed	Public magnet	Poor/Working
> 70% Black	Mixed	1 year US HS	Middle
> 70% Black	< 30% Black	Private	Middle
< 30% Black	< 30% Black	Private	Upper
Mixed	Mixed	Private (US)	Upper

TABLE C1. Characteristics of qualitative sample of Black students interviewed in conjunction with the NLSF (*continued*)

Name	Year	Nativity	Race	Country or region
Women (N = 38)				
Tiffany	SR	Native	Mono	USA
Shana	FR	Native	Mono	USA
Karen	SR	Native	Mono	USA
Destiny	SR	2nd gen	Mono	Belize
Kara	SR	2nd gen	Mono	Nigeria
Madison	SO	2nd gen	Mono	Trinidad/Belize
Miranda	SO	2nd gen	Mono	Ghana
Samantha	SO	2nd gen	Mono	Jamaica/Dominica
Eugena	SO	2nd gen	Mono	Nigeria
Agnes	SO	2nd gen	Mono	Belize
Ashley*	SR	1st gen	Mono	Jamaica
Denise*	SR	Native	Mono	USA
Julie	JR	Native	Mono	USA
April	SR	Native	Mono	USA
Sandra	SR	Native	Mono	USA
Tia	JR	Native	Mono	USA
Olivia	SR	2ns gen	Mono	Haiti/Nigeria
Nia	JR	2nd gen	Mono	Jamaica
Nina	SR	2nd gen	Mono	Panama
Veronica	SR	2nd gen	Mono	Haiti
Yolanda	FR	2nd gen	Mono	Sierra Leone
Ann*	SR	1st gen	Mixed/A	Taiwan/Nigeria
Paige	SO	2nd gen	Mixed/L	Mexico
Crystal*	SO	Native	Mixed/W	USA
Emily	FR	Native	Mixed/W	USA

Notes: Ashley became a citizen as a teenager; Denise's mom is second generation from Panama; Ann grew up in Taiwan where her neighborhood was all Asian, but she attended an American private high school in Taiwan, her mom is Taiwanese, and her dad is Nigerian and a naturalized citizen (as is Ann); Crystal lived with her White grandparents, who are upper middle class, but mom is working class.

Neighborhood racial composition	High school racial composition	High school type	Self-reported social class status
> 70% Black	> 70% Black	Public	Poor
Mixed	Mixed	Public	Middle
> 70% Black	> 70% Black	Public	Working
> 70% Black	< 30% Black	Public	Working/Lower middle
65% Black	Mixed/Black	Public	Middle
> 70% Black	< 30% Black	Private/ABC	Lower middle
< 30% Black	< 30% Black	Public	Upper middle
> 70% Black	< 30% Black	Private/P4P	Working
Mixed/White	< 30% Black	Private	Middle/Upper middle
> 70% Black	Mixed/Black	Public	Working/Lower middle
> 70% Black/WI	Mixed/White	Public	Working/Lower middle
> 70% Black	< 30% Black	Boarding/ABC	Working/Lower middle
> 70% Black	Mixed/White	Public magnet	Working/Lower middle
> 70% Black	Mixed	Public	Lower middle/Middle
Mixed/White	< 30% Black	Private	Middle/Upper middle
> 70% Black	> 80% White	Private	Lower middle
< 30% Black	< 30% Black	Public	Upper
< 30% Black	< 30% Black	Private	Upper middle
30-70% Black	30-70% Black	Public	Lower middle/Middle
> 70% Black	Mixed/White	Public magnet	Lower middle
> 70% Black	> 5% Black	Private/SEEDS	Lower Middle/middle
< 30% Black	< 30% Black	Private US int.	Upper middle
< 30% Black	Mixed/Latino	Public	Middle
< 30% Black	< 30% Black	Public	Working/Upper middle
< 30% Black	< 30% Black	Public	Upper

TABLE C1. Characteristics of qualitative sample of Black students interviewed in conjunction with the NLSF (*continued*)

Name	Year	Nativity	Race	Country or region
Candace*	SR	Native	Mixed/W	USA
Rachel*	JR	2nd gen	Mixed/W	Trinidad
Charlotte	JR	2nd gen	Mixed/W	PR, Guyana
Blair	FR	Native	Mixed/W	USA
Erica	JR	Native	Mixed//W	USA
Eve	JR	Native	Mixed/W	USA
Francheska	SR	2nd gen	Mixed/W	Haiti/Croatia
Jessica	JR	Native	Mixed/W	USA
Maryanna	FR	Native	Mixed/W	USA
Megan	SR	Native	Mixed/W	USA
Renee	SR	Native	Mixed/W	USA
Sadie	SR	2nd gen	Mixed/W	Panama
Jane	JR	2nd gen	Mixed/W	Curaçao

Notes: Candace's father is second generation from Dominican Republic (Black), mom is Jewish; Rachel's mom is Jewish.

Neighborhood racial composition	High school racial composition	High school type	Self-identified social class atatus
< 30% Black	< 30% Black	Public	Middle
< 30% Black	Mixed	Public	Middle/Upper middle
< 30% Black	< 30% Black	Private	Upper middle
< 30% Black	Mixed	Public	Middle
Mixed/Black	Mixed	Public	Middle
50-50 B/W	50-50 B/W	Public	Middle
Mixed	Mixed/W	Private	Middle
< 30% Black	30%–40% Black	Public	Working/Lower middle
< 30% Black	Mixed	Public magnet	Middle
< 30% Black	< 30% Black	Public	Upper
< 30% Black	< 30% Black	Public	Upper middle
< 30% Black	< 30% Black	Public	Upper
< 30% Black	Mixed	Public	Upper middle

Focus-Group Conversation Guide

Topic I (10 minutes): Racial and Ethnic Identification

- Everyone goes around the room and explains why they define themselves as Black American/not Black American. (Leader probes here for national origins of parents and grandparents, and how students ethnically and racially define themselves.)

Topic II (20 minutes): Blackness and Whiteness in Contemporary America

- What does it mean to be Black in contemporary United States? (Global question)
  Probes:
  - Characteristics of typical Black man/woman in the United States (Try to nail things down as much as possible—gender, social class, where living, what family looks like, etc.—what is their vision of the typical Black person nowadays.)
    - ✓ For the average/typical Black person living in the United States nowadays, what aspects of life are particularly difficult? (Ask here for where one lives, day-to-day interactions with people of varying racial/ethnic groups, social class, being a Black [institution name] student, etc.)
- What does it mean to be White in the contemporary United States? (Global question)
  Probes:
  - Characteristics of typical White man/woman in the United States (Try to nail things down as much as possible—gender, social class,

where living, what family looks like, etc.—what is their vision of the typical White person nowadays.)

    ✓ For the average/typical White person living in the United States nowadays, what aspects of life are particularly difficult? (Ask here for where one lives, day-to-day interactions with people of varying racial/ethnic groups, social class, being a White [institution name] student, etc.)

- What are the most salient differences between the average/typical Black/White person living in the United States nowadays? How so? (Probe here for lifestyle differences, cultural differences, interactions with different racial/ethnic groups, social class, gender issues, etc.)

Topic III (20 minutes): Blackness and Whiteness at [institution name]

- What does it mean to be a Black student at [institution name]?
  Probes:
  - What are the characteristics of the typical/average Black student (gender, social class, skin tone, etc.)?
  - Is the typical/average Black student different from the average/typical Black person (man/woman) in the United States nowadays? If so, how? (Probe for specific differences.)
- What does it mean to be a White student at [institution name]?
  Probes:
  - What are the characteristics of the typical/average White student (gender, social class, skin tone, etc.)?
  - Is the typical/average White [institution name] student different from the average/typical White person (man/woman) in the United States nowadays? If so, how? (Probe for specific differences here.)
- Compare/Contrast what it means to be a White/Black student at [institution name].
  Probes:
  - How are students' experiences different? How so? What aspects of college life are especially different or similar (social, academic, gender, class, regional differences)?

Topic IV (30 minutes): Racial Stereotypes and Race Relations at [institution name] and Beyond

- What are some of the most common stereotypes/perceptions about Black people in general? (Repeat question for Whites.)
  Probes:
  - How do these stereotypes/perceptions about Black (White) people affect race relations between/among Black and White students at [institution name]? And in contemporary America?
  - What are race relations like between/among Black and White students at [institution name]?
  - Are Black/White students concerned about how Black/White students perceive them? How so? Why?
  - Are Black/White students concerned about how professors/administrators perceive them? How so? Why?
- How common is it for White students to have close friends/partners who are Black students at [institution name] (and vice versa)?
  Probes:
  - Find out what the dynamics are of interracial friendships from group—do students have close friends who are White? Find out how many. How did they meet friends in primary social group?
  - Do they want to socialize with Black/White students more or less? Why/Why not?
  - If it is not common for Black students to be close friends with White students, why is that?
  - For Black/White students, what are the biggest barriers to developing friendships with White students here?
  - Do you think it is common for Black students to date White students at [institution name]? Why or why not? What is the gender composition of the Black-White relationships? How about just having sex with Black/White students? Is that more/less/equally acceptable as having a steady boyfriend/girlfriend of the other race? Why/Why not?

Topic V (20 minutes): Understanding Biracial Identity

- Now that we have talked about the most common/popular stereotypes/perceptions of Black and White people at [institution name] and in general, let us talk about what it means to be biracial at

[institution name] and beyond. For the purposes of our discussion, we will define biracial as having one Black parent and one White parent. *Probes:*
  - Where do biracial people fit into the racial perceptions/stereotypes about White people and Black people that we discussed?
  - How do these racial stereotypes/perceptions affect
biracial students' experiences at [institution name] and beyond?
- What does it mean to be a biracial student at [institution name]? What are the characteristics of the typical/average biracial [institution name] student? (Probe for gender, class, etc. differences.)
    ✓ Is the typical/average biracial student at [institution name] different from the average/typical biracial person living in the contemporary United States? Is so, how? (Probe for specific differences here.)
    ✓ Is the typical/average biracial student at [institution name] different from the average/typical Black student at [institution]? White student at [institution name]? Is so, how? (Probe here for specific differences.)
- In general, what are the characteristics of the average/typical biracial person (man/woman) in the contemporary United States? (Probe for specific characteristics: gender, social class, skin tone, etc.)
    ✓ For the average/typical biracial person (half Black/half White) living in the contemporary United States, what aspects of daily life are especially difficult? (<u>Probe here for where one lives, day-to-day interactions with people of varying racial/ethnic groups, social class, being a [institution name] student.</u>)
    ✓ Are there added difficulties (rather than being solely White or Black) to being a biracial person living in the contemporary United States? (<u>Probe here for where one lives, day-to-day interactions with people of varying racial/ethnic groups, social class, being a [institution name] student.</u>) If yes, how so? If not, why not?
- Finally, let us talk about intergroup friendships at [institution name]. *Probes:*
  - How common is it for biracial students to have close friends who are Black students at [institution name]?
  - How common is it for biracial students to have close friends who are White students at [institution name]?

- How common is it for biracial students to have close friends who are Black students at [institution name]?
- For biracial students, what are the biggest barriers to developing friendships with Black students here? How about with White students?
- Are biracial students welcomed into the Black student community at [institution name]? Why/Why not?
- Are biracial students welcomed into the White student community at [institution name]?

End of focus group. Thank students for participating.

REFERENCES

Addo, Fenaba, Jason N. Houle, and Daniel Simon. 2016. "Young, Black, and (Still) in the Red." *Race and Social Problems* 8(1):64–76.

Ainsworth, James. 2002. "Why Does It Take a Village? The Mediation of Neighborhood Effects on Educational Achievement." *Social Forces* 81(1):117–152.

Aizer, Anna. 2007. "Neighborhood Violence and Urban Youth." Pp. 275–308 in Jonathan Gruber, ed., *The Problems of Disadvantaged Youth: An Economic Perspective*. Chicago: University of Chicago Press.

Alba, Richard. 2020. *The Great Demographic Illusion: Majority, Minority, and the Expanding American Mainstream*. Princeton, NJ: Princeton University Press.

Alexander, Karl, Doris Entwisle, and Linda Olson. 2014. *The Long Shadow: Family Background, Disadvantaged Urban Youth, and the Transition to Adulthood*. New York: Russell Sage Foundation.

Alexander, Michelle. 2010. *The New Jim Crow: Mass Incarceration in the Age of Colorblindness*. New York: New Press.

Allen, Richard L., Michael C. Dawson, and Ronald E. Brown. 1989. "A Schema-Based Approach to Modeling an African American Racial Belief System." *American Political Science Review* 83(2):421–439.

Allen, Walter R. 1992. "The Color of Success: African-American College Student Outcomes at Predominantly White and Historically Black Colleges and Universities." *Harvard Educational Review* 62(1):26–44.

Allen, Walter R., Robert Teranishi, Gniesha Dinwiddie, and Gloria González. 2002. "Knocking at Freedom's Door: Race, Equity and Affirmative Action in U.S. Higher Education." *Journal of Public Health Policy* 23(4):440–452.

Allison, Paul D. 2001. *Missing Data*. Thousand Oaks, CA: Sage.

Allport, Gordon W. 1954. *The Nature of Prejudice*. Boston: Addison-Wesley.

Amato, Paul R., and Frieda Fowler. 2002. "Parenting Practices, Child Adjustment, and Family Diversity." *Journal of Marriage and Family* 64(3):703–716.

Anderson, Monica, and Gustavo López. 2018. "Key Facts about Black Immigrants in the U.S." Pew Research Center, January 24. http://pewrsr.ch/2E2rH4N.

Andrews, Jeff. 2018. "Ben Carson Removes Anti-discrimination Language from HUD's Mission Statement." Curbed.com. https://www.curbed.com/2018/3/7/17090716/ben-carson-hud -discrimination-mission-statement.

Ang, Desmond. 2020. "The Effects of Police Violence on Inner-City Students." *Quarterly Journal of Economics* 27. https://doi.org/10.1093/qje/qjaa027.

Arcidiacono, Peter, Esteban Aucejo, Andrew Hussey, and Kenneth Spenner. 2013. "Racial Seg-regation Patterns in Selective Universities." *Journal of Law & Economics* 56(4):1039–1060.

Armstrong, Elizabeth A., and Laura T. Hamilton. 2013. *Paying for the Party: How College Maintains Inequality.* Cambridge, MA: Harvard University Press.

Arnett, Jeffrey J. 2000. "Emerging Adulthood: A Theory of Development from the Late Teens through the Twenties." *American Psychologist* 55(5):469–480.

Arnett, Jeffrey J. 2003. "Conceptions of the Transition to Adulthood among Emerging Adults in American Ethnic Groups." *New Directions in Child and Adolescent Development* 100:63–75.

Arnett, Jeffrey J. 2016. "College Students as Emerging Adults: The Developmental Implications of the College Context." *Emerging Adulthood* 4(3):219–222.

Aronson, Joshua, Diana Burgess, Sean M. Phelan, and Lindsey Juarez. 2013. "Unhealthy Interactions: The Role of Stereotype Threat in Health Disparities." *American Journal of Public Health* 103(1):50–56.

Astin, Alexander W. 1982. *Minorities in American Higher Education.* San Francisco: Jossey-Bass.

Astin, Alexander W. 1993. *What Matters in College? Four Critical Years Revisited.* San Francisco: Jossey-Bass.

Azmitia, Margarita, Moin Syed, and Kimberly Radmacher. 2013. "Finding Your Niche: Identity and Emotional Support in Emerging Adults' Adjustment to the Transition to College." *Journal of Research on Adolescence* 23(4):744–761.

Baker, Christina N. 2008. "Under-represented College Students and Extracurricular Involvement: The Effects of Various Student Organizations on Academic Performance." *Social Psychology of Education* 11(3):273–298.

Banks, Ralph Richard. 2011. *"Is Marriage for White People?" How the African American Marriage Decline Affects Everyone.* New York: Penguin Random House.

Barajas, Heidi Lasley, and Jennifer L. Pierce. 2001. "The Significance of Race and Gender in School Success among Latinas and Latinos in College." *Gender and Society* 15(6):859–878.

Barrow, Christine. 1996. *Family in the Caribbean: Themes and Perspectives.* Kingston, Jamaica: Ian Randle and James Curry Publishers.

Bashi, Vilna F. 2007. *Survival of the Knitted: Immigrant Social Networks in a Stratified World.* Stanford, CA: Stanford University Press.

Baugh, John. 1983. "A Survey of Afro-American English." *Annual Review of Anthropology* 12:335–354.

Baum, Sandy, Jennifer Ma, Matera Pender, and D'Wayne Bell. 2015. *Trends in Student Aid, 2015.* New York: The College Board. http://files.eric.ed.gov/fulltext/ED572541.pdf.

Bauman, Kurt J., and Nikki L. Graf. 2003. "Educational Attainment: 2000." *U.S. Census 2000 Brief Series* C2KBR-24. Washington, DC: U.S. Census Bureau.

Baumrind, Diana. 1966. "Effects of Authoritative Parental Control on Child Behavior." *Child Development* 37(4):887–907.

Baumrind, Diana. 1972. "An Exploratory Study of Socialization Effects on Black Children: Some Black-White Comparisons." *Child Development* 43(1):261–267.

Beasley, Maya A. 2011. *Opting Out: Losing the Potential of America's Young Black Elite.* Chicago: University of Chicago Press.

Becker, Gary S. 1964. *Human Capital: A Theoretical and Empirical Analysis.* New York: National Bureau of Economic Research.

Becker, Howard. 1963. *The Outsiders: Studies in the Sociology of Deviance.* Glencoe, IL: Free Press.

Beland, Louis-Philippe, and Dongwoo Kim. 2016. "The Effect of High School Shootings on Schools and Student Performance." *Educational Evaluation and Policy Analysis* 38(1):113–126.

Bell, Derek. 2003. "Diversity's Distractions." *Columbia Law Review* 103(6):1622–1633.

Bempechat, Janine, Suzanne E. Graham, and Norma V. Jimenez. 1999. "The Socialization of Achievement in Poor and Minority Students: A Comparative Study." *Journal of Cross-Cultural Psychology* 30(2):139–168.

Benjamin, Lois. 2005. *The Black Elite: Still Facing the Color Line in the Twenty-First Century.* 2nd ed. Lanham, MD: Rowman & Littlefield.

Bennett, Pamela R., and Amy Lutz. 2009. "How African American Is the Net Black Advantage? Differences in College Attendance among Immigrant Blacks, Native Blacks, and Whites." *Sociology of Education* 82(1):70–100.

Benson, Janel E. 2020. "Exploring the Racial Identities of Black Immigrants in the United States." *Sociological Forum* 21(2):219–247.

Bentley-Edwards, Keisha L., and Collette Chapman-Hilliard. 2015. "Doing Race in Different Places: Black Racial Cohesion on Black and White College Campuses." *Journal of Diversity in Higher Education* 8(1):43–60.

Berlin, Lisa C., Christy J. Brady-Smith, and Jeanne Brooks-Gunn. 2002. "Links between Child-bearing Age and Observed Maternal Behaviors with 14-Month-Olds in the Early Head Start Research and Evaluation Project." *Infant Mental Health Journal* 23(2):104–109.

Bettez, Silvia Christina. 2002. *But Don't Call Me White: Mixed Race Women Exposing Nuances of Privilege and Oppression Politics.* Rotterdam: Sense.

Bielby, William T. 2012. "Minority Vulnerability in Privileged Occupations: Why Do African American Financial Advisers Earn Less than Whites in a Large Financial Services Firm?" *Annals of the American Academy of Political and Social Science* 639:3–32.

Bischoff, Kendra, and Ann Owens. 2019. "The Segregation of Opportunity: Social and Financial Resources in the Educational Contexts of Lower- and Higher-Income Children, 1990–2014." *Demography* 56(5):1635–1664.

Blackwell, Debra L., and Daniel T. Lichter. 2000. "Mate Selection among Married and Cohabitating Couples." *Journal of Family Issues* 21(3):275–302.

Blackwell, Debra L., and Daniel T. Lichter. 2005. "Homogamy among Dating, Cohabiting, and Married Couples." *Sociological Quarterly* 45(4):719–737.

Blalock, Hubert M. 1991. *Understanding Social Inequality: Modeling Allocation Processes.* New York: Sage.

Blascovich, Jim, Steven J. Spencer, Diane Quinn, and Claude Steele. 2001. "African Americans and High Blood Pressure: The Role of Stereotype Threat." *Psychological Science* 12(3):225–229.

Blauner, Bob. 2001. *Still the Big News: Racial Oppression in America.* Philadelphia: Temple University Press.

Blauner, Robert. 1972. *Racial Oppression in America.* New York: Harper and Row.

Bleske-Recheck, April, David Lubinski, and Camilla P. Benbow. 2004. "Meeting the Educational Needs of Special Populations: Advanced Placement's Role in Developing Exceptional Human Capital." *Psychological Science* 15(4):217–224.

Blockett, Reginald A., Pamela P. Felder, Walter Parrish III, and Joan Collier. 2016. "Pathways to the Professoriate: Exploring Black Doctoral Student Socialization and the Pipeline to the Academic Profession." *Western Journal of Black Studies* 40(2):95–110.

Bluestone, Cheryl, and Catherine S. Tamis-LeMonda. 1999. "Correlates of Parenting Styles in Predominately Working- and Middle-Class African American Mothers." *Journal of Marriage and Family* 61(4):881–893.

Bobo, L. (1988). "Group Conflict, Prejudice, and the Paradox of Contemporary Racial Attitudes." Pp. 85–114 in P. A. Katz and D. A. Taylor, eds., *Eliminating Racism: Profiles in Controversy*. New York: Plenum.

Bobo, Lawrence D., Camille Z. Charles, and Alicia D. Simmons. 2012. "The Real Record on Racial Attitudes." Pp. 38–83 in Peter V. Marsden, ed., *Social Trends in the United States: Evidence from the General Social Survey since 1972*. Princeton, NJ: Princeton University Press.

Bodovski, Katerina. 2010. "Parental Practices and Educational Achievement: Social Class, Race, and Habitus." *British Journal of Sociology of Education* 31(2):139–156.

Bodovski, Katerina, and George Farkas. 2007. "Mathematics Growth in Early Elementary School: The Roles of Beginning Knowledge, Student Engagement, and Instruction." *Elementary School Journal* 108(2):115–130.

Bohnert, Amy M., Julie W. Aikins, and Jennifer Edidin. 2007. "The Role of Organized Activities in Facilitating Social Adaptation across the Transition to College." *Journal of Adolescent Research* 22(2):189–208.

Bonczar, Thomas P. 2003. *Prevalence of Imprisonment in the U.S. Population, 1974–2001*. Washington, DC: U.S. Bureau of Justice Statistics.

Bourdieu, Pierre. 1977. *Outline of a Theory of Practice*. Trans. Richard Nice. Cambridge: Cambridge University Press.

Bourdieu, Pierre. 1986. "The Forms of Capital." Pp. 241–258 in J. G. Richardson, ed., *Handbook of Theory and Research for the Sociology of Education*. New York: Greenwood.

Bordieu, Pierre. 1998. *Practical Reason: On the Theory of Action*. Stanford, CA: Stanford University Press.

Bowen, Gary L., Roderick A. Rose, Joelle D. Powers, and Elizabeth J. Glennie. 2008. "The Joint Effects of Neighborhoods, Schools, Peers, and Families on Changes in the School Success of Middle School Students." *Family Relations* 57(4):504–516.

Bowen, William G., and Derek Bok. 1998. *The Shape of the River: Long-Term Consequences of Considering Race in College and University Admissions*. Princeton, NJ: Princeton University Press.

Bowen, William G., and Sarah A. Levin. 2003. *Reclaiming the Game: College Sports and Educational Values*. Princeton, NJ: Princeton University Press.

Bowman, Scott W. 2011. "Multigenerational Interactions in Black Middle Class Wealth and Asset Decision Making." *Journal of Family and Economic Issues* 32(1):15–26.

Bowman, Scott W. 2016. "Who and What You Know: Social and Human Capital in Black Middle-Class Economic Decision-Making." *Race and Social Problems* 8(1):93–102.

Boyd, Taylor B. H., and Donald Mitchell Jr. 2018. "Black Male Persistence in Spite of Facing Stereotypes in College: A Phenomenological Exploration." *Qualitative Report* 23(4):893–913.

Boyd-Franklin, Nancy. 2003. *Black Families in Therapy: Understanding the African American Experience*. New York: Guilford.

Branch, Taylor. 1988. *Parting the Waters: America in the King Years 1954–63*. New York: Simon & Schuster.

Branch, Taylor. 1998. *Pillar of Fire: America in the King Years 1963–65*. New York: Simon & Schuster.

Branch, Taylor. 2006. *At Canaan's Edge: America in the King Years, 1965–68*. New York: Simon & Schuster.

Brewster, Joe, Michele Stephenson, and Hilary Beard. 2013. *Promises Kept: Raising Black Boys to Succeed in Life*. New York: Spiegel & Grau.

Broman, Clifford L., Harold W. Neighbors, and James S. Jackson. 1988. "Racial Group Identification among Black Adults." *Social Forces* 67(1):146–158.

Brown, Eric. 2013. *The Black Professional Middle Class: Race, Class, and Community in the Post–Civil Rights Era*. New York: Routledge.

Brown, Hana, and Jennifer A. Jones. 2015. "Rethinking Panethnicity and the Race-Immigration Divide: An Ethnoracialization Model of Group Formation." *Sociology of Race and Ethnicity* 1(1):181–191.

Brown, Janet, and Sharon Johnson. 2008. "Childrearing and Child Participation in Jamaican Families." *International Journal of Early Years Education* 16(1):31–40.

Brown, Tamara L., Calendra M. Phillips, Tahirah Abdulla, Ebony Vinson, and Jermaine Robertson. 2011. "Dispositional versus Situational Coping: Are the Coping Strategies African Americans Use Different for General versus Racism-Related Stressors?" *Journal of Black Psychology* 37(3):311–335.

Brown, Ursula M. 2001. *The Interracial Experience: Growing Up Black/White Racially Mixed in the United States*. New York: Praeger.

Brownstein, Ronald. 2016. "The Challenge of Educational Inequality." *The Atlantic*, May 19. https://www.theatlantic.com/education/archive/2016/05/education-inequality-takes -center-stage/483405/.

Bryce-Laporte, Roy S. 1972. "Black Immigrants: The Experience of Invisibility and Inequality." *Journal of Black Studies* 3(1):29–56.

Buck, Stuart. 2010. *Acting White: The Ironic Legacy of Desegregation*. New Haven, CT: Yale University Press.

Bulcroft, Richard A., Diane C. Carmody, and Kris A. Bulcroft. 1996. "Patterns of Parental Independence Giving to Adolescents: Variations by Race, Age, and Gender of Child." *Journal of Marriage and Family* 58(4):866–883.

Bullock, Henry Allan. 1967. *A History of Negro Education in the South: From 1619 to the Present*. Cambridge, MA: Harvard University Press.

Burdick-Will, Julia. 2013. "School Violent Crime and Academic Achievement in Chicago." *Sociology of Education* 86(4):343–361.

Burke, Ruth, and Grace Kao. 2010. "Stability and Change in Racial Identities of Multiracial Adolescents." Pp. 39–50 in Kathleen O. Korgen, ed., *Multiracial Americans and Social Class: The Influence of Social Class on Racial Identity*. New York: Routledge.

Burnett, Christopher A. 2020. "Diversity under Review: HBCUs and Regional Accreditation Actions." *Innovative Higher Education* 45(1):3–15.

Butterfield, Sherri-Ann P. 2004. "'We're Just Black': The Racial and Ethnic Identities of Second-Generation West Indians in New York." Pp. 288–312 in Philip Kasinitz, John H. Mollenkopf, and Mary C. Waters, eds., *Becoming New Yorkers: Ethnographies of the New Second Generation*. New York: Russell Sage Foundation.

Byrd, W. Carson. 2017. *Poison in the Ivy: Race Relations and the Reproduction of Inequality on Elite College Campuses*. New Brunswick, NJ: Rutgers University Press.

Byrd, W. Carson, Rachelle Brunn-Bevel, and Parker J. Sexton. 2014. "'We Don't All Look Alike': The Academic Performance of Black Student Populations at Elite Colleges." *Du Bois Review: Social Science Research on Race* 11(2):353–385.

Calarco, Jessica McCoy. 2018. *Negotiating Opportunities: How the Middle Class Secures Advantages in School*. New York: Oxford University Press.

Capps, Randy, Kristen McCabe, and Michael Fix. 2011. *New Streams: Black African Migration to the United States*. Washington, DC: Migration Policy Institute. https://www.migrationpolicy .org/research/new-streams-black-african-migration-united-states.

Carolan, Brian V., and Sara J. Wasserman. 2015. "Does Parenting Style Matter? Concerted Cultivation, Education Expectations, and the Transmission of Educational Advantage." *Sociological Perspectives* 58(2):168–186.

Carson, E. Ann. 2020. *Prisoners in 2018*. Washington, DC: U.S. Bureau of Justice Statistics.

Carter, Prudence L. 2003. "'Black' Cultural Capital, Status Positioning, and Schooling Conflicts for Low-Income African American Youth." *Social Problems* 50(1):136–155.

Carter, Prudence L. 2005. *Keepin' It Real: School Success beyond Black and White*. New York: Oxford University Press.

Carter, Prudence L. 2010. "Cultural Flexibility among Students in Different Racial and Ethnic School Contexts." *Teachers College Record* 112(6):1529–1574.

Carter, Prudence L. 2012. *Stubborn Roots: Race, Culture, and Inequality in U.S. and South African Schools*. New York: Oxford University Press.

Cashin, Sheryll. 2014. *Place, Not Race: A New Vision of Opportunity in America*. Boston: Beacon.

Caughy, Margaret O'Brien, and Patricia J. O'Campo. 2006. "Neighborhood Poverty, Social Capital, and the Cognitive Development of African American Preschoolers." *American Journal of Community Psychology* 37(1–2):141–154.

Center for Responsible Lending. 2019. *Quicksand: Borrowers of Color and the Student Debt Crisis*. Durham, NC: Center for Responsible Lending. https://www.responsiblelending.org/sites /default/files/nodes/files/research-publication/crl-quicksand-student-debt-crisis-jul2019.pdf.

Center for Talent Innovation. 2021. *Being Black in Corporate America: An Intersectional Exploration*. New York: Center for Talent Innovation (renamed COQUAL). https://www .talentinnovation.org/_private/assets/BeingBlack-KeyFindings-CTI.pdf.

Chafe, William H., Raymond Gavins, and Robert Korstad, eds. 2001. *Remembering Jim Crow: African Americans Tell about Life in the Segregated South*. New York: New Press.

Chajewski, M., K. D. Mattern, and E. J. Shaw. 2011. "Examining the Role of Advanced Placement Exam Participation in 4-Year College Enrollment." *Educational Measurement: Issues and Practice* 30(4):16–27.

Charles, Camille Z. 2003. "The Dynamics of Racial Residential Segregation." *Annual Review of Sociology*, 29:167–207.

Charles, Camille Z., Gniesha Dinwiddie, and Douglas S. Massey. 2004. "The Continuing Consequences of Segregation." *Social Science Quarterly* 85(5):1353–1374.

Charles, Camille Z., Mary J. Fischer, Margarita Mooney, and Douglas S. Massey. 2009. *Taming the River: Negotiating the Academic, Financial, and Social Currents in America's Selective Colleges and Universities.* Princeton, NJ: Princeton University Press.

Charles, Camille Z., Rory A. Kramer, Kimberly C. Torres, and Rachelle Brunn-Bevel. 2015. "Intragroup Heterogeneity and Blackness: Effects of Racial Classification, Immigrant Origins, Social Class, and Social Context on the Racial Identity of Elite College Students." *Race and Social Problems* 7(4):281–299.

Charles, Camille Z., Vincent J. Roscigno, and Kimberly C. Torres. 2007. "Racial Inequality and College Attendance: The Mediating Role of Parental Investments." *Social Science Research* 36(1):329–352.

Charles, Camille Z., Kimberly C. Torres, and Rachelle J. Brunn. 2008. "Black Like Who? Exploring the Racial, Ethnic, and Class Diversity of Black Students at Selective Colleges and Universities." Pp. 247–266 in Charles A. Gallagher, ed., *Racism in Post-Race America: New Theories, New Directions.* Chapel Hill, NC: Social Forces.

Chavous, Tabbye M. 2000. "The Relations around Racial Identity, Perceived Ethnic Fit, and Organizational Involvement for African American Students at a Predominately White University." *Journal of Black Psychology* 26(1):79–100.

Chavous, Tabbye, and Seanna Leath. 2017. "'We Really Protested': The Influence of Sociopolitical Beliefs, Political Self-Efficacy, and Campus Racial Climate on Civic Engagement among Black College Students Attending Predominantly White Institutions." *Journal of Negro Education* 86(3):220–237.

Chavous, Tabbye M., Bridget L. Richardson, Felicia R. Webb, Gloryvee Fonseca-Bolorin, and Seanna Leath. 2018. "Shifting Contexts and Shifting Identities: Campus Race-Related Experiences, Racial Identity, and Academic Motivation among Black Students during the Transition to College." *Race and Social Problems* 10(1):1–18.

Cheadle, Jacob E. 2008. "Educational Investment, Family Context, and Children's Math and Reading Growth from Kindergarten through the Third Grade." *Sociology of Education* 81(1):1–31.

Cherlin, Andrew J. 2009. *The Marriage-Go-Round: The State of Marriage and Family in America Today.* New York: Vintage.

Chessman, Hollie, and Morgan Taylor. 2019. "College Student Mental Health and Well-Being: A Survey of Presidents." *Higher Education Today Blog.* Washington, DC: American Council on Education. https://www.higheredtoday.org/2019/08/12/college-student-mental-health-well-survey-college-presidents/.

Chetty, Raj, John N. Friedman, Nathaniel Hendren, Maggie R. Jones, and Sonya R. Potter. 2018. *The Opportunity Atlas: Mapping the Childhood Roots of Social Mobility.* NBER Working Paper No. 25147. https://opportunityinsights.org/paper/the-opportunity-atlas/.

Chetty, Raj, Nathaniel Hendren, Patrick Kline, and Emmanuel Saez. 2014. "Where is the Land of Opportunity? The Geography of Intergenerational Mobility in the United States." *Quarterly Journal of Economics* 129(4):1443–1623.

Chiswick, Barry R. 1978. "The Effect of Americanization on the Earnings of Foreign-Born Men." *Journal of Political Economy* 86(5):897–921.

Chiswick, Barry R., and Paul W. Miller. 1998. "English Language Fluency among Immigrants in the United States." *Research in Labor Economics* 17:151–200.

Chiswick, Barry R., and Paul W. Miller. 2010. "The Effects of School Quality in the Origin on the Payoff to Schooling for Immigrants." *IZA Discussion Papers No. 5075.*

Choi, Jung Hyun, Alanna McCargo, Michael Neal, Laurie Goodman, and Caitlin Young. 2019. *Explaining the Black-White Homeownership Gap: A Closer Look at Disparities across Local Markets.* Washington, DC: Urban Institute. https://www.urban.org/research/publication/explaining-black-white-homeownership-gap-closer-look-disparities-across-local-markets.

Choo, Hae Yeon, and Myra Marx Ferree. 2010. "Practicing Intersectionality in Sociological Research: A Critical Analysis of Inclusions, Interactions, and Institutions in the Study of Inequalities." *Sociological Theory* 28(2):129–149.

Christie, Ron. 2010. *The Curious History of a Racial Slur.* New York: Thomas Dunn.

Clark, Kenneth B. 1965. *Dark Ghetto: Dilemmas of Social Power.* New York: Harper and Row.

Clark-Ibáñez, Marisol, and Diane Felmlee. 2004. "Interethnic Relationships: The Role of Social Network Diversity." *Journal of Marriage and the Family* 66(2):293–305.

Clerge, Orly. 2014. "Toward a Minority Culture of Mobility: Immigrant Integration into the African-American Middle Class." *Sociology Compass* 8(10):1167–1182.

Clerge, Orly. 2019. *The New Noir: Race, Identity, and Diaspora in Black Suburbia.* Berkeley: University of California Press.

Coates, Ta-Nehisi. 2015. *Between the World and Me.* New York: Spiegel & Grau.

Cohen, Cathy. 1999. *The Boundaries of Blackness: AIDS and the Breakdown of Black Politics.* Chicago: University of Chicago Press.

Cole, Elizabeth R., and Safiya R. Omari. 2003. "Race, Class and the Dilemmas of Upward Mobility for African Americans." *Journal of Social Issues* 59(4):785–802.

Coleman, James S. 1988. "Social Capital in the Creation of Human Capital." *American Journal of Sociology* 94(Suppl):S95–S120.

Collins, Patricia H. 2000. *Black Feminist Thought.* 2nd ed. New York: Routledge.

Collins, Patricia H. 2019. *Intersectionality as Critical Social Theory.* Durham, NC: Duke University Press.

Collins, Patricia H., and Sirma Bilge. 2016. *Intersectionality (Key Concepts).* Cambridge, UK: Polity.

Condron, Dennis J. 2009. "Social Class, School and Non-school Environments, and Black/White Inequalities in Children's Learning." *American Sociological Review* 74(4):683–708.

Conley, Dalton. 2010. *Being Black, Living in the Red: Race, Wealth, and Social Policy in America.* 10th anniversary ed. Berkeley: University of California Press.

Cookson, Peter W., and Caroline H. Persell. 1985. *Preparing for Power: America's Elite Boarding Schools.* New York: Basic Books.

Cornell, Stephen E., and Douglas Hartmann. 1998. *Ethnicity and Race: Making Identities in a Changing World.* Thousand Oaks, CA: Pine Forge.

Cottrell, Catherine A., Steven L. Neuberg, and Norman P. Li. 2007. "What Do People Desire in Others? A Sociofunctional Perspective on the Importance of Different Functional Others." *Journal of Personality and Social Psychology* 92(2):208–231.

Cox, Daniel, Juhem Navarro-Rivera, and Robert P. Jones. 2016. *Race, Religion, and Political Affiliation of Americans' Core Social Networks.* Washington, DC: Public Religion Research Institute. https://www.prri.org/research/poll-race-religion-politics-americans-social-networks/.

Crenshaw, Kimberlé. 1989. "Demarginalizing the Intersection of Race and Sex: A Black Feminist Critique of Antidiscrimination Doctrine." *University of Chicago Legal Forum* 1(8):139–168.

Crenshaw, Kimberlé. 1991. "Mapping the Margins: Intersectionality, Identity Politics, and Violence against Women of Color." *Stanford Law Review* 42:1241–1299.

Crocker, Jennifer, Brenda Major, and Claude M. Steele. 1998. "Social Stigma." Pp. 504–553 in Daniele T. Gilbert and Susan T. Fiske, eds., *The Handbook of Social Psychology*, vol. 2. Boston: McGraw-Hill.

Crosnoe, Robert, Monica J. Johnson, and Glen H. Elder Jr. 2004. "School Size and the Interpersonal Side of Education: An Examination of Race/Ethnicity, and Organizational Context." *Social Science Quarterly* 85(5):1259–1274.

Crosnoe, Robert, Monica K. Johnson, and Glen H. Elder Jr. 2011. "Insights on Adolescence from a Life Course Perspective." *Journal of Research on Adolescence* 21(1):273–280.

Cross, William E. Jr. 1971. "The Negro-to-Black Conversion Experience: Toward a Psychology of Black Liberation." *Black World* 20(9):13–27.

Cross, William E. Jr. 1991. *Shades of Black: Diversity in African-American Identity*. Philadelphia: Temple University Press.

Cross, William E. Jr., Bruce O. Grant, and Ana Ventuneac. 2012. "Black Identity and Well-Being: Untangling Race and Ethnicity." Pp. 125–146 in Jas M. Sullivan and Ashraf M. Esmail, eds., *African American Identity: Racial and Cultural Dimensions of the Black Experience*. Lanham, MD: Rowman & Littlefield.

Crutcher, Michael E. 2010. *Tremé: Race and Place in a New Orleans Neighborhood*. Athens: University of Georgia Press.

Currington, Celeste V., Jennifer H. Lundquist, and Ken-Out Lin. 2021. *The Dating Divide: Race and Desire in the Era of Online Romance*. Berkeley: University of California Press.

Davenport, Lauren D. 2016. "The Role of Gender, Class, and Religion in Biracial Americans' Racial Labeling Decisions." *American Sociological Review* 81(1):57–84.

Davis, Angela. 2017. "The Prosecution of Black Men." Pp. 178–208 in Angela Davis, ed., *Policing the Black Man: Arrest, Prosecution, and Imprisonment*. New York: Random House.

Dawson, Michael C. 1994. *Behind the Mule: Race and Class in African American Politics*. Princeton, NJ: Princeton University Press.

Dawson, Michael C. 2001. *Black Visions: The Roots of Contemporary African-American Political Ideologies*. Chicago: University of Chicago Press.

Delpit, Lisa. 1988. "The Silenced Dialogue: Power and Pedagogy in Educating Other People's Children." *Harvard Educational Review* 58(3):280–299.

Demo, David H., and Michael Hughes. 1990. "Socialization and Racial Identity among Black Americans." *Social Psychology Quarterly* 53(4):364–374.

Desmond, Matthew. 2016. *Evicted: Poverty and Profit in the American City*. New York: Crown.

DeSousa, Jason. 2001. "Reexamining the Educational Pipeline for African American Students." Pp. 21–44 in Lee Jones, ed., *Retaining African Americans in Higher Education: Challenging Paradigms for Retaining Students, Faculty and Administrators*. Sterling, VA: Stylus.

de Souza Briggs, Xavier. 2002. "Social Capital and Segregation: Race, Connections, and Inequality in America." *KSG Faculty Research Working Papers Series RWP02-011*, February. Cambridge, MA: Kennedy School of Government. https://research.hks.harvard.edu/publications/getFile.aspx?Id=35.

Dickerson, Bette J. 1995. *African American Single Mothers: Understanding Their Lives and Families*. Thousand Oaks, CA: Sage.

DiMaggio, Paul. 1982. "Cultural Capital and School Success: The Impact of Status Culture Participation on the Grades of High School Students." *American Sociological Review* 47(2):189–201.

DiMaggio, Paul, and Francie Ostrower. 1990. "Participation in the Arts by Black and White Americans." *Social Forces* 68(3):753–778.

DiPrete, Thomas A., and Claudia Buchmann. 2013. *The Rise of Women: The Growing Gender Gap in Education and What It Means for American Schools.* New York: Russell Sage Foundation.

Dix, Willard. 2016. "What College 'Match' and 'Fit' Are All About." *Forbes*, May 9. https://www .forbes.com/sites/willarddix/2016/05/09/what-college-match-and-fit-are-all-about /#3d04f7506d1f.

Djama, Yanvi, and Sitawa R. Kimuna. 2014. "Are Americans Really in Favor of Interracial Marriage? A Closer Look at When They Are Asked about Black-White Marriage for Their Relatives." *Journal of Black Studies* 45(6):528–544.

Dodoo, Francis N. A. 1991. "Immigrant and Native Black Workers' Labor Force Participation in the United States." *National Journal of Sociology* 5(1):3–17.

Dodoo, Francis N. A. 1997. "Assimilation Differences among Africans in America." *Social Forces* 76(2):527–546.

Dodoo, Francis N. A. 1999. "Black and Immigrant Labor Force Participation in America." *Race and Society* 2(1):69–82.

Dollard, John. 1937. *Caste and Class in a Southern Town.* New Haven, CT: Yale University Press.

Dornbusch, Sanford M., Philip L. Ritter, P. Herbert Leiderman, Donald F. Roberts, and Michael J. Fraleigh. 1987. "The Relation of Parenting Style to Adolescent School Performance." *Child Development* 58(5):1244–1257.

Dow, Dawn M. 2016. "The Deadly Challenges of Raising African American Boys: Navigating the Controlling Image of the 'Thug.'" *Gender and Society* 30(2):161–188.

Dow, Dawn M. 2019. *Mothering while Black: Boundaries and Burdens of Middle-Class Parenthood.* Berkeley: University of California Press.

Dowd, Alicia C., John J. Cheslock, and Tatiana Melguizo. 2008. "Transfer Access from Community Colleges and the Distribution of Elite Higher Education." *Journal of Higher Education* 79(4):442–472.

Doyle, Jamie M., and Grace Kao. 2007. "Are Racial Identities of Multiracials Stable? Changing Self-Identification among Single and Multiple Race Individuals." *Social Psychology Quarterly* 70(4):405–423.

Drago, Edmund L. 1990. *Initiative, Paternalism, and Race Relations: Charleston's Avery Normal Institute.* Athens: University of Georgia Press.

Drake, St Clair, and Horace R. Cayton. 1945. *Black Metropolis: A Study of Life in a Northern City.* New York: Harcourt, Brace.

Du Bois, W. E. Burghardt. 1899. *The Philadelphia Negro: A Social Study.* Philadelphia: University of Pennsylvania Press.

Du Bois, W. E. Burghardt. 1903. *The Souls of Black Folk: Essays and Sketches.* Chicago: A. C. McClurg.

Du Bois, W. E. Burghardt. 1948. "The Talented Tenth." W. E. B. Du Bois Papers (MS 312). Special Collections and University Archives, University of Massachusetts Amherst Libraries.

Dudley-Grant, G. Rita. 2001. "Eastern Caribbean Family Psychology with Conduct-Disordered Adolescents from the Virgin Islands." *American Psychologist* 56(1):47–57.

Dufur, Mikaela J., Toby L. Parcel, and Kelly P. Troutman. 2013. "Does Capital at Home Matter More than Capital at School? Social Capital Effects on Academic Achievement." *Research in Social Stratification and Mobility* 31:1–12.

Dumais, Susan A. 2002. "Cultural Capital, Gender, and School Success: The Role of Habitus." *Sociology of Education* 75(1):44–68.

Dumais, Susan A. 2006. "Early Childhood Cultural Capital, Parental Habitus, and Teachers' Perceptions." *Poetics* 34(2):83–107.

Duncan, Otis Dudley. 1968. "Inheritance of Poverty or Inheritance of Race?" Pp. 85–110 in Daniel P. Moynihan, ed., *Understanding Poverty*. New York: Basic Books.

Eberhardt, Jennifer L. 2019. *Biased: Uncovering the Hidden Prejudice That Shapes What We See, Think, and Do*. New York: Viking.

Eberhardt, Jennifer L., Paul Davies, Valerie Purdie-Vaughns, and Sheri Johnson. 2006. "Looking Deathworthy: Perceived Stereotypicality of Black Defendants Predicts Capital-Sentencing Outcomes." *Psychological Science* 17(5):383–386.

Eccles, Jacquelynne, and Robert W. Roeser. 2010. "Schools as Developmental Contexts during Adolescence." *Journal of Research on Adolescence* 21(1):225–241.

Edin, Kathryn. 1991. "Surviving the Welfare System: How AFDC Recipients Make Ends Meet in Chicago." *Social Problems* 38:462–474.

Edmonds, Christina, and Melanie Killen. 2009. "Do Adolescents' Perceptions of Parental Racial Attitudes Relate to Their Intergroup Contact and Cross-Race Relationships." *Group Processes and Intergroup Relations* 12(1):5–21.

Eggerling-Boeck, Jennifer. 2002. "Issues of Black Identity: A Review of the Literature." *African American Research Perspectives* 8(1):17–26.

Ellwood, David T. 1988. *Poor Support: Poverty in the American Family*. New York: Basic Books.

Emerson, Katherine T. U., and Mary C. Murphy. 2014. "Identity Threat at Work: How Social Identity Threat and Situational Cues Contribute to Racial and Ethnic Disparities in the Workplace." *Cultural Diversity and Ethnic Minority Psychology* 20(4):508–520.

Espeland, Wendy, and Michael Sauder. 2007. "Rankings and Reactivity: How Public Measures Create Social Worlds." *American Journal of Sociology* 113(1):1–40.

Espenshade, Thomas J., Chang Y. Chung, and Joan L. Walling. 2004. "Admission Preferences for Minority Students, Athletes, and Legacies at Elite Universities." *Social Science Quarterly* 85(5):1422–1446.

Espenshade, Thomas J., and Alexandra W. Radford. 2009. *No Longer Separate, Not Yet Equal: Race and Class in Elite College Admission and Campus Life*. Princeton, NJ: Princeton University Press.

Evans, Hyacinth, and Rose Davies. 1996. "Overview Issues in Child Socialization in the Caribbean." Pp. 1–24 in Janet Brown and Jaipaul Roopnarine, eds., *Caribbean Families: Diversity among Ethnic Groups*. Greenwich, CT: Ablex.

Fahle, Erin M., Sean F. Reardon, Demetra Kalogrides, Ericka S. Weathers, and Heewon Jang. 2020. "Racial Segregation and School Poverty in the United States, 1999–2016." *Race and Social Problems* 12(1):42–56.

Farkas, George. 1996. *Human Capital or Cultural Capital? Ethnicity and Poverty Groups in an Urban School District*. New Brunswick, NJ: Transaction.

Farkas, George, Robert P. Grobe, Daniel Sheehan, and Yuan Shuan. 1990. "Cultural Resources and School Success: Gender, Ethnicity, and Poverty Groups within an Urban School District." *American Sociological Review* 55(1):127–142.

Faulk, Deborwah, Robert A. Bennett III, and James L. Moore III. 2017. "Gamed by the System: Exploring Black Youths' Motivation to Participate in Sports." *Boyhood Studies* 10(1):88–100.

Feagin, Joe R., Hernan Vera, and Nikitah Imani. 1996. *The Agony of Education: Black Students at White Colleges and Universities*. New Brunswick, NJ: Rutgers University Press.

Fears, Darryl. 2007. "In Diversity Push, Top Universities Enrolling More Black Immigrants." *Washington Post*, May 6, A2. https://www.washingtonpost. com/wp-dyn/content/article /2007/03/05/AR2007030501296.html.

Felmlee, Diane. 2001. "No Couple Is an Island: A Social Network Perspective on Dyadic Stability." *Social Forces* 79(4):1259–1287.

Ferber, Abby. 1998. *White Man Falling: Race, Gender and White Supremacy*. Lanham, MD: Rowman & Littlefield.

Ferguson, Ann. 2003. *Bad Boys: Public Schools in the Making of Black Masculinity*. Ann Arbor: University of Michigan Press.

Ferguson, Elizabeth A. 1938. "Race Consciousness among American Negroes." *Journal of Negro Education* 7(1):32–40.

Field, Carolyn J., Sitawa R. Kimuna, and Murray A. Straus. 2013. "Attitudes toward Interracial Relationships among College Students: Race, Class, Gender, and Perceptions of Parental Views." *Journal of Black Studies* 44(7):741–776.

Fischer, Mary J. 2008. "Does Campus Diversity Promote Friendship Diversity? A Look at Interracial Friendships in College." *Social Science Quarterly* 89(3):631–655.

Fischer, Mary J., and Julie A. Kmec. 2004. "Neighborhood Socioeconomic Conditions as Moderators of Family Resource Transmission: High School Completion among At-risk Youth." *Sociological Perspectives* 47(4):507–527.

Fischer, Mary J., and Douglas S. Massey. 2007. "The Effects of Affirmative Action in Higher Education." *Social Science Research* 36(2):531–549.

Fleming, Jacqueline. 1981. "Stress and Satisfaction in College Years of Black Students." *Journal of Negro Education* 50(3):307–318.

Fleming, Jacqueline. 1984. *Blacks in College*. San Francisco: Jossey-Bass.

Flood, Sarah, Miriam King, Renae Rodgers, Steven Ruggles, J. Robert Warren, and Michael Westberry. 2021. *Integrated Public Use Microdata Series, Current Population Survey: Version 9.0* [data set]. Minneapolis, MN: IPUMS. https://doi.org/10.18128/D030.V9.0.

Fogg-Davis, Hawley. 2001. "Navigating Race in the Market for Human Gametes." *Hastings Center Report* 31(5):13–21.

Ford, Richard T. 2009. "Barack Is the New Black: Obama and the Promise/Threat of the Post–Civil Rights Era." *Du Bois Review* 6(1):37–48.

Frazier, E. Franklin. 1957. *Black Bourgeoisie: The Rise of a New Middle Class in the United States*. Glencoe, IL: Free Press.

Friedman, Sam, and Daniel Laurison. 2019. *The Class Ceiling: Why It Pays to Be Privileged*. Bristol, UK: Policy Press.

Fries-Britt, Sharon L. 1998. "Moving beyond Black Achiever Isolation: Experiences of Gifted Collegians." *Journal of Higher Education* 69(5):556–576.

Fries-Britt, Sharon, and Bridget Turner. 2002. "Uneven Stories: Successful Black Collegians at a Black and a White Campus." *Review of Higher Education* 25(3):315–330.

Froyum, Carissa M. 2010. "The Reproduction of Inequalities through Emotional Capital: The Case of Socializing Low-Income Black Girls." *Qualitative Sociology* 33(1):37–54.

Fryer, Roland G. Jr., Lisa Kahn, Steven D. Levitt, and Jorg L. Spenkuch. 2012. "The Plight of Mixed Race Adolescents." *Review of Economics and Statistics* 94(3):621–634.

Fryer, Roland G., and Paul Torelli. 2005. *An Empirical Analysis of "Acting White."* NBER Working Paper No. 11334. Cambridge, MA: National Bureau of Economic Research. https://www.nber.org/papers/w11334.pdf.

Fu, Vincent K. 2001. "Racial Intermarriage Pairings." *Demography* 38(2):147–159.

Fuligni, Andrew J., and Kim M. Tsai. 2012. "Change in Ethnic Identity across the College Transition." *Developmental Psychology* 48(1):56–64.

Furstenberg, Frank F. Jr., Thomas D. Cook, Jacqueline Eccles, Glen H. Elder Jr., and Arnold Sameroff. 1999. *Managing to Make It: Urban Families and Adolescent Success.* Chicago: University of Chicago Press.

Gaines, Kevin K. 1996. *Uplifting the Race: Black Leadership, Politics, and Culture in the Twentieth Century.* Chapel Hill: University of North Carolina Press.

García, Jorge Luis, James J. Heckman, Duncan E. Leaf, and María J. Prados. 2020. "Quantifying the Life-Cycle Benefits of an Influential Early-Childhood Program." *Journal of Political Economy* 128(7):2502–2541.

Garza, Evan. 2015. "To Be Young, Gifted and Black: The Civil Rights Legacy of Nina Simone." *Blanton Museum of Art Blog,* February 16. http://blantonmuseum.org/2015/02/to-be-young-gifted-and-black-the-civil-rights-legacy-of-nina-simone-2/.

Gasman, Marybeth. 2008. "Minority-Serving Institutions: A Historical Backdrop." Pp. 18–27 in Marybeth Gasman, Benjamin Baez, and Caroline S. V. Turner, eds., *Understanding Minority-Serving Institutions.* Albany: State University of New York Press.

Gasman, Marybeth. 2013. *The Changing Faces of Historically Black Colleges and Universities.* Philadelphia: Center for Minority Serving Institutions, University of Pennsylvania Graduate School of Education. http://www.gse.upenn.edu/pdf/cmsi/Changing_Face_HBCUs.pdf.

Gatewood, Willard B. 2000. *Aristocrats of Color: The Black Elite, 1880–1920.* Fayetteville: University of Arkansas Press.

Gershenson, Seth, and Erdal Tekin. 2017. "The Effect of Community Traumatic Events on Student Achievement: Evidence from the Beltway Sniper Attacks." *Education Finance and Policy* 13(4):513–534.

Gibbs, Jewelle Taylor. 1989. "Biracial Adolescents." Pp. 322–350 in Jewelle T. Gibbs and Larke Nahme Huang, eds., *Children of Color: Psychological Intervention with Minority Youth.* San Francisco: Jossey-Bass.

Gibson, Campbell J., and Kay Jung. 2002. *Historical Census Statistics on Population Totals by Race, 1790 to 1990, and by Hispanic Origin, 1970 to 1990.* Population Division Working Paper 56. Washington, DC: U.S. Census Bureau.

Gibson, Campbell J., and Emily Lennon. 1999. *Historical Census Statistics on the Foreign-Born Population of the United States: 1850–1990.* Washington, DC: U.S. Census Bureau.

Giesler, Carly. 2019. *The Voices of #MeToo: From Grassroots Activism to a Viral Roar*. Lanham, MD: Rowman & Littlefield.

Gilens, Martin. 1999. *Why Americans Hate Welfare: Race, Media, and the Politics of Antipoverty Policy*. Chicago: University of Chicago Press.

Giles-Sims, Jean, Murray A. Straus, and David B. Sugarman. 1995. "Child, Maternal, and Family Characteristics Associated with Spanking." *Family Relations* 44(2):170–176.

Glaser, Barry G., and Anselm L. Strauss. 1967. *The Discovery of Grounded Theory: Strategies for Qualitative Research*. Chicago: Aldine.

Go, Julian. 2018. "Postcolonial Possibilities for the Sociology of Race." *Sociology of Race and Ethnicity* 4(4):439–451.

Goffman, Erving. 1961. *Asylums: Essays on the Social Situation of Mental Patients and Other Inmates*. New York: Doubleday.

Goldin, Claudia, and Lawrence F. Katz. 2008. "Transitions: Career and Family Life Cycles of the Educational Elite." *American Economic Review* 98(2):363–369.

Goldner, Jonathan S., Dakari Quimby, Maryse H. Richards, Arie Zakaryan, Steve Miller, Daniel Dickson, and Jessica Chilson. 2014. "Relations of Parenting to Adolescent Externalizing and Internalizing Distress Moderated by Perception of Neighborhood Danger." *Journal of Clinical Child and Adolescent Psychology* 45(2):141–154.

Goldrick-Rab, Sara. 2016. *Paying the Price: College Costs, Financial Aid, and the Betrayal of the American Dream*. Chicago: University of Chicago Press.

Gordon, April A. 1996. *Transforming Capitalism and Patriarchy: Gender and Development in Africa*. Boulder, CO: Lynne Rienner.

Gordon-Reed, Annette. 2008. *The Hemingses of Monticello: An American Family*. New York: Norton.

Graham, Lawrence O. 1999. *Our Kind of People: Inside America's Black Upper Class*. New York: Harper.

Granovetter, Mark S. 1973. "The Strength of Weak Ties." *American Journal of Sociology* 78(6): 1360–1380.

Grant, Ruth W., and Marion Orr. 1996. "Language, Race, and Politics: From 'Black' to 'African American.'" *Politics & Society* 24(2):137–152.

Gray, Marjory R., and Laurence Steinberg. 1999. "Unpacking Authoritative Parenting: Reassessing a Multidimensional Construct." *Journal of Marriage and the Family* 61(3):574–587.

Green, Adrienne. 2016. "The Cost of Balancing Academia and Racism." *The Atlantic*, January 21. https://www.theatlantic.com/education/archive/2016/01/balancing-academia-racism /424887.

Greenwald, Anthony G., and Mahzarin R. Banaji. 1995. "Implicit Social Cognition: Attitudes, Self-Esteem, and Stereotypes." *Psychological Review* 102(1):4–27.

Greer, Christina M. 2013. *Black Ethnics: Race, Immigration, and the Pursuit of the American Dream*. New York: Oxford University Press.

Greer, Tawanda M., and Kathleen Chwalisz. 2007. "Minority-Related Stressors and Coping Processes among African American College Students." *Journal of College Student Development* 48(4):388–404.

Gregory, Steven. 1998. *Black Corona: Race and Politics of Place in an Urban Community*. Princeton, NJ: Princeton University Press.

Griffin, Kimberly, Wilfredo del Pilar, Kadian McIntosh, and Autumn Griffin. 2012. "'Oh, of Course I'm Going to Go to College': Understanding How Habitus Shapes the College Choice Process of Black Immigrant Students." *Journal of Diversity in Higher Education* 5(2):96–111.

Griffin, Kimberly A., Meghan J. Pifer, Jordan R. Humphrey, and Ashley M. Hazelwood. 2011. "(Re)defining Departure: Exploring Black Professors' Experiences with and Responses to Race and Racism." *American Journal of Education* 117(4):495–526.

Guffrida, Douglas L. 2003. "African American Student Organizations as Agents of Socialization." *Journal of College Development* 44(3):304–319.

Gullickson, Aaron. 2006. "Education and Black-White Interracial Marriage." *Demography* 43(4):673–689.

Gurin, Patricia, Shirley Hatchett, and James S. Jackson. 1989. *Hope and Independence: Blacks' Response to Electoral and Party Politics*. New York: Russell Sage Foundation.

Gusa, Diane Lynn. 2010. "White Institutional Presence: The Impact of Whiteness on Campus Climate." *Harvard Educational Review* 80(4):464–489.

Gyekye, Kwame. 1996. *African Cultural Values: An Introduction*. Accra: Sankofa.

Hall, Ronald E. 2010. *An Historical Analysis of Skin Color Discrimination in America*. New York: Springer.

Hallet, Ronald E., and Kristan M. Venegas. 2011. "Is Increased Access Enough? Advanced Placement Courses, Quality, and Success in Low-Income Urban Schools." *Journal for the Education of the Gifted* 34(3):468–487.

Hamilton, Tod. 2012. "Arrival Cohort, Assimilation, and the Earnings of Caribbean Women." *Review of Black Political Economy* 39(4):445–460.

Hamilton, Tod. 2013. "Black Immigration." Pp. 263–267 in Patrick L. Mason, ed., *Encyclopedia of Race and Racism*. 2nd ed. New York: Macmillan Reference USA.

Hamilton, Tod. 2014. "Selection, Language Heritage, and the Earnings Trajectories of Black Immigrants in the United States." *Demography* 50(3):975–1002.

Hamilton, Tod. 2019. *Immigration and the Remaking of Black America*. New York: Russell Sage Foundation.

Hannon, Lance. 2015. "White Colorism." *Social Currents* 2(1):13–21.

Hannon, Lance, Robert DeFina, and Sarah Bruch. 2013. "The Relationship between Skin Tone and School Suspension for African Americans." *Race and Social Problems* 5(4):281–295.

Hansberry, Lorraine. 1969. *To Be Young, Gifted and Black: Lorraine Hansberry in Her Own Words*. Adapted by Robert Nemiroff. New York: Signet Classics.

Harper, Cassandra E., and Fanny G. Yeung. 2015. "College Student Characteristics and Experiences as Predictors of Interracial Dating." *College Student Journal* 49(4):599–609.

Harper, Shaun R. 2008. "Realizing the Intended Outcomes of Brown: African American Male Undergraduates and Social Capital." *American Behavioral Scientist* 51(7):1030–1053.

Harper, Shaun R. 2015. "Black Male College Achievers and Resistant Responses to Racist Stereotypes at Predominantly White Colleges and Universities." *Harvard Educational Review* 85(4):646–674.

Harris, Angel L. 2011. *Kids Don't Want to Fail: Oppositional Culture and the Black-White Achievement Gap*. Cambridge, MA: Harvard University Press.

Harris, David R., and Justin Thomas. 2002. *The Educational Costs of Being Multiracial: Evidence from a National Survey of Adolescents*. PSC Research Report 02-521. Ann Arbor: Population

Studies Center, University of Michigan. https://www.psc.isr.umich.edu/pubs/pdf.php?i=8984719362876604422464908749&f=rr02-521.pdf.

Harris, Herbert W. 1995. "Introduction: A Conceptual Overview of Race, Ethnicity and Identity." Pp. 1–25 in Herbert W. Harris, Howard C. Blue, and Ezra H. Griffith, eds., *Racial and Ethnic Identity: Psychological Development and Creative Expression*. New York: Routledge.

Haynes, Bruce D. 2001. *Red Lines, Black Spaces: The Politics of Race and Space in a Black Middle-Class Suburb*. New Haven, CT: Yale University Press.

Haynie, Aisha Cecilia. 2002. "Not 'Just Black' Policy Considerations: The Influence of Ethnicity on Pathways to Academic Success amongst Black Undergraduates at Harvard University." *Journal of Public and International Affairs* 13(1):40–62.

Heckman, James J. 2011. "The Economics of Inequality: The Value of Early Childhood Education." *American Educator* 25(1):31–47.

Heilemann, John. 1995. "Black Is Back." *New Yorker*, October 30, 33. https://www.newyorker.com/magazine/1995/10/30/black-is-back.

Heitzeg, Nancy A. 2016. *The School-to-Prison Pipeline: Education, Discipline, and Racialized Double Standards*. New York: Praeger.

Herman, Melissa R., and Mary E. Campbell. 2012. "I Wouldn't, but You Can: Attitudes toward Interracial Relationships." *Social Science Research* 41(2):343–358.

Herndon, Michael K., and Joan B. Hirt. 2004. "Black Students and Their Families: What Leads to Success in College." *Journal of Black Studies* 34(4):489–513.

Herring, Cedric, and Loren Henderson. 2016. "Wealth Inequality in Black and White: Cultural and Structural Sources of the Racial Wealth Gap." *Race and Social Problems* 8(1):4–17.

Herring, Cedric, Verna M. Keith, and Hayward Derrick Horton. 2004. *Skin Deep: How Race and Complexion Matter in the "Color-Blind" Era*. Urbana: University of Illinois Press.

Hersch, Joni. 2011. "The Persistence of Skin Color Discrimination for Immigrants." *Social Science Research* 40(5):1337–1349.

Higginbotham, Evelyn B. 1993. *Righteous Discontent: The Women's Movement in the Black Baptist Church, 1880–1920*. Cambridge, MA: Harvard University Press.

Hill, Mark. 2000. "Color Differences in the Socioeconomic Status of African American Men: Results of a Longitudinal Study." *Social Forces* 78(4):1437–1460.

Hill, Nancy, E. Domini R. Castellino, Jennifer E. Lansford, Patrick Nowlin, Kenneth A. Dodge, John E. Bates, and Gregory S. Pettit. 2004. "Parent Academic Involvement as Related to School Behavior, Achievement, and Aspirations: Demographic Variations across Adolescence." *Child Development* 75(5):1491–1509.

Hill, Shirley A. 2001. "Class, Race, and Gender Dimensions on Child Rearing in African American Families." *Journal of Black Studies* 31(4):494–508.

Hill, Shirley A. 2005. *Black Intimacies: A Gender Perspective on Families and Relationships*. Walnut Creek, CA: AltaMira.

Hirsch, Jennifer S., and Shamus Khan. 2020. *Sexual Citizens: A Landmark Study of Sex, Power, and Assault on Campus*. New York: Norton.

Hirschl, Thomas, Joyce Altobelli, and Mark R. Rank. 2003. "Does Marriage Increase the Odds of Affluence? Exploring the Life Course Probabilities." *Journal of Marriage and Family* 65(4):927–938.

Hobson, Charles J., Joseph Kamen, Jana Szostek, Carol M. Nerthercut, James Tiedmann, and Susan Wojnarowicz. 1998. "Stressful Life Events: A Revision and Update of the Social Re-adjustment Rating Scale." *International Journal of Stress Management* 5(1):1–23.

Hochschild, Jennifer L., and Vesla Weaver. 2007. "The Skin Color Paradox and the American Racial Order." *Social Forces* 86(2):643–670.

Holloway, S. R., M. Ellis, R. Wright, and M. Hudson. 2005. "Partnering 'Out' and Fitting In: Residential Segregation and the Neighbourhood Contexts of Mixed-Race Households." *Population, Space, and Place* 11(4):299–324.

Holt, Brianna. 2020. "Now I Understand Why My Parents Were So Strict." *The Atlantic*, June 30. https://www.theatlantic.com/family/archive/2020/06/my-black-parents-had-be-strict /612610/.

hooks, bell. 1981. *Ain't I a Woman: Black Women and Feminism.* Boston: South End.

Horn, Laura J., and C. Dennis Carroll. 1998. *Stopouts or Stayouts? Undergraduates Who Leave College in Their First Year.* Washington, DC: National Center for Educational Statistics.

Horowitz, Ruth E. 1939. "Racial Aspects of Self-Identification in Nursery School Children." *Journal of Psychology* 7(1):91–99.

Horvat, Erin M., and Anthony L. Antonio. 1999. "'Hey, Those Shoes Are Out of Uniform': African American Girls in an Elite High School and the Importance of Habitus." *Anthropology & Education Quarterly* 30(3):317–342.

Howard, Simon, and Alex M. Borgella. 2020. "Are Adewale and Ngochi More Employable than Jamal and Lakeisha? The Influence of Nationality and Ethnicity Cues on Employment-Related Evaluations of Blacks in the United States." *Journal of Social Psychology* 160(4):509–519.

Huelsman, Mark. 2015. *The Debt Divide: The Racial and Class Bias behind the "New Normal" of Student Borrowing.* New York: Demos.

Hughes, Everett C. 1963. "Race and the Sociological Imagination." *American Sociological Review* 28(6):879–890.

Hughes, Michael, and Bradley Hertel. 1990. "The Significance of Color Remains: A Study of Life Chances, Mate Selection, and Ethnic Consciousness among Black Americans." *Social Forces* 68(4):1105–1120.

Hunt, Matthew O. 2007. "African American, Hispanic, and White Beliefs about Black/White Inequality, 1977-2004." *American Sociological Review* 72(3):390–415.

Hunter, Lea, Ed Chung, and Akua Amaning. 2020. *Fact Sheet: Trump Says One Thing and Does Another on Criminal Justice.* Washington, DC: Center for American Progress. https://www .americanprogress.org/issues/criminal-justice/reports/2020/ 02/03/480028/fact-sheet -trump-says-one-thing-another-criminal-justice/.

Hunter, Marcus A. 2015. "W. E. B. Du Bois and Black Heterogeneity: How the Philadelphia Negro Shaped American Sociology." *American Sociologist* 46(2):219–233.

Hunter, Margaret L. 1998. "Colorstruck: Skin Color Stratification in the Lives of African American Women." *Sociological Inquiry* 68(4):517–535.

Hunter, Margaret L. 2002. "'If You're Light You're Alright': Light Skin Color as Social Capital for Women of Color." *Gender & Society* 16(2):175–193.

Hunter, Margaret L. 2007. "The Persistent Problem of Colorism: Skin Tone, Status, and Inequality." *Sociology Compass* 1(1):237–254.

Hurtado, Sylvia, Cynthia L. Alvarez, Chelsea Guillermo-Wann, Marcela Cuellar, and Lucy Arellano. 2012. "A Model for Diverse Learning Environments: The Scholarship on Creating and Assessing Conditions for Student Success." Pp. 41–122 in John C. Smart and Michael B. Paulsen, eds., *Higher Education: Handbook of Theory and Research*. New York: Springer.

Hurtado, Sylvia, Kimberly A. Griffin, Lucy Arellano, and Marcela Cuellar. 2008. "Assessing the Value of Climate Assessments: Progress and Future Directions." *Journal of Diversity in Higher Education* 1(4):204–221.

Hwang, Jackelyn. 2016. "The Social Construction of a Gentrifying Neighborhood: Reifying and Redefining Identity and Boundaries in Inequality." *Urban Affairs Review* 52(1):98–128.

Ingoldby, Bron, Paul Schvaneveldt, Andrew Supple, and Kevin Bush. 2003. "The Relationship between Parenting and Behaviors and Adolescent Achievement and Self-Efficacy in Chile and Ecuador." *Marriage and Family Review* 35(3–4):139–159.

Intrator, Jake, Jonathan Tannen, and Douglas S. Massey. 2016. "Segregation by Race and Income in the United States 1970–2010." *Social Science Research* 60(1):45–60.

Inzlicht, Michael, and Sonia K. Kang. 2010. "Stereotype Threat Spillover: How Coping with Threats to Social Identity Affects Aggression, Eating, Decision-Making, and Attention." *Journal of Personality and Social Psychology* 99(3):467–481.

Inzlicht, Michael, and Toni Schmader. 2012. *Stereotype Threat: Theory, Process, and Application*. New York: Oxford University Press.

Irizarry, Yasmiyn. 2013. "Is Measuring Interracial Contact Enough? Racial Concentration, Racial Balance, and Perceptions of Prejudice among Black Americans." *Social Science Quarterly* 94(3):591–615.

Jack, Anthony A. 2014. "Culture Shock Revisited: The Social and Cultural Contingencies to Class Marginality." *Sociological Forum* 29(2):453–475.

Jack, Anthony A. 2019. *The Privileged Poor: How Elite Colleges Are Failing Disadvantaged Students*. Cambridge, MA: Harvard University Press.

Jackson, Kenneth T. 1985. *Crabgrass Frontier: The Suburbanization of the United States*. New York: Oxford University Press.

James, Rosalina, Helene Starks, Valerie Segrest, and Wylie Burke. 2012. "From Leaky Pipeline to Irrigation System: Minority Education through the Lens of Community-Based Participatory Research." *Progressive Community Health Partnership* 6(4):471–479.

Jaret, Charles, and Donald C. Reitzes. 2009. "Currents in a Stream: College Student Identities and Ethnic Identities and Their Relationship with Self-esteem, Efficacy, and Grade Point Average in an Urban University." *Social Science Quarterly* 90(2):345–367.

Jargowsky, Paul, and Mary Jo Bane. 1990. "Ghetto Poverty: Basic Questions." Pp. 16–67 in Laurence E. Lynn and Michael G. H. McGeary, eds., *Inner-City Poverty in the United States*. Washington, DC: National Academies Press.

Jarrett, Robin L., Patrick J. Sullivan, and Natasha D. Watkins. 2005. "Developing Social Capital through Participation in Organized Youth Programs: Qualitative Insights from Three Programs." *Journal of Community Psychology* 33(1):41–55.

Johnson, Anne, Tobin Van Ostern, and Abraham White. 2012. *The Student Debt Crisis*. Washington, DC: Center for American Progress. https://www.americanprogress.org/issues/education-postsecondary/reports/2012/ 10/25/42905/the-student-debt-crisis/.

Johnson, Anthony M. 2019. "'I Can Turn It On When I Need To': Pre-college Integration, Culture, and Peer Academic Engagement among Black and Latino/a Engineering Students." *Sociology of Education* 92(1):1–20.

Johnson, Odis Jr. 2010. "Assessing Neighborhood Racial Segregation and Macroeconomic Effects in the Education of African Americans." *Review of Educational Research* 80(4): 527–575.

Johnson, Violet M. 2000. *The Other Black Bostonians: West Indians in Boston, 1900–1950.* Bloomington: Indiana University Press.

Jones, Antwan, Marcus Andrews, and Sarah Policastro. 2015. "Neighborhood Racial Composition, Institutional Socialization, and Intraracial Feelings of Closeness among Black Americans." *Urban Studies Research* 2015(712046):1–12. http://downloads.hindawi.com/archive/2015/712046.pdf.

Jones, Nicholas A., and Jungmiwha Bullock. 2012. "The Two or More Races Population: 2010." *2010 Census Briefs C2010BR-13.* Washington, DC: U.S. Census Bureau. https://www.census.gov/prod/cen2010/briefs/c2010br-13.pdf.

Jones, Nicholas A., and Amy S. Smith. 2001. "The Two or More Races Population: 2000." *Census 2000 Brief C2KBR/01-6.* Washington, DC: U.S. Census Bureau. https://www2.census.gov/library/publications/decennial/2000/briefs/c2kbr01-06.pdf.

Jones-White, Daniel R., Peter M. Radcliffe, Linda M. Lorenz, and Krista M. Soria. 2014. "Priced Out? The Influence of Financial Aid on the Educational Trajectories of First-Year Students Starting College at a Large Research University." *Research in Higher Education* 55(4): 329–350.

Jordan, Winthrop D. 2014. "Historical Origins of the One-Drop Racial Rule in the United States." *Emerging Paradigms in Critical Mixed Race Studies* 1(1):98–124.

Joyner, Kara, and Grace Kao. 2005. "Interracial Relationships and the Transition to Adulthood." *American Sociological Review* 70(4):563–581.

Judson, Eugene, and Angela Hobson. 2015. "Growth and Achievement Trends of Advanced Placement (AP) Exams in American High Schools." *American Secondary Education* 43(2):59–76.

Kalmijn, Matthijs, and Gerbert Kraaykamp. 1996. "Race, Cultural Capital, and Schooling: An Analysis of Trends in the United States." *Sociology of Education* 69(1):22–34.

Kaplan, Eric J. 2010. *Peer Social Networks among Low-Income Students at an Elite College.* PhD diss., University of Pennsylvania. https://repository.upenn.edu/dissertations/AAI3410479/.

Karp, David A., Lynda L. Holmstrom, and Paul S. Gray. 1998. "Leaving Home for College: Expectations for Selective Reconstruction of Self." *Symbolic Interaction* 21(3):253–276.

Kasinitz, Phillip, Mary C. Torres, and John H. Mollenkopf. 2009. *Inheriting the City: The Children of Immigrants Come of Age.* New York: Russell Sage Foundation.

Katznelson, Ira. 2005. *When Affirmative Action Was White: An Untold History of Racial Inequality in Twentieth-Century America.* New York: Norton.

Kaufman, Jason, and Jay Gabler. 2004. "Cultural Capital and the Extracurricular Activities of Girls and Boys in the College Attainment Process." *Poetics* 32(2):145–168.

Keels, Micera, and Keshia Harris. 2014. "Intercultural Dating at Predominantly White Universities in the United States: The Maintenance and Crossing of Group Borders." *Societies* 4(3):363–379.

Kelchen, Robert, Sara Goldrick-Rab, and Braden Hosch. 2017. "The Costs of College Attendance: Examining Variation and Consistency in Institutional Living Cost Allowances."
Journal of Higher Education 88(2):1–25.

Kelly, Andrew P., and Sara Goldrick-Rab. 2014. *Reinventing Financial Aid: Charting a New Course
to College Affordability*. Cambridge, MA: Harvard Education Press.

Kennedy, Louise V. 1968. *The Negro Peasant Turns Cityward*. Brooklyn, NY: AMS Press.

Kent, Mary M. 2007. "Immigration and America's Black Population." *Population Bulletin*
62(4):1–15.

Khan, Shamus R. 2011. *Privilege: The Making of an Adolescent Elite at St. Paul's School*. Princeton,
NJ: Princeton University Press.

Khanna, Nikki. 2011. *Biracial in America: Forming and Performing Racial Identity*. Boston: Lex-
ington Books.

Khanna, Nikki, and Cathryn Johnson. 2010. "Passing as Black: Racial Identity Work among
Biracial Americans." *Social Psychology Quarterly* 73(4):380–397.

Kilson, Martin. 2014. *Transformation of the African American Intelligentsia, 1880–1912*. Cambridge,
MA: Harvard University Press.

Kim, Catherine Y., Daniel J. Losen, and Damon T. Hewitt. 2012. *The School-to-Prison Pipeline:
Structuring Legal Reform*. New York: New York University Press.

Kim, Mikyong M., and Clifton F. Conrad. 2006. "The Impact of Historically Black Colleges and
Universities on the Academic Success of African American Students." *Research in Higher
Education* 47(4):399–427.

King, Noel and Walter Ray Watson. 2019. "Nina Simone's 'Lovely, Precious Dream' For Black
Children." National Public Radio (Morning Edition), January 8. https://www.npr.org
/2019/01/08/683021559/nina-simone-to-be-young-gifted-and-black-american
-anthem.

Klopfenstein, K. 2004. "Advanced Placement: Do Minorities Have Equal Opportunities?" *Economics of Education Review* 23(2):115–131.

Korgen, Kathleen O. 1998. *From Black to Biracial: Transforming Racial Identity among Americans*.
New York: Praeger.

Kozol, Jonathan. 1991. *Savage Inequalities: Children in America's Schools*. New York: Harper.

Kronus, Sidney. 1971. *The Black Middle Class*. Columbus, OH: Merrill.

Kuriloff, Peter, and Michael C. Reichert. 2003. "Boys of Class, Boys of Color: Negotiating the
Academic and Social Geography of an Elite Independent School." *Journal of Social Issues*
59(4):751–769.

Lacoe, Johanna. 2016. "Too Scared to Learn? The Academic Consequences of Feeling Unsafe
in the Classroom." *Urban Education Online*. https://doi.org/10.1177/0042085916674059.

Lacy, Karyn R. 2004. "Black Spaces, Black Places: Strategic Assimilation and Identity Construction in Middle-Class Suburbia." *Ethnic and Racial Studies* 27(6):908–930.

Lacy, Karyn R. 2007. *Blue-Chip Black: Race, Class, and Status in the New Black Middle Class*.
Berkeley: University of California Press.

Ladner, Joyce. 1971. *Tomorrow's Tomorrow: The Black Woman*. Garden City, NY: Doubleday.

Lamont, Michèle, and Crystal M. Fleming. 2005. "Everyday Antiracism: Culture and Religion
in the Cultural Repertoire of the African American Elite." *Du Bois Review: Social Science
Research on Race* 2(1):29–43.

Lamont, Michèle, and Annette Lareau. 1988. "Cultural Capital: Allusions, Gaps, and Glissandos in Recent Theoretical Developments." *Sociological Theory* 6(2):153–168.

Landor, Antoinette M., Leslie G. Simons, Ronald L. Simons, Gene H. Brody, Chalandra M. Bryant, Frederick X. Gibbons, Ellen M. Granberg, and Janet N. Melby. 2013. "Exploring the Impact of Skin Tone on Family Dynamics and Race-Related Outcomes." *Journal of Family Psychology* 27(5):817–826.

Landry, Bart. 1987. *The New Black Middle Class.* Berkeley: University of California Press.

Landry, Bart. 2018. *The New Black Middle Class in the Twenty-First Century.* New Brunswick, NJ: Rutgers University Press.

Lansford, Jennifer E., Kirby Deater-Deckard, Kenneth A. Dodge, John E. Bates, and Gregory S. Pettit. 2004. "Ethnic Differences in the Link between Physical Discipline and Later Adolescent Externalizing Behaviors." *Journal of Child Psychological Psychiatry* 45(4):801–812.

Lareau, Annette. 2003. *Unequal Childhoods: Class, Race, and Family Life.* Berkeley: University of California Press.

Lareau Annette, and Elliot B. Weininger. 2003. "Cultural Capital in Educational Research: A Critical Assessment." *Theory and Society* 32(5–6):567–606.

Lee, Barrett A., Sean F. Reardon, Glenn Firebaugh, Chad R. Farrell, Stephen A. Matthews, and David O'Sullivan. 2008. "Beyond the Census Tract: Patterns and Determinants of Racial Segregation at Multiple Geographic Scales." *American Sociological Review* 73(5):766–791.

Lee, Elizabeth A., and Rory Kramer. 2013. "Out with the Old, in with the New? Habitus and Social Mobility at Selective Colleges." *Sociology of Education* 86(1):18–35.

Lee, Jennifer, and Frank Bean. 2010. *The Diversity Paradox. Immigration and the Color Line in America.* New York: Russell Sage.

Lee, Jennifer, and Min Zhou. 2015. *The Asian American Achievement Paradox.* New York: Russell Sage Foundation.

Lemann, Nicholas. 1991. *The Promised Land: The Great Black Migration and How It Changed America.* New York: Knopf.

Leo-Rhynie, Elsa A. 1996. "Class, Race, and Gender Issues in Child Rearing in the Caribbean." Pp. 25–56 in Janet Brown and Jaipaul L. Roopnarine, eds., *Caribbean Families: Diversity among Ethnic Groups.* Greenwich, CT: Ablex.

Levin, Shana, Pamela L. Taylor, and Elena Caudle. 2007. "Interethnic and Interracial Dating in College: A Longitudinal Study." *Journal of Social and Personal Relationships* 23(4):323–341.

Lewis, Daniel Levering. 1995. "The Intellectual Luminaries of the Harlem Renaissance." *Journal of Blacks in Higher Education* 7:68–69.

Lieberson, Stanley. 1980. *A Piece of the Pie: Blacks and White Immigrants since 1880.* Berkeley: University of California Press.

Lipson, Sarah K., Adam Kern, Daniel Eisenberg, and Alfiee Breland-Noble. 2018. "Mental Health Disparities among College Students of Color." *Journal of Adolescent Health* 63(3):348–356.

Lipson, Sarah K., Emily G. Lattie, and Daniel Eisenberg. 2019. "Increased Rates of Mental Health Service Utilization by US College Students: 10-Year Population-Level Trends (2007–2017)." *Psychiatric Services* 70(1): 60–63.

Livingston, Gretchen, and Anna Brown. 2017. *Intermarriage in the U.S. 50 Years after* Loving v. Virginia. Washington, DC: Pew Research Center. https://www.pewsocialtrends.org/2017/05/18/intermarriage-in-the-u-s-50-years-after-loving-v-virginia/.

Lofton, Richard, and James Earl Davis. 2015. "Toward a Black Habitus: African Americans Navigating Systemic Inequalities within Home, School, and Community." *Journal of Negro Education* 84(3):214–230.

Logan, Rayford W. 1958. "The Evolution of Private Colleges for Negroes." *Journal of Negro Education* 27(3):213–220.

Lovallo, William J. 2016. *Stress and Health: Biological and Psychological Interactions.* 3rd ed. New York: Sage.

Lovett, Bobby L. 2011. *America's Historically Black Colleges: A Narrative History, 1837–2009.* Macon, GA: Mercer University Press.

Maddox, Keith B., and Stephanie A. Gray. 2002. "Cognitive Representations of Black Americans: Reexploring the Role of Skin Tone." *Personality and Social Psychology Bulletin* 28(2):250–259.

Magee, Joe C., and Pamela K. Smith. 2013. "The Social Distance Theory of Power." *Personality and Social Psychology Review* 17(2):158–186.

Mandara, Jelani, Fatima Varner, and Scott Richman. 2010. "Do African American Mothers Really 'Love' Their Sons and 'Raise' Their Daughters?" *Journal of Family Psychology* 24(1):41–50.

Manning, Alex. 2019. "The Age of Concerted Cultivation: A Racial Analysis of Parental Repertoires and Childhood Activities." *DuBois Review* 16(1):1–31.

Marks, Carole. 1989. *Farewell, We're Good and Gone: The Great Black Migration.* Bloomington: Indiana University Press.

Marques, Leonardo. 2016. *The United States and the Transatlantic Slave Trade to the Americas, 1776–1867.* New Haven, CT: Yale University Press.

Marsh, Kris, William Darity, Phillip N. Cohen, Lynne M. Casper, and Daniel Salters. 2007. "The Emerging Black Middle Class: Single and Living Alone." *Social Forces* 86(2):735–762.

Martin, Ben L. 1991. "From Negro to Black to African American: The Power of Names and Naming." *Political Science Quarterly* 106(1):83–107.

Martin, Lori L. 2010. 'Strategic Assimilation or Creation of Symbolic Blackness: Middle-Class Blacks in Suburban Contexts." *Journal of African American Studies* 14(2):234–246.

Marx, David M., and Philip A. Goff. 2006. "Clearing the Air: The Effect of Experimenter Race on Target's Test Performance and Subjective Experience." *British Journal of Social Psychology* 44(4):645–657.

Massey, Douglas S. 1990. "American Apartheid: Segregation and the Making of the Underclass." *American Journal of Sociology* 96:329–357.

Massey, Douglas S. 2007. *Categorically Unequal: The American Stratification System.* New York: Russell Sage.

Massey, Douglas S. 2013. "Inheritance of Poverty or Inheritance of Place? The Emerging Consensus on Neighborhoods and Stratification." *Contemporary Sociology* 42(5):690–697.

Massey, Douglas S. 2018. "Segregation in 21st Century America." *Journal of Catholic Social Thought* 15(2):235–260.

Massey, Douglas S. 2020. "Still the Linchpin: Segregation and Stratification in the USA." *Race and Social Problems* 12(1):1–12. https://doi.org/10.1007/s12552-019-09280-1.

Massey, Douglas S., Len Albright, Rebecca Casciano, Elizabeth Derickson, and David Kinsey. 2013. *Climbing Mount Laurel: The Struggle for Affordable Housing and Social Mobility in an American Suburb.* Princeton, NJ: Princeton University Press.

Massey, Douglas S., and Stefanie Brodmann. 2014. *Spheres of Influence: The Social Ecology of Racial and Class Inequality*. New York: Russell Sage Foundation.

Massey, Douglas S., Camille Charles, Garvey Lundy, and Mary J. Fischer. 2003. *Source of the River: The Social Origins of Freshmen at America's Selective Colleges and Universities*. Princeton, NJ: Princeton University Press.

Massey, Douglas S., and Nancy A. Denton. 1985. "Spatial Assimilation as a Socioeconomic Outcome." *American Sociological Review* 50:94–105

Massey, Douglas S., and Nancy A. Denton. 1989. "Hypersegregation in U.S. Metropolitan Areas: Black and Hispanic Segregation along Five Dimensions." *Demography* 26:373–93.

Massey, Douglas S., and Nancy A. Denton. 1993. *American Apartheid: Segregation and the Making of the Underclass*. Cambridge, MA: Harvard University Press.

Massey, Douglas S., and Mary J. Fischer. 2005. "Stereotype Threat and Academic Performance: New Findings from a Racially Diverse Sample of College Freshmen." *DuBois Review* 2(1):45–67.

Massey, Douglas S., and Mary J. Fischer. 2006. "The Effect of Childhood Segregation on Minority Academic Performance at Selective Colleges." *Ethnic and Racial Studies* 29(1):1–26.

Massey, Douglas S., and Margarita Mooney. 2007. "The Effects of America's Three Affirmative Action Programs on Academic Performance." *Social Problems* 54(1):99–117.

Massey, Douglas S., Margarita Mooney, Kimberly C. Torres, and Camille Z. Charles. 2007. "Black Immigrants and Black Natives Attending Selective Colleges and Universities in the United States." *American Journal of Education* 113(2):243–271.

Massey, Douglas S., and Jayanti Owens. 2014. "Mediators of Stereotype Threat among Black College Students." *Ethnic and Racial Studies* 37(3):557–575.

Massey, Douglas S., and LiErin Probasco. 2010. "Divergent Streams. Race-Gender Achievement Gaps at Selective Colleges and Universities." *Du Bois Review* 7(1):219–246.

Massey, Douglas S., and Jacob S. Rugh. 2018. "The Great Recession and the Destruction of Minority Wealth." *Current History* 117(802):298–303.

Massey, Douglas S., and Jacob S. Rugh. 2021. "America's Unequal Metropolitan Geography: Segregation and the Spatial Concentration of Affluence and Poverty." Pp. 161–187 in Frances Rosenbluth and Margaret Weir, eds., *The New Politics of Insecurity*. New York: Cambridge University Press.

Massey, Douglas S., Jacob S. Rugh, Justin P. Steil, and Len Albright. 2016. "'Riding the Stagecoach to Hell': A Qualitative Analysis of Racial Discrimination in Mortgage Lending." *City and Community* 15(2):118–136.

Massey, Douglas S., and Jonathan Tannen. 2015. "A Research Note on Trends in Black Hypersegregation." *Demography* 52(3):1025–1034.

Massey, Douglas S., and Jonathan Tannen. 2016. "Segregation, Race, and the Social Worlds of Rich and Poor." Pp. 13–33 in Henry Braun and Irwin Kirsch, eds., *The Dynamics of Opportunity in America: Evidence and Perspectives*. New York: Springer.

Massey, Douglas S., and Jonathan Tannen. 2017. "Suburbanization and Segregation in the United States." *Ethnic and Racial Studies* 41(9):1594–1611.

Mathurin, Melba N., Uwe P. Gielen, and Jennifer Lancaster. 2006. "Corporal Punishment and Personality Traits in the Children of St. Croix, United States Virgin Islands." *Cross-Cultural Research* 40(3):306–324.

Mattern, Kristin D., Emily J. Shaw, and Xinhui Xiong. 2009. *The Relationship between AP Exam Performance and College Outcomes*. College Board Research Report 2009-4. New York: College Board. http://files.eric.ed.gov/fulltext/ED561021.pdf.

McAdam, Doug. 1982. *Political Process and the Development of Black Insurgency, 1930–1970*. Chicago: University of Chicago Press.

McAdoo, Harriette P. 1997. "Upward Mobility across Generations in African American Families." Pp. 139–162 in Harriette P. McAdoo, ed., *Black Families*. 3rd ed. Thousand Oaks, CA: Sage.

McAdoo, Harriette P. 1988. "Transgenerational Patterns of Upward Mobility in African American Families." Pp. 148–168 in Harriet P. McAdoo, ed., *Black Families*. Newbury Park, CA: Sage.

McCall, Leslie. 2005. "The Complexity of Intersectionality." *Signs: Journal of Women in Culture and Society* 30(3):1771–1800.

McClain, Kevin, and April Perry. 2017. "Where Did They Go: Retention Rates for Students of Color at Predominantly White Institutions." *College Student Affairs Leadership* 4(1), Article 3:1–10. https://scholarworks.gvsu.edu/cgi/viewcontent.cgi?article=1047&context=csal.

McClendon, David, Janet C. L. Kuo, and Kelly R. Raley. 2014. "Opportunities to Meet: Occupational Education and Marriage Formation in Young Adulthood." *Demography* 51(4):1319–1344.

McFarland, Daniel A., James Moody, David Diehl, and Ruben J. Thomas. 2014. "Network Ecology and Adolescent Social Structure." *American Sociological Review* 79(6):1088–1121.

McLoyd, Vonnie, Ana Mari Cauce, David Takeuchi, and Leon Wilson. 2000. "Marital Processes and Parental Socialization in Families of Color: A Decade of Research." *Journal of Marriage and Family* 62(4):1070–1093.

McMillan Cottom, Tressie. 2019. *Thick: And Other Essays*. New York: New Press.

McPherson, Miller, Lynn Smith-Lovin, and Matthew E. Brashears. 2006. "Social Isolation in America: Changes in Core Discussion Networks over Two Decades." *American Sociological Review* 71(3):353–375.

Merton, Robert. 1941. "Intermarriage and the Social Structure: Fact and Theory." *Psychiatry: A Journal of the Biology and the Pathology of Interpersonal Relations* 4(3):361–374.

Milem, Jeffrey F. 1998. "Attitude Change in College Students: Examining the Effect of College Peer Groups and Faculty Normative Groups." *Journal of Higher Education* 69(2):117–140.

Milem, Jeffrey F., Mitchell J. Chang, and Anthony Lising. 2005. *Making Diversity Work on Campus: A Research-Based Perspective*. Washington, DC: American Association of Colleges and Universities.

Miller, Randall M., and John D. Smith. 1997. *Dictionary of Afro-American Slavery: Updated, with a New Introduction and Bibliography*. Westport, CT: Praeger.

Miller, Suzanne C., Michael A. Olson, and Russell H. Fazio. 2004. "Perceived Reactions to Interracial Romantic Relationships: When Race Is Used as a Cue to Status." *Group Processes Intergroup Relations* 7(4):354–369.

Min, Stella, and Miles G. Taylor. 2018. "Racial and Ethnic Variation in the Relationship between Student Loan Debt and the Transition to First Birth." *Demography* 55(1):165–188.

Model, Suzanne. 2011. *West Indian Immigrants: A Black Success Story?* New York: Russell Sage Foundation.

Monk, Ellis P. 2014. "Skin Tone Stratification among Black Americans, 2001–2003." *Social Forces* 92(4):1313–1337.

Monk, Ellis P. 2015. "The Cost of Color: Skin Color, Discrimination, and Health among African-Americans." *American Journal of Sociology* 121(2):396–444.

Monk, Ellis P. 2018. "The Color of Punishment: African Americans, Skin Tone, and the Criminal Justice System." *Ethnic and Racial Studies* 42(10):1593–1612.

Monk, Ellis P., Michael H. Esposito, and Hedwig Lee. 2021. "Beholding Inequality: Race, Gender, and Returns to Physical Attractiveness in the United States." *American Journal of Sociology* 127(1):194–241.

Moody, James. 2001. "Race, School Integration, and Friendship Segregation in America." *American Journal of Sociology* 107(3):679–716.

Mooney, Margarita. 2010. "Religion, College Grades and Satisfaction among Students at Elite Colleges and Universities." *Sociology of Religion* 71(2):179–215.

Moore, Jacqueline M. 1999. *The Transformation of the Black Elite in the Nation's Capital, 1880–1920*. Charlottesville: University of Virginia Press.

Moore, Kesha S. 2008. "Class Formations: Competing Forms of Black Middle-Class Identity." *Ethnicities* 8(4):492–517.

Morning, Ann. 2011. *The Nature of Race: How Scientists Think and Teach about Human Difference*. Berkeley: University of California Press.

Morris, Edward W. 2007. "'Ladies' or 'Loudies'? Perceptions and Experiences of Black Girls in Classrooms." *Youth and Society* 38(4):490–515.

Morris, Jerome E., and Adeoye Adeyemo. 2012. "Touchdowns and Honor Societies: Expanding the Focus of Black Male Excellence." *Phi Delta Kappan* 93(5):28–32.

Murry, Velma, Gene H. Brody, Lansford Ronald L. Simons, Carolyn E. Cutrona, and Frederick X. Gibbons. 2008. "Disentangling Ethnicity and Context as Predictors of Parenting within Rural Black American Families." *Applied Developmental Science* 12(4):202–210.

Murty, Komanduri, and Julian B. Roebuck. 2015. "African American HBCU Students' Attitudes and Actions toward Interracial Dating and Marriage: A Survey Analysis." *Race, Gender, and Class* 22(3–4):136–153.

Museus, Samuel D. 2014. "The Culturally Engaging Campus Environments (CECE) Model: A New Theory of Success among Racially Diverse College Student Populations." *Higher Education: Handbook of Theory and Research* 29:189–227.

Museus, Samuel D., and Stephen John Quaye. 2009. "Toward an Intercultural Perspective of Racial and Ethnic Minority College Student Persistence." *Review of Higher Education* 33(1):67–94.

Mwangi, Chrystal A. George. 2014. "Complicating Blackness: Black Immigrants & Racial Positioning in U.S. Higher Education." *Journal of Critical Thought and Praxis* 3(2):1–27.

Myrdal, Gunnar. 1944. *An American Dilemma: The Negro Problem and Modern Democracy, Volume I*. New York: Harper and Row.

National Association of College and University Business Officers. 2021. "U.S. and Canadian Institutions Listed by Fiscal Year (FY) 2020 Endowment Market Value and Change in Endowment Market Value from FY19 to FY20." February. https://www.nacubo.org/-/media /Documents/Research/2020-NTSE-Public-Tables—Endowment-Market-Values— FINAL-FEBRUARY-19-2021.ashx.

National Association of Real Estate Boards. 2020. *African American Homeownership Falls to 50-Year Low*. Lanham, MD: National Association of Real Estate Boards. https://www.nareb.com/african-american-homeownership-falls-50-year-low/.

National Student Clearinghouse Research Center. 2020. *Student Tracker*. Washington, DC: National Student Clearinghouse Research Center. https://www.studentclearinghouse.org/colleges/studenttracker/.

Neckerman, Kathryn, Prudence Carter, and Jennifer Lee. 1999. "Segmented Assimilation and Minority Cultures of Mobility." *Ethnic and Racial Studies* 22(6):848–865.

Norwood, Carolette. 2021. "Black Feminist Sociology and the Politics of Space and Place at the Intersection of Race, Class, Gender, and Sexuality." Chap. 10 in Zakiya Luna and Whitney Pirtle, eds., *Black Feminist Sociology: Perspectives and Praxis*. Milton Park, UK: Routledge.

Norwood, Kimberly J., and Violeta Solonova Foreman. 2014. "The Ubiquitousness of Colorism: Then and Now." Pp. 9–29 in Kimberly J. Norwood, ed., *Color Matters: Skin Tone Bias and the Myth of a Post-Racial America*. New York: Routledge.

Nussbaum, David A., and Claude M. Steele. 2007. "Situational Disengagement and Persistence in the Face of Adversity." *Journal of Experimental Psychology* 43(1):127–134.

Oeur, Blume Freeden. 2018. *Black Boys Apart: Racial Uplift and Respectability in All-Male Public School*. Minneapolis: University of Minnesota Press.

Oliver, Melvin L., and Thomas M. Shapiro. 2006. *Black Wealth, White Wealth: A New Perspective on Racial Inequality*. New York: Taylor & Francis.

Onwuachi-Willig, Angela. 2007. "The Admission of Legacy Blacks." *Vanderbilt Law Review* 60(4):1141–1231.

Otterbein, Keith F. 1965. "Caribbean Family Organization: A Comparative Analysis." *American Anthropologist* 67(1):66–79.

Owens, Ann. 2017. "Racial Residential Segregation of School-Age Children and Adults: The Role of Schooling as a Segregating force." *RSF: The Russell Sage Foundation Journal of the Social Sciences* 3(2):63–80.

Owens, Ann. 2018. "Income Segregation between School Districts and Inequality in Students' Achievement." *Sociology of Education* 91(1):1–27.

Owens, Ann. 2020. "Unequal Opportunity: School and Neighborhood Segregation." *Race and Social Problems* 12(1):29–41.

Owens, Ann, Sean F. Reardon, and Christopher Jencks. 2016. "Income Segregation between Schools and Districts." *American Education Research Journal* 53(4):1159–1197.

Owens, Jayanti, and Scott M. Lynch. 2012. "Black and Hispanic Immigrants' Resilience against Negative-Ability Stereotypes at Selective Colleges and Universities in the United States." *Sociology of Education* 85(4):303–328.

Owens, Jayanti, and Douglas S. Massey. 2011. "Stereotype Threat and College Academic Performance: A Latent Variables Approach." *Social Science Research* 40(1):150–166.

Packard, Gerald M. 2003. *American Nightmare: The History of Jim Crow*. New York: St. Martin's.

Painter, Nell I. 2010. *The History of White People*. New York: Norton.

Palmer, Robert, and Marybeth Gasman. 2008. "'It Takes a Village to Raise a Child': The Role of Social Capital in Promoting Academic Success for African American Men at a Black College." *Journal of College Student Development* 49(1):52–70.

Palmer, Robert T., J. Luke Wood, and Andrew Arroyo. 2015. "Toward a Model of Retention and Persistence for Black Men at Historically Black Colleges and Universities." *Spectrum: A Journal on Black Men* 4(1):5–20.

Parham, Thomas. 1989. "Cycles of Nigresence." *Counseling Psychologist* 17(2):187–226.

Parham, Thomas A., and Paris T. Williams. 1993. "The Relationship of Demographic and Background Factors to Racial Identity Attitudes." *Journal of Black Psychology* 19(1):7–24.

Park, Robert E. 1923. "Negro Race Consciousness as Reflected in Race Literature." *American Review* 1(5):505–517.

Parker, Kim, Juliana Menasce Horowitz, Rich Morin, and Mark Hugo Lopez. 2015. *Multiracial in America: Proud, Diverse and Growing in Numbers*. Washington, DC: Pew Research Center.

Pascarella, E., and P. Terenzini. 2005. *How College Affects Students (Vol. 2): A Third Decade of Research*. San Francisco: Jossey-Bass.

Pattillo, Mary. 1999. *Black Picket Fences: Privilege and Peril among the Black Middle Class*. Chicago: University of Chicago Press.

Pekkarinen, Tuomas. 2012. "Gender Differences in Education." *Nordic Economic Policy Review* 1:165–196.

Perna, Laura W. 2000. "Differences in the Decision to Attend College among African Americans, Hispanics, and Whites." *Journal of Higher Education* 71(2):117–141.

Perry, Teresa, Claude Steele, and Asa G. Hilliard III. 2003. *Young, Gifted, and Black: Promoting High Achievement among African-American Students*. Boston: Beacon.

Peterson, Ruth D., and Lauren J. Krivo. 2010. *Divergent Social Worlds: Neighborhood Crime and the Racial-Spatial Divide*. New York: Russell Sage Foundation.

Pettigrew, Thomas F. 1979. "Racial Change and Social Policy." *Annals of the American Academy of Political and Social Science* 441:114–131.

Pettigrew, Thomas F., and Linda R. Tropp. 2000. "A Meta-analytic Test of Intergroup Contact Theory." *Journal of Personality and Social Psychology* 90(5):751–783.

Pifer, Alan. 1973. *The Higher Education of Blacks in the United States*. New York: Carnegie Corporation.

Platt, Jonathan M., Lisa M. Bates, Justin Jager, Katie A. McLaughlin, and Katherine M. Keyes. 2020. "Changes in the Depression Gender Gap from 1992 to 2014: Cohort Effects and Mediation by Gendered Social Position." *Social Science & Medicine* 258:113088. https://doi.org/10.1016/j.socscimed.2020.113088.

Portes, Alejandro. 1998. "Social Capital: Its Origins and Applications in Modern Sociology." *Annual Review of Sociology* 24:1–24.

Portes, Alejandro, and Rubén G. Rumbaut. 2001. *Legacies: The Story of the Immigrant Generation*. Berkeley: University of California Press.

Portes, Alejandro, and Rubén G. Rumbaut. 2014. *Immigrant America: A Portrait*. 4th ed. Berkeley: University of California Press.

Powers, Daniel A., and Christopher G. Ellison. 1995. "Interracial Contact and Black Racial Attitudes: The Contact Hypothesis and Selectivity Bias." *Social Forces* 74(1):205–226.

Preston, E. Delorus. 1935. "William Syphax, a Pioneer in Negro Education in the District of Columbia." *Journal of Negro History* 20(4):448–476.

Prewitt, Kenneth. 2013. *What Is "Your" Race? The Census and Our Flawed Efforts to Classify Americans*. Princeton, NJ: Princeton University Press.

Public Religion Research Institute. 2013. *American Values Survey 2013*. Washington, DC: Public Religion Research Institute. https://www.prri.org/wp-content/uploads /2014/08/AVS -Topline-FINAL.pdf.

Qian, Zhenchao. 1997. "Breaking the Racial Barriers: Variations in Interracial Marriage between 1980 and 1990." *Demography* 34(2):263–276.

Quadlin, Natasha Yurk, and Daniel Rudel. 2015. "Responsibility or Liability? Student Loan Debt and Time Use in College." *Social Forces* 94(2):589–614.

Quillian, Lincoln. 2006. "New Approaches to Understanding Racial Prejudice and Discrimination." *Annual Review of Sociology* 32:299–328.

Quillian, Lincoln. 2012. "Segregation and Poverty Concentration: The Role of Three Segregations." *American Sociological Review* 77(3):354–379.

Quillian, Lincoln, Devah Pager, Ole Hexel, and Arnfinn Midtbøen. 2017. "Meta-analysis of Field Experiments Shows No Change in Racial Discrimination in Hiring over Time." *Proceedings of the National Academy of Sciences* 114(41):10870–10875.

Quillian, Lincoln, John J. Lee, and Brandon Honoré. 2020. "Racial Discrimination in the U.S. Housing and Mortgage Lending Markets: A Quantitative Review of Trends 1976–2016." *Race and Social Problems* 12(1):13–28.

Radloff, Lenore S. 1977. "The CES-D Scale: A Self-Report Depression Scale for Research in the General Population." *Applied Psychological Measurement* 1(3):385–401.

Raley, R. Kelly, Megan M. Sweeney, and Danielle Wondra. 2015. "The Growing Racial and Ethnic Divide in U.S. Marriage Patterns." *Future of Children* 25(2):89–109.

Reardon, Sean F. 2016. "School Segregation and Racial Academic Achievement Gaps." *RSF: Russell Sage Foundation Journal of the Social Sciences* 2(5):34–57.

Reardon, Sean F., Lindsay Fox, and Joseph Townsend. 2015. "Neighborhood Income Composition by Household Race and Income 1990–2009." *Annals of the American Academy of Political and Social Science* 660:78–97.

Reardon, Sean F., and Ann Owens. 2014. "60 Years after Brown: Trends and Consequences of School Segregation." *Annual Review of Sociology* 40:199–218.

Redford, Jeremy, Jennifer A. Johnson, and Julie Honnold. 2009. "Parenting Practices, Cultural Capital and Educational Outcomes: The Effects of Concerted Cultivation on Academic Achievement." *Race, Gender & Class* 16(1/2):25–44.

Reed, Adolph L., and Merlin Chowkwanyun. 2012. "Race, Class, Crisis: The Discourse of Racial Disparity and Its Analytical Discontents." *Socialist Register* 48:149–175.

Reese, Frederick. 2017. "Twenty-Five Percent of HBCU's Student Body Is Non-Black: Is This the End of Majority Black Schools?" *Atlanta Black Star*, November 20. https://atlantablackstar .com/2017/11/20/twenty-five-percent-hbcus-student-body-non-black-end-majority-black -schools/.

Reeves, Richard V. 2017. *Dream Hoarders: How the American Upper Middle Class Is Leaving Everyone Else in the Dust, Why That Is a Problem, and What to Do about It*. Washington, DC: Brookings Institution Press.

Reeves, Richard V., and Edward Rodrigue. 2015. *Single Black Female BA Seeks Educated Husband: Race, Assortative Mating and Inequality*. Washington, DC: Brookings Institution. https:// www.brookings.edu/research/single-black-female-ba-seeks-educated-husband-race -assortative-mating-and-inequality/.

Reid, Ira D. A. 1939. *The Negro Immigrant: His Background, Characteristics and Social Adjustment, 1899–1937*. New York: Columbia University Press.

Reyes, Daisy Verduzco. 2017. "Disparate Lessons: Racial Climates and Identity-Formation Processes among Latino Students." *Du Bois Review* 14(2):447–470.

Rich, Dorothy. 1998. "What Parents Want from Teachers." *Educational Leadership* 55(8):32–39.

Richardson, Joseph B., Mischelle Van Brakle, and Christopher St. Vil. 2014. "Taking Boys Out of the Hood: Exile as a Parenting Strategy for African American Male Youth." *New Directions for Child and Adolescent Development* 2014(143):11–31.

Rimer, Sara, and Karen W. Arenson. 2004. "Top Colleges Take More Blacks, but Which Ones?" *New York Times*, June 24. https://www.nytimes.com/2004/06/24/us/top-colleges-take-more-blacks-but-which-ones.html.

Roberson, Loriann, and Carol T. Kulik. 2007. "Stereotype Threat at Work." *Academy of Management Perspectives* 21(2):24–40.

Robertson, Ray V., Aditit Mitra, and Jean Van Delinder. 2005. "The Social Adjustment of African American Females at a Predominantly White Midwestern University." *Journal of African American Studies* 8(4):31–45.

Robinson, Eugene. 2016. *Disintegration: The Splintering of Black America*. New York: Doubleday.

Robinson, Keith, and Angel L. Harris. 2014. *The Broken Compass: Parental Involvement with Children's Education*. Cambridge, MA: Harvard University Press.

Rockquemore, Kerry Ann, and David L. Brunsma. 2007. *Beyond Black: Biracial Identity in America*. 2nd ed. Lanham, MD: Rowman & Littlefield.

Roksa, Josipa, and Daniel Potter. 2011. "Parenting and Academic Achievement: Intergenerational Transmission of Educational Advantage." *Sociology of Education* 84(4):299–321.

Rollock, Nicola, David Gillborn, Carol Vincent, and Stephen Ball. 2011. "The Public Identities of the Black Middle Classes: Managing Race in Public Spaces." *Sociology* 46(6):1078–1093.

Roscigno, Vincent J., and James W. Ainsworth-Darnell. 1999. "Race, Cultural Capital, and Educational Resources: Persistent Inequalities and Achievement Returns." *Sociology of Education* 72(3):158–178.

Ross, Stephen L., and John Yinger. 2002. *The Color of Credit: Mortgage Discrimination, Research Methodology, and Fair-Lending Enforcement*. Cambridge, MA: MIT Press.

Rothstein, Richard. 2017. *The Color of Law: A Forgotten History of How Our Government Segregated America*. New York: Norton.

Rothwell, Jonathan, and Douglas S. Massey. 2015. "Geographic Effects on Intergenerational Income Mobility." *Economic Geography* 91(1):83–106.

Ruggles, Steven, Catherine A. Fitch, Ronald Goeken, J. David Hacker, Matt A. Nelson, Evan Roberts, Megan Schouweiler, and Matthew Sobek. 2021. *IPUMS Ancestry Full Count Data: Version 3.0* [data set]. Minneapolis, MN: IPUMS.

Ruggles, Steven, Sarah Flood, Sophia Foster, Ronald Goeken, Jose Pacas, Megan Schouweiler, and Matthew Sobek. 2021. *IPUMS USA: Version 11.0* [data set]. Minneapolis: IPUMS. https://doi.org/10.18128/D010.V11.0.

Rugh, Jacob S., and Douglas S. Massey. 2010. "Racial Segregation and the American Foreclosure Crisis." *American Sociological Review* 75(5):629–651.

Rugh, Jacob S., and Douglas S. Massey. 2014. "Segregation in Post–Civil Rights America: Stalled Integration or End of the Segregated Century?" *Du Bois Review* 1(2):202–232.

Russell, Kathy, Midge Wilson, and Ronald Hall. 2013. *The Color Complex: The Politics of Skin Color in a New Millennium.* Rev. ed. New York: Anchor.

Russell-Brown, Kathryn. 1998. *The Color of Crime: Racial Hoaxes, White Fear, Black Protectionism, Police Harassment and Other Macroaggressions.* New York: New York University Press.

Sampson, Robert J. 1992. "Family Management and Child Development: Insights from Social Disorganization Theory." Pp. 63–93 in Joan McCord, ed., *Facts, Frameworks, and Forecasts: Advances in Criminological Theory,* vol. 3. New Brunswick, NJ: Transactions.

Sampson, Robert J. 2012. *Great American City: Chicago and the Enduring Neighborhood Effect.* Chicago: University of Chicago Press.

Sampson, Robert J., Patrick Sharkey, and Stephen W. Raudenbush. 2008. "Durable Effects of Concentrated Disadvantage on Verbal Ability among African-American Children." *Proceedings of the National Academy of Sciences* 105(3):845–852.

Sampson, William A. 2007. *Race, Class, and Family Intervention: Engaging Parents and Families for Academic Success.* Lanham, MD: Rowman & Littlefield Education.

Sanchez, Gabriel. 2008. "Latino Group Consciousness and Perceptions of Commonality with African Americans." *Social Science Quarterly* 89(2):428–444.

Schoepflin, Todd. 2009. "Perspectives of Interracial Dating at a Predominately White University." *Sociological Spectrum* 29(3):346–370.

Schultz, Theodore W. 1961. "Investment in Human Capital." *American Economic Review* 51(1):1–17.

Schultz, Theodore W. 1981. *Investing in People: The Economics of Population Quality.* Berkeley: University of California Press.

Schuman, Howard, Charlotte Steeh, Lawrence Bobo, and Maria Krysan. 1998. *Racial Attitudes in America: Trends and Interpretations.* Cambridge, MA: Harvard University Press.

Schwartz, Seth J., James E. Côté, and Jeffrey H. Arnett. 2005. "Identity and Agency in Emerging Adulthood: Two Developmental Routes in the Individualization Process." *Youth and Society* 37(2):201–229.

Seamster, Louise, and Raphaël Charron-Chénier. 2017. "Predatory Inclusion and Education Debt: Rethinking the Racial Wealth Gap." *Social Currents* 4(3):199–207.

Seamster, Louise, and Victor Ray. 2018. "Against Teleology in the Study of Race: Toward the Abolition of the Progress Paradigm." *Sociological Theory* 36(4):315–342.

Sears, David O., Mingying Fu, P. J. Henry, and Kerra Bui. 2008. "The Origins and Persistence of Ethnic Identity among 'New Immigrant' Groups.'" *Social Psychology Quarterly* 66(4):419–437.

Sellers, Robert M., Cleopatra H. Caldwell, Karen H. Schmeelk-Cone, and Marc A. Zimmerman. 2003. "Racial Identity, Racial Discrimination, Perceived Stress, and Psychological Distress among African American Young Adults." *Journal of Health and Social Behavior* 44(3):302–317.

Sellers, Robert M., Stephanie A. J. Rowley, Tabbye M. Chavous, J. Nicole Shelton, and Mia A. Smith. 1997. "Multidimensional Inventory of Black Identity: A Preliminary Investigation of Reliability and Construct Validity." *Journal of Personality and Social Psychology* 73(4): 805–815.

Sellers, Robert M., Mia A. Smith, J. Nicole Shelton, Stephanie A. J. Rowley, and Tabbye M. Chavous. 1998. "Multidimensional Model of Racial Identity: A Reconceptualization of African American Racial Identity." *Personality and Social Psychology Review* 2(1): 18–39.

Sellin, Thorsten, and Marvin E. Wolfgang. 1964. *The Measurement of Delinquency.* New York: Wiley.

Shapiro, Thomas. 2004. *The Hidden Cost of Being African American: How Wealth Perpetuates Inequality*. New York: Oxford University Press.

Shapiro, Thomas, Tatjana Meschede, and Sam Osoro. 2013. *The Roots of the Widening Racial Wealth Gap: Explaining the Black-White Economic Divide*. Waltham, MA: Institute on Assets and Social Policy, Brandeis University. https://heller.brandeis.edu /iasp/pdfs/racial-wealth -equity/racial-wealth-gap/roots-widening-racial-wealth-gap.pdf.

Sharkey, Patrick. 2010. "The Acute Effect of Local Homicides on Children's Cognitive Performance." *Proceedings of the National Academy of Sciences* 107(26):11733–11738.

Sharkey, Patrick. 2013. *Stuck in Place: Urban Neighborhoods and the End of Progress toward Racial Equality*. Chicago: University of Chicago Press.

Sharkey, Patrick. 2018. "The Long Reach of Violence: A Broader Perspective on Data, Theory, and Evidence on the Prevalence and Consequences of Exposure to Violence." *Annual Review of Criminology* 1:85–102.

Sharkey, Patrick, and George Galster. 2017. "Spatial Foundations of Inequality: A Conceptual Model and Empirical Overview." *RSF: Russell Sage Foundation Journal of the Social Sciences* 3(2):1–33.

Sharkey, Patrick, Amy Ellen Schwartz, Ingrid Gould Ellen, and Johanna Lacoe. 2014. "High Stakes in the Classroom, High Stakes on the Street: The Effects of Community Violence on Students' Standardized Test Performance." *Sociological Science* 1(1):199–220.

Sharkey, Patrick, Nicole Strayer, Andrew Papachristos, and Cybele Raver. 2012. "The Effect of Local Violence on Children's Attention and Impulse Control." *American Journal of Public Health* 102:2287–2293.

Sharpe, Jacqueline. 1996. "Mental Health Issues and Family Socialization in the Caribbean." Pp. 259–274 in Janet Brown and Jaipaul Roopnarine, eds., *Caribbean Families: Diversity among Ethnic Groups*. Greenwich, CT: Ablex.

Shaw, Clifford, and Henry D. McKay. 1969. *Juvenile Delinquency and Urban Areas*. Chicago: University of Chicago Press.

Shaw-Taylor, Yoku, and Steven A. Tuch. 2007. *The Other African Americans: Contemporary African and Caribbean Immigrants in the United States*. Lanham, MD: Rowman & Littlefield.

Shedd, Carla. 2015. *Unequal City: Race, Schools, and Perceptions of Injustice*. New York: Russell Sage Foundation.

Siegelman, Lee, Steven Tuch, and Jack Martin. 2005. "What's in a Name? Preference for 'Black' versus 'African-American' among Americans of African Descent." *Public Opinion Quarterly* 69(3):429–438.

Simons, Ronald L., Leslie Gordon Simons, Callie Harbin Burt, Holli Drummund, Eric Stewart, Gene H. Brody, Frederick X. Gibbons, and Carolyn Cutrona. 2006. "Supportive Parenting Moderates the Effect of Discrimination upon Anger, Hostile View of Relationships, and Violence among African American Boys." *Journal of Health and Social Behavior* 47:373–389.

Simpson, Andrea Y. 1998. *The Tie That Binds: Identity and Political Attitudes in the Post–Civil Rights Generation*. New York: New York University Press.

Siy, John Oliver, and Cheryan, Sapna. 2013. "When Compliments Fail to Flatter: American Individualism and Responses to Positive Stereotypes." *Journal of Personality and Social Psychology* 104:87–102.

Skrentny, John R. 1996. *The Ironies of Affirmative Action: Politics, Culture, and Justice in America*. Chicago: University of Chicago Press.

Smetana, Judith G. 2000. "Middle-Class African American Adolescents' and Parents' Conceptions of Parental Authority and Parenting Practices: A Longitudinal Investigation." *Child Development* 71(167):1672–1686.

Smetana, Judith G., Nicole Campione-Barr, and Aaron Metzger. 2006. "Adolescent Development in Interpersonal and Societal Contexts." *Annual Review of Psychology* 57:255–284.

Smetana, Judith G., and Cheryl Gaines. 1999. "Adolescent-Parent Conflict in Middle-Class African American Families." *Child Development* 70(6):1447–1463.

Smith, Candis Watts. 2014. *Black Mosaic: The Politics of Pan-Ethnic Diversity*. New York: New York University Press.

Smith, Delores E., and Todd M. Moore. 2013. "Parenting Style and Psychosocial Outcomes in a Sample of Jamaican Adolescents." *International Journal of Adolescence and Youth* 18(3):176–190.

Smith, Delores E., and Gail Mosby. 2003. "Jamaican Child-Rearing Practices: The Role of Corporal Punishment." *Adolescence* 38(150):369–381.

Smith, Jeffrey A., Miller McPherson, and Lynn Smith-Lovin. 2014. "Social Distance in the United States: Sex, Race, Religion, Age, and Education Homophily among Confidants, 1985 to 2004." *American Sociological Review* 79(3):432–456.

Smith, Raymond T. 1996. *The Matrifocal Family*. New York: Routledge.

Smith, Sandra, and Mignon Moore. 2000. "Intraracial Diversity and Relations among African-Americans: Closeness among Black Students at a Predominantly White University." *American Journal of Sociology* 106(1):1–39.

Smith, Sandra, and Mignon Moore. 2002. "Expectations of Campus Racial Climate and Social Adjustment among African American College Students." Pp. 93–119 in Walter R. Allen, Margaret B. Spencer, and Carla O'Connor, eds., *African American Education: Race, Community, Inequality and Achievement*. New York: Elsevier Science.

Solórzano, Daniel, Miguel Ceja, and Tara Yosso. 2000. "Critical Race Theory, Racial Microaggressions, and Campus Racial Climate: The Experiences of African American College Students." *Journal of Negro Education* 69(1/2):60–73.

Sorin, Gretchen. 2020. *Driving while Black: African American Travel and the Road to Civil Rights*. New York: Liveright.

Spencer, Rainier. 2011. *Reproducing Race: The Paradox of Generation Mix*. Boulder, CO: Lynne Rienner.

Spencer, Steven J., Claude M. Steele, and Diane M. Quinn. 1999. "Stereotype Threat and Women's Math Performance." *Journal of Experimental Social Psychology* 35(1):4–28.

Spickard, Paul R. 1989. *Mixed Blood: Intermarriage and Ethnic Identity in Twentieth-Century America*. Madison: University of Wisconsin Press.

Stackman, Valerie R., Rebecca Reviere, and Barbara C. Medley. 2016. "Attitudes toward Marriage, Partner Availability, and Interracial Dating among Black College Students from Historically Black and Predominantly White Institutions." *Journal of Black Studies* 47(2):169–192.

Stanton-Salazar, Ricardo. 1997. "A Social Capital Framework for Understanding the Socialization of Racial Minority Children and Youths." *Harvard Educational Review* 67(1):1–41.

Stanton-Salazar, Ricardo. 2011. "A Social Capital Framework or the Study of Institutional Agents and the Empowerment of Low-Status Students and Youth." *Youth and Society* 43(3): 1066–1109.

Staples, Robert. 1981. "The Myth of Black Matriarchy." Pp. 335–348 in Filomina C. Steady, ed., *The Black Woman Cross Culturally*. Cambridge, MA: Schenkman.

Stearns, Elizabeth, Claudia Buchmann, and Kara Bonneau. 2009. "Interracial Friendships in the Transition to College: Do Birds of a Feather Flock Together Once They Leave the Nest?" *Sociology of Education* 82(2):173–195.

Steele, Claude M. 1997. "A Threat in the Air: How Stereotypes Shape Intellectual Identity and Performance." *American Psychologist* 52(6):613–629.

Steele, Claude M., and Joshua Aronson. 1995. "Stereotype Threat and the Intellectual Test Performance of African Americans." *Journal of Personality and Social Psychology* 69(5): 797–811.

Steele, Claude M., Steven J. Spencer, and Joshua Aronson. 2002. "Contending with Group Image: The Psychology of Stereotype and Social Identity Threat." *Advances in Experimental Psychology* 34:379–440.

Steele, Ric G., Jill S. Nesbitt-Daly, Robert C. Daniel, and Rex Forehand. 2005. "Factor Structure of the Parenting Scale in a Low-Income African American Sample." *Journal of Child and Family Studies* 14(4):535–549.

Steil, Justin P., Len Albright, Jacob S. Rugh, and Douglas S. Massey. 2018. "The Social Structure of Mortgage Discrimination." *Housing Studies* 33(5):759–776.

Steinberg, Lawrence, Susie D. Lamborn, Sanford M. Dornbusch, and Nancy Darling. 1992. "Impact of Parenting Practice on Adolescent Achievement: Authoritative Parenting, School Involvement, and Encouragement to Succeed." *Child Development* 63(5):1266–1281.

Stephens, Nicole M., Stephanie A. Fryberg, Hazel R. Markus, Camille S. Johnson, and Rebecca Covarrubias. 2012. "Unseen Disadvantage: How American Universities' Focus on Independence Undermines the Academic Performance of First-Generation College Students." *Journal of Personality and Social Psychology* 102(6):1178–1197.

Stockman, Farah. 2019. "'We're Self-Interested': The Growing Identity Debate in Black America." *New York Times*, November 8. https://www.nytimes.com/2019/11/08/us/slavery-black-immigrants-ados.html.

Strage, Amy, and Tamara S. Brandt. 1999. "Authoritative Parenting and College Students' Academic Adjustment and Success." *Journal of Educational Psychology* 91(1):146–156.

Strassmann, Mark. 2019. "Millennials Struggle under the Burden of Student Loan Debt." *CBS Evening News with Norah O'Donnell*, April 30. https://www.cbsnews.com/news/student-loan-debt-i-had-a-panic-attack-millennials-struggle-under-the-burden-of-student-loan-debt/.

Strauss, Anselm, and Juliet Corbin. 1990. *Basics of Qualitative Research: Techniques and Procedures for Developing Grounded Theory*. Thousand Oaks, CA: Sage.

Strayhorn, Terrell L. 2011. "Bridging the Pipeline: Increasing Underrepresented Students' Preparation for College through a Summer Bridge Program." *American Behavioral Scientist* 55(2):142–159.

Stripling, Jack. 2019. "'It's an Aristocracy': What the Admissions-Bribery Scandal Has Exposed about Class on Campus." *Chronicle of Higher Education*, April 17. https://www.chronicle.com/article/It-s-an-Aristocracy-/246131.

Stryker, Sheldon, and Peter J. Burke. 2000. "The Past, Present and Future of Identity Theory." *Social Psychology Quarterly* 63(4):284–297.

Suárez-Orozco, Carola, and Manuel Suárez-Orozco. 1995. *Transformations: Immigration, Family Life, and Achievement Motivation among Latino Adolescents*. Stanford, CA: Stanford University Press.

Sudman, Seymour, and Norman M. Bradburn. 1982. *Asking Questions: A Practical Guide to Questionnaire Design*. San Francisco: Jossey-Bass.

Swidler, Anne. 1986. "Culture in Action: Symbols and Strategies." *American Sociological Review* 51(2):273–386.

Syed, Moin, and Margarita Azmitia. 2010. "Narrative and Ethnic Identity Exploration: A Longitudinal Account of Emerging Adults' Ethnicity-Related Experiences." *Developmental Psychology* 46(1):208–219.

Tajfel, Henri, and John C. Turner. 1986. "The Social Identity Theory of Intergroup Behaviour." Pp. 7–24 in William G. Austin and Stephen Worchel, eds., *Psychology of Intergroup Relations*. 2nd ed. Chicago: Nelson-Hall.

Tamborini, Christopher R., Chang Hwan Kim, and Arthur Sakamoto. 2015. "Education and Lifetime Earnings in the United States." *Demography* 52(4):1383–1407.

Tamis-LeMonda, Catherine S., Rahil D. Brigges, Sandra G. McClowry, and David L. Snow. 2008. "Challenges to the Study of African American Parenting: Conceptualization, Sampling, Research Approaches, Measurement, and Design." *Parenting: Science and Practice* 8(4):319–358.

Tate, Katherine. 1993. *From Protest to Politics: The New Black Voters in American Elections*. Cambridge, MA: Harvard University Press.

Taylor, Elizabeth D. 2017. *The Original Black Elite: Daniel Murray and the Story of a Forgotten Era*. New York: Harper-Collins.

Taylor, Kate. 2020. "Former Pimco C.E.O. Gets 9 Months in Prison in College Admissions Case." *New York Times*, February 7. https://www.nytimes.com/2020/02/07/us/douglas-hodge-college-admissions-scandal.html.

Taylor, Keeanga-Yamahtta. 2019. *Race for Profit: How Banks and the Real Estate Industry Undermined Black Home Ownership*. Chapel Hill: University of North Carolina Press.

Taylor, Robert J., Linda M. Chatters, M. Belinda Tucker, and Edith Lewis. 1990. "Developments in Research on Black Families: A Decade Review." *Journal of Marriage and the Family* 52(4):993–1014.

Terkel, Amanda. 2018. "Ben Carson Removes Anti-discrimination Language from HUD Mission Statement." *Huffington Post*, June 6. https://www.huffpost.com/entry/hud-mission-statement_n_5a9f5db0e4b002df2c5ec617.

Thomas, Courtney A. 2015. "A New Look at the Black Middle Class: Research Trends and Challenges." *Sociological Focus* 48(3):191–207.

Thomas, Duane E., and Howard Stevenson. 2009. "Gender Risks and Education: The Particular Classroom Challenges for Urban Low-Income African American Boys." *Review of Research in Education* 33(1):160–180.

Thomas, Scott L. 2000. "Deferred Costs and Economic Returns to College Quality, Major and Academic Performance: An Analysis of Recent Graduates in Baccalaureate and Beyond." *Research in Higher Education* 41(3):281–313.

Thomas, William I., and Dorothy S. Thomas. 1928. *The Child in America: Behavior Problems and Programs*. New York: Knopf.

Thompson, Jeffrey P., and Gustavo A. Suarez. 2015. *Exploring the Racial Wealth Gap Using the Survey of Consumer Finances*. Finance and Economics Discussion Series 2015-076. Washington, DC: Board of Governors of the Federal Reserve System. http://dx.doi.org/10.17016/FEDS.2015.076.

Thornhill, Ted. 2015. "Racial Salience and the Consequences of Making White People Uncomfortable: Intra-racial Discrimination, Racial Screening, and the Maintenance of White Supremacy." *Sociology Compass* 9(8):694–703.

Thornton, Michael C., Robert Joseph Taylor, and Linda M. Chatters. 2014. "African American and Black Caribbean Mutual Feelings of Closeness: Findings from a National Probability Survey." *Journal of Black Studies* 44(6):798–828.

Thornton, Michael C., Thanh V. Tran, and Robert J. Taylor. 1997. "Multiple Dimensions of Racial Group Identification among Adult Black Americans." *Journal of Black Psychology* 23(3):293–309.

Tinto, Vincent. 1993. *Leaving College: Rethinking the Causes and Cures of Student Attrition*. 2nd ed. Chicago: University of Chicago Press.

Tomaskovic-Devey, Donald, Marcinda Mason, and Matthew Zingraff. 2004. "Looking for the Driving while Black Phenomena: Conceptualizing Racial Bias Processes and Their Associated Distributions." *Police Quarterly* 7(1):3–29.

Torche, Florencia, and Peter Rich. 2017. "Declining Racial Stratification in Marriage Choices? Trends in Black/White Status Exchange in the United States, 1980 to 2010." *Sociology of Race and Ethnicity* 3(1):31–49.

Torres, Kimberly. 2009. "'Culture Shock': Black Students Account for Their Distinctiveness at an Elite College." *Ethnic and Racial Studies* 32(5):883–905.

Torres, Kimberly C., and Camille Z. Charles. 2004. "Metastereotypes and the Black-White Divide: A Qualitative View of Race on an Elite College Campus." *Du Bois Review* 1(1):115–149.

Torres, Kimberly C., and Douglas S. Massey. 2012. "Fitting In: Segregation, Social Class, and the Experiences of Black Students at Selective Colleges and Universities." *Race and Social Problems* 1(4):171–192.

Tovar, Jessica, and Cynthia Feliciano. 2009. "'Not Mexican-American, but Mexican': Shifting Ethnic Self-Identifications among Children of Mexican Immigrants." *Latino Studies* 7(2):197–221.

Travis, Dnika J., Jennifer Thorpe-Moscon, and Courtney McCluney. 2016. *Emotional Tax: How Black Women and Men Pay More at Work and How Leaders Can Take Action*. New York: Catalyst: Workplaces That Work for Women. https://www.catalyst.org/wp-content/uploads/2019/01/emotional_tax_how_black_women_and_men_pay_more.pdf.

Turner, Erlanger A., Megan Chandler, and Robert W. Heffer. 2009. "The Influence of Parenting Styles, Achievement Motivation, and Self-Efficacy on Academic Performance in College Students." *Journal of College Student Development* 50(3):337–346.

Turner, Ronald. 1995. "The Color Complex: Intraracial Discrimination in the Workplace." *Labor Law Journal* 46(11):678–684.

Tutwiler, Sandra Winn. 2016. *Mixed Race Youth and Schooling: The Fifth Minority*. New York: Routledge.

Twine, France W. 1996. "Brown-Skinned White Girls: Class, Culture, and the Construction of White Identity in Suburban Communities." *Gender, Place, and Culture* 3(2):205–224.

Tyson, Karolyn. 2011. *Integration Interrupted: Tracking, Black Students, and Acting White after Brown*. New York: Oxford University Press.

Tyson, Karolyn, William Darity Jr., and Domini R. Castellino. 2005. "It's Not 'a Black Thing': Understanding the Burden of Acting White and Other Dilemmas of High Achievement." *American Sociological Review* 70(4):582–695.

Ukpokodu, Omiunota. 2018. "African Immigrants, the 'New Model Minority': Examining the Reality in U.S. K–12 Schools." *Urban Review* 50(1):69–96.

Urban Institute. 2018. *Segregated Neighborhoods, Segregated Schools?* Washington, DC: Urban Institute. https://www.urban.org/features/segregated-neighborhoods-segregated-schools.

U.S. Census Bureau. 2018. *Foreign Born ACS Data Tables*. Washington, DC: U.S. Census Bureau. https://www.census.gov/topics/population/foreign-born/data/tables/acs-tables.html.

U.S. Census Bureau. 2020. *Educational Attainment in the United States: 2019*. Washington, DC: U.S. Census Bureau. https://www.census.gov/data/tables/2019/demo/education-attainment/cps-detailed-tables.html.

U.S. Census Bureau. 2021. *CPS Income Data Tables*. Washington, DC: U.S. Census Bureau. https://www.census.gov/topics/income-poverty/income/data/tables/cps.html.

U.S. Federal Reserve. 2019. *Report on the Economic Well-Being of U.S. Households in 2018*. Washington, DC: U.S. Federal Reserve. https://www.federalreserve.gov/publications/2019-economic-well-being-of-us-households-in-2018-student-loans-and-other-education-debt.htm.

U.S. National Center for Educational Statistics. 2018. *State Education Reforms Data Tables*. Washington, DC: U.S. Department of Education. https://nces.ed.gov/programs/statereform/tab5_1.asp.

U.S. National Center for Educational Statistics. 2020a. "Percentage of 18- to 24-Year-Olds Enrolled in College, by Level of Institution and Sex and Race/Ethnicity of Student: 1970 through 2016." *Digest of Educational Statistics*, Table 302.60. Washington, DC: National Center for Educational Statistics. https://nces.ed.gov/programs/digest/ d17/tables/dt17_302.60.asp?referer=raceindicators.

U.S. National Center for Educational Statistics. 2020b. *Status and Trends in the Education of Racial and Ethnic Groups Indicator 23: Postsecondary Graduation Rates*. Washington, DC: National Center for Educational Statistics. https://nces.ed.gov/programs/raceindicators/indicator_red.asp.

U.S. National Center for Educational Statistics. 2020c. *Digest of Educational Statistics*, Table 303.70. Washington, DC: National Center for Educational Statistics. https://nces.ed.gov/programs/digest/d19/tables/dt19_303.70.asp.

U.S. Office of Immigration Statistics. 2019. *2018 Yearbook of Immigration Statistics*. Washington, DC: U.S. Department of Homeland Security.

Uslaner, Eric M. 2012. *Segregation and Mistrust: Diversity, Isolation, and Social Cohesion*. New York: Cambridge University Press.

Van Hek, Margriet, Gerbert Kraaykamp, and Maarten H. J. Wolbers. 2016. "Comparing the Gender Gap in Educational Attainment: The Impact of Emancipatory Contexts in 33 Cohorts across 33 Countries." *Educational Research and Evaluation* 22(5–6):260–282.

Vaquera, Elizabeth, and Grace Kao. 2005. "Private and Public Displays of Affection among Interracial and Intra-racial Adolescent Couples." *Social Science Quarterly* 86(2):484–508.

Verplanken, Bas, Jolanda Jetten, and Ad van Knippenberg. 1996. "Effects of Stereotypicality and Perceived Group Variability on the Use of Attitudinal Information in Impression Formation." *Personality and Social Psychology Bulletin* 22(9):960–971.

Vickerman, Milton. 1999. *Crosscurrents: West Indian Immigrants and Race.* New York: Oxford University Press.

Voisin, Dexter H., Kathy M. Berringer, Lois Takahashi, Sean Burr, and Jessica A. M. Kuhnen. 2016. "No Safe Havens: Protective Parenting Strategies for African American Youth Living in Violent Communities." *Violence and Victims* 31(3):523–536.

Wacquant, Loïc J. D., and William Julius Wilson. 1989. "The Cost of Racial and Class Exclusion in the Inner City." *Annals of the American Academic of Political and Social Science* 601:8–25.

Wade, Joel, Melanie Romano, and Leslie Blue. 2004. "The Effect of African American Skin Color on Hiring Preferences." *Journal of Applied Social Psychology* 34(12):2550–2558.

Wallace, Derron. 2017. "Reading 'Race' in Bourdieu? Examining Black Cultural Capital among Black Caribbean Youth in South London." *Sociology* 51(5):907–923.

Wang, Wendy. 2012. *The Rise of Intermarriage: Rates, Characteristics Vary by Race and Gender.* Washington, DC: Pew Research Center. http://www.pewsocialtrends.org/2012/02/16/the-rise-of-intermarriage/.

Ward, Lee, Michael J. Siegel, and Zebulun Davenport. 2012. *First-Generation College Students: Understanding and Improving the Experience from Recruitment to Commencement.* San Francisco: Jossey-Bass.

Warikoo, Natasha, and Prudence Carter. 2009. "Cultural Explanations for Racial and Ethnic Stratification in Academic Achievement: A Call for a New and Improved Theory." *Review of Educational Research* 79(1):366–394.

Warner, W. Lloyd. 1936. "American Caste and Class." *American Journal of Sociology* 42(2):234–237.

Washington, Scott L. 2011. "Hypodescent: A History of the Crystallization of the One-Drop Rule in the United States, 1880–1940." PhD diss., Princeton University. https://catalog.princeton.edu/catalog/6818243.

Watabe, Akiko, and David R. Hibbard. 2014. "The Influence of Authoritarian and Authoritative Parenting on Children's Academic Achievement Motivation: A Comparison between the United States and Japan." *North American Journal of Psychology* 16(2):359–382.

Waters, Mary C. 1999. *Black Identities: West Indian Immigrant Dreams and American Realities.* Cambridge, MA: Harvard University Press.

Waters, Mary C., Philip Kasinitz, and Asad L. Asad. 2014. "Immigrants and African Americans." *Annual Review of Sociology* 40:369–390.

Waters, Mary C., and Marisa Gerstein Pineau. 2016. *The Integration of Immigrants into American Society.* Washington, DC: National Academies Press.

Watson, Camilla E. 2018. "Federal Financing of Higher Education at a Crossroads: The Evolution of the Student Loan Debt Crisis and the Reauthorization of the Higher Education Act of 1965." *University of Georgia School of Law Legal Studies Research Paper No. 2018-43.* https://ssrn.com/abstract=3279667.

Weiss, Robert S. 1994. *Learning from Strangers: The Art and Method of Qualitative Interview Studies.* New York: Free Press.

Welburn, Jessica S. 2016. "Dual Consciousness, Social Mobility, and the Experiences of Middle-Income African Americans in the Post–Civil Rights Era." *Journal of African American Studies* 20(2):202–227.

Welburn, Jessica S., and Cassi L. Pittman. 2012. "Stop 'Blaming the Man': Perceptions of Inequality and Opportunities for Success in the Obama Era among Middle-Class African Americans." *Ethnic and Racial Studies* 35(3):523–540.

Weldon, S. Laurel. 2008. "Intersectionality." Pp. 193–218 in Gary Goertz and Amy G. Mazur, eds., *Politics, Gender, and Concepts: Theory and Methodology*. New York: Cambridge University Press.

Western, Bruce. 2006. *Punishment and Inequality in America*. New York: Russell Sage Foundation.

White-Johnson, Rhonda L. 2012. "Prosocial Involvement among African American Young Adults: Considering Racial Discrimination and Racial Identity." *Journal of Black Psychology* 38(3):313–341.

Wichowsky, Amber. 2019. "Civic Life in the Divided Metropolis: Social Capital, Collective Action, and Residential Income Segregation." *Urban Affairs Review* 55(1):257–287.

Wilder, JeffriAnne, and Colleen Cain. 2011. "Teaching and Learning Color Consciousness in Black Families: Exploring Family Process and Women's Experiences with Colorism." *Journal of Family Issues* 32(5):577–604.

Wilkerson, Isabel. 2010. *The Warmth of Other Suns: The Epic Story of America's Great Migration*. New York: Random House.

Wilkins, Rhonda. 2008. *Swimming Upstream: A Study of Black Males and the Academic Pipeline*. Saarbrücken: VDM Verlag.

Williams, Amber D., Meeta Banerjee, Fantasy Lozada-Smith, Danny Lambouths, and Stephanie J. Rowley. 2017. "Black Mothers' Perceptions of the Role of Race in Children's Education." *Journal of Marriage and Family* 79(4):932–946.

Williams, David R., and Selina A. Mohammed. 2013. "Racism and Health I: Pathways and Scientific Evidence." *American Behavioral Scientist* 57(8):1152–1173.

Williams, Deadric T. 2019. "A Call to Focus on Racial Domination and Oppression: A Response to 'Racial and Ethnic Inequality in Poverty and Affluence, 1959–2015.'" *Population Research and Policy Review* 38(5):655–663.

Williams, Juan. 1987. *Eyes on the Prize: America's Civil Rights Years 1954–1965*. New York: Viking Penguin.

Willie, Charles V., and Donald Cunnigen. 1981. "Black Students in Higher Education: A Review of Studies, 1965–1980." *Annual Review of Sociology* 7:177–198.

Willie, Sarah. 2003. *Acting Black: College, Identity, and the Performance of Race*. New York: Routledge.

Wilson, William Julius. 1987. *The Truly Disadvantaged: The Inner City, the Underclass, and Public Policy*. Chicago: University of Chicago Press.

Wilson, William Julius. 1996. *When Work Disappears: The World of the New Urban Poor*. New York: Random House.

Wing, Kelisa J. 2018. *Promises and Possibilities: Dismantling the School-to-Prison Pipeline*. Scotts Valley, CA: CreateSpace.

Wingfield, Adia Harvey, and Koji Chavez. 2020. "Getting in, Getting Hired, Getting Sideways Looks: Organizational Hierarchy and Perceptions of Workplace Racial Discrimination." *American Sociological Review* 85(1):31–57.

Wolfgang, Marvin E., Robert M. Figlio, Paul E. Tracy, and Simon I. Singer. 1985. *The National Survey Crime Severity (NCJ-96017)*. Washington, DC: U.S. Government Printing Office.

Woodward, C. Vann. 1957. *The Strange Career of Jim Crow*. New York: Oxford University Press.

Woodward, C. Vann. 1981. *Mary Chestnut's Civil War*. New Haven, CT: Yale University Press.

Wright, Richard, Steven Holloway, and Mark Ellis. 2013. "Gender and the Neighborhood Location of Mixed-Race Couples." *Demography* 50(2):393–420.

Wu, Ellen D. 2013. *The Color of Success: Asian Americans and the Origins of the Model Minority*. Princeton, NJ: Princeton University Press.

Yamaguchi, Kazuo, and Yantao Wang. 2002. "Class Identification of Married Employed Women and Men in America." *American Journal of Sociology* 108(2):440–475.

Yancey, George. 2007. *Interracial Contact and Social Change*. Boulder, CO: Lynne Rienner.

Yancey, George A., and Richard Lewis, Jr. 2009. *Interracial Families: Current Concepts and Controversies*. New York: Routledge.

Yosso, Tara J. 2005. "Whose Culture Has Capital? A Critical Race Theory Discussion of Community Cultural Wealth." *Race, Ethnicity, and Education* 8(1):69–91.

Yosso, Tara J. 2006. *Critical Race Counterstories along the Chicana/Chicano Educational Pipeline*. Milton Park, UK: Taylor & Francis.

Yosso, Tara J., William A. Smith, Miguel Ceja, and Daniel Solórzano. 2009. "Critical Race Theory, Racial Microaggressions, and Campus Racial Climate for Latina/o Undergraduates." *Harvard Educational Review* 79(4):659–691.

Zarate, Maria E., and Harry P. Pachon. 2006. *Equity in Offering Advanced Placement Courses in California High Schools, 1997–2003*. Los Angeles: Tomas Rivera Policy Institute.

INDEX

ABOUT THE AUTHORS

CAMILLE Z. CHARLES is the Walter H. and Leonore C. Annenberg Professor in the Social Sciences, and professor of sociology and Africana studies at the University of Pennsylvania.

RORY KRAMER is associate professor of sociology and criminology at Villanova University.

DOUGLAS S. MASSEY is the Henry G. Bryant Professor of Sociology and Public Affairs at Princeton University.

KIMBERLY C. TORRES is an affiliated faculty member in organizational dynamics and the Center for Africana Studies at the University of Pennsylvania.

CPSIA information can be obtained
at www.ICGtesting.com
Printed in the USA
JSHW022246010722
27784JS00003B/3